RECASTING THE
EUROPEAN ORDER

EUROPE IN CHANGE

SERIES EDITOR EMIL KIRCHNER

Already published

Greece in a changing Europe: between European integration and Balkan disintegration?
KEVIN FEATHERSTONE AND KOSTAS IFANTIS (EDS)

forthcoming titles

The new Eastern Question
ANDREW COTTEY

Seeking asylum: Germany and migration into Europe
BARBARA MARSHALL

Turkey's relations with a changing Europe
MELTEM MUFTULER

Democratic theory and the European Union
ALBERT WEALE

RECASTING THE EUROPEAN ORDER

James Sperling
& Emil Kirchner

RECASTING THE EUROPEAN ORDER

Security architectures
and economic cooperation

MANCHESTER UNIVERSITY PRESS
Manchester and New York

distributed exclusively in the USA by St. Martin's Press

Copyright © James Sperling and Emil Kirchner 1997

Published by Manchester University Press
Oxford Road, Manchester M13 9NR, UK
and Room 400, 175 Fifth Avenue, New York, NY 10010, USA

Distributed exclusively in the USA
by St. Martin's Press, Inc., 175 Fifth Avenue, New York, NY 10010, USA

British Library Cataloguing-in-Publication Data
A catalogue record is available from the British Library

Library of Congress Cataloging-in-Publication Data
Sperling, James.
   Recasting the European order : security architectures and economic cooperation / James Sperling and Emil Kirchner.
     p.   cm.—(Europe in change)
  ISBN 0–7190–3986–X.—ISBN 0–7190–3987–8
  1. Europe—Foreign economic relations.   2. International cooperation
3. Decommunization—Europe. 4. Economic security—Europe. 5. National security—Europes.   I. Kirchner, Emil Joseph.
II. Title.   III. Series.
HF1531.S684   1997
337.4—dc20   95–25061
                                                                            CIP

ISBN 0 7190 3986 X *hardback*
     0 7190 3987 8 *paperback*

First published in 1997

00 99 98 97   10 9 8 7 6 5 4 3 2 1

Typeset in Great Britain
by Northern Phototypesetting Co Ltd, Bolton
Printed in Great Britain
by Redwood Books, Trowbridge

Contents

	Figures and tables	*page* vi
	Preface	vii
	Abbreviations	ix
1	Introduction: economic security and the problem of cooperation	1
2	The regional institutions of security: the Council of Europe, the European Union and the Western European Union	28
3	The Atlantic institutions of security: NATO, the OSCE and the UN	57
4	The economic dimension of security: managing the macroeconomy	85
5	The economic dimension of security: binding trade ties	130
6	The economic dimension of security: financing the transition	162
7	The economic dimension of security: financing environmental security	201
8	Conclusion: security architectures and institutional futures	234
	Bibliography	268
	Index	285

Figure and tables

Figure

1	Transformation and utility curves of a hypothetical state	page 7

Tables

1	Military force strength and budgets, 1985–93/97	43
2	Maastricht convergence criteria, 1988	117
3	Maastrict criteria, 1994	117
4	Maastricht criteria, EU on a weighted basis, 1986–95	118
5	Maastricht criteria, Visegrad countries, 1994	129
6	Annual percentage change in intra-CMEA trade, 1989–93	148
7	Regional concentration of trade in 1993, EU	148
8	Geographical distribution of trade, 1989 and 1993	149
9	Regional concentration of trade in 1993, Germany	150
10	Regional concentration of trade in 1993, United States	150
11	Bloc concentration of US, German and EU exports, 1993	150
12	Export concentration ratio of selected former member states of CMEA, 1993	151
13	Herfindahl–Hirschman trade concentration ratios, 1938 and 1993	153
14	Long-term debt, by creditor, 1990	173
15	Regional debt ratios, 1992	174
16	Debt indicators for eastern Europe and the Russian Federation, 1989–93	175
17	Investment flows and G-24 aid to selected CEE states, 1990–94	188
18	Direct foreign and portfolio investment as a share of GNP for selected CEE and industrialised countries, 1993	189
19	ERP aid as a share of 1949 GNP of recipient countries	190
20	G-24 aid as a share of 1990 GNP of recipient countries	190
21	Debt ratios for selected individual countries in transition and for Mexico and Brazil, 1991–93	195
22	Arrears, 1990–91	195
23	Real short-term interest rates, 1986–93	195
24	Trade growth, 1989–92	196
25	National GDP growth rates, 1990–92	196
26	Regional GDP growth rates, 1990–94	196
27	Real total domestic demand, 1988–94	196
28	Convertible currency current account balances, 1990–93	197
29	Project investment loans, on an annual basis, 1990–93	231
30	Project investment loans: total outstanding, 1990–93	231
31	EBRD environmental lending, 1990–93	232

Preface

The dramatic events since the late 1980s, which witnessed the end of the Cold War, the dissolution of the Warsaw Pact, the fragmentation of the Soviet Union and the emergence of a united Germany, have set in motion a recasting of the European security order. There has been a shift of emphasis from territorial defence to 'out-of-area' engagements and from military to economic and environmental security. These developments raise important questions about the *raison d'être* of existing security organisations. Are they simply relics of the Cold War that have outlived their usefulness or can they adjust to new threats, challenges and roles?

This book examines the process of change and adjustment since 1989, places particular emphasis on the non-military elements of security, and analyses the forces and institutions which contribute to peaceful and cooperative relations between eastern and western Europe. The place and relevance of the non-military aspects of security and the role of international organisations in European security are the subject of debate if not controversy, especially in the realist camp of international relations theory. Realists reject the autonomy of the economic dimension of security, seeing it instead as an adjunct of military security or as a simple problem of welfare maximisation. Similarly, the role of international organisations is assigned a marginal role in explaining the behaviour of states or in shaping the dynamic of the international system.

Whilst recognising the continued role of the military dimension in European security, albeit a diminishing and changed one, this study highlights the growing importance of the economic, financial and environmental dimensions of security which make important contributions to the process of marketisation and democratisation in the transition societies of central and eastern Europe. The outcome of those transitions will have significant bearings on the future shape of the European security order and the prospects for peace and stability in Europe.

Individual chapters, especially the introduction, which provides the conceptualisation of the approach taken in this study, were presented at various conferences. We would like to thank those who provided helpful comments, in particular Clive Archer, Simon Bulmer, Barry Buzan, Phil Cerny, C. Randall Henning, Mike Huelshoff, Zaki Laidi, Carl Lankowski, Yogi Malik, John Peterson, Jean-Jacques Roche, Michael Smith and Hugh Ward. We are also extremely grateful to Kevin Wright for compiling the bibliography and for providing valuable research assistance in the completion of the manuscript. A special word of thanks to Richard Purslow, our editor, for his encouragement and assistance throughout the gestation of the book. Finally, we would like to extend our gratitude for financial assistance provided by the Nuffield Foundation, the European Commission and the University of Akron.

James Sperling and Emil Kirchner
December 1995

Abbreviations

APEC	Asia Pacific Economic Cooperation
ARRC	Allied Rapid Reaction Corps
ASEAN	Association of South East Asian Nations
AWACS	airborne warning and control system
BIP	Baltic Investment Programme
BIS	Bank for International Settlements
BSEC	Black Sea Economic Cooperation
C³	command, control and communications
CAP	common agricultural policy
CCMS	Committee on the Challenges of Modern Society
CEE	central and eastern European
CEFTA	Central European Free Trade Association
CFE	Conventional Forces in Europe
CFSP	common foreign and security policy
CIDIE	Committee of International Development Institutions on the Environment
CIS	Commonwealth of Independent States
CJTF	combined joint task force
CMEA	Council on Mutual Economic Cooperation
COCOM	Coordinating Committee controlling East–West Trade
CSBM	confidence and security-building measure
DDSR	debt and debt service reduction
DSU	dispute settlement understanding
EAP	environmental action programme
EBRD	European Bank for Reconstruction and Development
EC	European Community
ECOFIN	Council of Economic and Finance Ministers
EDC	European Defence Community
EEA	European Economic Area
EECU	East European Clearing Union
EFF	extended Fund facility
EFTA	European Free Trade Association
EIB	European Investment Bank
EIS	European Information Service
EMCF	European Monetary Cooperation Fund
EMI	European Monetary Institute
EMS	European Monetary System
EMU	economic and monetary union
EPC	European Political Cooperation
ERM	exchange rate mechanism
ERP	European Recovery Programme

ESAF	enhanced structural adjustment facility
ESCB	European System of Central Banks
ESI	European security identity
EU	European Union
FOC	forum of consultation
FSC	Forum of Security Cooperation
GATS	General Agreement on Trade in Services
GATT	General Agreement on Tariffs and Trade
GDP	gross domestic product
GNP	gross national product
G-7	Group of Seven
G-24	Group of Twenty-four
IAEA	International Atomic Energy Authority
IBRD	International Bank for Reconstruction and Development (World Bank)
IEPG	Independent European Programme Group
IFOR	implementation force
IMF	International Monetary Fund
INSAG	International Nuclear Safety Advisory Group
LIBOR	London inter-bank offer rate
MAFF	market access fact-finding
NACC	North Atlantic Cooperation Council
NAFTA	North American Free Trade Agreement
NATO	North Atlantic Treaty Organisation
NEFCO	Nordic Environment Finance Corporation
NIB	Nordic Investment Bank
NORTHAG	North European Army Group
NoPEF	Nordic Project Fund
NUSS	IAEA nuclear safety standards
OECD	Organisation for Economic Cooperation and Development
OMA	orderly marketing agreement
OSCE	Organisation for Security and Cooperation in Europe
PfP	Partnership for Peace
SACEUR	Supreme Allied Command, Europe
SALT	strategic arms limitation talks
SHAPE	Supreme Headquarters, Allied Powers in Europe
SII	Structural Impediment Initiative
START	strategic arms reduction talks
STF	systemic transformation facility
TRIPS	trade-related intellectual property rights
UN	United Nations
UNEP	United Nations Environmental Programme
UNHCR	United Nations High Commission on Refugees
UNPROFOR	United Nations Protection Force
VER	voluntary export restraint
WEAG	Western European Armaments Group
WEU	Western European Union
WTO	World Trade Organisation

For Victoria Walker-Sperling
    Tristan and Stefan Kirchner

1

Introduction
Economic security and the problem of cooperation

A reconfiguration of Europe's strategic landscape and a redefinition of security have taken place in Europe. The security concerns of the European and North American states have expanded and now not only embrace the preoccupation with territorial integrity, defence and deterrence, but also include the non-military elements of security that range from macroeconomic stability to environmental degradation. After the onset of the Korean War, security was conceived primarily, if not exclusively, in terms of military security. The major European powers were preoccupied with sustaining the nuclear balance of terror between the superpowers and the conventional balance of power on the Eurasian land mass. Despite the heavy emphasis upon the military element of national security, attention was paid to the economic underpinnings of military prowess. Nonetheless, economic issues were subordinated and treated as an adjunct of the more important and pressing issue of military security. Economic security was not a relevant analytical category until the late 1960s.

Economic issues grew more salient in the late 1960s and were increasingly treated as important political and broader architectural elements of both national security and the larger security order. A few studies of the Western alliance in the late 1960s and early 1970s emphasised the importance of economic relations between the members of the Atlantic alliance; they focused on the importance of those economic relationships as critical struts undergirding the alliance and the security of its member states.[1] The growing remoteness of a military threat to European security combined with an increase in the frequency of economic conflict within the Atlantic area during the 1970s and 1980s. This period saw the erosion of American hegemony and the rise of Germany and Japan, the slow collapse of the Bretton Woods monetary system between 1971 and 1973, the two oil shocks of 1973 and 1979, and the consequent concern over access to critical raw materials, the divergence of macroeconomic policies throughout the 1980s, and a marked preference on both sides of the Atlantic for bilateralism in trade relations. Economic issues moved to the 'top table' of diplomatic discourse within the Atlantic area.[2] By the end of the 1980s, the security concerns of the Europeans, particularly the Germans, were increasingly expressed in an economic rather than military idiom.[3] The collapse of the post-Yalta security order has initiated the process of recalibrating national interests to conform with the pressures and opportunities presented by the emerging European security order.

The sudden transformation of the Cold War security order in 1989 altered the structure of the European state system, intensified the relationship between military security and economic security and possibly inverted their relative importance, raised new possibilities of cooperation in military and economic affairs, and necessitated the striking of a new balance between the economic, political and military requirements of security. The end of the Cold War and the erasure of the stark political and military lines dividing the European continent have not unified Europe. Europe remains divided by differences in the level of *per capita* GDP, the level of economic development, the stability of democratic institutions, and differential membership of the key institutions of the European security order, particularly the North Atlantic Treaty Organisation (NATO) and the European Union (EU). Overcoming the continuing division of Europe and assuring the future stability of the European security order are contingent upon the successful transition of the central and eastern European states to the market economy and multi-party democracy. The *sine qua non* of the successful transition of those countries is a stable economic and political environment. Consequently, until that transition is completed and consolidated, issues of political economy must be treated as elements of the new security order rather than as simple issues of welfare maximisation. This perspective requires a redefinition of security. It suggests that the European security system has two mutually constitutive elements, the political-military and the economic. The interdependence of these two elements of the security architecture raises a set of important and interrelated questions. Does a stable security architecture require the parallel construction of the institutions of military and economic security? What are the limits of asymmetrical progress in the construction of those institutions? If the parallel construction of those institutions is not possible, what does it imply about the future European security order?

The change in the definition of security and the presumed necessity of the parallel construction of the institutions of the European security order requires a convincing case to be made that the post-Cold War security problematique differs significantly from that posed by the post-war period (and perhaps any other epoch of modern European history); and a convincing case to be made that the provision of security in the post-Cold War era will be best supplied by international institutions. It is our purpose to make the case for both propositions.

The changing attributes of the European state system

From the perspective of national policy-makers in North America or Europe, the world has experienced fundamental changes. The Warsaw Pact has dissolved and NATO has been robbed of its post-war *raison d'être*. The Soviet Union has fragmented into a large number of independent republics, some of which are tenuously connected with Russia by pre-existing economic ties and a paper confederation. Not only are the nations of central and eastern Europe undergoing a political and economic transformation simultaneously, but many of them seek membership of the Western clubs, particularly NATO, the Western European Union (WEU) and the EU. Germany is united and has gained a new centrality, both geographically and politically, in the 'new' Europe. More broadly, the ideological enmity that marked relations among the two post-war blocs has given way to growing ideological conformity and growing amity.

Yet, from the vantage point provided by neo-realist theory, it is not clear that anything has fundamentally changed. For the neo-realists, the 'deep structure' of the international system remains anarchical and competitive.[4] States are still driven by concern over the relative gains from cooperation and by the pursuit of power. The political change that was set in motion in 1989 did little to change the actual distribution of capabilities within the system; the system is still characterised by military bipolarity.[4] Likewise, from the vantage point of neo-liberal institutionalist theory, not much has changed, either. The system remains essentially anarchical, but anarchy is modified generally within issue areas by sets of rules and institutions that shape and constrain state preferences. States are still driven by the imperative of absolute gain and economic welfare maximisation; states consequently prefer strategies of sustained cooperation.[5] The contemporary international system supplies ample empirical evidence to support either set of propositions. It is our view, however, that the changes that have taken place in Europe suggest that the emergent European security order casts a doubt on the usefulness of either theory if it requires the exclusion of the other. From a historical perspective, the changes that took place in 1989 do not appear to be a marked departure from other significant junctures in the history of the modern European state system. Yet, at the same time, the domestication of international politics that has slowly evolved during the twentieth century suggests that the prospects for sustained cooperation within the European political space are greater than they have ever been in the past. Important changes have taken place in the European state system which point to the growing importance of institutions in managing European conflicts of interest and the necessity of reconsidering the domain of security.

Although it remains the primary actor in the contemporary international system, the state is changing in a number of important ways. First, the national economies of Europe and North America are experiencing greater levels of openness, in the real as well as in the financial sectors of the economy. Second, the tension between autonomy and interdependence in the conduct of economic affairs is slowly being resolved in favour of the latter; it is increasingly true that 'internal state power is sustained by external cooperation'.[6] Third, external cooperation has taken the form of ceding some sovereign power to non-state actors, ranging from supranational actors (most notably the EU in the case of the western European states) to international organisations (for instance, the International Monetary Fund, the IMF, and International Atomic Energy Agency, or IAEA). States increasingly face external constraints in the formation or execution of policy; in fact, state preferences are increasingly shaped by the principles, norms and rules of international institutions.[7] And finally, the process of democratisation and the embrace of the market economy in eastern and central Europe are producing a more homogeneous European state system. One consequence of this development is the creation of a common frame of reference among the nations of the European security space that should facilitate cooperation, just as the previous ideological opposition formed a barrier to cooperation between the two halves of Europe.[8]

A second category of change is the currency of power in the security space occupied by the states of North America and Europe. While it is true that the primacy of military security, the residual preoccupation with nuclear war and the concern with national survival remain the paramount concerns of the major European powers, it is also the case that a perceptible shift has taken place in the relative importance of military security and economic welfare that favours the latter. As economic issues increased in salience in the 1970s and 1980s military issues and the concern with military security suffered a corresponding decline. This shift of emphasis, already under way, was transformed by the end of the Cold War. The end of the Cold War, in redirecting attention to the underlying importance of economic capacity, has changed the perception of power and consequently its redistribution. The absence of a stark military threat to the West has made the process of America's relative economic decline more meaningful and resonant in Atlantic relations.[9] Thus the currency of military power has been devalued, particularly in the relations among the wealthy states of the European security space, and is being driven out by the currencies of commercial competitiveness and economic capacity. The dominance of the technological frontier, essential for sustaining commercial competitiveness in world markets, has become the arena of intense competition between the North American and western European states. Moreover, only the economic capacity of the NATO member states can finance the long-term transition to the market economy and democracy in the former member states of the Warsaw Pact. The new currency of power has thus altered the distribution of capabilities in the European security space. Whereas Cold War Europe was characterised by political-military bipolarity dominated by the United States and the Soviet Union, post-Cold War Europe is characterised by an economic multipolarity conjoined by a military bipolarity that has been eclipsed, for the time being, by the economic and environmental security concerns of the states occupying the European security space.

The third category of change that has taken place is located in the resolution of the debate about state preferences offered by Robert Powell. Powell has argued convincingly that preferences are not immutable but are linked quite closely with the external constraints facing a state, and that those constraints are linked with the level of amity and enmity in the international system.[10] Where there are high levels of enmity, cooperation is unlikely: states are compelled to focus on relative gains, since an unequal absolute gain derived from cooperation today could lead to military defeat tomorrow. Where there are high levels of amity, on the other hand, cooperation is more likely: states are free to focus on absolute gains, since a state's relative loss today is unlikely to be employed against it tomorrow and lead to defeat on the battlefield. The implications of Powell's argument are of significance for the institutional architecture and likely patterns of cooperation in the post-Cold War European security space.

It is relatively safe to assume that the resort to interstate war is no longer at issue in the 'new Europe', notwithstanding the civil conflicts raging in the former Yugoslavia and percolating along the periphery of the former Soviet Union. The enmity of the pre-1989 European security area, generated by two mutually opposed and ideologically antagonistic military alliances, is no more. In its place we find a Europe where ideological fragmentation and opposition are being replaced by growing ideological conformity; where opposed military alliances have been replaced by a single military alliance, NATO, in search of a pan-European security role; and where the wealthy states of Europe are actively seeking to assist the economic and political transformation undertaken by the states of central and eastern Europe (CEE). Amity, then, has become the contextual hallmark of interstate relations in the 'new Europe'. This change of context should lead us to expect, then, greater cooperation between the former member states of the two Cold War alliances. And that cooperation is in fact taking place in economic, political and military affairs. The fear of relative gains has been replaced with concern for ensuring cooperative outcomes that deliver an optimum level of absolute gains for all.

Non-reciprocated cooperation during the Cold War between the NATO and Warsaw Pact states carried potentially high costs for individual and collective security.[10] The necessity of military cooperation within each alliance created an incentive to minimise conflict and non-cooperation within the alliance on economic issues.[11] The potential use of force against NATO member states by the Warsaw Pact created a context that encouraged cooperation in economic affairs to ensure large absolute gains to meet the welfare and military security demands of NATO states. With the end of the Cold War, however, the costs of defection in economic matters have declined precipitously: the absence of cooperation between Europe and North America in economic affairs, for example, no longer carries with it a high cost in military terms. And, perhaps more important, the benefits of defection have risen markedly: if, as we have argued above, the most important currency of power is economic and the source of that power is dominance of the technological frontier, then we should expect less cooperation in economic affairs among the NATO allies today than occurred during the Cold War.[12]

The confluence of three developments – a process of change in the structural characteristics of the state, in the currency of power and in the contextual environment – suggests that the prospects for cooperation have increased in the European security space. But these changes are important only in so far as they contribute to the resolution of the post-war security dilemmas that stymied pan-European cooperation.

The transformation of the post-war security dilemmas

The new-found amity in the European security space has also transformed the two security dilemmas that confronted states historically. The first, elaborated by Robert Jervis, locates the security dilemma in the unhappy circumstance that 'many of the means by which a state tries to increase its security decrease the security of others'.[13] The intensity of this security dilemma varies with four variables. The fear of exploitation exacerbates the security dilemma: the less (more) secure a state is, the more (less) vigilant it must be in making a decision to cooperate and run the risk of defection by another. The security dilemma is accentuated by the subjective security requirements of decision-makers: the lower (higher) the perceived security threat, the less (more) intense will be the security dilemma. Thirdly, the inward (outward) orientation of policy-makers combined with the rising (falling) opportunity cost of military expenditures also acts to reduce (increase) the intensity of the security dilemma.[14] The intensity of the security dilemma is dependent upon a final characteristic of the security environment: the offensive-defensive balance. Jervis argues that where the defence has the advantage in war, and where an offensive posture is distinguishable from a defensive posture, the strategic environment will be 'doubly stable': the advantage is possessed by the defender, which lessens the incentive to and likelihood of war, since a successful attack is unlikely; and the ability to distinguish between offensive and defensive capabilities forces the potential aggressor to signal its intentions by the act of acquiring offensive capabilities. The opposite combination (offence has the advantage and the two postures are indistinguishable) is 'doubly dangerous': the advantage is possessed by offensive forces, the inability to distinguish between offensive and defensive weaponry generates unstable arms races, and states have a powerful incentive to strike first in a crisis.[15]

A second security dilemma facing decision-makers is the division of national resources as between economic welfare and military security, or, more colloquially, the competition between guns and butter.[16] The division of resources between guns and butter, and the actual level of consumption of both goods, are determined by two factors: the production capacity of a society and its preferences. The production capacity of a society may be represented by a transformation curve plotting the different combinations of guns and butter that the society can produce, given its endowment of land, labour, capital and technology. The transformation curve, *ab*, is represented in Figure 1. The preferences of a society may be sketched by a series of indifference curves that represent different 'bundles' of guns and butter that are equally satisfying at any point along any given indifference curve, where a bundle of goods along indifference curve *Ub* (e.g. point *e*) is preferable to a bundle of goods along indifference curve *Ua* (e.g. points *c* or *d*). The most efficient point of consumption is found at the point of tangency between the indifference curve and the transformation curve – in this example, at point *e*. At point *e* our hypothetical state will consume 0*x* of guns and 0*y* of butter.

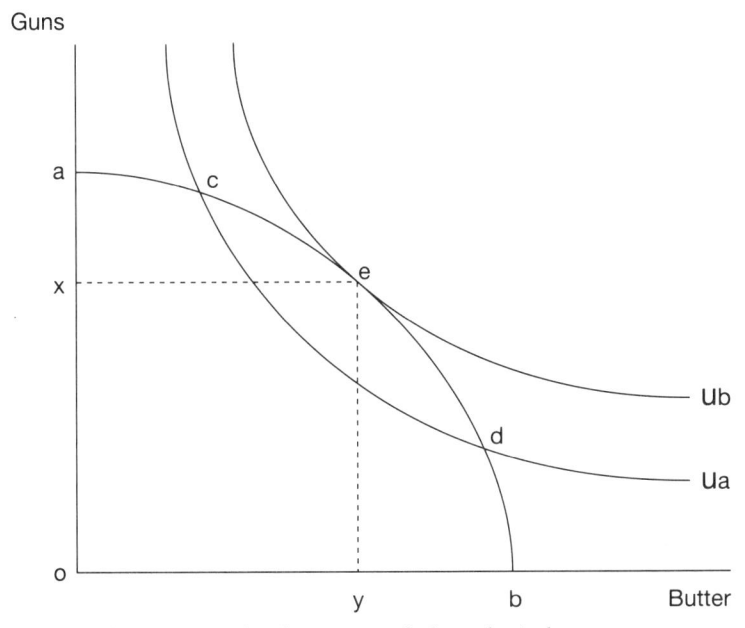

Figure 1 Transformation and utility curves of a hypothetical state

The slope of indifference curves and the shape of transformation curves vary from state to state. Variations in national transformation curves reflect different combinations of the factors of production and different levels of productivity in the sectors producing guns and butter. Variations in the slope of the indifference curves between societies reflect, for example, changes in elite preferences or domestic political coalitions, changes in the geopolitical context of a state or in the technology of war, or an increase (or decrease) in a state's economic capacity.[17] More generally, the 'spectre of war' determines the allocation of national resources between guns and butter; it determines the bias of the indifference curve towards the consumption of guns as opposed to butter. The larger the shadow cast by war, the more immediate is the military security threat to a state, and the greater the level of national resources devoted to guns. Conversely, the more the shadow of war recedes into the background, the more distant is the military security threat to a state, and the greater the level of national resources devoted to butter.[18]

Do these two security dilemmas continue to constrain state choice in the new Europe? The short answer is no. The two security dilemmas have become less intense and have been transformed by the transition to post-Cold War Europe. The security dilemma identified by Jervis has become inverted with the end of the Cold War. The nations of the West fear the negative consequences of political and economic insecurity in the east. Consequently, any measures taken by the nations of the east that enhance national security, defined broadly in its military or economic dimensions, are viewed as a positive contribution to European security rather than as a threat to the security of the west. They also provide the incentive and the opportunity for the nations of western Europe to cooperate with their eastern neighbours even at the risk of being exploited: free riding by the central and eastern Europeans poses a lesser threat to the NATO states than does the re-emergence of authoritarian regimes or economic collapse that could shatter the fragile post-Cold War peace. The perception of a security threat has dwindled as well. The confrontation of the two post-war alliances has ended. The threat once posed to the West has become not only hypothetical but improbable as well. The military threat to the West is limited to residual concern over Russia's intentions in its former internal empire and the 'near abroad', and that residual concern is strongest in the United States and weakest among the states of western Europe.

The security dilemma has been muted by the domestic economic and political difficulties experienced in Europe and North America. In western Europe and North America attention has been directed to the need to overcome structural unemployment and to (re)discover the grail of non-inflationary growth with full employment. Publics and elites in the West have demanded that the 'peace dividend' be employed to redress pressing social, budgetary, economic, and even environmental problems caused by or ignored during the Cold War. In the east, publics and elites are preoccupied with the task of recasting national economies, national polities and habits of mind. The problems associated with the transition to market economies and democracy have pushed the problem of military security into a residual category, whose immediacy rises and falls in response to temporary threats, real or imagined, emanating primarily from Russia.

The security dilemma has also been eased by the change that has taken place in the offensive-defensive balance: Russian military forces have largely retreated to their national boundaries, nations in the east and west have adopted some variation of the concept of 'defensive-defence', NATO's 'new strategic concept' emphasises the importance of out-of-area tasks for NATO and has undergone a major restructuring of forces to meet that need. Moreover, the reduction of conventional force levels embodied in the CFE agreements makes an offensive attack unlikely; the warning time of a major land assault has been increased to at least a year on the European continent, and continuing declines in defence budgets seem likely into the medium term. In our view, it would be closer to the mark to argue that many of the means by which European states attempt to increase their own security *increase* the security of others in post-Cold War Europe.

The distribution of the national product between guns and butter has also been largely resolved with the end of the Cold War. Preferences, capabilities and the procurement of military security have all been changed, and that change has been fundamental in the east. There has been a shift in preferences in post-Cold War Europe: for all the countries located in the European security space there has been rightward shift of national utility curves. The sharp decline in the absolute level of real defence expenditures and in the share of central government expenditures devoted to defence indicates that there is now a decided preference for welfare expenditures. For the CEE states this shift in preferences reflects the combined effect of new political elites organising the transition to democracy and the market economy, a less threatening geopolitical context (namely the end of the Soviet imperium and the disintegration of the Soviet Union itself) and greater cooperation between the west and east enabling (and requiring) that shift to take place.

The nations of the former Warsaw Pact have also experienced a precipitous decline in their gross domestic products, which reflects the collapse of the pre-1989 patterns of trade, the efforts to eradicate rigidities in labour, property and capital markets, and the run-down of the defence sector of their economies. This decline in gross domestic product means that the CEE nations have experienced not only a shift in the composition of the bundle of goods they prefer but a contraction of the amount of guns and butter available for consumption. Thus a change in the shape of the transformation curve in combination with a rightward shift of utility curves have combined to increase the demand for welfare expenditure, to decrease the demand for military expenditure, and to reduce the total amount of both that is available for consumption. In the West, the shift in preferences reflects the political demand and expectation among the governed as well as among those who govern that there would be a 'peace dividend' expended on social, economic and environmental ills, that defence-related industries would be converted to civilian commercial production, and that the geopolitical context facing most western European states would become more reassuring. Thus the rightward shift of North American and European indifference curves has been driven by a variety of factors that may be summarised by the simple observation that the Cold War has ended.

The increased demand for non-defence goods in the east suggests that a new dilemma over the division of the national product now faces the West. Whereas security during the Cold War was defined primarily in terms of military security, and the shadow of war loomed over the European continent, security in post-Cold War Europe is defined increasingly in economic terms and the shadow of war has been displaced by the threat of political and economic chaos in central and eastern Europe. The military instrument is an inappropriate policy instrument with which to meet this new threat, although it could be used to alleviate its symptoms – spreading civil war and mass migration. The most effective instruments in the diplomatic toolbox of the Western democracies are economic and financial: the extension of free-trade agreements, a stable and calculable macroeconomic environment, financial aid and technical assistance to ease the transition to the market economy, and financial support to redress the environmental degradation and ease the debt inherited from fifty years of economic mismanagement. The 'peace dividend' cannot be devoted solely to narrow national welfare objectives; some of it must be diverted to supporting the indirect systemic task of minimising the threat of political and societal chaos in the east. But unlike conventional defence expenditures, which arguably provide direct benefits to the national economy, these systemic expenditures provide diffuse benefits at best and their contribution to systemic stability remains questionable. Although the political return on this type of expenditure is uncertain and defies exact measurement, it is nonetheless essential to the systemic stability of the European security space.

The two post-war security dilemmas have been resolved in a way that removes once intractable barriers to security cooperation between the two halves of Europe. The resolution of these dilemmas has created a new one, namely the necessity of devoting scarce resources to the task of purchasing systemic stability. Systemic stability and the prospect of a peaceful and cooperative pan-European security order are largely contingent upon the successful transition to the market and multi-party democracy in central and eastern Europe. And those transitions, in turn, are contingent upon a stable economic and military environment. This line of reasoning raises two questions. What is the relationship between these economic and military elements of the security order? Do we need to expand the definition of security to account for the relevant economic dimensions of the security equation in post-Cold War Europe? It is our position that the economic tasks facing the states of Europe should no longer be viewed as devoid of a security dimension and treated as a problem of welfare maximisation unencumbered by security considerations; and that the economic dimension of security cannot be merely subordinated to the military dimension of security. Rather, the concept of security must be broadened to envelop all its elements. To that task we now turn.

Towards an economic definition of security

Mercantilist thought has been more conscious of the connection between the economic and military elements of national security than much of the contemporary literature on either security studies or political economy. The critical roles played by economic capacity and wealth as essential components of state security and state power are central concerns of mercantilist thought, even though the precise relationship between 'power' and 'plenty' varies considerably.[19] Many contemporary analysts do not embrace the broad mercantilist view that economic capacity is not only an essential instrumental objective of national security policy but a proper end of state policy as well. Rather, the relationship between power and plenty is reduced to a narrower instrumental approach.

At the most general level, the instrumental treatment of economic security focuses on the connection between economic growth and national security, particularly on determining how or whether the rate of economic growth constrains the ability to achieve a desired level of military security. A second instrumental treatment of European security reduces the problem to that of determining the consequences of defence spending on national economic growth. Depending upon the analyst, defence spending is viewed as either a drag on or the motor driving domestic economic growth.[20] A third variation focuses on the division of the national budget between defence and non-defence expenditures. Here the dominant concern is distribution within the narrow confines of the national budgetary process. In this case the relationship between the economy and military security is reduced to examining the allocation of scarce budgetary resources within a closed domestic political system.[21]

A second approach addresses the connection between the erosion of national autonomy and the openness of the national economy. Here the level of trade, financial integration and monetary interdependence becomes the Achilles' heel of national security policy. Other analysts contract this concern to a focus upon the necessity of technological dominance to guarantee military security.[22] These analysts are concerned with the necessity of maintaining a state's position on the technological frontier, of translating technological dominance into a competitive edge in the production and deployment of military forces, and of guaranteeing the domestic viability and international competitiveness of the national industrial base.

A final category of analysis focuses on the connection between government macroeconomic policy and national security policy. Here the inability of the state to correct chronic balance of payments or budgetary deficits is treated as a threat to national security. Such concerns are perhaps best captured by the concept of 'strategic overextension' which describes the seemingly inevitable incompatibility between the commitments and the capabilities of great powers.[23] These instrumental views of the relationship between economics and security are overly narrow and parochial. They are overly narrow because they neither consider nor investigate the concept or the content of economic security. Economic issues are important only in so far as they affect the military dimension of the security equation. These views are parochial because they are fixated on security from a national rather than a systemic or societal perspective.

A broader concept of economic security deserves attention and elaboration, although such a conceptualisation faces a number of difficulties. First, there is the question of what is to be protected. As Barry Buzan argues, 'the state's responsibilities are nowhere near so clearly defined in the economic sector as they are in the political and military ones'.[24] Moreover, the market economy, and the accompanying market ideology sustaining it, are premised upon the insecurity of economic actors, particularly at the firm and individual level. The problem, then, becomes one of disentangling desirable adjustments at the level of the individual and firm from undesirable developments at the level of society, the state or the system.

In one of the more sustained treatments of economic security, Barry Buzan concludes that economic security can have meaning only in restricted circumstances and where there is a demonstrable linkage between the economy, on the one hand, and military capability, power or social identity on the other. Yet issues impinging upon the content of economic capacity and national identity, ranging from monetary relations to macroeconomic policy to debt repudiation, are treated as essential and critical elements of the inexorable ebb and flow of the market mechanism.[25] While it is a superficially attractive proposition that anarchy 'is the optimal political environment for the market',[26] this formulation runs the risk of conflating the absence of centralised power, law and effective sanction at the level of the international system with the construction of a legal system, enforced by a political authority, necessary for the market mechanism to flourish at the level of the state. In other words, advanced capitalism and the allocation of goods by the market are not politically neutral constructs or limited by national boundaries. Rather, the market is a social convention that requires both political support and protection at the national and international levels – requirements that are provided by the state for internal transactions and by treaty, conventions and international institutions for external transactions.

There are, then, any number of definitions of economic security. We believe that economic security has three identifiable and separable elements. First, economic security reflects concern over the ability of the state to protect the social and economic fabric of a society. Second, economic security involves the ability of the state to act as an effective gatekeeper and to maintain societal integrity. Third, economic security concerns the ability of the state in cooperation with others to foster a stable international economic environment in order to reinforce cooperation in the military sector as well as to extract the welfare gains of openness. This conceptualisation of economic security suffers from a number of disabilities: it lacks the historical primacy and intellectual currency assigned to military security; it suffers from diffuseness of both potential threats and remedies; and its content resists neat categories of threat. It is also clear that the economic dimension of the national security is not as well demarcated as the military dimension of security. Military threats to national security are both specific and intentional; economic threats are both diffuse and systemic, they may be unintended or a secondary consequence of state action.[27] But these troubling characteristics do not relieve us of the need to consider economic security as a distinct concept. The consequences of macroeconomic malfeasance by a major economic power, the collapse of financial markets triggered by a major debt repudiation, a generalised hyperinflation, or the collapse of currency markets could, singly or in combination, threaten the very survival of the state or nullify the economic clauses of the domestic social contract, upend the economic foundation of national political stability, or reintroduce the corrosive competition between states that preceded the Second World War. The resolution of the security problem facing post-Cold War Europe cannot be achieved by dodging the problem of economic security or by treating the economy as an instrumental adjunct of the military requirements of security. Nor can we be satisfied with simply displacing the military definition of security with an economic conceptualisation of security – the military dimension remains too important. The security of post-Cold War Europe demands a broader, systemic definition of the relationship between the economic and military dimensions of security; it requires that the economic dimension be treated as an integral part of the overall security system rather than as an adjunct to the military dimension of security at the national level. The concern embedded in this conceptualisation of economic security is that the international economic system be constructed in such a manner that it creates a stable and secure environment, supporting not only the political and military sectors of interstate relations but the economic sector as well.

It also suggests that an analysis of the institutions and architectures of the post-Cold War European security space should be framed by concern not only with these two components of security but with how the two elements of security intersect and the consequences of that intersection for the formulation of a stable European security architecture. Yet such concern presumes that the barriers to the institutionalisation of the European security architecture that existed in the post-war period have been surmounted. Such an assumption would appear to be supported by the argument up to this point: the external context of state action in the European security space is now characterised by amity rather than enmity, and the security dilemmas of the post-war period have been largely resolved. The potential for cooperation may not be directly translated into the institutionalisation of that cooperation. It may be that the core characteristics of military competition preclude the institutionalisation of cooperation; and the changing currency of power may also serve to limit the feasibility of institutionalising the economic dimension of security.

A continuing problem of cooperation?

The provision of military and economic security poses the problem of collective action for the member states of the European security space. Yet the problem of defining the exact content of those public goods and of reducing the incentives and opportunities to free-ride suggest the creation of multilateral institutions.[28] Yet the military and economic sectors have been held to pose quite different barriers to cooperation and effective institutionalisation.

Charles Lipson characterised economic and security affairs as two fundamentally different forms of strategic interaction that account, in turn, for 'significantly different institutional arrangements' in these two sectors of international politics. He notes that although both economic and security affairs experience bouts of cooperation and conflict, economic interactions, unlike security interactions, are often mediated by sets of norms, rules and decision-making institutions that constrain state choice and establish convergent expectations. The prevalence of institutional governance in economic affairs and the relative absence of institutional governance in military affairs need explaining, since both issue areas meet the primary criterion for institutionalised cooperation: each offers an 'opportunity for joint gains [complicated] by interdependent but autonomous decision making'.[29]

Two important environmental conditions distinguished these two sectors of interaction during the post-war era: the potentially high cost of betrayal in military affairs as compared with the generally low (and reversible) cost of betrayal in the economic sector; and the (subsequent) treatment of military affairs as strictly competitive and of economic affairs as conditionally cooperative. These two environmental conditions, in turn, suggested three categories of difference between military and economic issues. First, economic interactions between competitors were normally defined as cooperative games, whereas security interactions between adversaries were normally defined as non-cooperative games. Cooperation in the economic realm was expected to improve national welfare, whereas cooperation in the military realm was restricted to the strengthening of intra-alliance political relations and the enhancement of alliance military efficacy. Second, the penalty imposed on a state for unreciprocated cooperation in the economic realm was not considered to be perilous to the state's survival, while the penalty imposed on a state for unreciprocated cooperation in the military realm was considered so. And, third, it was generally assumed that states focus upon absolute gains in choosing whether or not to cooperate in economic affairs, whereas in the intensely competitive military sector states were assumed to focus upon relative gains in choosing whether or not to cooperate. It was moreover assumed that only with great difficulty could cooperative economic games be translated into non-cooperative games; and that it was highly unlikely that the non-cooperative military game could be transformed into a cooperative game.[30] It is doubtful whether these differences have survived the end of the Cold War.

In the post-Cold War European security space, there have been changes in the choices states face: as argued above, the resolution of the security dilemmas has transformed the military sector into a cooperative game. Cooperation between states on military issues holds out the prospect of a reciprocal enhancement of national security. The downgrading of the military element of power, the downsizing of military establishments across Europe, and the transition to strategies of defensive defence have diminished the severity of the penalty associated with unreciprocated cooperation. Thus the prospect of confidence-building measures and an institutionalised system of cooperation in military affairs seems less remote. Unfortunately, the change in the currency of power, the new emphasis on the economic elements of power, may increase the penalty for unilateral cooperation in economic affairs. The shifting of inter-state competition from the military realm to the economic realm, substituting the shadow of a trade war for the shadow of a hot war, may have the paradoxical effect of making cooperation more difficult in the economic realm just as cooperation is facilitated in the military realm.

These changes have two implications for economic and military security cooperation in the new Europe. First, the elaboration of pan-European institutions fostering cooperation in the military realm does not face the insuperable obstacles that existed in the post-war period, because the military dimension of security has been transformed into a cooperative game – a development driven by the favourable change in the international context, the growing homogenisation of the European state system, and the resolution of the security dilemmas. Nonetheless, military cooperation within NATO may be burdened, since the costs associated with defection within the NATO alliance have declined owing to the dissolution of the Warsaw Pact and the enfeeblement of Russia. Likewise, the prospects for the development of pan-European institutions managing the economic dimensions of security have vastly improved, but it remains the case that the NATO allies now face barriers to economic cooperation that were largely absent over the course of the post-war period. The potential burdening of economic relations between these countries may be located in the shift in the relevant currencies of power conjoined with the location of the 'new' centres of economic power within the compass of the NATO alliance.

Cooperation in economic and military affairs remains a problem, but it is not as intense or worrisome as in the post-war period. Nonetheless, one difficulty in sustaining cooperation in economic and military affairs has been carried over from the Cold War period: there remains wide variation in the emphasis on and definition of security found among the member states of NATO. The United States, for example, retains a largely military definition of security as well as the conventional understanding of economic security, namely that the economy is important only to the extent that it affects military capability. France, on the other hand, takes a broader view of security, but that view by and large reflects the concern of classical realists with the pursuit of power and plenty as the separable but reciprocally dependent elements of national security. And the Germans, of the major European states, have gone furthest in abandoning the military definition of security and embracing a definition that reflects the preoccupations of a civilian power. These different conceptions of security, which are shared by the other nations of the European security space to differing degrees and intensities, preclude a common frame of reference and the prospect of identical interests that would make international institutions redundant. Thus the divergent interests and conceptions of security held by the European and extra-European powers underline the difficulty of and necessity for elaborating, extending and establishing international cooperation in the European security space.

The requirements of a comprehensive security system

The institutional configuration of the post-Cold War security order is in a state of becoming. The architecture of the emerging European security order, the relationships between institutions of security in the military and economic domains, and the coordination of those domains remain ambiguous and plastic. The most important question facing the future security order revolves around those institutional relationships within those two security domains and, perhaps more important, the interplay and interdependence of those domains. The architectural dimension of the emerging European security order revolves around the problem of establishing coherence within each security domain as well as complementarity between them.

The management of economic competition among the NATO allies and the successful transition to the market economy and multi-party democracy in the former member states of the Warsaw Pact are the basic building blocks of the new European security architecture. The passing of the Cold War diminished the force of anarchy in the shaping of the European security environment and enhanced the 'interaction capacity' of the European state system.[31] The interaction capacity of a security system captures not only 'the ability and the willingness of [states] to interact, but also determines what types and levels of interaction are both possible and desired'.[32] One element of the system's interaction capacity is the extent to which states share norms and are governed by common institutions. Institutions, according to Buzan et al., 'greatly facilitate, and even promote, interactions that shared norms and values make possible and desired ... Institutions provide not only more opportunities to communicate, but also more obligations and more incentives to do so.'[33] The states of the European security space increasingly share common norms and state interaction is increasingly governed by a common set of institutions. Common membership of institutions fostering those norms on a pan-European basis has created a greater interaction capacity within the European security space.

This focus on the interaction capacity of the system presumes the importance of norms and institutions as constraints on state choice in an anarchical system. The role of institutions in international relations is shaped by the conceptual pre-eminence attained by both the international regimes and the 'new institutionalism' literature, both of which highlight the autonomy of political institutions in shaping state preferences and constraining state choice.[34] Both bodies of literature demonstrate that international institutions must be treated as something other than a clearing house for information or preferences; both suggest, rather, how international institutions shape state preferences, how those preferences develop and change, and why states deviate from power-based explanations of state action. Institutions also serve the important function of supplying historical and normative order in an anarchical world.[35] Historical order refers to the role played by institutions in shaping historical processes. Although this role can be judged only *ex post*, awareness of the potential historical role institutional choice may play in a given element of a security architecture underlines the importance of institutional design and choice. Flaws in institutional design, as in the 1930s, can contribute to the collapse of the international system.[36] Normative order directs attention to the consideration of 'the relations among norms, the significance of ambiguity and inconsistency in norms, and the time path of the transformation of normative structures'.[37] Both historical order and normative order suggest that the institutional design of the emerging European security order must meet the criteria of regime congruence and interdependence.

The stability of the emerging European security architecture depends upon the congruence and interdependence of the economic and military security regimes governing the European security space. Regime congruence refers to the requirement that the norms governing these separate regimes are mutually reinforcing and that those norms do not conflict in purpose. The interdependence of the military and economic security regimes refers to the requirement that the norms of military (economic) regimes should generate positive externalities that support the norms and institutions of the economic (military) regimes. It also implies that the regimes supporting the economic and military components of the overall security architecture are mutually dependent: instability or incoherence in one element of the security architecture will undo the stability or coherence of the other element. The stability and effectiveness of the future European security order require the satisfaction of these two criteria, both of which were met under the American and Soviet-dominated economic and military alliance systems.

The problem of institutional design precedes the emergence of the new Europe, but has only recently emerged as a focal point of either the theoretical or the policy-orientated literature.[38] The variation in institutional design is either attributed to the indeterminacy of a cooperative outcome – i.e. the problem of cooperation could be solved by any number of institutional possibilities – or it is attributed to the observation that different categories of problem require different types of institutional solution.[39] But, with the end of the Cold War, the process of institution-building and adaptation has given a new prominence and urgency to the problem and criteria of institutional choice.

There are three categories of enquiry that pertain to the issue of institutional choice: the problems associated with the institutional configuration of the security architecture; the problems associated with resolving the dilemmas of cooperation that states (and other actors) face within and between issue areas; and the problem of identifying the content of the emergent security architecture. The resolution of these problems provides a basis for assessing the levels of regime congruence and interdependence within the European security space.

The problems associated with the issue of institutional configuration revolve around three issues: institutional scope; institutional membership; and the character of the institutional clusters governing specific issue areas. Institutional scope reflects concern with the geographical scope of the institution. The various institutions of the post-Cold War security architecture range from the regional to the Atlantic, to the global. Membership of these institutions is both selective and universal within a particular geographical demarcation – as the overlapping but incongruent memberships of the UN, the Organisation for Security and Cooperation in Europe (OSCE), NATO and the WEU demonstrate. The problem of scope and membership raises a number of questions. Is one particular combination of geographical scope and membership optimal for the supply of security? Are the problems of institutional redundancy or competition mediated or intensified by different or overlapping institutional memberships? How do choices of inclusion and exclusion affect the quality of systemic security and stability?

The emergence of institutional clusters within issue areas raises a set of more compelling questions about the congruence and interdependence of the institutions of the European security space. Institutional clusters, defined as the set of institutions that govern a specific issue area within the economic or military dimension of security, raise three general questions. The first question to be posed is: does a single institution hold a monopoly of competence within an issue area or does it share its competence with other institutions? If there is more than one institution involved in the management of a specific issue area, another question arises. Can the institutional interrelationships within the issue area be best described as a hierarchy or as a polyarchy? The answer to that question is both descriptive and prescriptive: it determines whether institutions act in conformity with the principle of subsidiarity or in accordance with the market metaphor; and it enables analysts to assess the relative merits of each form of organisation in terms of efficiency of effort and efficacy of outcome. The second general question – is there a differentiation or conflation of issue areas? – directs attention to the necessity of compartmentalising the different elements of the security order without divorcing them from one another and thereby precluding necessary or successful cross-issue area linkages. A third area of enquiry focuses on whether a single institution has a monopoly of competence within an issue area or shares its competence with another. The more diluted is the competence for any single issue area within a cluster, and the less hierarchically those institutions are ordered, the more likely will be the potential level of institutional dissonance. The final question asks whether there is a surfeit or a deficit of institutions governing an issue area, whether there is an institutional disequilibrium. An institutional disequilibrium can be of two sorts. First, there can be a surfeit of institutions where too many institutions seek to manage too small a policy space, as in the case of providing finance for the reconstruction of central and eastern Europe – the World Bank (IBRD), the European Bank for Reconstruction and Development (EBRD), the European Investment Bank (EIB) and the European Community's Phare programme largely duplicate each other's efforts. Second, there can be a deficit of institutions where too few (or unempowered) institutions seek to manage too large a policy space, as is the case with restructuring the nuclear power industry in central and eastern Europe as well as in the former Soviet Union – no single institution has the authority or resources to address the most pressing environmental threat to Europe. While this concept of institutional (dis)equilibrium is difficult to define or measure with any precision, it requires careful consideration nonetheless.

The next set of issues that need to be addressed focuses on whether the existing and proposed institutional frameworks facilitate the coordination of state action within and between the economic and military components of the security order. First, it is essential to assure the operation of mechanisms facilitating the coordination of common problems within an issue area (e.g. the need to coordinate debt negotiations between commercial and official creditors). Second, there is a similar need for policy coordination between issue areas (e.g. the need for the 'greening' of EIB finance for eastern and central European in accordance with the Fifth Environmental Action Plan of the EU). And, finally, there is a need to coordinate the economic and military dimensions of security where they intersect (e.g. coordinating the reduction of forces in Europe with the microeconomic policies aiding defence conversion).

A comprehensive treatment of the emerging European security architecture requires the deconstruction of that architecture into sets of interlocking institutional clusters. There are three institutional clusters defining the post-Cold War security architecture. The first is the well known and easily accepted political-military cluster that is rooted in the realist tradition. The second and third clusters, which contain the economic institutions of security, reflect the close connection between the future stability of the European security space and the successful political and economic transformation of central and eastern Europe: one cluster encompasses exchange rate stability, the freeing of trade, and macroeconomic stability; the other cluster encompasses the interconnected problems of financing the large debt overhang of the CEE countries, the political and economic transition of those countries, and the resolution of regional environmental threats. The stability of the emerging architecture depends upon the normative congruence within and interdependence between those clusters. The argument presented above suggests that careful attention must be paid to institutional choice and identified some criteria for that choice.

Conclusion

Institutional choice in shaping the future European security order has become a central element of American and European foreign policy strategies. The policy importance attached to the institutional elaboration of European security raises two final questions. What are the likely sources of institutional supply in the new Europe? What are the limits of the dysynchronous construction of the economic and military components of the European security architecture?

There is clearly a demand for institutions governing the military and economic elements of the post-Cold War European security space.[40] The problem rests in the supply of those institutions and their transformation. Hegemony, leadership and small-n multilateralism are the three sources of institutional supply that are potentially relevant to the post-Cold War security architecture.

The hegemonic stability thesis holds that, in an anarchical international system, only a hegemonic power can provide the collective good of international stability and foster international cooperation. The ability of a hegemonic power to do so is logically and empirically compelling: it is logically compelling because hegemonic powers have both the self-interest and the ability to establish international institutions; and a cursory examination of European history makes it an empirically compelling proposition. It is also the case, however, that a state falling short of hegemonic pretensions, but nonetheless capable of exerting international leadership, can also contribute to the provision of international institutions. A state can solve what Peter F. Cowhey calls the 'top dog' problem of institutional supply if it has 'the means to motivate self-interested [states] to participate in collective action'.[41] But the ability of a state to assume or seek a position of leadership depends upon its ability, first, to distinguish between states that can be induced to cooperate and those that cannot, and, second, to reward the former and to penalise the latter. International institutions may also be the result of small-n multilateralism. Small-n multilateralism, for example in the form of the Group of Seven (G-7) or Group of Three (G-3), occurs when the significant states in an issue area agree to cooperate in the creation or adaptation of international institutions.[42] Small-n multilateralism offers a greater probability of sustained cooperation than large-n multilateralism, although it carries a price: restricting the number of participating states reduces the gains from cooperation.

Since the United States appears to be undergoing a prolonged process of hegemonic decline and Germany can stake a claim only to regional dominance, leadership and small-n multilateralism are likely to be the important sources of institutional supply in the post-Cold War European security space. The majority of the relevant economic and security regimes have been carried over from the Cold War order; many are now in the process of adaptation to the new international environment. While many international institutions have their origin in the immediate post-war period and owe their existence to American hegemony, it is also the case that the adaptation of these regimes to the post-Cold

War security landscape has been and will remain the result of small-n multilateralism within the G-7 or of leadership exercised by the United States on issues affecting Atlantic cooperation or by Germany on issues affecting European cooperation. The absence of a hegemonic power in the post-Cold War European security space suggests that the evolution of existing regimes and the creation of new regimes will require intensive negotiation. The prospect of a regime being imposed in any issue area by a single European or North American power is unlikely. As a consequence, the task of regime construction and adaptation facilitating cooperation in issue areas ranging from the environment to macroeconomic stability to defence will be greatly complicated.

The preferred institutions of security in both the military and the economic dimensions differ across national boundaries; competition to deliver the blueprint of that architecture is particularly marked between the United States, the major western European states (Britain, France and Germany) and Russia. The diverse definitions of security and the competition to supply the outlines of the security architecture pose barriers to great-power cooperation in constructing a coherent European security system. Moreover, it remains likely that some institutions will fail to play their intended roles in the new security environment.[43] The proliferation of institutions and new forms of cooperation that are spanning Europe across the economic and military dimensions of security will undoubtedly generate both intended and unintended consequences. The process of small-n multilateralism, which may be the only politically viable avenue of institutional supply, may have the flawed outcome of putting into place a set of security institutions that reflect an incompatible jumble of great-power preferences that pleases no one and erodes the quality of European security.

An assessment of the emerging security architecture requires an assessment of its parts, the three critical institutional clusters outlined above. A successful security architecture requires these institutional clusters to generate positive externalities, which requires their interdependence. Institutional interdependence suggests, in turn, the necessity of parallel progress in the development and elaboration of the constituent elements of the security architecture. But the parallel progress of those clusters cannot be taken for granted; it is probably more reasonable to assume that progress will be dysynchronous rather than synchronous. What are the causes and consequences of uneven progress? A potential barrier to even progress and a source of potential regress is the inability of the states of the former Warsaw Pact to conclude successfully the economic and political transformation of their societies. Membership of the core institutions of European security, the EU and NATO, is contingent upon the transformation of those nations into democracies with market economies. Consequently, continued and deepened economic and military cooperation depends in large part upon the increasing homogeneity of the European nation states; or the creation of a common political and economic frame of reference, generating a common and legitimate normative order governing Europe. A failure at this level, which suggests the failure of the institutions of economic security, implies the inevitable collapse of a cooperative pan-European security order.

The transformation of these societies has been made possible and has been supported by the changes enumerated above that have taken place in the European state system. Yet it is more than likely that progress in the construction of the economic dimension of the security architecture will outstrip the construction of the military dimension. As compared with the military sector, the pay-offs and costs of cooperation in the economic sector are relatively certain, the costs of compliance and non-compliance are relatively well established, the constraints on adverse state conduct are relatively well established, and the institutional mechanisms facilitating cooperation are long-standing and highly developed. The same cannot be said of the military element of security. Here we find that the pay-offs and costs of cooperation, particularly between former adversaries, are uncertain, the costs of compliance and non-compliance are high and difficult to reverse, and the institutional mechanisms facilitating cooperation are relatively underdeveloped and experience of them is chequered. The process of uneven progress is affected by yet another consideration: the incongruity between the economic and military pay-offs derived from cooperation combined with the domestic political costs of cooperating in either dimension. It may be that the high symbolic cost of cooperation on the military dimension of security, calculated in terms of lost national prestige and autonomy, may present too high a political barrier to military cooperation on a pan-European basis. And it may be that the measurable pay-offs from cooperation on the economic dimension of security may be likewise stymied by domestic political resistance. These considerations, which establish the linkage between domestic politics and interstate cooperation, suggest that there may be some unique level of interstate cooperation on the military and economic dimensions of security that is domestically sustainable. The tolerance of external cooperation to sustain domestic welfare and security objectives will vary between states and will set a limit on the overall level of cooperation within post-Cold War Europe. Although cooperation in both issue areas may be derailed by domestic political resistance, it is unlikely that the economic and military trains will both leave the tracks at the same point of institutional development. The possibility of dysynchronous development of the two elements of the post-Cold War security architecture raises the important question of whether autonomous or differentiated progress in the economic and military elements of the security order can be safely tolerated if the overall stability of the system is to be assured.

Uneven institutional development or uneven progress in the supply of military and economic security could have disastrous results for Europe. Although there has been a real decrease in the likelihood of major war, it remains the case that there is no comprehensive set of institutions that effectively monitor and manage the military dimension of European security. There are no countervailing sets of institutions in operation that could foster greater economic or military security in eastern and central Europe, not to mention the former Soviet Union. The exclusion of the CEE states from full participation in the existing military institutions of security (e.g. NATO or the WEU), combined with the inclusion of those same nations in the institutions of Atlantic economic security, if not the EU, precludes the development of a sustained and interdependent community of interests that will engender and foster cooperation across both the economic and the military dimensions of security.

This potential imbalance suggests a reconsideration of the future course of Europe. If the minimum level of interdependence between the economic and military elements of security cannot be realised with the existing institutions of security, it may counsel the creation of a security architecture that tolerates if not encourages the economic and military differentiation of the European area. It may counsel a return to a set of security institutions mimicking those established in the aftermath of the Second World War, but not marred by the ideological enmity or competition between Russia and the United States. If the minimum level of interdependence is sufficiently low, and is met by the existing institutions of security, it may counsel a less drastic course: economic differentiation or integration complemented by cooperation in a less formal or inclusive set of security institutions.

The resolution of this dilemma may be found in the distribution of capabilities in post-Cold War Europe. The distribution of capabilities raises the issue of polarity and re-emerges as a critical variable in the determination of the broad contours of the European security system. If military power recedes into the deep background of diplomacy, if military power becomes merely the foundation of interstate relations and no longer functions as an instrument of statecraft, the states occupying the European security space will be driven by one of the many logics ascribed to economic multi-polarity: at one extreme, it will provide a more fertile basis for cooperation and stability; at the other, it promises a return to the competitive and non-cooperative world of neo-mercantilism. The choice of institutions in both the economic and the military dimensions of security will largely define the pathway that is eventually chosen for Europe.

Notes

1   See Richard N. Cooper, *The Economics of Interdependence* (New York: McGraw-Hill for the Council on Foreign Relations, 1968); and David P. Calleo and Benjamin M. Rowland, *America and the World Political Economy: Atlantic Dreams and National Realities* (Bloomington: Indiana University Press, 1973). By the mid-1970s, however, the importance of the economic dimension of national policy, if not national security policy, was established by the turbulence in international economic affairs and by the publication of Robert O. Keohane and Joseph S. Nye's *Power and Interdependence: World Politics in Transition* (Boston: Little Brown, 1977) and Robert Gilpin's *US Power and the Multinational Corporation* (New York: Basic Books, 1975).

2   This development was given institutional form with the G-7 economic summits. For a history of the G-7, see Robert D. Putnam and Nicholas Bayne, *Hanging Together: the seven-power Summits* (Cambridge, Mass.: Harvard University Press, 1984); and G. John Ikenberry's brief update in 'Salvaging the G-7,' *Foreign Affairs*, vol. 72, no. 2 (spring 1993), pp. 132–40.

3   See Hans Maull, 'Germany and Japan: the New Civilian Powers,' *Foreign Affairs*, vol. 69, no. 5 (winter 1990/91), pp. 91–106; and James Sperling, 'America, NATO, and West German Foreign Economic Policies, 1949–1989' in Emil J. Kirchner and James Sperling, *The Federal Republic of Germany and NATO: Forty Years After* (London: Macmillan, 1992), pp. 157–93; 'German Security Policy and the Future European Security Order' in Michael G. Huelshoff, Andrei S. Markovits and Simon Reich (eds), *From Bundesrepublik to Deutschland: German Politics after Unification* (Ann Arbor: University of Michigan Press, 1993), pp. 321–46.

4   The classic statement of the neo-realist position is found in Kenneth Waltz, *Theory of International Politics* (New York: Random House, 1979). Critiques of neo-realism include John Gerard Ruggie, 'Continuity and Transformation in the World Polity: toward a Neorealist Synthesis,' *World Politics*, vol. 35, no. 2 (January 1983), pp. 261-85; Robert O. Keohane, 'Theory of World Politics: Structural Realism and Beyond,' in Robert O. Keohane (ed.), *Neorealism and its Critics* (New York: Columbia University Press, 1986), pp. 158–203); and Barry Buzan, Charles Jones and Richard Little, *The Logic of Anarchy: Neorealism to Structural Realism* (New York: Columbia University Press, 1993). For neo-realist interpretations of the post-Cold War international system see Kenneth Waltz, 'The Emerging Structure of International Politics,' *International Security*, vol. 18, no. 2 (fall 1993), pp. 59–60; and John Mearsheimer, 'Back to the Future: Instability in Europe after the Cold War,' *International Security*, vol. 15, no. 1 (summer 1990), pp. 5–56.

5   The neo-liberal position is foreshadowed and informed by Hedley Bull's distinction between an anarchical international system and an anarchical society. He suggests the importance of rules and institutions that states commonly assent to in their own self-interest. See Hedley Bull, *The Anarchical Society: a Study of Order in World Politics* (London: Macmillan, 1977) and Barry Buzan, 'From International System to International Society: Structural Realism and Regime Theory meet the English School,' *International Organization*, vol. 47, no. 3 (summer 1993), pp. 327–52. The theoretical approaches that may be broadly labelled neo-liberal include: regime analysis (e.g. Stephen D. Krasner, ed., *International Regimes*, Ithaca: Cornell University Press, 1983, and Robert O. Keohane, *After Hegemony: Cooperation and Discord in the World Political Economy*, Princeton: Princeton University Press, 1984); multilateralism (John Gerard Ruggie, ed., *Multilateralism Matters: the Theory and Praxis of an Institutional Form*, New York: Columbia University Press, 1993); and epistemic communities (Peter M. Haas, *Knowledge, Power and International Policy Coordination*, special issue of *International Organization*, vol. 46, no. 1, winter 1992). Game-theoretic treatments of the possibility of cooperation and the (occasional) need for institutions to facilitate cooperation include Arthur Stein, *Why Nations Cooperate: Circumstance and Choice in International Relations* (Ithaca: Cornell University Press, 1990), and Robert Axelrod, *The Evolution of Cooperation* (New York: Basic Books, 1984). For a comparison of the neo-liberal and neo-realist positions that places the assumptions and conclusions of each position into sharp relief see Joseph Grieco, *Cooperation among Nations: Europe, America, and Non-tariff Barriers to Trade* (Ithaca: Cornell University Press, 1990), especially chapter 2.

6   Wolfram F. Hanrieder, 'Dissolving International Politics: Reflections on the Nation-State,' *American Political Science Review*, vol. 72, no. 3 (September 1978), pp. 1276–87. On the contest between autonomy and interdependence see Thomas Ilgen, *Autonomy and Interdependence* (Totowa: Rowman & Littlefield, 1985).

7   International institutions must be viewed as shapers of preferences rather than as simply functioning as the clearing house of competing state preferences. This view of institutions is found in James G. March and Johan P. Olsen, 'The New Institutionalism: Organizational Factors in Political Life,' *American Political Science Review*, vol. 78, no. 3 (September 1984), pp. 734–9.
8   Raymond Aron, *Peace and War: a Theory of International Relations* (New York: Anchor Press, 1973). See also Bruce Russett, 'Correspondence – the Democratic Peace', *International Security*, vol. 19, no. 4 (spring 1995), pp. 164–75.
9   On the issue of hegemonic rise and decline see Charles P. Kindleberger, *The World in Depression, 1929–39* (Berkeley: University of California Press, 1973); Robert Gilpin, *War and Change in World Politics* (Princeton: Princeton University Press, 1981), and Robert O. Keohane, *After Hegemony: Cooperation and Discord in the World Political Economy* (Princeton: Princeton University Press, 1984).
10 Robert Powell, 'Absolute and Relative Gains in International Relations Theory,' *American Political Science Review*, vol. 85, no. 4 (December 1991), pp. 1303–20. The importance of amity and enmity in shaping interstate relations is found in Arnold Wolfers, *Discord and Collaboration* (Baltimore: Johns Hopkins University Press, 1962).
11 Joanne Gowa, 'Bipolarity, Multipolarity, and Free Trade,' *American Political Science Review*, vol. 83, no. 4 (December 1989), pp. 1245–56.
12 Powell briefly discusses the problem of cooperation even when force is not at issue; Duncan Snidal suggests that Powell's formulation is too extreme to capture state interaction in a less restrictive universe. Robert Powell, 'Absolute and Relative Gains …', p. 1316; and Duncan Snidal, 'Relative Gains Problem for International Cooperation – Comment,' *American Political Science Review*, vol. 87, no. 3 (September 1993), p. 740. Another way of putting it is that the games played in the West during the Cold War were coordination or a battle of the sexes, but that the end of the Cold War may have transformed those games into a prisoners' dilemma. The focus of competition shifted from interbloc comparisons to intrabloc comparisons of (relative) gains from cooperation; the intensity of relative gains concerns increased for intrabloc interaction and decreased for interbloc interaction. For the transformation of games see Duncan Snidal, 'Relative Gains and the Pattern of International Cooperation,' *American Political Science Review*, vol. 85, no. 3 (September 1991), pp. 701–26.
13 Robert Jervis, 'Cooperation under the Security Dilemma,' *World Politics*, vol. 30, no. 2 (January 1978), pp. 167–214. He attributes this formulation of the security dilemma to John Herz, 'Idealist Internationalism and the Security Dilemma,' *World Politics*, vol. 2, no. 2 (January 1950), pp. 157–80, and to Herbert Butterfield, *History and Human Relations* (London: Collins, 1950), pp. 19–20.
14 Jervis, 'Cooperaton …', p. 175.
15 Jervis, 'Cooperation …', pp. 211ff.
16 Robert Powell, 'Guns, Butter, and Anarchy,' *American Political Science Review*, vol. 87, no. 1 (March 1993), p. 116.
17 This discussion draws on Robert Gilpin, *War and Change in World Politics* (Princeton: Princeton University Press, 1981), pp. 21ff.
18 Powell, 'Guns, Butter, and Anarchy,' p. 116.
19 See Jacob Viner, 'Power versus Plenty,' *World Politics*, vol. 1, no. 1 (October 1949), pp. 1–27; David Baldwin, *Economic Statecraft* (Princeton: Princeton University Press, 1985).
20 Michael D. Ward and David R. Davis, 'Sizing up the Peace Dividend: Economic Growth and Military Spending in the United States, 1948–96,' *American Political Science Review*, vol. 86, no. 3 (September 1992), pp. 748–55; Steve Chan, 'The Impact of Defense Spending on Economic Performance: a Survey of Evidence and Problems,' *Orbis*, summer 1985, pp. 403–34; Charles Kupchan, 'Defence Spending and Economic Performance,'

Survival, autumn 1989, pp. 447–61; Lloyd J. Dumas, *The Overburdened Economy* (Berkeley: University of California Press, 1986).

21   Penelope Hartland-Thunberg, 'From Guns and Butter to Guns *v.* Butter: the Relation between Economics and Security in the United States,' *Washington Quarterly*, vol. 11, no. 4 (autumn 1988), pp. 47–54.

22   See Theodore H. Moran, 'An Economics Agenda for Neorealists,' *International Security*, vol. 18, no. 2 (fall 1993), pp. 214–15; *American Economic Policy and National Security* (New York: Council of Foreign Relations Press, 1993), pp. 41–70; Ethan Barnaby Kapstein, *The Political Economy of National Security: a Global Perspective* (New York: McGraw-Hill, 1992), pp. 188ff.

23   Paul Kennedy, *The Rise and Fall of the Great Powers* (New York: Random House, 1987); David P. Calleo, *Beyond American Hegemony* (New York: Basic Books, 1987) and *The Imperious Economy* (Cambridge, MA: Harvard University Press, 1982);

24   Barry Buzan, *People, States and Fear: an Agenda for International Security Studies in the post-Cold War Era*, second edition (Boulder: Lynne Rienner, 1991), p. 124.

25   Buzan, *People, States and Fear*, pp. 124–31; 241–8.

26   Buzan, *People, States and Fear*, p. 249.

27   Martin C. McGuire, 'The Revolution in International Security,' *Challenge*, vol. 33, no. 2 (March/April 1990), p. 6.

28   There is a large literature devoted to the role played by institutions in facilitating cooperation and resolving the problem of free riding. See Arthur Stein, *Why Nations Cooperate*, Robert O. Keohane, *After Hegemony: Cooperation and Discord in the World Political Economy* (Princeton: Princeton University Press, 1984); Stephen Krasner (ed.), *International Regimes* (Ithaca: Cornell University Press, 1983); Lisa L. Martin, 'Interests, Power, and Multilateralism,' *International Organization*, vol. 46, no. 4 (autumn 1992), pp. 765–93.

29   Charles Lipson, 'International Cooperation in Economic and Security Affairs,' *World Politics*, vol. 37, no. 1 (October 1984), p. 2. See also R. Harrison Wagner, 'The Theory of Games and the Problem of International Cooperation,' *American Political Science Review*, vol. 70, no. 2 (June 1983), pp. 330–46.

30   Lipson, 'International Cooperation ...,'pp. 12ff. Duncan Snidal has demonstrated formally the difficulty of transforming a variable-sum game into the constant-sum game of pure conflict. See Duncan Snidal, 'Relative Gains and the Pattern of International Cooperation,' *American Political Science Review*, vol. 85, no. 3 (September 1991), pp. 701–26.

31   For an extended discussion of interaction capacity as an element of the international system structuring the relations between states see Barry Buzan, Charles Jones and Richard Little, *The Logic of Anarchy: Neorealism to Structural Realism* (New York: Columbia University Press, 1993), pp. 69–80.

32   Buzan *et al.*, *The Logic of Anarchy*, p. 69.

33   Buzan *et al.*, *The Logic of Anarchy*, pp. 70–1.

34   James G. March and Johan P. Olsen, 'The New Institutionalism: Organizational Factors in Political Life,' *American Political Science Review*, vol. 78, no. 3 (September 1984), p. 738. See also Elisabeth R. Gerber and John E. Jackson, 'Endogenous Preferences and the Study of Institutions,' *American Political Science Review*, vol. 87, no. 3 (September 1993), p. 652, and Geoffrey Garrett, 'The European Community's Internal Market,' *International Organization*, vol. 46, no. 2 (spring 1992), pp. 534–45. For two representative volumes on regime-based understandings of international politics see Stephen Krasner (ed.), *International Regimes* (Ithaca: Cornell University Press, 1983); and Paul F. Diehl (ed.), *The Politics of International Organizations* (Chicago: University of Chicago Press, 1989), p. 15.

35   March and Olsen, 'The New Institutionalism,' pp. 743–4.

36 Kenneth Oye, *Economic Discrimination and Political Exchange* (Princeton: Princeton University Press, 1992).
37 March and Olsen, 'The New Institutionalism,' p. 744.
38 See Miles Kahler, *International Institutions and the Political Economy of Integration* (Washington, DC: Brookings Institution, 1995), chapter one, and Lisa L. Martin, *Coercive Diplomacy: Explaining Multilateral Economic Sanctions* (Princeton: Princeton University Press, 1992).
39 The categories of problem are derived from the strategic interaction states face. See Duncan Snidal, 'Coordination versus Prisoners' Dilemma: Implications for International Cooperation and Regimes,' *American Political Science Review*, vol. 79, no. 4 (December 1985), pp. 923–4; Arthur Stein, 'Coordination and Collaboration: Regimes in an Anarchic World', in Stephen D. Krasner, ed., *International Regimes* (Ithaca: Cornell University Press, 1982), pp. 115–41; and Lisa Martin, 'Interests, Power, and Multilateralism,' pp. 768–83.
40 The literature on the supply of regimes is less well developed. See Oran R. Young, 'Regime Dynamics: the Rise and Fall of Regimes,' in Krasner, *International Regimes*, pp. 93–113.
41 Peter F. Cowhey, 'Domestic Institutions and International Communication,' *International Organization*, vol. 47, no. 2 (spring 1993), p. 300. What remains unaddressed, however, is the actual *need* for international regimes. The usefulness of a regime is found to be heavily dependent upon the type of cooperation problem faced by states. See Martin, 'Interests, Power, and Multilateralism.' The requirements of leadership are drawn from William T. Bates and Robert H. Bianco, 'Cooperation by Design: Leadership, Structure, and Collective Dilemmas,' *American Political Science Review*, vol. 84, no. 1 (March 1990), pp. 138–48. See also Duncan Snidal, 'The Limits of Hegemonic Stability Theory,' *International Organization*, vol. 39, no. 3 (summer 1985), pp. 579–614.
42 See Kenneth A. Oye, 'Explaining Cooperation under Anarchy: Hypotheses and Strategies,' *World Politics*, vol. 38, no. 1 (October 1985), p. 21, and Miles Kahler, 'Multilateralism with Small and Large Numbers,' *International Organization*, vol. 46, no. 3 (summer 1992), pp. 684–5.
43 The European Bank for Reconstruction and Development is a good case in point. Designed as the engine of economic growth and political transformation in central and eastern Europe, the EBRD has failed to deliver on its original promise. It has become a relatively inconsequential force in the recasting of eastern and central Europe playing a distant second to its primary competitor (and shareholder), the European Investment Bank.

2

The regional institutions of European security
The Council of Europe, the European Union and the Western European Union

Although the EU, the WEU and the Council of Europe have contributed to peaceful relations in Europe, their contribution to the territorial defence of western Europe in the pre-1989 period was limited. A combination of internal and external factors successfully conspired against greater effectiveness. Uncertainties over Germany and the existence of the Cold War prevented initial attempts to establish a European Defence Community (EDC) in the 1950s. Over a forty-year period NATO established an effective collective defence arrangement which would either make alternative security structures superfluous or, as particularly perceived by the United States, make the establishment of separate or autonomous security organisations intolerable. Attempts to substantially upgrade the role of the WEU, like the 1987 Platform, or to make the WEU a strengthened and autonomous defence arm of the EU, as in the Maastricht treaty negotiations, have therefore failed. Although the Single European Act actually called for the establishment of the necessary economic conditions for greater progress towards eventual political union, it maintained that all such efforts must be compatible with NATO and WEU aims, and did not lift the limits imposed by Article 223 of the Rome Treaty. Similarly, the Council of Europe was confined to the promotion of democratic values, human rights and cultural traits.

Can these limitations be maintained in the post-1989 period, given the change in threat perception by the West, the level of ethnic conflict in central and eastern Europe and elsewhere in the world, the existence of a unified Germany, the potential for EU enlargement, and the possible reduction of US military commitment to Europe? With NATO lacking a clear mandate for out-of-area interventions, can these three European institutions, individually or collectively, take on major tasks in the security field? In what areas, and to what extent, could these institutions contribute to the prevention or resolution of conflict and to peaceful relations in Europe and elsewhere in the world? On what basis, or equity, could collaboration with NATO, the OSCE or the UN be conducted?

Answers to these questions require an analysis of the genesis and evolution of the Council of Europe, the EU and the WEU, the changing circumstances in which the three organisations have found themselves after 1989, and the potential they have for contributing to security and stability in Europe and elsewhere in the world. This chapter will deal firstly with the development of the three organisations and their role in European security. It will then proceed with an analysis of the factors which are likely to shape future security developments in Europe and suggest ways in which the policies of these three organisations might be strengthened in post-communist Europe.

Pre-1989 western European security

The Council of Europe, the EU and the WEU have all made important contributions to the peace and stability that prevailed in western Europe prior to 1989; examples range from Franco-German reconciliation and the consolidation of democratisation in Greece, Spain and Portugal. The success of the EU, primarily in economic and democratic terms, acted as a magnet for the CEE states and indirectly contributed to the break-up of the Soviet bloc and the demise of the Cold War. In contrast to the other two organisations, only the WEU has a specific defence and security dimension. The WEU owes much of its origin to the defeat of plans for a European Defence Community by the French National Assembly in 1954. It was formed in 1954 as a device to facilitate rearming the then West Germany and bringing it into NATO. Although all three organisations have increased in size, their evolution has been markedly different. The Council of Europe, by and large, has stuck to its original task of promoting cultural and democratic values. Like the OSCE, the Council of Europe spans both parts of Europe, drawing twenty-four members from western Europe and fifteen from central and eastern Europe. The fifteen EU members act as a distinct entity within the Council of Europe. In contrast to the Council of Europe, the EU has undergone considerable task expansion in a number of fields, including foreign and security policy. Specific efforts to establish a common European security or defence policy have failed to be ratified in treaty form, like the EDC in 1954, or have been stillborn, like the French attempt in the early 1960s, known as the Fouchet plan, and the Genscher-Colombo plan of 1980. Subsequently, for much of the 1960s, 1970s and early 1980s, defence and security policy remained a taboo subject, with EU affairs restricted to the ambit of what Stanley Hoffmann has described as 'low politics'.[1] The assumption was that the EU, preoccupied with trade and economic issues (low politics), would not be able to engage in issues of defence and security (high politics) which were controlled or influenced by the prevailing bipolar world and were 'core' elements of sovereignty. Whilst this description held some validity for the period in question, there were (and are) existing EU policies which effectively either have security implications or contribute to the development of a common foreign and security policy (CFSP). These policies relate to aid and development policy, as carried out through the Yaoundé and Lomé conventions; the EU's external commercial policy, where the EU has exclusive competence to represent the member states, as pursued through trade treaties, association agreements and GATT negotiations; monetary cooperation, and the alignment of exchange rates which touches upon both internal and external aspects of the EU; and the Single Market programme, which strengthens the economic base of the EU and enhances its international stature.

Furthermore, the establishment of European Political Cooperation (EPC) in the early 1970s was a direct attempt to coordinate the foreign policy of EU member states. EPC enables member states to consult and exchange information in order to encourage collective discussion and action in foreign policy. It provides the opportunity for *démarches* and joint negotiations and declarations with third countries, and representation in international bodies. However, EPC is not an exclusive instrument. Rather it is an additional channel for member states to pursue their foreign policy goals. What impairs the effectiveness of EPC is the principle of unanimity and the fact that the majority of actions remain non-binding and declaratory. This presents the possibility for member states to take unilateral action which may not be in the interests of other member states or of the EU. Often EPC decisions are also so broadly defined that they are open to interpretation by each of the member states. The absence of steering or sanctioning instruments is an additional failing associated with EPC.

With EPC restricted to the coordination of national foreign policies rather than designing a common foreign policy prior to 1989, and with security aspects left largely untouched, developments in the WEU were no more encouraging. On the contrary, even after efforts to strengthen its role in promoting collective security and facilitating 'out-of-area' military operations, via the Platform on European Security Interests of 27 October 1987, the WEU appeared to be moribund.[2] It did, however, play a coordinating role in naval monitoring during the Iran–Iraq war, involving Belgian, British, French, Dutch and Italian forces. Portugal and Spain became WEU members in 1988 and Greece joined in 1992. Consequently in 1995 the WEU had nine full members, three associate members and three observers. Iceland, Norway and Turkey as associate members have the right to speak at meetings of the WEU council, but may not block decisions that are required to be made by consensus; Austria, Denmark and Ireland as observer states are permitted to attend WEU council meetings and working groups.

Since its reactivation, WEU has been a forum for consultation on arms control issues. It has discussed practical arrangements among member states for implementing the CFE treaty verification regime. An expert group has been working on the development of national inspection teams and the creation of multinational inspection teams with the participation of inspectors from CEE countries, as well as training CEE inspectors. The WEU satellite centre at Torejon has been cited as a means by which data gathered under the Open Skies Treaty could be jointly analysed and distributed to national capitals, permitting cost saving and also allowing more effective mission planning and resource management among WEU members.[3]

The consequences of the tumultuous changes of late 1989, bringing in their wake the end of the Cold War, German unification, the break-up of the Soviet Union, and instability in central and eastern Europe, gave the Council of Europe, the WEU and the EU a new opportunity in the foreign and security field. The Gulf conflict of 1991 gave the WEU an additional chance to play, once again, a coordinating role for military intervention (the coordination of a naval blockade). How have these organisations responded to these changes and opportunities?

New opportunities and challenges

It is a well known fact that institutions generally respond slowly to external change.[4] In the case of the Council of Europe, the WEU and the EU this response is subject to the diverse interests of members. However, given its more limited range of organisational objectives, on the one hand, and its specifically Europe-wide focus, on the other, the Council of Europe was able to adapt more swiftly to events in eastern Europe by granting membership to the states of the region.[5] Membership does not entail security guarantees or economic aid, but can be considered as one of the prerequisites of EU membership, and possibly of WEU membership. Among its main tasks are the promotion of Europe's common heritage, the protection of minorities and the safeguarding of democracies. Responding to the needs of the CEE members, the Council of Europe has expanded its activities to cover the judiciary, law enforcement, the training of lawyers and civil servants, local and regional democracy, and education.[6] By focusing on local and grass-roots initiatives, it has helped to reduce tension and has established links between otherwise antagonistic groups within and across states. Its European Charter for Regional or Minority Languages and the Framework Convention on the Protection of National Minorities set important guidelines for easing community relations.[7] Although the Council of Europe has made impressive strides in extending its values and orientations to the CEE area, mainly through membership, it faces the difficult task of deciding to admit countries with apparent human rights violations such as Russia (Chechnya). Whilst membership of a wide range of countries with varying records on democracy and human rights would create internal strains on the organisation, exclusion can create resentment, and isolation, and may abet the return of authoritarian regimes. If membership is not feasible for some CEE countries, then other ways must be found whereby the Council of Europe can foster their democratic development. What should be avoided is a new division in Europe caused by membership inclusion and exclusion.

Whereas the Council of Europe has had some success in responding to the problems posed by the transition of former communist regimes to democracy, the EU has found it much more difficult to adjust. EU members, especially the larger ones, found themselves caught between the need to respond to events such as German unification, changes in eastern Europe and the Gulf conflict of 1990–91, and the desire to preserve national sovereignty and acquired power status. The Maastricht treaty, forged through the Franco-German initiative in the spring of 1990, was a compromise between the two countervailing tendencies which left in its wake an acrimonious change of leadership in Britain.

Whether the Maastricht treaty is sufficient to accommodate or integrate a unified Germany into the EU, whether it allows the EU to develop a genuine CFSP and become an effective external actor, and whether it will contribute to the erosion of national sovereignty or alter power positions within the EU, remain to be seen. To obtain a better understanding of what the treaty entails we have to consider its objectives, achievements and prospects.

The Treaty on European Union sets out to establish the framework and processes necessary to achieve a CFSP. The aims of that policy are to: (1) safeguard the common values, fundamental interests and independence of the EU; (2) strengthen the security of the EU and its member states in all ways; (3) preserve world peace and strengthen international security in accordance with the principles of the UN charter as well as the principles and objectives of the OSCE; (4) promote international cooperation; and (5) develop and consolidate democracy and the rule of law, and respect for human rights and fundamental freedoms. It calls for joint action in these fields and for closer ties between the EU and WEU. Joint action is to be attempted within the OSCE on disarmament and arms control measures in Europe, nuclear non-proliferation, and the economic aspects of security, particularly the transfer of military technology. Overall the aim is to ensure the coherence of external relations (trade, aid, EPC). The method of operation, however, remains intergovernmental. The Council of Ministers will be required to define a common position only when 'it is deemed necessary'. Governments are permitted to pursue their foreign policy as long as they follow the common position; they are required to inform and consult other members if the matter is of 'general concern'. To a certain extent this can be regarded as a retrograde step from the Single European Act, which required member states to endeavour to reach a common position. National governments remain the most decisive actors in the field of foreign and security affairs, where state-to-state bargaining is allowed to dominate the policy-making process. Decisions on CFSP are to be taken by unanimity on guidelines and questions of principle; the guidelines and principles can be implemented by majority voting.

The WEU is to become the defence component of the EU, while at the same time being the instrument for strengthening the European pillar of NATO. The

WEU is requested 'to elaborate and implement decisions and actions of the EU which have defence implications'. Already, there is WEU-EU cooperation in the protection, policing and administering of the Bosnian town of Mostar.[8] Maastricht left open the political and legal question of whether the WEU should operate under the ultimate responsibility of the EU or of NATO.[9] The EU intergovernmental conference in 1996 will probably make progress towards clarifying this situation. Meanwhile, since the WEU has no structure or role by which to function independently, attention has turned to how the WEU's effectiveness can be enhanced or used actively to pursue EU objectives.

At the St Petersberg summit of June 1992 the WEU decided to strengthen its virtually non-existent operational capabilities by outlining a procedure for the assignment of forces and the creation of a planning cell. The latter was established in Brussels in October 1992 to identify and update lists of units from member states that could be earmarked for WEU use on certain missions. Other tasks that have been given to it include recommending proposals on command, control and communications (C^3) arrangements for operational missions and preparing contingency plans for operations. Under these arrangements the WEU will be activated only for specific purposes, rather than constituted as a standing operational force.[10] However, this 'cell' has not yet succeeded in organising exercises.[11] It can also be said that the Torejon satellite interpretation centre, which is to promote satellite intelligence gathering and analysis, suffers from a shortage of funds. The WEU council and secretariat moved from London to Brussels in January 1993 to facilitate relations with the EU and NATO. These WEU innovations have increased the complementarity in aims and task performance with the EU's CFSP. What is being done to improve the operational capabilities of the WEU?

The Eurocorps is seen as the foundation for the establishment of WEU military forces and command structures. The joint Franco-German brigade established in 1988, with a strength of 4,000 soldiers, is the basis of multi-national forces, the basic concept of Eurocorps. Since 1993 a number of Eurocorps formations have been in existence. The main one comprises a planned military strength of 50,000 from France, Germany, Belgium and Spain. Luxembourg also intends to join. France, Italy and Spain envisage both an air maritime force and a ground force answerable to the WEU. France and Britain have established a so-called Euro-Air Group, based at High Wycombe, where the unit's task will be to draw up requirements and procedures for all operations in support of joint peace-keeping and humanitarian action. Britain and the Netherlands have also established an amphibious force. Plans also exist for a Dutch-German corps under alternate command and for the formation of an air mobile brigade between Britain, Germany and Belgium. The Dutch navy is to merge its naval headquarters with Belgium's.[12] However, the effectiveness of the Eurocorps formations has been questioned. Critics maintain that they will be ill suited to rapid deployment and mobile operations outside Europe, since they are largely composed of heavy units designed for battle on the central European front.[13]

This factor plus the general lack of forces, equipment logistics, intelligence gathering and airlift capability indicates that the WEU may find it difficult to establish an autonomous operational capability and will have to rely on NATO for some years to come.[14]

Even if the WEU's organisational capacity can be improved, Denmark, Germany and Ireland may not participate in military interventions. Denmark has only associate status and Ireland is a mere observer. No clear line had emerged in 1995 as to what relationship the new EU members, Austria, Finland and Sweden, would seek with the WEU.[15] Until the judgement of the German Constitutional Court in July 1994, Germany had felt inhibited by its constitution, which had been interpreted as preventing it from participating in military interventions in NATO out-of-area operations.[16] After the Constitutional Court decision, the government declared that its future military missions would be based on UN or OSCE mandates and decided on a 'case by case' basis. Given the country's size and status, the absence of German participation is not only particularly crucial to the scale of operations but may also provoke resentment from those countries that regularly supply military forces to future WEU peacekeeping missions. On the other hand, even if Germany were to participate fully in WEU operations, the sending of German troops to international trouble spots like Bosnia or the Middle East might provoke controversy because of Germany's past.

There is also a question over the WEU's identity. Having been founded primarily as a defence organisation, to what extent can it, or will some of its members allow it, to engage in out-of-area security tasks? For nearly identical reasons, a similar 'role search' is taking place within NATO. Both organisations are undergoing a painful adjustment process. In turn this adjustment process affects the relationship between NATO and the WEU, raising questions over complementarity and rivalry as well as cost and benefit considerations. How autonomous can the WEU become within NATO without endangering the cohesion and effectiveness of the latter organisation? This delicate balancing act is further complicated by the WEU's relationship with the EU. Differences in the composition of these two organisations, as well as stark differences between France and the United Kingdom over the future role of the WEU,[17] pose serious questions as to who is representing what between the organisations. In part because of calls for an 'inner core' of EU countries by members of the German governing party in September 1994, there were anxieties on the part of certain WEU members that such an inner core could gradually erode powers hitherto belonging to the WEU as the sole organisation responsible for European security and defence.[18] Would it imply a division of labour in the future, with the WEU mostly confined to tasks of defence and the EU primarily entrusted with issues of security? Given the intertwining of defence and security, such a separation could not easily be established. However, the EU actually insists it will examine, case by case, whether security questions discussed in the framework of the CFSP have implications in the defence area and whether the WEU should be called upon. On the other hand, there are also calls for independent WEU action. In other words, contrary to the Maastricht treaty, under which the WEU must receive a mandate from the EU before acting, some suggest that, should the EU be unable to reach agreement on an initiative from the WEU, the latter should be free to forge ahead.[19] There is thus a question over which nucleus is more important: the WEU as a defence and security organisation, or a possible inner core of the EU through a strengthened CFSP.

These problems have so far prevented the WEU from playing an effective role on its own. Rather, it has been forced to act with or through NATO and to elicit UN legitimation or mandates, which have introduced their own limitations on efforts to resolve the ethnic conflict in the former Yugoslavia.[20]

Lessons to be learned

Given the constraints experienced by both the EU and the WEU, what lessons can be drawn and how does the EU intend to rectify the shortcomings? In one sense it can be argued that the EU and the WEU effectively failed to translate opportunities into action between 1990 and 1995; no coherent foreign security policy emerged to deal with, for example, the ethnic conflict in Bosnia. There has been too much reliance on economic and diplomatic measures, which took the form of trade, aid, air and financial sanctions against Serbia as well as the dispatching of monitors for information gathering, the assessment of various troop movements, and the implementation of negotiated cease-fires.[21]

In contrast, military interventions have been kept to a minimum. Organisational difficulties within the WEU are among, but not necessarily the major, factors in this. As the example of NATO showed, the existence of adequate military intervention forces between 1992 and the end of 1995 was no guarantee that those forces would be used in a crisis if it happened to be defined as 'out of area'. The key aspect is the political will on the part of member states over when and how to employ military force.

Whether such a decision could be reached more easily among a few individual countries on an *ad hoc* basis, as in the Gulf conflict of 1991, rather than in organisations of either twelve or fifteen members, is a point of debate. Whereas in the Gulf conflict the United States, Britain and France agreed on the objectives of engagement, the same cannot be said of the Bosnian conflict. Not only did the United States fail to commit ground forces to UN peace-keeping operations but the Americans were at odds with Britain and France over the extent to which military intervention should be used and the arming of the Bosnian Muslims. Germany, whilst unable for constitutional reasons to send ground forces to Bosnia, adopted the US line on the supply of weapons to the Muslims. A lack of common objectives among EU and NATO members in the Bosnian case provided a stark contrast with the Gulf conflict, where a confluence of interests supported joint military action.[22] Dissimilar national interests, rather than the question of whether a few large countries would have done better than the WEU or NATO, appears to have been the crucial explanation for the lack of effectiveness until mid-1995 of the WEU and NATO in resolving the Bosnian conflict.

Moreover, it could be argued that the EU/WEU, NATO and the UN introduced measures which helped to contain the Bosnian conflict and provided much-needed humanitarian relief operations. The EU was a key actor in the establishment of a permanent peace conference in Geneva where the protagonists were able to come and discuss a possible resolution of the conflict. Despite the fact that the Geneva peace conferences were not exclusive to the EU, rather a partnership with the UN, it can be argued that the EU had acted as a catalyst of cooperation between European and international organisations. In late 1993 the EU also sought to increase the number of military personnel under UNPROFOR command and so enable that command to overcome those trying to obstruct aid convoys by the 'use of all appropriate means'. Finally, by hanging together the Western powers denied the Balkan combatants the chance to play one state off against another. Comforting as this may sound, it was no substitute for resolving a situation which lingered on for several years with enormous bloodshed.

What lessons, then, are to be learned and improvements to be made if, for example, the EU/WEU is to become effective in the future? Both external and internal factors are of relevance. The US attitude towards the role of the WEU is of crucial importance. For a considerable time the United States viewed the WEU either as duplicating NATO missions or as possibly dragging Americans against their will into conflicts along Europe's periphery. Changes brought about by the end of the Cold War, increased interest in Asia, domestic budgetary constraints, and the perceived need to bring central and parts of eastern Europe closer into the EU fold in order to prevent a re-emergence of Russian influence in that region, have brought about new American thinking. It appears also that the Eurocorps meets American congressional concerns about burden sharing and free riders. Evidence of the changing US attitude can be found in the NATO summit declaration of January 1994, which recognised the need for the development of a European security identity. A similar pledge was made by US President Clinton on his visit to Europe in June 1994.[23] There is now a US willingness to share military assets with the European allies. As suggested by the NATO declaration of January 1994, there will be Combined Joint Task Forces (CJTFs are technically under NACC/NATO auspices) between NATO and the WEU. Whilst the practicalities have yet to be worked out, the introduction of CJTFs will be of significance to EU/WEU development, an aspect which will be examined in the following chapter. It will probably also enhance the role of Eurocorps. In spite of these favourable external developments, the EU needs to overcome a number of internal obstacles if it is to develop an effective CFSP.

For the CFSP to become more effective, it must be able to do at least two things. It must become proactive and use forward planning in European and international matters rather than depend on reactive measures. Secondly, it must be able to back up its economic and diplomatic measures, especially with regard to peace-keeping, with the use of force. There is truth in the late Manfred Wörner's statement that political solutions and diplomatic efforts will work only if they are backed by the necessary military power and the credible resolve to use it against an aggressor.[24]

More efficient planning requires clarity of objective, coherence and consistency in the formulation of policies and synchronisation between the EU and WEU. The latter necessitates, according to Van Eekelen, the former secretary-general of the WEU, common working procedures, including joint planning between the two organisations. As he sees it, the security, if not the military, dimension of common actions of the EU will always be present one way or another. The early involvement of the WEU is therefore fully justified.[25] However, given prevailing differences over, for example, the extent to which member states feel their interests are compromised in the Bosnian conflict, the role of the WEU, further EU enlargement, and voting in the Council of Ministers, clarity in CFSP objectives is a daunting task. EU objectives are therefore often of a general, if not bland, nature, espousing such principles as responsibility in the world, international equilibrium, the maintenance of peace, the reduction of international tension, and cooperation among nations, rather than prioritising aims or spelling out the means necessary to implement policy objectives. The Maastricht treaty falls into this category, being long on general aims and short on specific priorities, and even shorter on detailed means. Nevertheless, there are a number of developments where EU policy objectives are being pursued in a more focused and specific manner. Among them are attempts to resolve and prevent conflict in central and eastern Europe, promoting political stability in the region, and fostering Europe-wide cooperation. It is important to briefly examine these attempts in order to establish their significance and future potential.

Two areas of concentration have emerged in which the EU seeks to (1) prevent the events of Bosnia from recurring elsewhere in central Europe, and to promote stability in central Europe, (2) strengthen ties with Russia, Ukraine, the Baltic countries and some of the CIS states, like Kasakhstan, and to defuse the conflict between Russia and Ukraine and between the Baltic republics and Russia. The first area of concentration may be overshadowed, at least in the medium term, by EU enlargement considerations. In any case, given the severity of existing ethnic conflicts and the potential for further conflicts, the EU and the WEU envisage the use of two main types of activities to relate to both areas of concentration. These two activities are crisis management and conflict prevention. Crisis management relates to cases where both organisations can engage in peace-making or peace-keeping operations, the resolution of ethnic and regional conflicts, humanitarian aid (disaster relief operations) and assistance to countries at war. Conflict prevention activities seek to strengthen the establishment of democratic regimes in CEE countries (based on the rule of law, a pluralist system and respect for human rights), the introduction of market-based economies in the region, and the promotion of Europe-wide cooperation. The logic is that peace and stability depend on democracy and prosperity. Conflict prevention is coupled with cooperation, mutual interests and solidarity. It reflects concerns expressed by Vaclav Havel and Hans-Dietrich Genscher that any attempts by the west to distance itself from its responsibility for the rest of Europe would have serious consequences for western Europe as well, e.g. affect its tranquillity, peace and prosperity.[26]

Parallel with efforts at crisis management in the former Yugoslavia, the EU started in 1991 to establish ties and relations with the CEE area.[27] Since then Europe Agreements[28] with Poland, Hungary, the Czech Republic and Slovakia have come into force, and have been signed with Bulgaria and Romania. Whilst the content of these initial agreements was mostly of an economic nature and entailed conditions at least as favourable to the EU as to the CEE countries, it laid the foundations of political dialogue and established a framework for closer ties. It is the political dialogue and the framework of greater cooperation, rather than the economic content of the agreements, which will be analysed here. Details of the economic aspects of the agreements and technical assistance programmes will be found in Chapters 5 and 6.

Since 1992 a qualitative evolution of relations between the EU and the CEE countries can be observed. A multilateral dialogue has been established which goes beyond both economic and informal arrangements. Upgrading this dialogue was particularly pronounced at the Copenhagen European Council meeting in June 1993. Significantly, the EU committed itself to an interpretation of the purpose of the Europe Agreements as being the framework for preparing associates for eventual full membership. It calls on prospective associates to 'assume the obligations of membership by satisfying the requisite economic and political conditions'. These stipulations were reiterated at the Essen summit in December 1994. However, no specific deadlines or precise criteria of 'readiness' were laid down. What it did initiate was an array of meetings, between the two entities, including some at the highest level,[29] and an increase in the range of subjects to be discussed, such as a CFSP, justice and home affairs. Although the meetings have only consultative status, they demonstrate the importance the EU attaches to relations with these countries. At a minimum it ensures that the CEE countries are regularly informed on issues dealt within the EPC/CFSP area.

Consultation with the EU is to be further promoted by the decision of the Visegrad countries to establish among other things a system of defence coordination, to encourage economic and political reform, to build upon the existing free-trade zone, and to ensure speedy and full integration within the EU.[30] There can be little doubt, however, that what the CEE countries really want is full membership as soon as possible. Already, in the spring of 1994, Hungary and Poland had submitted applications for full EU membership. The question of membership defies easy answers, not only for the EU but also for the WEU and NATO. As Shea argues:

the spread of nationalism presents a dilemma as to whether to admit states with nationalist ambitions to regional organisations in order to dampen these tendencies early, and risk being infected with their instability, or shut them out and thereby exacerbate the conflict which may spread in any case.[31]

There is of course a question whether it is reasonable of the EU to demand from potential CEE members that they should solve their problems before joining when what the EU claims as one of its greatest achievements was to have established a situation where no war is likely to occur in the future and where in the process historic national enmities have been overcome. This point is made more strongly by Vaclav Havel, who suggests that what CEE states need is more than structures. In his view what is required is expressions of solidarity, symbols and effective means which can be fostered only through full membership of the EU and WEU. He therefore praises the Council of Europe, which has admitted most CEE states, as helping to balance national differences, promote common norms and cultivate the values from which the spirit and ethos of European integration may grow.[32] Membership of the Council of Europe may also bring with it a new legally binding dimension on the rights of minorities.

Whilst all CEE states seek EU and WEU membership, the consummation of their desire is not universally shared by the existing EU and WEU members. Whilst Germany favours admitting them to both organisations, Britain prefers EU membership rather than WEU membership, whereas France desires the reverse. France is concerned that enlargement may dilute EU integration efforts and possibly strengthen German influence; the United Kingdom seems to be prepared to accept a dilution of the EU but not of the WEU, fearing that admission to the latter may adversely affect the relationship between the WEU and NATO.

The St Petersberg WEU summit offered associate co-operation partnership membership to CEE states, much along the same lines as the North Atlantic Cooperation Council (NACC).[33] At this summit a Forum of Consultation (FOC) was created. Like the arrangement made under the NACC it seeks to strengthen existing relations by restructuring the dialogue, consultations and cooperation between the WEU and the east. The FOC can be considered less diverse than the NACC, and may therefore be a useful vehicle to enable those countries to acquaint themselves with the future security and defence policy of the EU and find new opportunities to cooperate with the WEU.[34] In May 1994 nine CEE countries became 'Associate Partners' of the WEU.[35] However, this status will not provide them, at least for the foreseeable future, with security guarantees.[36] A closer link with the WEU could also forge more direct links with NATO through the 'European pillar' and with the EU. Curiously, whilst the WEU has offered associate membership to nine CEE countries, the EU has accorded such status, as well as indications of eventual membership, only to six CEE states. There is also a possibility that CEE states will be prepared to offer troops in support of WEU peace-keeping operations.[37]

With these issues simmering, the EU and WEU have pursued a parallel strategy of conflict prevention. In the opinion of the former secretary-general of the WEU, Wilhelm van Eekelen, this means diminishing the perceived significance of frontiers, settling the problems of minorities in the spirit of Helsinki and through arbitration, investing boldly in economic reconstruction, and associating these future partners of the EU with the dialogue on the current status of the security of the European continent and its future prospects.[38] The so-called Balladur proposal for a European Stability Pact, launched in 1993, is the most concrete expression of this aim. It stems from the realisation that political stability is an essential condition of economic and social progress in eastern Europe. It intends to reinforce stability to the east of the EU and can be considered an exercise in preventive diplomacy. Motivated partly by the wish to make up for failure in the former Yugoslavia, it is an effort to persuade CEE states to work together, in the hope of similar success to that which the United States achieved with the Marshall Plan in western Europe. The aim is to guarantee the rights of minorities and the inviolability of frontiers in Europe so that tragedies like that of the former Yugoslavia do not recur. Beyond that, the thinking is that, if these countries are to join the EU, they must not bring unresolved conflicts with them. The Balladur proposal would build on the activities within the Phare programme, the Europe Agreements with the Visegrad countries, the cooperation agreements with CEE states, and the aid and technical assistance which the EU provides to the CEE area. The pact is limited to Poland, Hungary, the Czech Republic, Slovakia, Romania, Bulgaria and the three Baltic republics. It would help to tie together the existing European security and human rights organisations -OSCE, the Council of Europe, NATO and the WEU. As well as the pact itself, there were a series of 'round tables' between neighbouring states, and bilateral agreements between particular states. At the inaugural conference in Paris in May 1994, attended by the foreign ministers of some forty European countries and representatives of European organisations. It did not deal with areas of conflict in the former Yugoslavia and the Caucasus, and the countries in those areas were not invited to the conference, with the exception of Slovenia. The conference agreed to establish two round tables, on the treatment of the Russian minority in the Baltic states and on Hungarian minorities in Slovakia and Romania. The aim of the round tables was to produce bilateral accords of 'good neighbourliness' which would be endorsed in a concluding session of the conference and then registered with the OSCE. Poland, with only tiny ethnic minorities left, has already concluded bilateral treaties with all seven neighbouring states. These goals were largely realised with the final conference of the pact, held in Paris in March 1995.

Whilst the Stability Pact has been seen as the foundation of a European *Ostpolitik*, Russia has expressed reservations that the Stability Pact clashes with the OSCE, the Partnership for Peace (PfP) initiative and the NACC. Thus the EU has the difficult task of balancing the need to provide security for CEE against the risk of alienating Russia. Much of the concern which central European states have with regard to security relates to Russia and the successor states of the

Soviet Union. Whilst the fragmentation of the former Soviet Union has resulted in a less powerful adversary for the West, there are many remaining and newly emerging problems which have significant implications for the whole of Europe. These relate to existing levels of military forces and weapons of mass destruction; nuclear blackmail, made possible by the abundant and unregulated stocks of weapons and nuclear waste; and the proliferation of weapons of mass destruction. There are also dangers of large-scale migration from the Commonwealth of Independent States (CIS) to central and western Europe. For the EU the challenge is how to normalise and promote relations with Russia and the successor states of the former Soviet Union and contribute to economic and political stability in that region, e.g. to avoid the occurrence of excessive nationalism, violence and ultimately a return to authoritarian regimes and repression.[39]

The EU has singled out relations with Russia, Ukraine, Kazakhstan and the Baltic republics as a top priority. Part of the reason is that the first three states possess nuclear weapons, and the Baltic states have close historical and cultural links with Poland and the northern European countries. The twofold objective of the EU is to bring these countries rapidly within the European cooperation system; and to defuse tension between Kiev and Moscow, and between the Baltic republics and Russia, as well as to draw the Baltic states closer to the Union. In line with these objectives the EU has concluded partnership and cooperation agreements with Kazakhstan, Kyrgyzstan, Ukraine and Russia, and has signed free-trade agreements with Latvia, Lithuania and Estonia. The latter envisage the creation of a free-trade zone for industrial goods within four years. The aim of the partnership and cooperation agreements is to provide a solid global framework for the development of deeper bilateral relations. They cover political dialogue in addition to trade in goods and services, capital, intellectual and industrial property protection and economic cooperation. They also stress democratic values, respect for human rights and a market economy as essential elements of the partnership. Finally, they emphasise the importance of regional cooperation to safeguard the future prosperity and stability of the ex-Soviet republics. Although similar in aims, the partnership and cooperation agreements differ in scope and importance.

The agreements with Ukraine and Russia are the most comprehensive. Both agreements hold out the prospect of a free-trade area at the turn of the century and are to encourage foreign investment and liberalise trade. In the case of Ukraine concern over nuclear weapons and power stations and the specific issue of the Crimea played a key role. The initial refusal by Ukraine to sign the nuclear non-proliferation treaty, the storage of nuclear weapons on Ukraine soil and the overhaul of the Chernobyl nuclear power plant were central to such concern. As a consequence, the EU was willing to provide Ecu 500 million towards the shutdown of the Chernobyl plant and to insist on a framework of adequate standards for continued operation of the other existing nuclear power plants in Ukraine. It also donated Ecu 79 million in emergency food aid. The agreement with Russia can be seen as a central plank in the Western strategy of stabilising post-communist Russia. It also aims to ease Russian nationalist fears of encirclement as more countries which were formerly Soviet satellites or neutrals are drawn into the democratic, market-orientated orbit of the EU. On the other hand, there are also EU hopes that this agreement will encourage Russia to play a constructive and stabilising rather than intrusive role in CIS states, especially in the Caucasus region, where Russia has already stationed peacekeeping forces in certain states to deal with ethnic conflicts. The West wants to avoid being drawn into conflicts over which it may have little control. Finally, the EU is attempting to bind Russia into the European security and cooperation framework and so avoid a situation where Russia once again deals direct with the United States to the exclusion of the Europeans.

Consistency and coherence in EU policy

It is one thing to declare objectives and priorities, quite another to execute and implement them with consistency, coherence and efficiency. One way of assessing EU activities in the external field is to consider the number and types of so-called joint actions undertaken by the EU. Crucial to these joint actions is the principle declared in the Maastricht treaty that there should be consistency and coherence in activities between the EU and member states, on the one hand, and between CFSP and the EU on the other. The wider implications of this principle are evident in the Treaty on European Union, which declares that the CFSP shall include all questions relating to the security of the EU, including the eventual framing of a common defence policy, which may lead to common defence. It also requests the WEU to elaborate and implement decisions and actions of the EU which have defence implications. This entails the interconnection of all three pillars and involves coordination between internal and external issues (trade and aid). The task of ensuring consistency and coherence in CFSP action, as well as between CFSP actions and other EU policies, falls to the Commission and the Council of Ministers. This sharing of responsibility could create its own problems over who should be the determinant in those areas where security cooperation and other EU matters as such meet or are superimposed (as in the field of external relations).

General areas in which joint action is to prevail concern the OSCE process (disarmament and arms control, including confidence-building measures), nuclear non-proliferation issues, and the economic aspects of security, in particular control of the transfer of military technology to third countries and control of arms exports. At the special European Council Meeting of October 1993 the first areas of joint action were selected, involving the Middle East peace process, war in the former Yugoslavia, elections in Russia, democracy in South Africa, and preventive diplomacy in the form of the creation of a stability pact with the CEE states. Other joint action has involved the dispatching of observers to the Russian and South African general elections, the mobilisation of financial and economic means of advancing the peace process in the Middle East, and cooperation with other international organisations to fulfil the UN Security Council's resolution regarding humanitarian aid to Bosnia. These are small steps in themselves. An expansion in scope is required. If that takes place more attention will have to be paid to the relationship between (1) economic, trade and aid policy and CFSP and (2) internal security policy and CFSP. A few examples will illustrate the difficulty and importance of achieving consistency and coherence between these policy objectives.

The western Europeans will be required to expand their defence effort to meet challenges posed by ethnic conflicts in CEE, international crises, as in Somalia or Rwanda and a continued reduction in the American defence commitment. This involves not only troops but also military equipment, which in turn requires appropriate levels of defence spending and an adequate defence industry base – a requirement that could compel the WEU countries to raise the proportion of GDP spending on defence by an extra 1.5 per cent and sustain that increase for about five years.[40] Yet judging from the current free fall in defence spending of most west European countries (except France) the opposite seems to happening, a decrease rather than an increase in military capacity for cooperative WEU missions (see Table 1). To mitigate this erosion, west European states have tried to ensure greater integration of forces through the establishment of multinational forces of which the Eurocorps is a leading example. Falling defence expenditures, caused by the demand for a peace dividend after the Cold War, also affect the defence industry base and raise questions about acceptable threshold levels below which defence autonomy is impossible to sustain.

Table 1 Military force strength and budgets, 1985–93/97

	Force strength			Budget ($ million)	
	1985	1994	1997	1985	1993
Belgium	91,600	80,700	40,000	2,428	1,866
Denmark	29,600	28,000	25,000	1,259	1,256
France	476,600	431,700	371,000	20,780	21,890
Germany	478,000	408,000	300,000	19,222	19,252
Greece	159,000	159,300	159,300	2,331	1,903
Ireland	13,700	13,000	n.a.	320	283
Italy	385,100	325,000	287,000	9,733	10,690
Luxembourg	800	800	800	38	57
Netherlands	101,600	74,000	70,000	3,884	3,818
Portugal	73,000	58,300	n.a.	2,428	1,866
Spain	320,000	201,000	180,000	3,969	3,735
UK	327,100	293,500	241,000	23,791	20,726

Source: Ian Mather, 'Old armies battle to find a common front', The European, 22–8 July 1994.

Ideally, this would require the establishment of a common policy on military procurement. However, efforts at standardising military equipment have had mixed results. Among the encouraging signs is the December 1992 decision to transfer the functions of the Independent European Programme Group (IEPG) to the WEU. The Western European Armaments Group (WEAG) – which inherits the work formerly done by the IEPG – will help to promote European cooperation in the field of armaments. However, given the difficulties encountered in the former IEPG of monitoring, promoting and coordinating armaments cooperation, high expectations should not be held of the WEAG. Prevailing national interests, issues of national sovereignty and interdependence, prevent the development of a Euro-wide military industrial dimension. In part this is evident in the problems experienced with cross-border cooperation in military aviation, with Germany deciding in 1994 to go slow on the Eurofighter 2000 aircraft, and the United Kingdom agreeing in January 1995 to hedge its bets by purchasing twenty-five C-130Js and developing a new European military transport (FLA). However, the Eurofighter represents Europe's largest industrial project, at approximately £40 billion. Only slow progress has been made towards liberalising European defence procurement. Mention should also be made of cooperation on the Helos (reconnaissance satellite) project. However, there is still too much reliance on national preferences in the awarding of defence contracts and too little intra-European competition, despite the efforts of ministers working through the IEPG.[41] Even within the single market, the EU has so far failed to abolish Article 223 of the Rome treaty, which specifies that weapons and war *matériél* are exempt from EU competition rules. It is likely that the intergovernmental conference of 1996 will lift the restriction. Another option, suggested by Trevor Taylor, would be for the WEAG to procure some of the major and most expensive systems, which could perhaps then be operated on a joint basis by European armed forces, but which would be too costly if purchased separately on a national basis.[42] The work sharing at the WEU satellite centre at Torejon in Spain is an example which could be extended to the domain of procurement. Clearly the cost of duplication is enormous, but whether considerations of national interest and sovereignty will allow such collaboration is as yet an open question. The establishment of a French–German arms procurement body in 1994 might signal the arrival of a number of bilateral arrangements.

In the field of economic affairs, external trade, aid and development, difficulties also emerge with regard to consistency and coherence. For example, the association agreement with CEE states make it evident that the EU is not yet ready to meet the expectations of the associate states, as can be seen with the EU's reluctance to expose itself to the competitiveness of some European low-wage economies in 'sensitive areas' of the economy. Yet failure to provide CEE states with the necessary economic opportunities could harm their prospects of political stability, such stability being the very thing the EU seeks to promote through the Stability Pact. The EU does somewhat better with regard to aid and development policy, where it has generally managed to ensure that the principle of respect for human rights is taken seriously by the cooperation partners.

An area where consistency and coherence appear particularly important is internal security, the so-called 'third pillar' of European Union. As domestic politics cannot easily be separated from foreign policies, the line between internal and external security becomes increasingly blurred. This is particularly relevant to the EU as it tries to eliminate internal border controls and to add new members. Efforts against cross-border terrorism, drug-trafficking, money laundering and organised crime are necessary not only between EU member states but also between EU member states and CEE countries. In addition, there is considerable worry about the smuggling of plutonium out of eastern Europe and the former Soviet Union.

Not all existing EU member states are willing to abolish border controls and, with the EU facing enlargement, this opens a number of questions. Can EU member states agree on sharing a joint information system, creating an effective Europol, establishing a common asylum policy, and extraditing alleged criminals? In late 1993 some progress was made in this respect with the establishment of a group of national security officials – known as the K4 Committee – to deal with internal security matters in the EU. A major concern is the question of illegal immigrants into the Union, which has given rise to public and parliamentary debate of growing intensity and occasional acts of violence. It was this sensitivity which prevented the Maastricht treaty from containing a more robust commitment to a common immigration policy. Even though slow progress is being made, the EU realises that, if it is to control immigration and to keep it within manageable bounds, cooperation with the main source countries of 'would-be emigrants' is required. Another task of the committee is the establishment of a police intelligence database containing a vast number of files on criminals and suspected illegal immigrants. The European Information Service (EIS), which will link the security services of the Fifteen, will be based on an existing information system operated by the nine Schengen group countries on their land, sea and air borders. This group of EU countries abolished all internal barriers in March 1995 and collates data on stolen vehicles, counterfeit currency and other offences. The data bank of this group will eventually store about 1.5 million items of information on individuals and their movements. The EU is also considering the establishment of Europol, a European police network based in the Netherlands which would focus on the illegal drugs trade as well as on terrorism. Other plans involve the establishment of a European Prosecutor's Office and giving the European Court of Justice jurisdiction in some criminal matters.

Meanwhile, there are attempts, especially among the British, German and Italian secret services, to combat cross-border terrorism and organised crime. Intelligence agencies from eastern Europe are being drawn into the fray. However, whilst there is cooperation on this as on many other aspects of the EPC field, it is also the case that individual member-state secret service agencies do not generally share intelligence information with each other. As a matter of fact member states are still in the business of spying on each other.[43]

Prospects for collective EU/WEU action

As the above examination has demonstrated, achieving consistency and coherence between member states and EU policies and between EU policies and CFSP remains a distant goal. The same can be said about the prospects of collective action. The contrast between the desirable and the possible has been most visible with regard to EU policy in the former Yugoslavia, stretching from problems with recognition of the successor states in ex-Yugoslavia, and inability to intervene effectively in the conflict over Bosnia, to the unilateral action by Greece to block trade with Macedonia.

Whilst the EU has responded with a host of economic and diplomatic measures to upheavals and developments in CEE states, it has not been able, either on its own or in conjunction with the WEU, to respond with effective military measures to conflicts such as that in Bosnia. Lack of consensus, inadequate preparation by and relations with the WEU, and ambiguous lines of demarcation between the UN, NATO and OSCE have largely prevented such undertakings. The EU has moved away from a predominantly economic model of foreign policy in the Bosnian conflict, but it has not moved fully to a position that can be described as a political mode. The absence of a military capacity is the dominant factor here. However, it is too early to condemn the EU's CFSP. After all, the CFSP has been in existence only for a relatively short time and, given the diversity of national interests, it will take a few years to elucidate such a policy. An evaluation of its future prospects is therefore in order.

The prospects for collective action must be seen in the context of factors such as external pressure, the American commitment to European defence, and the development of EU integration generally. It is highly probable that ethnic conflicts will continue in central and eastern Europe. Whilst this is in itself an element of instability, there is also a danger that such conflicts could spread to parts of western Europe and/or cause substantial increases in migration from east to west, thus affecting the cohesion and stability of EU member states. Similar concerns prevail over developments in North Africa, particularly with regard to the rise of Islamic fundamentalism in Algeria. Demographic trends in the Maghreb, combined with economic difficulties, also have a direct effect on the EU in the form of increasing migration. Other potential threats relate to the proliferation of nuclear weapons and the resurgence of nationalism in CEE countries. With indications of a waning American defence commitment to Europe, the EU needs to upgrade its capabilities in the foreign and security areas if it is to respond to existing and potential external problems. The unpredictable role of Russia as a re-emerging regional actor is another factor which could contribute positively to a CFSP, as are potentially international conflicts, such as those in Somalia and Rwanda. There is another way in which the prospects for future joint action can be viewed. Individual WEU members can no longer afford to acquire all the necessary assets for deterrence in Europe or for force projection outside Europe. Cooperation is the only way of coping with the steady shrinkage in national defence budgets, notably in the fields of space, strategic transport, logistics and telecommunications.[44] The same holds for national military procurement and the survival of much of the defence industry base.[45]

These factors will undoubtedly increase pressure for a more effective CFSP. But how widespread the willingness to take collective action will be, and how quickly it can be taken, is still an open question. The tendency so far has been to 'coordinate' rather than design a CFSP, e.g. emphasis on the common rather than single elements of such a policy. As a report of the WEU Parliamentary Assembly indicates, 'The simple enumeration of objectives in matters of peace policy and stability that are general and therefore not binding to any great extent, such as those mentioned so far in the framework of the CFSP, is of little use.' In other words, what is needed is the specification of common interests, the clarification of priorities, and an indication of whether the EU/WEU would be prepared to support those interests by force if necessary.

Such willingness to act when agreed conditions exist would represent a qualitative jump in EU development since nearly everything the EU did in Bosnia took the form of designing a policy to meet a specific problem rather than applying an existing policy where the willingness to act in agreed circumstances existed.[46] No such policy had emerged by 1995, though the Commission had asked a group of high-level experts to prepare a report, which identified why and how the EU should adopt explicit objectives, procedures and instruments for the CFSP.[47] This report pleaded for a definition of the joint military resources available to be placed at the disposal of the EU in support of the CFSP, as well as for the specification of a timetable and objective conditions for participation by member states. Concretely, it recommended:

(1) the build-up of Eurocorps and other multinational units designated for the WEU into a sizeable European intervention force (around 150,000 soldiers) with the necessary command, intelligence and logistical components,
(2) mapping out an irrevocable course towards collective defence by the year 2000,
(3) the creation of a politically independent central (analysis and evaluation) capability with the (non-exclusive) right of initiative, which could facilitate joint Commission/WEU/Council Presidency proposals and be headed by a prominent personality,
(4) the introduction of qualified majority voting, though subject to a special weighting (reflecting the size of member states), on decisions not having military implications.

Some of these ideas were also echoed in the Balladur proposal for a White Paper on security in Europe which would highlight Europe's specific interests and define the means necessary for defending them in liaison with the Atlantic alliance.[48] Invariably, all these efforts entail the development of a European security identity as the European pillar of a reinforced NATO, and capable of effective, independent action in consultation with the other alliance members; the establishment of a stable immediate neighbourhood (including Russia, Ukraine, the Balkans, the Mediterranean and the Middle East) to reduce any potential threat to the EU; and the promotion of democracy and human rights in central and eastern Europe, as well as elsewhere in the world.[49]

Yet recognising the need for collective action is not the same as executing or implementing such a policy. In between lie key aspects of sovereignty, mutual trust and interests. The Cold War may be over but opportunism among nations and the quest for power are not. The tendency for states to define their national interests in terms of relative power gains dies hard. Or, to put it in another way, the desire among member states for unity is less than their interest in sovereignty. Nation states in eastern Europe have re-emerged with vigour, while member states of western Europe cling resolutely to sovereignty. This is most manifest in Britain, where Prime Minister John Major insists that 'it is for nations to build Europe, not for Europe to attempt to supersede nations. I want to see the Community become a wide union, embracing the whole of democratic Europe, in a single market and with common security arrangements firmly linked to NATO.'[50] Further evidence of this came in the White Papers on defence by the governments of France, Germany and the United Kingdom in 1994. Whilst all three White Papers allude to the importance of European and transatlantic cooperation, it is defined in terms of purely national interests. There is nothing to imply that the harmonisation of national interests constitutes an important goal, nor is inspiration drawn from the objectives of the CFSP.[51] The establishment of a single EU seat at the UN is as remote as ever. On the contrary, we can even detect a disregard for common objectives. For example, France decided in January 1995 to establish a diplomatic presence in Iraq, unilaterally deviating from the diplomatic freeze of the West. In addition, Germany, having been weaned on security dependence and a heavy dose of pacifism during the Cold War period, has found it hard even after the 1994 constitutional change to play a more active role in the WEU and to carry out peace-keeping missions in Europe and elsewhere in the world.

As a consequence of these prevailing national conditions the role of the EU and WEU in the security field is constrained. In a way this points to a circular problem: the lack of a strategy on where and when to engage in external conflicts or events prevents the development of WEU military capabilities, and inadequate development of WEU capacity impedes a CFSP strategy on where and when to engage. Subsequently, there is confusion over the function and direction of WEU, which prevents WEU from obtaining the necessary intelligence, command and logistical resources.

These circumstances would seem to refute integration theory and tend to support neo-realist arguments. But we may need to differentiate between the short- and long-term implications. Central to this is the question whether we should expect the renationalisation of defence policies or whether despite existing shortcomings a strengthening of the EU and WEU will occur. The answer tends to suggest the latter rather than the former. As Volker Rühe, the German defence minister, maintains, 'within the EU, no country can go its own way, nor can there be any possibility of thinking in terms of spheres of influence, coalitions and counter-coalitions, containment and hegemony ... All Europeans are dependent, in their own interest, on integration within the community.... Stable currencies, common diplomacy and common security are the indispensable components for a strong community.'[52]

What this implies is that whilst organisations like the EU and WEU are challenged by centrifugal forces of diverging national interests, structured and patterned relations provided by regional organisations are being preferred by governments to anarchical situations. It also suggests, as is argued by Peter van Ham, that in times of rapid and unanticipated change governments are disinclined to redesign regional institutions.[53] We will therefore not see any swift fundamental shift towards a full-blown EU security and defence policy, but rather a continuation of the pooling of sovereignties in sensitive areas of defence and foreign policy. Member states will stress a common rather than a single CFSP. Intergovernmentalism, though in a modified form (less reliance on the lowest common denominator), will continue to be the main practice. This will have two consequences. Firstly, the gap identified by Christopher Hill between capabilities and expectations will continue.[54] Internal differences over EU developments and diverging interests in foreign and security matters will impede capabilities for some time to come. Secondly, it will have repercussions at the 1996 intergovernmental conference in terms of consideration for greater efficiency in EU external action and in terms of a multi-speed Europe. Already there are indications that the 1996 intergovernmental conference will result in clashes of fundamental interests over voting procedures in the Council of Ministers, e.g. whether unanimity should be maintained, and if more majority voting were to be introduced, what form it should take. One of the forms that might be considered is the German suggestion of double majority voting, requiring both a majority of member states and a majority taking into account the size of their populations.

Whether progress will be made towards lifting the prevailing system of multiple-layered vetoes remains to be seen. Under the Maastricht treaty, it takes unanimity for the European Council to request the WEU to act, unanimity for the WEU to act, and the consent of individual nations to do so.[55] An interim solution which might be attempted at the 1996 intergovernmental conference would be to prevent a minority from blocking a majority, always subject to a reserved national right to withhold its forces. In other words, those who are as a result empowered to act should be able to use joint WEU facilities.[56] A parallel, or counter, British proposal, advanced in 1995, called for another layer of Euro-summitry, whereby European heads of state and government would meet apart from their six-monthly EU summits with different hats on - those of the WEU - to discuss defence issues. No doubt, if adopted, such an arrangement would complicate the existing system of decision-making of CFSP and WEU; it would also underline the intergovernmental character of the WEU and its distinctiveness from the EU.

Institutional reforms will most likely be affected by EU and WEU enlargement. In the first place this will relate to accession by members of the European Free Trade Association (EFTA), some of which have traditionally pursued a policy of neutrality and therefore may refuse membership of the WEU. How will the WEU relate to the CFSP after enlargement? Further discrepancies in membership between the EU and WEU may raise questions about the coherence and efficiency of the CFSP. How long could a form of neutrality with military non-participation as its core principle endure within the EU? Already there is an expectation of solidarity among EU members. For instance, how would a neutral member react if one or more EU countries were attacked from outside the EU? On the other hand, a CFSP competence for collective security could pave the way for the constructive integration of neutral countries into EU security policy. UN-mandated peace-keeping operations have traditionally made up the bulk of neutral countries' military activities. In addition, if present practices continue with regard to Denmark and Germany, then not all WEU members need to participate fully.

Different implications and proceedings can be expected with regard to enlargement by the admittance of CEE members. Apart from the economic and financial costs of incorporating new members, there are serious questions about the EU's capacity to absorb them while maintaining the momentum of European integration and its own cohesiveness and effectiveness. Significant reform of decision-making procedures would probably be necessary, as well as radical changes in policies, e.g. the Common Agricultural Policy (CAP). There may also be consideration of whether existing procedures can be used in a more elastic manner to meet the economic and political needs of new members.[57] Many of the Mediterranean countries are opposed to CEE enlargement, fearing that the benefits and subsidies they draw from the EU may be adversely affected. Hence enlargement or a large-scale coordination policy towards the CEE may cause serious divisions within the EU, yet inaction may promote unilateral intervention by some EU members.

Conclusion

Over a twenty-five-year period the EU has accumulated collective strength in trade negotiations and has created effective links with less developed countries in the form of aid and development policy. But the apparent strength in these areas has not been matched in EPC or CFSP terms. Here, especially in view of destabilising events in central and eastern Europe, reality has fallen short of expectations. The EU has been largely unable to act collectively and lacks many of the foreign-policy mechanisms necessary to project itself abroad. A number of factors are responsible. Chief among them is the unwillingness of member states to forgo a sufficient degree of sovereignty. Diverging national interests and jockeying for power among member states are the outward expression of the desire to preserve sovereignty. The issue is not so much institutional as a matter of insufficient identification of common political and security interests that guarantee unity.

In one sense the change from a predominantly military to a more economically orientated security dimension in the post-1989 period would seem to favour collective EU action. The Union's economic strength and activities together with its image as a 'civilian power' seemed suited to the post-Cold War environment. However, as Werner Link notes, compared with earlier problems, the new threats to security policy are diffuse, occur intermittently, with each case being totally different and unique, and do not have a uniform impact.[58] Rather than helping, these new threats exacerbate the problem of defining the conditions of when and how the EU should intervene in external crises. The consequence is a reactive rather than a proactive policy approach where tried and accustomed patterns of behaviour can be used. The result is a tendency to rely on the economic and diplomatic aspects of external action, reinforcing the idea that somehow defence and security matters are not really part of the EU remit but belong to NATO and are the responsibility of the United States. Conflict prevention rather than crisis management activities hence becomes the chosen method of engagement. Ample evidence of this can be found in the association agreements with CEE countries, the partnership and cooperation agreements with countries of the former Soviet Union, and the free-trade agreements with the Baltic republics. It also implies forsaking the Bosnian crisis and an orientation towards the avoidance of such a conflict elsewhere in central and eastern Europe. No doubt measures directed at conflict prevention are important, especially as a long-term objective, but circumstances show that actual developments do not correspond to the design of policy. Ethnic conflicts have their own dynamics. Besides, a United States less committed to European defence necessitates an increased level of EU preparedness and engagement in crisis management situations.

The ability to act on these issues will depend on whether WEU operations can be upgraded, EU decision-making improved, and connections between all three Maastricht pillars achieved. To expand WEU tasks and develop an effective European security identity requires among other things additional resources in order to achieve adequate force levels as well as strengthen relations with NATO in order to obtain access to required military assets (airlift, communication, surveillance capabilities, etc.). It also necessitates clarification of the division of labour between NATO and the WEU in terms of the authority and scope of operations to be undertaken by the WEU. To achieve agreement on these issues will not be easy, given the prevailing problems over resources and the sensitivity over defence and security issues in relation to national sovereignty. Even more problems can be expected with CFSP efficiency. The extent to which WEU should be incorporated into the EU or the degree of responsibility the EU should hold over WEU operations will be strongly contested among EU members, especially on the part of those with an Atlanticist orientation or of a neutralist persuasion. The ultimate contest will be over decision-making procedures and the extent to which majority voting should become a feature of the CFSP. There were strong indications that certain countries, like the United Kingdom and the Netherlands, were unwilling to accept such far-reaching developments. Whether the anticipated EU intergovernmental conference or the fifty years' review of the WEU in 1998 will split the ranks into groups (major versus minor reformers) or whether a compromise position would be possible is at this stage speculative. Given EU history, however, the latter rather than the former appears the more likely outcome.

Even a modest reform of the EU security dimension would allow the EU to complement its economic and diplomatic activities more effectively. It would add legitimacy to the WEU, make it the defence and security arm of the EU and promote the establishment of a European security identity. However, the CFSP would probably continue to function largely through intergovernmental means with the associated limitations on the binding nature of EU action and/or the continuation of parallel national action. A European security identity would therefore continue to represent a common rather than a single policy approach and give added legitimacy to the WEU. It would make it stronger to intervene in the case of ethnic conflicts and to ensure that such conflicts do not escalate or spread to other parts of Europe or possibly give rise to large migratory movements. However, in the end, the military capability of WEU will be the acid test of how effective the EU/WEU can be in peace-keeping missions or conflict resolution. Additional resources on the part of western European governments and collaboration with NATO are both required to overcome the existing inadequate military capability. This in turn requires consideration of the role of the OSCE and UN in European affairs, e.g. who decides the rules or legitimation of engagement in ethnic conflicts? Ambiguous demarcation lines between the UN, NATO, OSCE and WEU were partly responsible for inaction in the Bosnian conflict.

Important questions in this context will be whether certain military capabilities could be sub-contracted from NATO, and whether the WEU could take the initiatives over military operations on its own or be mandated by the OSCE or UN. Maastricht temporarily defused the controversy between Atlanticists and Europeanists over security architectures, and represented the first shifting away from dependence on American leadership in the security field.[59] But tensions still prevail between Atlanticists and Europeanists. The former secretary-general of the WEU, Wilhelm van Eekelen, has described the WEU as a 'hinge';

being the defence component of the EU, the potential military tool of the CFSP, and a pillar of NATO.[60] How far this is true will be partly explored in the following chapter.

Notes

1. Stanley Hoffmann, 'Obstinate or Obsolete? The Fate of the Nation-state and the Case of Western Europe,' *Daedalus* (1966), pp. 862–915.
2. For a review of WEU developments see Reimund Seidelmann (ed.), *Auf dem Weg zu einer westeuropäischen Sicherheitspolitik* (Baden-Baden: Nomos, 1989).
3. For further details see Kevin Wright, 'Open Skies,' *Air Force Monthly*, vol. 7, no. 7 (July 1994), pp. 15–19.
4. Samuel Huntington, 'Political Development and Political Decay,' *World Politics*, vol. XVII, no. 3 (April 1965), pp. 386–430.
5. In 1996 the Council of Europe had thirty-nine members. The CEE members were: Albania, Bulgaria, the Czech Republic, Estonia, Hungary, Latvia, Lithuania, Macedonia, Moldova, Poland, Romania, Russia, Slovakia, Slovenia and Ukraine. By this time, the following CEE countries had applied for membership: Belarus and Croatia.
6. See Daniel Tarschys, 'The Council of Europe: the challenge of enlargement,' *The World Today*, vol. 51, no. 4 (April 1995), pp. 62–4.
7. Ibid.
8. Nicole Gnesotto, 'Lessons of Yugoslavia,' *Chaillot Papers* 14 (Paris: WEU) Institute for Security Studies, March 1994, p. 19.
9. Gabriella Grasselli, 'Western Europe's Security after Maastricht,' *European Access* (October 1992), pp. 7–9.
10. Saadet Deger, 'World Military Expenditure,' *SIPRI Yearbook 1993* (Stockholm: SIPRI, 1993), p. 381.
11. Trevor Taylor, 'West European Security and Defence Cooperation: Maastricht and Beyond,' *International Affairs*, vol. 70, no. 1 (1994), pp. 1–16.
12. For further details see Ian Mather, 'Old Armies battle to find a Common Front,' *European*, 22–8 July 1994.
13. Taylor, 'West European Security and Defence Cooperation,' p. 2.
14. See, for example, Franco Algieri, *Integration*, no. 7/8 (Bonn, 1993), p. 176, and Alexis Seydoux and Jerome Paolini, 'From Western Security Interblocking to Institutional Evolutionism,' in M. Curtis, O. Diel, J. Paolini, A. Seydoux and R. Wolf, *Challenges and Responses to Future European Security: British, French and German Perspectives*, (London: European Strategy Group, 1993), pp. 171–202.
15. For an exploration of potential WEU development with regard to these countries see the *SIPRI Yearbook 1994* (Stockholm: SIPRI, 1994).
16. Emil J. Kirchner, 'The Impact of German Unification on the New European Order,' in Hugh Miall (ed.), *Redefining Europe: New Patterns of Conflict and Cooperation* (London: Royal Institute of International Affairs, 1994), pp. 206–26.
17. For example, there was a debate in 1992 over whether a joint WEU military force could be deployed for peace-keeping missions and the provision of armed escorts for humanitarian aid. The use of force was circumscribed by a division between Britain, which insisted on a strictly peace-keeping function, and France, Germany and Italy, which argued for a peacemaking mission and that involvement in the Balkans would be a first major step towards WEU as a component of CFSP. See James Gow, 'The Use of Coercion in the Yugoslav Crisis,' *The World Today*, vol. 48 (November 1992), pp. 198–202.
18. See Report submitted on Behalf of the Committee for Parliamentary and Public Rela-

tions, by Mr Roman, Rapporteur (Paris: WEU Institute for Security Studies, 31 October 1994).

19 Support for such an interpretation can be found in the report of the high-level group of experts on the CFSP, which stated that if a number WEU members were unwilling or unable to commit themselves to full participation in the European intervention force, this 'would make it necessary to set up new institutional machinery reserved for the countries participating in the European intervention force, at the interface between the European Council, the CFSP and the WEU. The WEU would accordingly retain *only* the defence responsibilities covered by Article 5 of the Brussels treaty (italics added). See High-level Group of Experts on the CFSP, First report on 'European Security Policy towards 2000: Ways and Means to establish genuine Credibility,' Brussels, 19 December 1994, p. 16.

20 François Heisbourg, 'The Future Direction of European Security Policy,' in M. Wörner, H. Cetin, F. Heisbourg, S. Lunn and J. Onyszkiewicz, *What is European Security after the Cold War?* (Brussels: Philip Morris Institute for Public Policy Research, December 1993), pp. 36–49.

21 For an account of the failings of the Western institutions in the conflict in ex-Yugoslavia see Gnesotto, 'Lessons of Yugoslavia,' M. Glenny, *The Fall of Yugoslavia: the Third Balkan War* (London: Penguin Books, 1992), p. 158, and Lawrence Freedman, 'The Balkan Tragedy,' *Foreign Policy*, no. 97 (winter 1994–95), pp. 53–69.

22 Catherine McArdle Kelleher, 'A New Security Order: the United States and the European Community in the 1990s,' Occasional Paper of the European Community Studies Association, US-EC Relations Project (Pittsburgh: ECSA, 1993).

23 During his D-day anniversary tour of Europe, President Clinton promised that the United States would 'remain engaged' in Europe and honour its NATO commitments, but added: 'we also want Europe to be strong. That's why America supports Europe's own steps so far toward greater unity in the EU, the WEU and the development of a European security identity.' Quoted in *The Financial Times*, 17. June 1994.

24 Manfred Wörner, 'European Security: Political will plus Military Might,' in Wörner *et al.*, *What is European Security after the Cold War?*, p. 18.

25 Wilhelm van Eekelen, 'WEU after two Brussels Summits: a new Approach to Common Tasks,' paper presented at the Royal Institute for International Relations, Brussels, 27 January 1994, p. 13.

26 Vaclav Havel, address to the European Parliament, reported in *EP News*, 7–11 March 1994, and Hans-Dietrich Genscher, 'Turning a Warhorse into a Peacemaker,' *European*, 27 May–2 June 1994.

27 There are other regional formations whose operations may in turn have beneficial implications for EU–CEE relations. One of these is the Council of Baltic Sea States, set up in May 1990, which serves as a platform for cooperation on a wide range of issues of interest to the states around the Baltic Sea. It has no elaborate structure, but will organise periodic ministerial meetings as well as several official committees. Another is the Central European Initiative, initiated by Italy in August 1990, which encompasses the CEE countries and the Balkans.

28 For details of these agreements see David Shumaker, 'The Origins and Development of Central European Cooperation, 1989–1992,' *East European Quarterly* (September 1993), pp. 351–73, and Andras Inotai, 'Die Beziehungen zwischen der EU und den assoziierten Staaten Mittel- und Osteuropas,' *Vierteljahreszeitschrift für Politik, Wirtschaft und Zeitgeschichte*, twenty-second year, no. 94/3 (summer 1994), pp. 19–35.

29 This involves meetings of the presidents of the association countries, the president of the European Council and the president of the European Commission; foreign ministers within the Association Council (meeting once a year); at the level of political directors; within the traditional framework of diplomacy; and at the parliamentary level

within the Parliamentary Association Committee (meetings as convenient).
30 See Andras Inotai, 'Die Regionale Zusammenarbeit der Visegrad-Staaten. Mehr Wettbewerb als Kooperation,' *Integration*, no. 1/94, pp. 21–9.
31 Jamie Shea, 'Security: the Future,' in J. Lodge (ed.), *The European Community and the Challenge of the Future*, second edition (London: Pinter, 1993), p. 362.
32 Vaclav Havel, address to the General Assembly of the Council of Europe, Vienna, 9 October 1992, translated by Paul Wilson and printed in *The New York Review of Books*, August 1993.
33 Eekelen, 'WEU after two Brussels Summits,' p. 9.
34 Mark Curtis, 'Western European Security and the Third World,' in Curtis *et al.*, *Challenges and Responses*, pp. 69–112.
35 These nine Associates are: Bulgaria, the Czech Republic, Estonia, Hungary, Latvia, Lithuania, Poland, Romania and Slovakia.
36 Eekelen, 'WEU after two Brussels Summits,' p. 12.
37 *WEU Newsletter*, no. 10 (November 1993), p. 3.
38 Eekelen, 'WEU prepares the Way for new Missions,' *NATO Review*, no. 5 (October 1993), pp. 19–23.
39 See Peter van Ham, 'Ukraine, Russia and European Security: Implications for Western Policy,' *Chaillot Papers* 13 (Paris: WEU Institute for Security Studies, February 1994).
40 Information provided by the Royal United Service Institute, quoted in *The Economist*, 25 February 1995.
41 Taylor, 'West European Security and Defence Cooperation.'
42 *Ibid.*
43 For details of spying activities between Britain and Germany see Annika Savill, 'Inside File,' *Independent*, 11 November 1993.
44 Eekelen, 'WEU after two Brussels Summits,' p. 14.
45 Taylor, 'West European Security and Defence Cooperation.'
46 Simon Lunn, 'A Reassessment of European Security,' in Wörner *et al.*, *What is European Security after the Cold War?*, pp. 50–67.
47 This report calls for a set of minimum requirements for participation in terms of allocation of forces, integration of command structures and effective support for the concomitant technology and logistical programme; participating countries must from the outset receive financial backing from those member states which do not wish to participate. See High-level Group of Experts on the CFSP, First report on 'European Security Policy towards 2000: Ways and Means to establish genuine Credibility,' Brussels, 19 December 1994, p. 16.
48 Balladur also called for improved defence cooperation between EU members, including weapons development. One of the French aims was to develop a military spy satellite system independent of the United States.
49 For further details see Günter Burghardt, 'The New Europe,' paper given at the sixteenth World Congress of the International Political Science Association, Berlin, 23 August 1994.
50 John Major, 'On Europe,' *Economist*, 25 September 1993, p. 29.
51 See Report submitted on behalf of the Committee for Parliamentary and Public Relations, by Mr Roman, Rapporteur, published by the WEU Institute for Security Studies, Document 1430, 31 October 1994.
52 Volker Rühe, 'The Konrad Adenauer Memorial Lecture, 1994: Germany's Responsibility in and for Europe,' St Antony's College, Oxford, and Konrad Adenauer Foundation, 1994.
53 Peter van Ham, 'Can Institutions hold Europe together?', in Miall, *Redefining Europe*.
54 Christopher Hill, 'The Capability–Expectations Gap, or, Conceptualizing Europe's International Role,' *Journal of Common Market Studies*, vol. 31, no. 3 (September 1993),

pp. 305–28.
55 See Martin and Roper, 'Introduction,' p. 4.
56 *Ibid.*, p. 5
57 Helen Wallace, 'The EC and Western Europe after Maastricht,' in Hugh Miall (ed.), *Redefining Europe*, pp. 19–29.
58 Werner Link, 'Serving World Peace as an equal Partner in the United Europe: Germany's Stance in Europe,' *German Comments: Review of Politics and Culture*, 33 (January 1994), pp. 13–19.
59 Hugh Miall, 'Wider Europe, Fortress Europe, Fragmented Europe?' in H. Miall (ed.), *Redefining Europe*, pp 1–16.
60 Eekelen, 'WEU after two Brussels Summits,' p. 1.

3

The Atlantic institutions of security
NATO, the OSCE and the UN

Both NATO and OSCE[1] have contributed enormously to the end of the Cold War and to peace and stability in Europe. Whether they can make a similar contribution to peace and stability in the post-Cold War period is one of the key questions of the 1990s and beyond. Both being creations of the Cold War and initially instigated for purposes of either territorial defence or the managing and reduction of tension between the two superpowers, neither has been capable of dealing effectively with the spate of ethnic conflicts which have occurred since 1989 and threaten to destabilise central and eastern Europe. Surprisingly, it has been the UN which has intervened more speedily, at least in military terms, than NATO or the OSCE. Surprising, because the UN was for a long time considered as weak, Third World-orientated, and inferior to NATO and the OSCE. Its role in the 1990–91 Gulf conflict, owing to the unprecedented cooperation among the five permanent members of the Security Council, helped to change this image. Yet, in the final analysis, UN effectiveness in Europe depends on NATO, the OSCE and the WEU either to carry out its instructions or to support its interventions.

Curiously, whilst circumstances require all four organisations to acquire new roles individually, their success also depends on how well they interact with each other. Both NATO and the WEU are essentially defence organisations, but both seek to add new security roles in order to deal with the challenges of the post-1989 era. Both organisations start from slightly different bases and perspectives. The WEU's fledgling partnership with the EU will help, in time, to combine military with economic and diplomatic objectives, as well as promote CEE membership. For NATO, the primary defence organisation in Europe, to add out-of-area military commitments in the form of peace-keeping and peace enforcement missions poses difficult questions (among Europeans as well as between Europeans and Americans) and discussion of eastern enlargement provokes strong Russian reservations. The effectiveness of both organisations in peace-keeping and peace enforcement roles will be affected by the extent to which their activities interlock rather than duplicate or interblock. Efforts to arrive at harmonious formulas will encounter thorny subjects such as leadership and burden sharing. There is consensus, however, that NATO represents the main guarantee against the uncertainties surrounding Russia or potential nuclear attack from anywhere in the world.

Although a pan-European rather than a purely Western body, the OSCE has become an important vehicle of Western policy towards post-communist Europe. The OSCE has undergone an evolutionary process, taking on new roles in conflict prevention and mediation, whilst carrying on its previous task as a forum for negotiating arms control and military confidence-building measures. In addition, because of its comprehensive membership (most of Europe and North America) and aims the OSCE can provide a legitimising function for military intervention by member states or outside organisations such as the WEU or NATO. Russia is particularly keen on seeking OSCE authorisation for its peace-keeping operations in the 'near abroad', especially in the Caucasus.

Besides NATO, the WEU and OSCE, the UN is becoming more engaged in aspects of European security. The UN's main objective has always been 'to restore peace and security' in the world. However, it was not until the 1991 Gulf conflict that the UN was able to demonstrate that it could participate effectively in large-scale international crises. A combination of expectations in the newly found role of 'restoring or maintaining world order', indecision by other organisations such as NATO, the OSCE and WEU, and Russian insistence on UN involvement has elevated the importance of the UN's role in European peace-keeping and peace enforcement missions.[2]

How NATO, the OSCE and the UN are adapting to the multi-faceted challenges of the post-1989 era, which comprise military as well as non-military aspects (economic, environmental, weapons proliferation, migration and refugees), is the focus of this chapter. It will first examine the evolution of the roles of these organisations, then proceed with an assessment of how the organisations interact with each other, with the EU, the WEU and the Council of Europe, and thereafter consider the future prospects of European security institutions.

NATO, the OSCE and the UN in search of new roles

The post-Cold War period has created fundamental challenges for NATO, the OSCE and the UN. For both NATO and the OSCE the East–West conflict and the stand-off between the two superpowers was of paramount importance. The disappearance of the Iron Curtain, the Warsaw Pact and the Soviet Union on the one hand, and the emergence of a united Germany, on the other, have drastically changed the objectives and functions, if not the *raison d'être* of NATO and the OSCE.[3] The single threat posed by the former Soviet Union and the

Warsaw Pact has given way to a multitude of threats sparked off by ethnic conflicts in central and eastern Europe which have the potential to affect western Europe through, for example, mass migration. How to adjust from defensive military postures to actual out-of-area military intervention raises important questions, particularly for NATO.

NATO

The dictum of Lord Ismay, the first secretary-general of NATO, has been widely seen as encapsulating pre-1989 NATO objectives: 'keep the Soviets out, the Americans in, and the Germans down'. Events since 1989 signify far-reaching changes in two of these areas (with regard to the Soviet Union and Germany) as well as with regard to the American defence commitment to Europe. The implications of the changes are worth highlighting. The disappearance of both the Warsaw Pact and the Soviet Union has made an attack on NATO territory, by either Russia or CIS states, a remote possibility. NATO has therefore responded with the introduction of a new military strategy, improved links with CEE states via the NACC and the PfP initiative.

Yet NATO is left with a number of problems which the end of the Cold War either did not resolve or actually helped to cause. Among them is the remaining large military strength of Russia, and to some extent that of Ukraine,[4] the danger of nuclear accidents due to inadequate storage or poor maintenance of weapons[5] and the threat of nuclear proliferation.[6] Uncertainties caused by ethnic strife, rising nationalism and the potential re-emergence of authoritarian regimes in Russia and many of the Soviet successor states dictate caution on the part of NATO and give rise to calls for a continuation of its role as the most credible and foremost defence organisation in Europe.[7] The task of trying to integrate a united (and therefore strengthened) Germany into a European security framework is seen as a complementary aspect of NATO's continued role. Whilst dealing with potential nuclear attacks or nuclear proliferation requires primarily a passive role in maintaining adequate military strength, ethnic conflicts, such as the one in ex-Yugoslavia, do require an active role; engagement not for the defence of NATO territory but for the securing and the promotion of stability in areas adjacent to NATO territory. To undertake such missions, which are not confined solely to the CEE region,[8] necessitates a rethinking of the principle of collective defence, extended deterrence, the role of the alliance, and NATO's relationship with the OSCE and the UN.

The new strategic concept of NATO which describes the new risks facing NATO as 'multi-faceted and multi-directional' goes some way towards meeting the post-1989 challenges.[9] It calls for a force structure which will permit measured, flexible and timely responses to crisis situations. The emphasis is on forward presence, crisis management and rapid reaction forces, and the abandonment of 'flexible response' and 'forward defence'. NATO will continue to rely on an appropriate mix of nuclear and conventional forces, although the level of these forces will be greatly reduced and the reliance on nuclear weapons will be decreased. The Allied Rapid Reaction Corps (ARRC) is the centrepiece of NATO's crisis management contingency planning structure. When fully operational, the headquarters should be able to command up to four divisions with 80,000 troops drawn from up to thirteen nations, able to be fielded within seven days. According to the new strategic concept, NATO defences will increasingly rely on multinational forces, because multinational units reinforce alliance solidarity and provide a way of developing more capable formations than might be available purely nationally.[10] Such arrangements would also stimulate greater cooperation among military forces. Already, as pointed out in Chapter 2, several such forces and units have been established since 1992. At its January 1994 meeting, NATO adopted a new set of 'force goals' as planning targets for the allies in developing the forces and capabilities needed to implement the strategic concept. However, these goals do not represent a formal commitment. Rather they represent a consensus that nations should be willing to adjust their force plans and priorities to meet collectively agreed force goals.

Some of the post-1989 challenges might, however, be met through conflict prevention measures or through peace-keeping and peace enforcement missions under UN or OSCE auspices. The first poses the question of how best to transmit Western-style security to central and eastern Europe. Can NATO give formal guarantees of the security of CEE states without them being full members of NATO or the WEU? On the other hand, in the absence of full membership, how can CEE countries be effectively brought into NATO or WEU peace-keeping and peace enforcement operations?

Both the issue of membership and the issue of links with the UN and the OSCE have caused a great deal of concern within as well as outside NATO, particularly in Russia, the country most concerned about any such expansion of the alliance. NATO has been both cautious and careful in its liaison with CEE countries in order not to offend Russia. The NACC, established in December 1991, and the PfP, introduced in January 1994, were designed to promote cooperation between NATO countries and CEE states and to increase stability in central and eastern Europe. A major task of the NACC has been to manage the allocation of conventional force reductions among the states of the former Soviet Union required under the CFE treaty. Its other function is to act as a forum for the exchange of information among the NATO and former Warsaw Pact countries on many security issues, including peace-keeping. The NACC also promotes joint training and the conduct of military exercises among these countries. The PfP covers a wider scope of activities than NACC whilst at the same time allowing for specific programmes of cooperation. PfP, almost in a League of Nations manner, offers a flexible forum to develop cooperation in the field of security and defence at a speed and pace that each nation is able and willing to sustain. Prospective members will have to demonstrate not only that they seek privileges from the alliance but also that they are committed to alliance principles, particularly the promotion of and commitment to democracy, and that they are determined to take the many practical steps necessary to prepare for alliance responsibilities.[11] The PfP purports to represent an evolutionary step for NATO in the direction of both membership expansion and the assumption of common security functions. Although it presents the appearance of a bridge-building mechanism, the PfP, in practice, can be considered a fudge: it envisages greater cooperation between NATO and CEE countries but NATO does not give any clear security guarantees. It provides a temporary respite, but will not prevent pressure from CEE states for full membership. Nonetheless, a perhaps unintended – but critical – eventuality of the PfP may be that partner states will progressively become so closely bound to NATO that the alliance will be committed *de facto* to the security of the partners.[12] What remains uncertain, however, is whether this would involve all partners from CEE countries or only some.

Irrespective of whether the latter will arise, the issue of security guarantees is of growing importance to NATO. Security in this context implies out-of-area missions – something NATO must conduct on its own or in conjunction with the UN and the OSCE. The latter poses difficulties over the degree of 'obligation' and autonomy. In other words, NATO has to decide what autonomy it wants to preserve over its own actions, and how far it should commit itself to performing tasks either as a regional organisation of the UN or under the mandate of the OSCE. This, in turn, leads to considerations of what types of units, infrastructure, communications, headquarters, etc., it should make available to UN missions.

In 1992 NATO agreed to undertake action if requested by either the UN or the OSCE on a case-by-case basis. Since then NATO has offered support to the UN in providing humanitarian assistance and controlling heavy weapons in Bosnia. NATO aircraft are monitoring Bosnian air space. In the Adriatic, the Standing Naval Force Mediterranean is helping to impose the UN-sanctioned embargo. A headquarters drawn from NORTHAG headquarters is coordinating action by troops made available to the UN in Bosnia. NATO has provided air power to prevent the strangulation of Sarejevo and it has supplied aircraft for the relief of UN troops garrisoned in Srebrenica. The use of air strikes in 1994 in Bosnia marked the first occasion on which NATO as an alliance had decided to engage its forces in operational military action. This action was repeated on a rather massive scale with the deployment of 60,000 troops in Bosnia in December 1995, known as the Implementation Force (IFOR) of the Dayton peace agreement. However, until now, several allies have ensured that contributions to out-of-area operations were clearly seen to emanate from individual countries. In this way, they wish the Atlantic alliance to retain its main defence function and remain within the territorial and juridical limits of the treaty. Others again, like Germany, prefer NATO, as well as WEU, missions to be coupled with UN or OSCE authorisation and legitimation. To assess the relationship of NATO with either of these two organisations requires a closer examination of them.

United Nations

The UN has been able to alter its image from that of an inactive to an active organisation. A major factor in this change was an agreement among the five permanent members of the Security Council in 1987 to use the UN more effectively in world affairs, particularly with regard to conflict and disarmament issues. The active involvement of the UN in the 1990–91 Gulf conflict added further credence to the UN. As a consequence, as suggested by Patrick Keatinge, the major powers now saw the UN

> as a forum of creative multilateral diplomacy rather than the sterile ritual of confrontation. There was renewed interest in the UN Charter as the central source of global norms, and a change in emphasis from the General Assembly, with its inherent Third World bias, to the original concept of a United Nations with strong political leadership exercised in the Council.[13]

Since the end of 1989, Security Council debates have ceased to be characterised by familiar Cold War polemics, and the council is taking decisions. The veto, used more than 190 times between 1946 and 1990, was used only once between 1991 and 1995.[14] As a consequence the UN was able to play an important role in, for example, the Iran–Iraq war, the civil war in El Salvador, the Soviet withdrawal from Afghanistan, the release of hostages from Lebanon, and the settlement of the conflict in Cambodia. Conflict in the former Yugoslavia was the first crisis on the European mainland that the UN had been asked to manage until it was replaced by NATO's IFOR. The UN had two operations in Bosnia: the blue-helmeted UN Protection Force (UNPROFOR), with 23,600 soldiers at the end of 1994; and the humanitarian mission run by the UN High Commissioner for Refugees (UNHCR). Between them, they undertook three main tasks: (1) providing aid to around 3.8 million people in the former Yugoslavia; (2) protecting minorities, e.g. UNHCR protection officers monitored the fate of minorities caught 'behind the lines'; and (3) peace-keeping, e.g. the policing of cease-fires, or the guarding of weapon depots by the UN under the policy of establishing 'total exclusion zones'. It carried out these tasks despite a lack of financial resources and the operational means to carry out peace-keeping missions. The engagement in Bosnia presented the UN with the choice of whether to rely on regional organisations such as the WEU or NATO; to delegate the conduct of operations to a lead state or *ad hoc* group of nations; or to build up its own peace-keeping forces (a UN stand-by peace-keeping force).[15] The UN has mandated a stand-by force planning group, which consists of a team of officers from France (chairman), Argentina, Canada, Denmark, Ghana, Pakistan and Poland, to study past and present peace-keeping operations to determine the 'building blocks' upon which future peace-keeping operations may be constructed. The countries concerned have been chosen on the basis of an equitable geographical representation and in the light of their past peace-keeping experience. The terms of reference require the group 'to develop a system of stand-by forces able to be deployed as a whole or in parts anywhere in the world at the secretary-general's request within an agreed response time for UN duties as mandated by the Security Council'. Already France has declared its willingness to make 1,000 soldiers available within forty-eight hours and a further 1,000 within a week.[16] From 1996 onwards Denmark intends to establish an international brigade comprising some 4,500 soldiers which will be available to serve under UN, NATO or OSCE command and also to undertake combat missions.[17] However, decisions on the deployment of these forces in a crisis will remain with the member states.

Before considering the objections which may be raised against such an arrangement, let us briefly deal with the questions of how such a force would be assembled and how it could be employed. According to UN sources there would be no difficulty in staffing a so-called 'foreign legion' force, indicating that it gets a dozen applications from would-be mercenaries each week.[18] As to employment considerations, there are three areas where specialist personnel and self-sufficient support elements would dramatically improve the UN's ability to respond rapidly to deployment requests: logistics and especially movement control units to establish priorities at the outset of an operation; communication units employing tactical satellite equipment which would be responsible for operating facilities in the early and critical phase of an operation; and multi-role and field engineer units to carry out a range of support operations. It is one thing to demonstrate how such a force could be established and for what purpose, quite another to obtain approval from member states. Opponents of the idea raise financial objections (for example, the need to pay, train, house and pension the soldiers). What such opposition really reflects, however, is abhorrence of the idea of handing over control to the Secretary General.

With regard to 'stand-by forces', while WEU countries do not generally have formal arrangements for the earmarking of forces for UN operations, most have contingency arrangements for the fairly rapid deployment of some force elements. Tied to this is the obvious need for both adequate airlift and sealift resources to 'reach the right place at the right time'. Such matters were under consideration in the WEU during 1994 and raise questions over WEU's access to strategic military assets over which NATO and more especially the United States has a monopoly. In other words, few large-scale operations could take place without active American involvement, given the United States' virtual monopoly of strategic sea transport, airlift, and intelligence-gathering capabilities.

The UN has been pushed into a more central position in world affairs, but has raised more expectations than it can meet. It is unclear what role the UN will play in the future, although the Yugoslav precedent suggests that the UN will be more important and necessary on the European scene than seemed likely when the Cold War ended. It remains the primary legitimising agent for collective security operations as well as a credible honest broker in conflict situations. It also has long years of experience of peace-keeping.

However, the UN is increasingly confronted with an imbalance between the demands imposed on it by member governments, such as peace-keeping, peace enforcement and humanitarian work, and the resources which have been made available to it. Whereas the UN undertook only thirteen peace-keeping missions in the first forty years of its existence, it was engaged in seventeen such operations in Bosnia by the beginning of 1995, spending more on the latter than it had spent in the previous forty-eight years combined.[19] The twelve EU member states contribute with around 70,000 troops to UN peace-keeping operations. Yet the UN labours under great difficulties. Complex military missions are still being patched together. Internal paralysis prevails all too often and can be overcome only when the United States unequivocally takes command, as in Korea in 1950, or in Operation Desert Storm in 1991, and then the blue UN flag is used only as a fig leaf for great-power intervention.[20] Funding is begged and borrowed and always late. There is no mechanism for learning the lessons of past mistakes or identifying what worked well. Also troublesome is that peacemaking and humanitarian aid are fundamentally incompatible in one crucial respect. Humanitarian relief demands strict neutrality. Peacemakers must often recognise one side as the aggressor. Failure to do so – as in Bosnia – detrimentally affects the mission. When two such dissimilar operations are entangled, as most often they now are, both suffer. As Jessica Mathews explains:

> Neutrality undermined every aspect of policy in Bosnia. It snagged diplomacy by undermining the greater legitimacy of the Bosnian government. It undermined economic sanctions by delivering a lot of fungible supplies (supplies for civilians free up other supplies for soldiers) to the Serbs. And it blocked military options because of the need to protect the relief work.[21]

Not only are sufficient resources and forces so far absent, the UN also suffers from political difficulties among the permanent members of the Security Council. Russia, through the use of its veto in the Security Council, has been accused of trying to turn the UN into an instrument of its own policy. The Chinese position on North Korea is seen as another detrimental factor for UN decisions. These shortcomings lead Dieter Mahncke to conclude that the UN cannot be considered as a 'primary instrument for ensuring western European security, nor perhaps overall European stability'.[22] With these shortcomings, what alternative does the OSCE provide as the core institution of the future European security architecture?

OSCE
Whilst confirming the inviolability of frontiers resulting from the Second World War, the OSCE, established in 1971, allowed *détente* to be pursued more rigorously. Its stated aims are to strengthen pluralist democracy and the observance of human rights, and to promote the peaceful settlement of disputes between member states. Through its emphasis on disarmament, confidence-building measures and human rights, the OSCE contributed significantly to the

end of the Cold War. It encompasses the broader definition of security, including military confidence-building, arms control, and economic, scientific, technological, environmental and humanitarian cooperation. The OSCE with its fifty-three member states (by the end of 1995, including the suspended membership of Yugoslavia) represents a forum for political consultation and cooperation that includes both a transatlantic and a Russian presence. As agreed under the Paris Charter in 1990, the OSCE now has at its disposal an impressive array of instruments to meet the differing requirements of early warning, cooperation and, if need be, confrontational conflict management. Through these instruments it seeks to effect a transition from its role as a forum for negotiation and dialogue to a more operational structure. Early warning, conflict prevention and crisis management have become the main features of the new OSCE.[23]

The early warning function takes the form of the introduction of confidence- and security-building measures (CSBMs); the formation of a Conflict Prevention Centre in Vienna as a focal point for the reporting of unusual or hazardous military activities and a computerised communication system between the signatories; the appointment of a High Commissioner on National Minorities; and the establishment of the Warsaw-based Office of Democratic Institutions and Human Rights. Conflict prevention measures and all verification regimes are co-ordinated via the Conflict Prevention Centre.

The next step on the ladder of conflict prevention is early action, for which the OSCE has created a number of mechanisms, such as fact-finding missions, long-term missions (to counter the imminent danger of the spillover of a conflict), and the Convention on Conciliation and Arbitration, established in September 1992.

Finally, in cases of seriously advanced conflicts, the OSCE will apply crisis management instruments. The overall responsibility for crisis management rests with the OSCE's political bodies, the Senior Council or the Permanent Committee, which meet weekly. In the first instance, the OSCE will send missions to deal with conflicts, composed of political, civilian and military representatives to facilitate dialogue, encourage conciliation, advise on legal and political arrangements, follow developments and, when necessary, investigate incidents. To strengthen its crisis management capacity, the OSCE formed in July 1992 a Forum for Security Cooperation (FSC) which in this context aims to apply stabilising measures in local crisis situations. It has drawn up a list and detailed description of possible military measures designed to complement a process of political settlement and comprising, among other things, various forms of military information exchange, local demilitarisation, constraining measures, and on-site verification and monitoring.

By 1995 the OSCE was involved in long-term conflict prevention missions in nine CEE countries and had seven Sanctions Assistance Missions in the countries surrounding Serbia/Montenegro.[24] The OSCE also has a clear mandate to deal with crises within states. In 1991, immediately after the abortive

Moscow *coup*, the OSCE states declared that commitments entered into in the field of the human dimension 'are matters of direct and legitimate concern to all participating states and do not belong exclusively to the international affairs of the states concerned'.[25]

In 1992 the OSCE declared itself to be a regional organisation within the meaning of chapter VIII of the United Nations charter. Accordingly, the OSCE will intervene only with the consent of all parties to a conflict and after the establishment of a true cease-fire. Interventions may cover a wide range of activities: the deployment of a buffer force; assistance to governments; observing respect for cease-fires, disarmament or the withdrawal of belligerents; humanitarian assistance and the protection of refugees. Like the UN it can legitimise international measures and actions in a political sense. For example, the OSCE has developed a set of rules for Russian-led peace-keeping operations within the CIS. It can also act as an executive organ for collective action on the part of the UN. Moreover, the OSCE could provide an umbrella function for regional groupings like the Nordic and Baltic Councils, the Black Sea Cooperation Council and the Central European Initiative.

The drawback of the OSCE is that it has hardly any effective instruments for settling disputes, as in the former Yugoslavia, and preventing crises. It has no military apparatus of its own and is weakened by the need for unanimity. This latter problem, as in the UN, is exacerbated by its large membership. Only since the Stockholm meeting in December 1992 has it had a permanent secretary-general. The Crisis Prevention Centre set up after the Paris conference in November 1990 and the High Commissioner for Minorities, appointed on 15 December 1992, have yet to prove their effectiveness. Recourse to the court of arbitration, also set up in 1992, is not compulsory and the court's verdicts are not binding. Evidence of the OSCE's weakness in crisis management came when the OSCE could not comply with the call by the UN Secretary General for assistance in mediating peace-keeping requirements in the former Yugoslavia, in particular in managing a mechanism for supervising the heavy weapons of the warring parties in Bosnia. It merely sent a mission to examine the situation in the detention camps and sent observers to Vojvodina, Kosovo and the Sanjak to try to prevent the conflict from spreading. While that was at least a start, the OSCE will need considerable reinforcement if it is to be effective.

There is also a question of whether the OSCE can adapt to post-Cold War conditions. Its emphasis, as stated in the Helsinki document of 1992, is 'to complement the political process of dispute resolution'[26] by means of 'good offices' and quiet diplomacy. This amounts to a self-imposed restriction with regard to crisis management and the enforcement of settlements. The restriction suggests to some observers that the OSCE may have served its purpose.[27] This view is challenged by Hans-Dietrich Genscher, the former German foreign minister, who argues that 'Far from ending with the resolution of the East–West conflict, its role has only just begun. Its task is to build up functioning pan-European structures.'[28] The fact that it is the only European security organisation in which

Russia has full membership is a clear advantage for such a task.

At its Budapest conference Russia tried to elevate the OSCE into a kind of superstructure, subsuming NATO and the CIS, and to be headed by a UN-style ten-nation steering committee. As envisaged, the OSCE would mandate NATO or CIS forces to intervene in regional conflicts. Owing to Western objections, Russia modified its proposal by suggesting that the OSCE should be the major moving force in European security, but that there was no need to set up a hierarchical system. The idea of strengthening the OSCE originates from Russian concern that Russia's influence in Europe was being undermined by NATO. Critics have suggested that Russia wants to use the OSCE to gain as much influence as possible over the decisions of NATO, while gaining maximum freedom of action for its own military activities in the southern republics of the CIS. For its part the United States has indicated support for an interim suggestion, by Germany, that OSCE members should refer any conflicts to the OSCE as a 'halfway house' before resorting to the UN. The United States also wants the OSCE to develop stronger early warning mechanisms which would give notice of potential conflicts and help to defuse them without resort to force.

Whilst it is questionable whether the OSCE can, as mandated by the 1994 Budapest conference, develop 'a common and comprehensive security model', there are indications that it is moving from norm-setting to operational activities. Two pending issues will help to determine the extent to which such a transformation is taking place. The first relates to the monitoring role assigned to the OSCE in the implementation of the Dayton peace agreement in Bosnia. The second will be the fate of its long-standing effort to set up a peace-keeping force in Nagorno-Karabakh. The measures, if implemented, would constitute the first such peace-keeping venture undertaken by the OSCE. However, Russia wants any peace-keeping force to be mainly Russian, while Azerbaijan has been pressing, with Western support, for a multinational effort. Russia's insistence on as free a hand as possible for its peace-keeping activities has fuelled Western fears that Moscow simply wants to use the OSCE to license its military presence in the southern republics of the CIS.

For the time being, it appears that the OSCE will continue to play *a* rather than *the* role in matters concerning European security. Its greatest drawback seems to be its organisational weakness and lack of military capacities – two aspects in which NATO has a clear advantage.

NATO-WEU relations: discord or harmony?

Whilst the role of OSCE, and especially the UN, in European security is of growing importance, it is the role of NATO and the WEU, and the relationship between these two organisations, which are crucial to European security. Although they differ in capability terms, they take top rank both as collective defence and as collective security organisations in Europe, e.g. defending the respective territories of member states and making contributions to out-of-area, mainly peace enforcement, operations. Given the overlap in membership, the relationship between the two organisations is of importance in terms of equity, complementarity and leadership. The WEU is the European pillar within NATO – a pillar, however, of considerably less influence in NATO affairs than the United States. This inferior role was largely a consequence of the Cold War and the then prevailing superpower bi-polarity. The collapse of the Warsaw Pact and the Soviet Union, the emergence of a unified Germany and the rise of ethnic conflicts have brought pressures and opportunities for each organisation. As is often the case when opportunities present themselves, different points of view emerge. Such is the case within both NATO and the WEU concerning their future directions. A few of these different perceptions are worth mentioning. Although Britain and France both tried to preserve NATO primarily as a defence organisation, their motivations differ. Britain tried to introduce a stronger role for European states within NATO through the establishment of the ARRC. The French view seems to be 'to reduce NATO to a classical alliance with political commitments' but without any substance to bolster those commitments. The United States would be a last resort, to be called upon only when European stability was disrupted to such an extent that the Europeans could no longer deal with the situation by themselves.[29] As a counterweight France pushed for the development of a more flexible and independent WEU within NATO. As Peter Schmidt points out, a strengthened WEU is a political instrument designed to realise certain missions of a political union, which stands next to the Atlantic alliance but is itself completely independent.[30] In contrast, ARRC has a British commander and its missions are planned by a dedicated staff at SHAPE.

The sense of competitiveness was particularly acute in 1992, after both organisations had decided to develop a peace-keeping competence for implementation of the embargo in the Adriatic and the military protection of humanitarian convoys.[31] Each established its own on-site command structures and procedures, even though most of the countries contributing units to the task were members of both organisations.[32] However, after June 1993 WEU naval forces deployed in the Adriatic and on the Danube to enforce sanctions on Serbia operated alongside NATO units and were placed under operational NATO control as part of operation Sharp Guard.

Formally, WEU seeks to undertake more comprehensive missions than NATO by declaring that it will use both the WEU treaty, the Washington treaty and OSCE and UN requests as the basis of its operations. According to the St Petersberg declaration, WEU forces can undertake three types of missions – humanitarian and rescue tasks, peace-keeping tasks and combat tasks – as parts of crisis management, including peace enforcement. In contrast, NATO's room for manoeuvre remains formally restricted to a peace-keeping mission in the framework of OSCE or UN mandates. However, in practice NATO has moved beyond these formal restrictions, for example by enforcing the no-fly zone over

Bosnia, by controlling the application of UN sanctions in the Adriatic, and by establishing IFOR.[33] Yet the establishment of a military command for peace-keeping purposes is not without difficulties. For example, the placing of elements of a NATO headquarters (NORTHAG) at the disposal of UNPROFOR was only possible by rearranging its structure, in doing so excluding the Germans, whilst including the French, Egyptians and Ukrainians.[34]

Two consequences emerge from the undertaking of peace-keeping missions by NATO and the WEU. Firstly, duplication in planning and administration seems unavoidable. There will be two planning staffs, for two military organisations which share some of the same units for the same or similar missions. Secondly, there could be tension between the formal tasking and the relative capacities of both organisations: whereas NATO has a restricted mission but greater capability, the WEU has fewer restrictions but more limited military capabilities.

The WEU intends to form a multinational European rapid reaction force. According to François Léotard, the former French defence minister, such a force would be both multinational and would have integrated (air, land and sea) forces.[35] It would not, however, be an attempt to establish independent standing forces, only a headquarters staff with a planning and coordination cell. The units assigned to it by NATO would have two hats, one NATO and one WEU, which means that the French forces would be subject first to tasking from the NATO command.[36] Hence, as long as the WEU does not create its own integrated military structure for the defence of the WEU states, the duplication of NATO's military structure is avoided. The trick is how to make the WEU more independent and efficient without undermining NATO's leading role in defence and security matters. This issue was addressed in January 1994 with the NATO concept of Combined Joint Task Forces, designed to resolve the problem of sharing military assets between the organisations.

The CJTF was introduced to help restructure NATO command arrangements and forces to meet the more varied military security demands of the post-Cold War era. The intention is to give NATO more flexible military options for dealing with contingencies in and beyond Europe. For the WEU, which lacks a full range of airlift, command and control, and intelligence capabilities to take on missions beyond members' national borders, this would be a welcome development. Overall, it would allow more effective sharing of global military burdens between the United States and Europe and pave the way for missions in which the United Stats had little or no direct interest or involvement. In addition, it could accommodate participation by forces from non-NATO allies, for example, from the CEE countries.

Particular attention has been paid to France's position within NATO by ensuring that CJTFs would remain under the direct sponsorship of the North Atlantic Council, which gives France a full say. This arrangement also suits Spain, which, like France, is only a political member of NATO. The CJTF would normally be available for missions accepted and conducted by NATO as a whole, including the United States. But the CJTF could also be used for missions undertaken by the NATO European allies who are also members of the WEU. In such a case, the CJTF commander, instead of receiving guidance from and reporting through NATO channels, would wear a WEU hat and report through a WEU command structure ultimately under the political direction of the WEU Council of Ministers. If NATO assets (for example, NATO's Airborne Warning and Control System aircraft) were to be used by WEU they could be placed under the operational control of the WEU commander when supporting a WEU operation.[37]

Once a command structure with operational procedures was in place, the allies could start identifying national units that could be combined to constitute a task force. Command post and planning exercises could be conducted, and eventually field exercises to test the complete range of cooperation that would be required to make the CJTF operational. For it to work, it needs a number of things, including the promotion of standardisation, or at least interoperability, among military equipment, supplies and operational procedures. It will also necessitate commitment, resources and goodwill on both sides. Some improvement was made with the January 1995 decision to establish a new NATO Standardisation Organisation,[38] the purpose of which is to give fresh impetus to alliance work on the coordination of allied policies and programmes for material, technical and operational standardisation. It will also support the Partnership for Peace initiative by addressing specific proposals for improved standardisation put forward by partner countries. Developments over standardisation have not been matched by specific indications either that the United States will continue to commit significant military assets to NATO or that the European allies will stem the recent decline in defence spending, as well as orientate some of their forces to support CJTF missions. Even more important, it must be emphasised that, at least until the end of 1995, the WEU's permanent staff declined to enter into discussion about how to organise task forces in line with CJTF objectives on the grounds that they had no mandate to do so from the member governments.[39]

Undoubtedly, CJTF arrangements would significantly enhance the likelihood of the WEU undertaking an (independent) operation in an optimum time frame and in a cost-effective manner. The WEU would benefit from additional joint headquarters and expanded peacetime planning possibilities.[40] It would be able to make a more effective contribution to UN operations, particularly those requiring more effective enforcement activities than are usually contemplated in traditional peace-keeping. The CJTF concept does not, however, provide for the automatic availability of assets. The United States would not transfer operational control of strategic assets to WEU command, but would provide services to WEU, such as force transport and intelligence support. Hence, as Stanley Sloan observes, 'for some time, the need for United States support will likely give the United States decisive influence over the choice of missions'.[41] This may not please France and Britain which want to be able to borrow NATO's military assets whenever it suits them. Part of the problem might be that Congress would not want American military equipment to be used in a confrontation over which America had no control. Already France is arguing that similar problems over joint authority as was experienced in Bosnia between the UN and NATO could occur between NATO and the WEU. To prepare against a United States default, WEU will therefore retain its autonomous planning capability and, as argued by the former secretary-general of the WEU, Wilhelm van Eekelen, should continue to develop its operational role so that it can act independently or implement requests from the EU.[42]

The introduction of the CJTF concept is an example of the United States preference for 'separable but not separate' force structures within NATO. Together with the Franco-German willingness to place Eurocorps under NATO or WEU command it signals an interim solution and a moving away from the zero-sum perception which prevailed until the end of 1992, viz. the view that the WEU will either undermine or replace NATO. One consequence of Bosnia has been to make it easier for France to accept the need for a transnational security structure. The problems of managing air operations (France participates in operations Sharp Guard and Deny Flight) confirmed for French leaders that any action with France's allies would need to be coordinated by an integrated command.[43] France now also accepts that NATO should be ready to undertake military operations outside its own territory. In 1995 in Seville France attended a NATO meeting for the first time since its withdrawal in 1966. But France rejects a pre-eminent role for NATO in European security. It still prefers the United States to become a bilateral partner of the EU on security matters. What is emerging, though, is a perception of 'joint gains', based on a relationship of transparency and complementarity. The spirit of this is encapsulated in the observation by the late NATO secretary-general, Manfred Wörner, that:

> Neither organisation can be effective if it considers the other as a rival, or if we waste time in debates on institutional prerogatives, or if we duplicate each other's efforts. There is enough to do for both organisations. In any crisis, we must decide which organisation can use our resources in the most cost-effective way, basing the judgment on pragmatism and the specific requirements of each situation.[44]

Nonetheless, how CJTF will work in practice remains somewhat unclear. Certainly, further clarification over command structures is needed in order to avoid the possibility of WEU troops receiving orders from both NATO headquarters and the WEU operational staff. Unresolved also is the problem of the extent to which the WEU rather than NATO should be involved in a given conflict. Should it be decided according to interest perception, e.g. whether a particular situation is primarily of European interest or is of more general concern to the alliance as a whole? A precise division of tasks along either functional or geographical lines seems difficult to achieve, since it is not always clear 'whose' interest will be involved. This will have particular relevance, in the often used phrase, if the WEU is to be capable of independent action 'only when NATO may not be willing or able to act'. In an attempt to clarify these ambiguities, Mahncke envisages four cases for the build-up of European capacity to act alone: (1) when the United States is generally supportive but chooses not to participate; (2) when the United States is uninterested; (3) when the United States is against such action; and (4) when the United States withdraws from Europe altogether.[45] These still leave some unanswered questions in the relationship between Europe and the United States, such as whether to replace the American SACEUR with a European commander on a rotating basis.[46] It lends, however, further credence to the argument that United States support for a stronger European pillar is related to less reliance on United States forces. The implications, however, are not universally accepted. On the contrary, countries like the United Kingdom associate a number of fears with such a development. They argue that if the WEU develops too far it could undermine United States commitment or call NATO's relevance into question, because it could convey the erroneous message to the United States that Europe is more capable than it really is and that the US contribution is superfluous. This they fear would set in motion a form of self-fulfilling prophecy.[47] To counteract such a development, Januzzi recommends synergy between the two organisations' structures, relying on NATO's military capabilities as the linchpin, without, however, any political subordination of one organisation to the other.[48] To achieve such synergy would require greater transparency within NATO.

The latter has not always been apparent. The United States, when it was still in the business of negotiating with the former Soviet Union over SALT and START, did not always adhere to this principle, which left a bitter aftertaste with some Europeans. Meanwhile, steps have been taken to harmonise working methods between NATO and WEU. The coordination of NATO and WEU meetings was introduced and the WEU has agreed to provide information on its activities to NATO. Nonetheless, problems of coordination continue, particularly over the conflict in Bosnia.[49] A troubling example occurred when the United States announced in November 1994 that it would no longer help enforce the arms embargo against the Bosnian government; never before had a NATO member declared that it would cease to carry out agreed NATO policy. Since it will be the European Council which gives political guidance to the WEU, the relation between the European Council and the NATO Council also needs clarification.

Another potential obstacle to coordination between the WEU and NATO involves the question of the membership of both organisations. So far the WEU has avoided problems of membership, but it is unclear whether this can be maintained. The WEU adjusted to NATO by granting Norway and Turkey associate and Denmark observer status, but if the WEU Forum for Consultation works, and if new members are admitted, that could pose problems for NATO and the United States. The current members of the WEU do not have the choice of keeping new EU members out, while 'candidates for NATO membership' have to be accepted by all NATO's current members. Under these circumstances

Turkey could block the admission of a new member in retaliation for not being accepted as a full WEU member. Moreover, granting security guarantees through the WEU and not through NATO would be likely to undermine the alliance.[50] Already the WEU Forum for Consultation runs the risk of duplicating some of the NACC's tasks.

NATO membership for CEE countries is more complicated than WEU enlargement, largely because of the United States role in NATO. The PfP arrangement helped temporarily and conveniently to postpone a decision which, when taken, will have internal and external implications, affecting both the cohesion of NATO and the future role of Russia in European security.

NATO, unlike the EU, cannot choose between 'deepening' and 'widening' according to the preference of its members. There is either a collective defence structure or there is none.[51] Anything less would approximate NACC-type status by another name.[52] But it is unclear whether the United States would accept an automatic nuclear response under predetermined conditions. On the other hand, there is also uncertainty over whether CEE countries would accept the necessary stationing of foreign troops and possibly nuclear deployments; or be able and willing to pay the cost of meeting NATO standards of military modernisation. This issue, plus concern over domestic uncertainties in potential member states, raises fears that the eastward enlargement of NATO would put intolerable strains on NATO's communication and decision-making processes, and might reduce it to the level of a loose collective security system.[53] Similar reasons are put forward by existing NATO members in discussions of whether CEE members could opt for the French version of NATO membership, i.e. join the political but not the military or integrated command structure.

That NATO is in a dilemma is obvious. Stating the fact does not provide an answer to pressing problems. How is NATO to respond to the existing power and security vacuum, spanning approximately the German and Russian borders? How is it to meet the security needs and perceived anxieties of the countries living in that region other than through enlargement? How is it to avoid the resentment, negative reactions or isolation of Russia that an eastward enlargement seems to promise?

The anxiety of CEE states not to be caught again between Russian and German power aspirations takes two forms. One is to seek NATO membership in case EU integration should fail and/or entice Germany to pursue unilateral strategies, such as bilateral arrangements with Russia. The other is the worry over a return to authoritarian rule in a Russia with expansionist aspirations. Whilst both reasons amount to an 'insurance policy' against future developments, they also culminate in the point that enlargement must take place now before a more deep-seated crisis occurs either in Russia or in the CEE region as a whole.

Unfortunately, enlargement entails choices over inclusion and exclusion and brings with it the danger of creating new lines of divisions in Europe, something that the PfP has avoided. This particularly affects Russia. In a sense, Russia is too big to be let in and too large to be left out. It is unclear whether Russia wishes to be part of NATO, but exclusion or rejection could have two likely consequences, one of which has primarily domestic repercussions while the other affects Russian cooperation.

Firstly, exclusion might stimulate a nationalist backlash, so jeopardising the position of the pro-Western reformers. Anti-Western reform campaigners could argue that the West attempts to fill the power vacuum in central and eastern Europe at the expense of Russia, and that the United States wants to secure a one-sided position of power and retain a military presence in Europe as a non-European country. Nationalists within Russia could portray this as tantamount to a policy of neo–containment.[54] It could accelerate rather than minimise pressure for Russian expansion. Already there are pressures either to intervene on behalf of some of the 20 million Russians trapped outside Russian territory as a consequence of the disintegration of the Soviet Union, in the 'near abroad',[55] or to reconstitute part of the former Soviet Union, at least economically.[56] Such an expansion, if accelerated, would not only cause anxiety within CEE states but could slow down the critical defence spending cuts that are necessary to rejuvenate the Russian economy. Other likely reactions by Russia to an eastward expansion of NATO from which it was excluded would be more anti-European and anti-Western sentiment and a negation of arms control obligations (SALT, START and CFE).

Secondly, exclusion might drive Russia into isolation. To observers like Brzezinski, it appears unwise to isolate, or for that matter to antagonise, Russia over NATO enlargement.[57] Russia, as a permanent member of the UN Security Council with the power to veto all UN resolutions on peace-keeping or crisis management the United States and NATO may wish to pass, still retains the potential to influence developments far beyond its own borders.[58] Cooperation in the sale of dual-purpose technologies and more conventional weapons, above all in conflict zones, is an aspect of great importance to the West. Another is the disarmament process. There are still 20,000 to 35,000 nuclear warheads in Russia and there is no guarantee that Russia is dismantling 2,000 to 3,000 per year as envisaged in the SALT treaty. Nor is there any certainty that Russia is keeping all this material under control and disposing of it safely. There is also a question mark over the safety of nuclear power stations. For all these reasons Russian cooperation and trust are required rather than discord and suspicion. This line is echoed in Foreign Minister Kozyrev's statement that

> It is important for Russia precisely now that it is making its choice to realise that the world needs our country not as 'the sick man' of Europe and Asia but as a strong partner holding a fitting place in the family of free, law-governed and democratic states. A policy in keeping with these expectations would be the best investment that the West could make in stability in Russia and the world, the strongest barrier against a re-emergence of 'Russian imperialism'. Conversely, aloofness on the part of the West, attempts to keep Russia out by means of new 'iron curtains' and *cordons sanitaires*, would merely provide fertile ground for nationalist and imperial extremism.[59]

For NATO the problem remains how to reassure Russia of a respected place in a European security arrangement, while denying it a veto over NATO action.[60] One of the ways forward would be to proceed simultaneously with NATO enlargement of some CEE states (excluding Ukraine and the Baltic countries, over which Russia expresses most sensitivity) and invite Russia to help create a new transcontinental system of collective security. The latter proposal, according to Brzezinski, should have two components: first, a formal treaty of global security cooperation between NATO and the Russian Federation; second, a new mechanism for special security consultations with the OSCE, including peace-keeping operations.[61] Included in such an arrangement could be the formal recognition of the CIS as a security organisation; and a revision in Russia's favour of the CFE treaty. In return certain guarantees might be sought with Russia over sanctions relief on, for example, Iraq and Serbia.

Although enlargement and good relations with Russia are necessary ingredients of NATO's viability, by themselves they are not sufficient to solve the problems of NATO's effectiveness, whether NATO can retain its status as the primary security institution in Europe in the future, whether it can represent the embryo of a new European defence structure in western Europe, or whether its main purpose should be to effect its gradual replacement through a new European Security Identity (ESI), of which the EU and WEU would be crucial components.

Future prospects of security institutions: interlocking versus interblocking

What contribution can security institutions make in the post-1989 era? Whereas it was mainly NATO that acted in the defence and security field in the Cold War period, the scope of institutional application has widened considerably. As was explicitly recognised in the November 1991 North Atlantic Council declaration, no single organisation can act alone any more. However, the proliferation of security institutions has resulted in overlapping functions and memberships, and poses questions about competences, competition, duplication, the division of labour and cooperation. This has resulted in a blurring of the dividing lines and the mandates of these organisations. Who does what, where, how and with what means has become a major issue. 'Interblocking' is heard as much as the term 'interlocking' when reference is made to the performance of security institutions in the conflict in ex-Yugoslavia. Part of the problem is that some organisations, like the UN or the OSCE, have legitimating powers but lack military capability, whilst others, such as NATO or the WEU, have the latter but not the former.

There is considerable interaction among the major institutions dealing with European security. For example, the WEU and NATO engaged in joint action in mounting a naval blockade against Serbia and monitoring Bosnian air space. The OSCE has cooperated with NATO and the Council of Europe in fact-finding missions. There is cooperation in the human rights sphere between the Council of Europe and the OSCE, particularly through the latter's Office of Democratic Institutions and Human Rights and its High Commissioner on National Minorities. UN officials are often present at OSCE meetings and there are regular cross-references to NATO and the OSCE in their respective communiqués.

In spite of these interactions, no efficient division of labour has emerged between the main security institutions, and duplication as well as 'interblocking' occurs. A few examples may illustrate the point. Up till now NATO and the UN have had considerable difficulty in coordinating their efforts. This was clearly illustrated in March 1994 by the disagreement between the UN commander, General Michael Rose, and the UN representative, Yasushi Akasiki, over the possibility of initiating air strikes following Serbian non-compliance with a NATO cease-fire ultimatum. There are problems of overlapping responsibilities and lack of coordination that also exist between NATO and the OSCE. NATO's commitment to consult with PfP participants if a partner perceives a direct threat to its territorial integrity, political independence or security has not yet been harmonised with existing OSCE mandates in the field of political consultation. The remits of NACC and the PfP programme are viewed with some trepidation by Wilhelm Hoeynck, the secretary-general of the OSCE. He warns that if insufficient care is exercised over crisis management missions, international organisations could find themselves being played off against one another by the conflicting parties.[62] Recognising growing similarities in terms both of membership and of tasks, James Goodby sees NACC as better positioned than the OSCE to be the main consultation forum for collective security operations between eastern and western Europe. Therefore, in his opinion, the NACC could also accept some of the operations and investigative missions currently assigned to the OSCE. This would reduce the role of the OSCE to that of establishing and monitoring standards of human rights and the treatment of minorities and long-term conflict resolution assistance, while NATO and NACC, armed with mandates, would perform 'the time-urgent fire brigade role'.[63] But even such a reduced function for the OSCE would clash with similar tasks carried out by the Council of Europe or would fail to meet aspects of the EU's Stability Pact. There are also different UN, NACC, NATO (minus France) and SHAPE peace-keeping doctrines, with the WEU also developing its own concept – not to mention national doctrines and concepts.[64]

The problem of who does what, where, how and with what means is further complicated by the need for legitimation. For example, certain countries like Germany insist that legitimation of military intervention or humanitarian operations is sought by means of either a UN or an OSCE mandate. This insistence could be further extended if peace-keeping operations involve Russia, via either NACC or the PfP. These issues indicate that no effective division of labour has yet emerged, rather there are signs of duplication and paralysis.

In view of these difficulties, should there be a 'lead' or 'core' security institution? Should NATO remain the central element of European security, despite accusations that this might be an attempt to capture and preserve Cold War hierarchies, both between and within various institutions? A 'yes' answer to this question derives partly from the uncertainties surrounding Russia and parts of eastern Europe, the Middle East and North Africa; partly from NATO's ability to improve relations with the WEU and to mount peace-keeping missions; and partly from the weakness of the UN, WEU and OSCE as viable alternatives. NATO is the only alliance with a functioning command and force structure. NATO capabilities are superior to those of the Europeans alone, and will remain so even if and when the Europeans develop their own capability.[65] There is no indication that the European countries are prepared to spend the extra 2-3 per cent of GDP annually needed to achieve a minimum level of autonomy from NATO and the United States.

Yet there are also drawbacks associated with NATO as a lead or core security institution. Different problems demand differing responses from various security institutions, and institutions such as the Council of Europe, the EU, the WEU and the OSCE could or should assume responsibility for many of the non-military aspects of security, especially problems of refugee movements, economic stabilisation, arbitration and conciliation alongside CSBMs.[66] NATO has no real experience in these fields. NATO has found it difficult to project stability to the CEE area, which involves dealing with issues of democratic and economic reconstruction, nuclear proliferation, disarmament and the maintenance of nuclear stockpiles. If NATO strategies of peace enforcement, including conventional deterrence techniques, are to be successful, they need to be nested in a broader set of policies and strategies including preventative peace-keeping and early warning, which in turn requires cooperation with member states of the UN, OSCE, WEU and PfP programme.[67]

Another continuing problem for NATO is how to maintain unity between North America and western Europe. There is no agreement within NATO on the extent to which NATO's main function of collective defence should be retained or new functions of collective security (crisis management and conflict prevention) undertaken. The shortcomings of *ad hoc* decision-making in the case of Yugoslavia are all too apparent. Internally, NATO is being challenged by American neo-isolationism,[68] on the one hand, and the formation of a strong ESI on the other. Signs of the former can be seen in US commitment to collective defence rather than collective security, and in the United States' predilection for maintaining NATO at all costs.[69] With regard to ESI, progress has been made with both the CJTF concept and the arrangements for Eurocorps, which enshrine the principle of 'separable but not separate' force. This could also strengthen the European pillar of NATO and therefore augment the European voice within the alliance and provide it with firm foundations on both sides of the Atlantic.[70] Such an arrangement could even enable 'WEU to become the out-of-area branch of NATO, which could in effect extend the geographical legs of NATO while also preserving it'.[71] Unclear, in such a perspective, is what is to become of the WEU, torn between a dual loyalty: should it become the European pillar of NATO or the centre of a European alternative to the transnational ties?[72] Until clarity in this area emerges, NATO seems poised to remain the prime security organisation in Europe for the foreseeable future. As Anne Marie Le Gloannec suggests, 'the dissolution of NATO would be either a recipe for disaster – a recreation of nineteenth-century Europe – or for success – but only if it promoted a European defence community'.[73]

Yet the debate about the purpose of NATO and the American and European roles can also be viewed from another angle. As Peter Schmidt notes, political and military situations provoke differing reactions in the NATO and WEU member countries when it comes to the actual decision to use military force, as the example of Yugoslavia clearly shows.[74] This makes it unlikely that the WEU and NATO will be militarily active with full participation of all member states. Under current conditions, alliances in general will more than likely play the role of back-up instruments, as in the Gulf War, rather than that of political and military coordination bodies. In the final analysis this calls into question the utility of having integrated transatlantic military structures and standing peacetime alliances.[75] This logic is likely to also affect the development of CFSP and of Eurocorps and points to the principle of 'variable geometry', whereby only a smaller number of EU members will commit themselves to specific CFSP goals and actions whilst others either 'opt out' or abstain from voting. Such a development may rend the fabric of European security institutions and promote a renationalisation of defence and security policy. However, as Peter van Ham suggests, the choice between 'all hanging together or hanging separately' is not a new one.[76]

The Bosnian crisis has once again emphasised that no organisation of sovereign states can function any more effectively than the consensus among its members permits. The success of any institution depends upon two factors: the willingness of the major powers to work through the institution and, second, leadership and initiative within a given institution.[77] Leadership and initiative will to a large extent influence which of the various security institutions will flourish and which will wither, as well as the extent to which they reflect a transatlantic or a European bias in terms of membership and agenda.[78] In designing an agenda there has to be a clear understanding of what security institutions should be used for. In the past, the global Soviet threat concentrated the allies' minds and limited the intensity of their quarrels, but this is no longer the case. What is required now is vision and conviction, through common ideas and concepts.[79] They are particularly needed with regard to ethnic conflicts and out-of-area military operations. However, it is here that governments note a lack of public enthusiasm for prolonged and confused operations other than war where missions are assigned other than those initially agreed. In the final analysis it is national differences that need to be overcome for security institutions to work effectively. This requires clarification on the part of the key actors comprising such institutions. For example, the United States has to decide what level of involvement it anticipates for itself and its partners, the French have to identify institutions that they can work through, and the British have to make a clear-cut decision about whether to endorse wholeheartedly the political aspects of European union, which includes the murky commitment to 'common defence'.[80] There is also uncertainty over the eventual role Germany is going to play in security collaboration. Those outside the formal western European institutional structure must be given guidance as to what criteria are to be satisfied if they are to achieve full integration into select western European 'clubs', particularly the EU and NATO.

Conclusion

There is a growing impression that the period of grace that followed the end of the Cold War and of the communist system is giving way to a feeling of growing perplexity regarding the path to be followed to give Europe a security architecture satisfactory to all concerned.[81] The security agenda of the past forty years has given way to a new agenda, comprising military security as well as non-military security matters (economic, political, nuclear-proliferation and storage – etc.). Crisis management and conflict prevention take a prominent place. Because many of the military operations have to be undertaken 'outside' NATO or EU territory, the term 'collective security' is an important addition to the existing concept of collective defence. Collective security 'embraces a collective response to intra-state violations of international norms in the name of international peace and security, as well as the long-understood responsibility for international norms in relations between states'.[82] The aim is to localise an actual conflict or potential conflict of either an intra-state or inter-state kind in order to prevent it from spreading.

Manfred Wörner, the late secretary-general of NATO, believed that the Cold War's abatement created an opportunity, denied to previous generations, to create lasting peace in Europe. This belief is dampened by Nicole Gnesotto, who argues that the end of the Cold War signifies the beginning of real wars, and that the conflict in ex-Yugoslavia demonstrates that collective security in Europe simply does not exist.[83] The outbreak of wars and the inability to cope with ethnic conflicts were predicted by John Mearsheimer in 1990.[84] Mearsheimer could also agree with Gnesotto's explanation that collective security does not work because of 'lack of agreement on principles and the interpretation of international laws, dilemmas within democracies regarding the use of force, the return to national reflexes rather than collective solidarity and the inappropriateness of institutions'.[85] Any international organisation – and NATO and the EU are no exception – is to a large extent only the sum of its parts and can subsequently be only as competent as it is allowed to be through the consensual decision-making process adopted by participating states. In other words, international organisations are often hostage to the willingness of member states to strike a compromise and act.

All security institutions are in the process of adjusting to the new circumstances by adopting new roles and functions, and by learning where cooperation with other organisations is possible, beneficial or necessary. Through this adaptation process they may help to prevent conflicts similar to the one in Bosnia from escalating. However, there are a number of remaining problems. Although interrelated, they fall into three categories: the issue of the legitimation of peace-keeping interventions, the cohesion of NATO, and the geographical expansion of security institutions.

First, the extent to which NATO and the WEU peace-keeping activities should be legitimised by the UN or the OSCE remains contentious. With UN and OSCE action either hampered by lack of resources, or subject to veto in the Security Council, both NATO and the WEU need to establish when and how independent action (without explicit authorisation) should be undertaken. Equally, for the UN, and possibly the OSCE, there is the question whether in view of the lax attitude taken by some member states on resources or peace-keeping missions, 'stand-by' forces should be established. There are still grey areas surrounding the issues of 'autonomy' and 'obligation'.

Second, although CJTF and Eurocorps arrangements have gone some way to secure the future of NATO and to improve its flexibility, NATO is by no means solidly assured of its future direction. Both the future of the United States and that of the EU remain uncertain. According to Anthony Lake, the US National Security Adviser, in the absence of a Russian military threat the future of the Euro-American relationship is almost bound to be decided on a case-by-case basis. Further US commitments to European security will probably be determined by the degree of success the CJTF concept will have. If the latter fails, the US commitment is likely to weaken. Equally, for the CJTF to work it will require Europe increasingly to perform a leadership role. In view of the disappointment expressed by the French over the lack of EU support in its UN initiative in Rwanda, an EU leadership role seems a long way off. Rather Europe seems still to be unable to resolve its own security problems collectively. NATO may therefore suffer from the impact of reduced US commitment and European inability to counteract. On the other hand, the argument that NATO needs to redefine its role will become less important as NATO becomes more involved in resolving international crises.[86] Caution is therefore as much called for as optimism.[87]

Third, membership is a problem not only for the UN and the OSCE, which both have large memberships, but it also causes problems for NATO and the EU. The geographical expansion of the latter two organisations is partly linked with the issue of legitimation and partly raises sensitive aspects of security guarantees and the consequences of exclusion, especially for Russia. With Russia insisting on UN authorisation for peace-keeping missions via the PfP programme, full membership would exacerbate this problem and might undermine its autonomous actions. A similar consequence may arise if full membership is envisaged of the WEU.[88] In the cooperative arrangements which the WEU and NATO have made with CEE states, the issues of security guarantees and the potential isolation of Russia (including the creation of new barriers/borders in Europe) have so far been avoided. Both, together with the EU, have tried to transfer and project stability to CEE and to act as guardians of regional stability. All have tried also to provide the CEE states with an active role in European security matters and to ensure that Russia especially does not feel isolated from these developments. Still open is the question whether or not to cooperate fully with Russia, to treat it as an equal, or to entrust it with a leadership (security provider) role in the CIS. Although they represent only limited adjustments to fill the security vacuum in CEE, these moves can be seen as attempts to lay the foundations of a new security order spanning the whole of Europe. But the issue of security guarantees will not go away. On the contrary, with uncertainty surrounding Russia, central European countries will continue to press for a decision.

Notes

1   The CSCE changed its name to OSCE in December 1994, to underline the body's permanent status.
2   See Luisa Vierucci, 'WEU: a Regional Partner of the United Nations?' *Chaillot Papers* 12 (Paris: WEU Institute for Security Studies, December 1993).
3   For further details see Colin McInnes (ed.), *Security Strategy in the New Europe* (London: Routledge, 1992); Peter Schmidt (ed.), *In the Midst of Change: on the Development of West European Security and Defence Cooperation* (Baden-Baden: Nomos, 1992); and Thomas-Durell Young and William T. Johnsen, 'Reforming NATO's Command and Operational Control Structures: Progress and Problems,' *SSI Special Report* (Carlisle, PA: Strategic Studies Institute, US Army War College, April 1992).
4   See Peter van Ham, 'Ukraine, Russia and European Security: Implications for Western Policy,' *Chaillot Papers* 13 (Paris: WEU Institute for Security Studies February 1994).
5   Together with NATO, the EU has offered full technical assistance in questions of nuclear storage, safety, and dismantlement. See Catherine McArdle Kelleher, 'A New Security Order: the United States and the European Community in the 1990s,' Occasional Paper of the European Community Studies Association (Pittsburgh: ECSA, June 1993), p. 27.
6   See John Simpson, 'Nuclear Non-proliferation in the post-Cold War Era,' *International Affairs*, vol. 70, no. 1 (1994), pp. 17–39.
7   See Michael Quinlan, 'The Future of Nuclear Weapons: Policy for Western Possessors,' *International Affairs*, vol. 69, no. 3, (1993) pp. 483–96.
8   See R. D. Asmus, R. L. Kugler and F. S. Larrabee, 'Building a New NATO,' *Foreign Affairs*, vol. 72, no. 4 (September/October 1993), pp. 28–40; and Esther Barbe, 'Spanish Responses to the Security Institutions of the new Europe: Mediterranean Objectives and European Instruments,' Working Paper, Centre d'Estudios sobre la Pau i el Desarmament, Autonomous University of Barcelona, no. 1, 1992.
9   See 'The Alliance's New Strategic Concept,' Press Communiqué S-1(91)85, Brussels, NATO Press Service, 7 November 1991.
10 For details see Stanley R. Sloan, 'Combined Joint Task Forces (CJTF) and New Missions for NATO,' *CRS Report for Congress*, 17 March 1994, p. 2.

11 See William Johnson and Thomas-Durell Young, 'Partnership for Peace: Discerning Fact from Fiction,' (Carlisle, PA: Strategic Studies Institute, US Army War College, August 1994), p. 16.
12 Ibid., p. 13.
13 Patrick Keatinge, 'The Twelve, the United Nations, and Somalia: the Mirage of Global Interventions,' paper delivered at the TEPSA conference, Brussels, 27–9 January 1994.
14 Helen Leigh-Phippard, 'Remaking the Security Council: the Options,' *The World Today*, vol. 50, nos. 8–9 (August–September 1994), pp. 167–72.
15 For an elaboration of this point see Giandomenico Picco, 'The UN and the Use of Force: Leave the Secretary General out of it,' *Foreign Affairs*, vol. 73, no. 5 (September/October 1994), pp. 15–18.
16 Karl Lamers, 'The Future Shape of United Nations Military Operations: Lessons of past UN Peace Missions,' *German Comments*, 35 (July 1994), p. 59.
17 Ibid., pp. 59–60.
18 Quoted in *The Economist*, 21 February 1995.
19 See Jessica Matthews, 'Don't abandon Peace-keeping,' *Washington Post*, reprinted in *The Japanese Times*, 8 December 1994.
20 See Peter Scholl-Latour, 'Anti-Islamic Alliance of the former Superpowers? Europe must press for Dialogue and Containment: Eurocorps,' *German Comment*, 38 (April 1995), pp. 11–20. For further critical views on the UN see G. Evans, 'Cooperative Security and Intrastate Conflict,' *Foreign Policy*, 56 (fall 1994), pp. 3–20, and for a general overview of UN development see Richard Falk, 'Appraising the UN at Fifty: the Looming Challenge,' *Journal of International Affairs*, vol. 48 (winter 1995), pp. 625–43.
21 Matthews, 'Don't abandon Peace-keeping.'
22 Dieter Mahncke, 'Parameters of European Security,' *Chaillot Papers* 10 (Paris: WEU Institute for Security Studies, September 1993).
23 See Wilhelm Hoeynck, 'CSCE works to develop its Conflict Prevention Potential,' *NATO Review* (April 1994), pp. 16–22.
24 Ibid.
25 Ibid.
26 See OSCE Helsinki Decisions 1992.
27 See Mahncke, 'Parameters of European Security,' and Goodby, *Collective Security in Europe after the Cold War*.
28 Hans-Dietrich Genscher, 'Turning a Warhorse into a Peacemaker,' *European*, 27 May–2 June 1994. For a similar view see Werner Bauwens, Bruno Colson, Wim De Haar, Koen De Feyter, Oliver Paye and Nic Vertongen, 'The CSCE and the changing Role of NATO and the European Union,' *NATO Review* (June 1994), pp. 21–5.
29 Nicole Gnesotto, 'Lessons of Yugoslavia,' *Chaillot Papers* 14 (Paris: WEU Institute for Security Studies March 1994), p. 27.
30 Peter Schmidt, 'The Western European Union in the 1990s: Searching for a Role,' *SSI Special Report* (Carlisle, PA: Strategic Studies Institute, US Army College, May 1993).
31 Ibid.
32 Alexis Seydoux and Jerome Paolini, 'From Western Security Interblocking to Institutional Evolutionism,' in M. Curtis, O. Diel, J. Paolini, A. Seydoux and R. Wolf (eds), *Challenges and Responses to Future European Security: British, French and German Perspectives* (London: European Strategy Group, 1993), p. 192.
33 See Draft Interim Report (Henk Vos and James Bilbray, co-rapporteurs) of the Sub-committee on Defence and Security Cooperation between Europe and North America, NATODAT, 14 July 1994, point 50.
34 Ibid.
35 See statement by M. François Léotard, French minister of defence, quoted in the *Financial Times*, 4 March 1994.

36 See Kelleher, 'A New Security Order,' p. 15
37 See Sloan, 'Combined Joint Task Forces and New Missions for NATO.'
38 This organisation will comprise a Committee on Standardisation, composed of high-level national representatives, an internal NATO Headquarters Standardisation Liaison Board, and an Office of NATO Standardisation composed of existing joint civilian and military NATO staff. See *NATO Review*, 2 (March 1995), p. 32.
39 This statement by the British Air Vice Marshal John Cheshire was quoted in the *Financial Times*, 20 July 1994.
40 Wilhelm van Eekelen, 'WEU after two Brussels Summits: a new Approach to Common Tasks,' paper delivered at the Royal Insititute for International Relations, Brussels, 27 January 1994, p. 5.
41 Sloan, 'Combined Joint Task Forces and New Missions for NATO,' p. 4.
42 Eekelen, 'WEU after two Brussels Summits,' p. 6.
43 Jolyon Howorth, 'The Debate in France over Military Intervention in Europe," in Lawrence Freedman (ed.), *Military Intervention in European Conflicts* (Oxford: Blackwell, 1994), pp. 106–24.
44 Manfred Wörner, 'European Security: Political will plus Military Might' in Wörner *et al.*, *What is European Security after the Cold War?*, p. 17.
45 Mahncke, 'Parameters of European Security,' p. 35.
46 Under an informal agreement within NATO, its supreme military commander is traditionally an American, while a European has always filled the post of secretary-general.
47 Simon Lunn, 'A Reassessment of European Security,' in Wörner *et al.*, *What is European Security after the Cold War?*, pp. 50–67.
48 Giovanni Jannuzzi, 'NATO's Outlook: a Perspective from Italy,' *NATO Review*, vol. 41, no. 6 (December 1993), p. 13.
49 John Newhouse, 'No Exit, no Entrance,' *New Yorker*, 28 June 1993.
50 R. D. Asmus *et. al.*, 'Building a New NATO.'
51 Karl-Heinz Kamp, 'The Folly of Rapid NATO Expansion,' *Foreign Policy*, 98 (spring 1995), p. 127.
52 Karsten Voigt (Working Group Rapporteur) supported by Senator William Roth, Carlie Rose, 'The Enlargement of the Alliânce,' Draft Special Report of the Working Group on NATO Enlargement,' NATO Integrated Data Service, 28 November 1994.
53 *Ibid.*, and Kamp, 'The Folly of Rapid NATO Expansion,' p. 122.
54 Gerhard Wettig, "Controversial Foundations of Security in Europe,' *Aussenpolitik*, vol. 46, no. 1 (1991), p. 46.
55 As Andrei Kozyrev, the Russian foreign minister, points out, almost every Russian has relatives in the 'near abroad' who are either discriminated against in one way or another or are becoming refugees. Nevertheless, the West does not raise its voice in their defence. And this is a circumstance which extreme nationalists actively exploit. Andrei Kozyrev, 'Leaders of World Diplomacy: a Strategy for Partnership,' *International Affairs*, 8 (1994), p.12.
56 Andrei Kozyrev compares the EU with CIS development, claiming that as in the former big countries such as France or Germany take the economic leadership there should be nothing wrong with Russia's declaration that it is seeking a gradual, primarily economic reintegration of the post-Soviet area on a voluntary and equal basis. See Kozyrev, 'Leaders of World Diplomacy,' p. 12.
57 Zbigniew Brzezinski, 'A Plan for Europe,' *Foreign Affairs*, vol. 74, no 1 (January/February 1995), pp. 26–42.
58 Kamp, 'The Folly of Rapid NATO Expansion, p. 125.
59 Kozyrev, 'Leaders of World Diplomacy,' p. 6.
60 Stanley Sloan, 'US Perspectives on NATO's Future,' *International Affairs*, vol. 71, no. 2 (April 1995), p. 229.

61 Brzezinski, 'A Plan for Europe,' p. 35.
62 Wilhelm Hoeynck, 'CSCE works to develop its Conflict Prevention Potential,' *NATO Review*, 2 (April 1994), pp. 16–21.
63 Goodby, 'Collective Security in Europe after the Cold War.'
64 Bruce George (General Rapporteur), 'Continental Drift, Draft General Report,' NATO Integrated Data Service, 9 December 1994, point 16.
65 Bauwens et al., 'The CSCE and the changing Role of NATO and the European Union,' p. 21.
66 See Simon Duke, *The New European Security Disorder* (London: Macmillan Press, 1994), p. 273.
67 David Carment, 'The International Politics of Ethnic Conflict: a NATO Perspective on Theory and Policy,' paper delivered at the APSA Convention, New York, September 1994, p. 3.
68 Anthony Lake, US national security adviser, warned in April 1994 against a spreading of new isolationism in the United States, indicating that there were threats to US foreign aid programmes, participation in peace-keeping, and the battles against terrorism and drug trafficking. Quoted in the *Financial Times*, 28 April 1995.
69 Duke, *The New European Security Disorder*, p. 347.
70 Volker Rühe, 'Adapting the Alliance in the Face of great Challenges,' *NATO Review*, December 1993, pp. 3–6.
71 Duke, *The New European Security Disorder*, p. 269.
72 *Ibid.*, pp. 26 and 246.
73 Talk given at the conference on United Germany in the European Union, Birmingham University, March 1995.
74 Peter Schmidt (with a summary of discussion by Maria Alngi), "Germany, France and NATO,' Strategic Studies Institute: Strategic Outreach Roundtable Paper and Conference Report, US Army War College, October 1994. See also Sloan, 'US Perspectives on NATO's Future,' p. 229, and Alan Lee Williams and Geoffrey Lee Williams, 'NATO's Future in the Balance: Time for a Rethink' (London: Atlantic Council of the United Kingdom, 1995), p. 19.
75 Geoffrey Lee Williams, 'Does Europe need an American Ally?' *European Brief*, vol. 2, no. 6 (March/April 1995), pp. 27–8.
76 Peter van Ham, 'Can Institutions Hold Europe Together?' in Hugh Miall (ed.), *Redefining Europe: New Patterns of Conflict and Cooperation* (London: Royal Institute of International Affairs, 1994), pp. 186–205.
77 Duke, *The New European Security Disorder*, p. 93.
78 *Ibid.*, p. 216.
79 For a further elaboration of this point see Herman von Richthofen (German ambassador to NATO), letter printed in the *Financial Times*, 2 December 1994.
80 George, 'Continental Drift,' point 8.
81 Duke, *The New European Security Disorder*, p. 369.
82 George, 'Continental Drift,' point 14.
83 Bauwens et. al., 'The CSCE and the changing role of NATO and the European Union.'
84 Goodby, 'Collective Security in Europe after the Cold War.'
85 Gnesotto, 'Lessons of Yugoslavia.'
86 John Mearsheimer, 'Back to the Future: Instability in Europe after the Cold War,' *International Security*, vol. 15, no. 1 (summer 1990), pp. 5–56.
87 Gnesotto, 'Lessons of Yugoslavia.'
88 Schmidt, 'The Western European Union in the 1990s.'

4

The economic dimension of security
Managing the macroeconomy

The security dimension of macroeconomic stability has been given resonance by the efforts of the eastern and central European countries to make the transition to the market economy and competitive multiparty democracy after 1989. The role of a stable macroeconomic environment in the European security order is indirect, but may be nonetheless critical to the successful construction of a stable pan-European security order. Macroeconomic stability and favourable macroeconomic conditions in western Europe and the United States will help shape the pace and success of the transition to the market economy in central and eastern Europe; it will also increase the prospects for a successful and lasting transition to democracy in those countries and consequently retard a return to non-democratic forms of governance. The linkage between macroeconomic stability and prosperity in the Atlantic economy for the success of the internal reform of the nations of central and eastern Europe is found in the causal connection established in the minds of Europe's ruling elites between the macroeconomic collapse after 1929 and the ensuing political chaos of the 1930s: the competitive devaluations and the rise of currency and trading blocs in the 1930s were an ill-conceived response to the macroeconomic collapse beginning in 1929. And these economic developments, in turn, facilitated the rise of fascism and established a basis for the outbreak of war in Europe. Just as the success of the Marshall Plan in fostering the recovery of the European nations after the Second World War framed the debate about the level and types of aid to be given to the nations of central and eastern Europe after the end of the Cold War, the failure to cope with the macroeconomic instability of Europe prior to the Second World War informs the preoccupation with the necessity of ensuring macroeconomic stability in the Atlantic economy to preclude a return to authoritarian government in central and eastern Europe.

The inclusion of macroeconomic policy in a discussion of the future European security order is not inconsistent with NATO communiqués since the

Atlantic Declaration in 1990 and may be reasonably inferred as a new security concern, albeit one which the alliance is uniquely ill equipped to meet. It is also the case, however, that simply stating that macroeconomic policy is an essential element of the post-Cold War security order does not make it one. What is certain, however, is that national macroeconomic policies, particularly where there is asymmetry in economic size and openness between the national actors, have the potential to generate international economic (dis)economies that can prove to be highly disruptive in a state system that enjoys a high level of economic interdependence, particularly in the financial sphere.[1]

The interpenetration of national economies impinges upon the autonomy of national authorities and constrains their ability to fulfil the welfare objectives of society. National autonomy in economic affairs depends upon the separation of domestic markets. The line between the national economy and the global economy has been significantly blurred; national markets are no longer separated and political and economic boundaries no longer coincide. External economic developments frequently dominate domestic economic activity and confound the efforts of national authorities to manage the domestic economy. Although national authorities retain much of their autonomy in the setting of policy objectives and in the choosing of policy instruments, they no longer exercise complete or effective control over policy outcomes.[2] This loss of control over outcomes and the limitation imposed upon the choice and effectiveness of instruments generated much of the conflict and cooperation between the states of the Atlantic economy prior to the end of the Cold War; it follows that much of the conflict and cooperation in the post-Cold War world will continue to be driven by the effort to reduce the external diseconomies arising from the autonomous exercise of macroeconomic policy instruments.

Yet macroeconomic policy remains an ambiguous candidate for inclusion in the security architecture of the post-Cold War world. Prior to 1989, the problem of macroeconomic policy cooperation within the context of the EU remained largely confined to the task of maintaining exchange rate stability within the European Monetary System (EMS) to protect intra-European trade from exchange rate disruptions stemming from wayward exchange rate and macroeconomic policies in the United States; and to further the prospects of the future monetary union of the European currencies that would parallel and support the political unification of Europe. The importance of macroeconomic policy cooperation within the Atlantic context was likewise restricted to the impact exchange rate instability would have upon the patterns of trade and investment within the Atlantic economy. It also reflected renewed erosion of national autonomy in the conduct of monetary policy: the progressive integration of Atlantic financial markets amplified the impact of divergent monetary and fiscal policies on bilateral exchange rates and reduced the autonomy of national authorities in the conduct of macroeconomic policy.[3] Where macroeconomic policy did impinge upon security issues, however, was in the corrosive effect macroeconomic conflicts had upon political cooperation in the security sphere. Yet the interdependence of macroeconomic policy and security policy traditionally defined in the Atlantic context was limited and has been easily short-circuited up to now: in the 1970s the Europeans in particular made a successful effort to preclude the linkage of security concerns and macroeconomic policy in the aftermath of the first oil crisis in 1973-74.[4]

The connection between the macroeconomic policies pursued by the G-7 nations (the United States, Japan, Germany, France, Italy, the United Kingdom and Canada) and the consequences of those policies for the nations in transition is direct and incontrovertible. The future stability of the European security order rests largely upon the successful transition of those nations to the market economy and the embrace of democratic forms of governance. The twin expectations of marketisation and democratisation serve as the criteria these nations must meet to continue extracting concessions on issues ranging from debt forgiveness to receiving financial support from international financial institutions (the European Bank for Reconstruction and Development) or special facilities within those institutions (the Structural Transformation Facility of the IMF). The future European security order, then, depends upon a stable macroeconomic environment facilitating trade between the eastern and western halves of the Atlantic economy and investment in the eastern half of Europe. Trade and financial flows, however, require a stable macroeconomic environment. And without that international context, the prospects for the successful transition to democracy and the market economy are significantly reduced, as are the prospects for the evolution of a peaceful and stable pan-European security order.

Macroeconomic stability shapes the prospects for a stable European security order in a number of ways. First, it plays an indirect role in supporting the transition to the market economy in eastern and central Europe and in the successful embrace of democracy in those countries. Second, macroeconomic stability has become the *sine qua non* of progress towards a single Europe, towards the fulfilment of the Maastricht treaty ambition of a single European currency. The criteria of macroeconomic policy stability established in the treaty, it will be argued, have become, at a minimum, the macroeconomic policy criteria for the whole of Europe, west, east and central. There is then a nascent macroeconomic regime that embraces the whole of Europe and therefore creates a common standard of macroeconomic performance that will not only act as a potential gatekeeper for future aspirants to join the EU and WEU (and potentially NATO as well), but which bears upon the continued deepening of the enlarged EU, particularly with respect to its ambitions in the security and foreign policy fields. And third, the inability of the nations of Europe and North America to sustain macroeconomic policy coordination may reintroduce an enmity in economic relations that will spill over and corrode efforts at cooperation and integration in the military sphere of the pan-European security architecture.

The prospects for a stable macroeconomic environment supporting the European security order are dependent at a minimum upon the provision of stable national macroeconomic policies and ideally upon the ability of the major states of the Atlantic area to coordinate their macroeconomic policies. The desirability of macroeconomic cooperation reflects the difficulty of sustaining divergences in monetary and fiscal policies in the contemporary international system; the current structure of these nations' economies – a high share of tradables as a proportion of GNP, high levels of capital mobility, and exchange rates free from control or segmentation – increasingly precludes macroeconomic autonomy, particularly monetary autonomy, as a realistic assumption or goal in the formation of policy. This loss of autonomy and the interdependence of macroeconomic policies create the demand for macroeconomic policy coordination between the nations of western Europe and North America and have generated efforts to achieve macroeconomic convergence within Europe itself.[5] Macroeconomic divergences in the Atlantic economy, in combination with the formal advantages associated with macroeconomic coordination, have produced episodic and generally unsuccessful efforts at coordination.[6] The relative failure to sustain macroeconomic coordination among the G-7 countries is attributed to a number of factors ranging from disagreements among policy-makers on the appropriate model of the world economy[7] to domestic bargaining and uncertainty about the policy and political consequences of policy coordination,[8] to institutional rigidities and dissimilarities that make the coordination of monetary and fiscal policy difficult,[9] to non-cooperation as a strategy maximising national utility,[10] to simple scepticism about the benefits of coordination.[11] Nonetheless, a persuasive case can be made in favour of the position that macroeconomic policy coordination is superior to the non-coordination of macroeconomic policy from both a national and a global perspective.[12]

The institutions of macroeconomic coordination and convergence

Despite the structural and institutional barriers to macroeconomic coordination, as well as doubts about the efficacy of policy coordination, the G-7 and IMF have established mechanisms for reaping the joint gains to be achieved from the coordination of monetary and fiscal policies. Within Europe, however, the more ambitious objective of policy convergence was established with the Maastricht treaty and managed by a cluster of EU institutions, including ECOFIN and the European Monetary Institute (EMI). The economic stabilisation and transformation of central and eastern Europe depend upon an accommodating international macroeconomic context. The provision of that context appears to depend at this juncture upon the stabilisation of the Atlantic macroeconomy and the coordination of national macroeconomic policies by the G-7 nations. And if those nations are to realise the objective of EU membership by the new millennium, they must embrace monetary and fiscal policies that correspond with the macroeconomic targets established by the Maastricht treaty.

International macroeconomic policy coordination has invariably taken place between the G-7 nations, and that coordination is usually preceded by a prearranged deal between the G-3 nations – the United States, Japan and Germany. The IMF continues to play a critical role in facilitating the joint management of the global macroeconomy in a number of important ways, although the specific competencey and role of the IMF flow from its responsibilities for overseeing the international monetary system. Its articles of agreement obligate the IMF to exercise 'firm surveillance' over the exchange rate system as well as the exchange rate policies of individual countries. The IMF has developed a set of principles guiding member state policies with respect to the management of national exchange rates. States are required to abstain from manipulating exchange rates or the international monetary system with the intention of avoiding necessary internal macroeconomic adjustment or of achieving an unfair trading advantage; to intervene in the exchange markets 'to counter disorderly conditions'; and to take into consideration the impact of intervention in the foreign exchange market on the economies of other countries. The IMF carries out its surveillance responsibilities with several procedures. First, there is the world economic outlook exercise which provides IMF members with a global frame of reference for the conduct of national macroeconomic and exchange rate policies compatible with the underlying global trends. Second, there are the Article IV consultations that take place between the IMF and the member states, which focus upon the viability of national exchange rates in view of the interrelationship of national macroeconomic and structural policies. Article IV consultations have helped the IMF establish three macroeconomic norms for its member states: reasonable price stability, a sustainable external position, and orderly economic growth. And the third mechanism facilitating the surveillance responsibility of the IMF is the participation of the IMF managing director in the deliberations of the annual G-7 economic summits. In this role, the IMF can fulfil some of the functions ascribed to an effective international regime: it lowers the transaction costs of macroeconomic coordination because the IMF provides all participants with an unbiased and symmetrical source of information about the macroeconomic and exchange rate polices of the major economies to all the participants and serves as a neutral source of policy recommendations that are relatively free of the parochial concerns of national leaders and finance ministers. The IMF may enter into discussions with a member state outside the regularised Article IV procedures in one of three circumstances: when a state engages in prolonged and large-scale one-way intervention in the foreign exchange market; when a state engages in an unsustainable level of borrowing to finance a balance of payments deficit; or when a state introduces restrictions on either the capital or the current account for balance of payments purposes. Even though the IMF is empowered to offer unsought advice to a state manipulating its exchange rate or otherwise disrupting the international monetary system, it lacks any real mechanism for enforcing its views unless the member state seeks IMF financing and thereby subjects itself to IMF conditionality.

Surveillance has not proved an effective mechanism for effecting cooperative solutions to the macroeconomic difficulties facing the nations of the G-7 or the global economy at large. Yet there are a number of reasons for strengthening surveillance. First, the IMF needs to strengthen its ability to oversee the macroeconomic policies of the advanced industrial countries, because it is their macroeconomic policies that have the largest spill-over effects on the global economy and the stability of the international monetary system. Second, the globalisation of financial markets and the emergence of three anchor currencies in the international monetary system raise the potential for international monetary instability in the event of significant divergences between the macroeconomic policies of Germany, Japan and the United States. Third, the significant systemic impacts of regional macroeconomic imbalances or exchange rate turmoil, like those associated with the progress towards European monetary union, suggest a broadening of IMF prerogatives. And finally, the effectiveness of surveillance remains largely dependent upon the willingness of national authorities 'to give due consideration to the views of the international community' in the formulation of national economic and exchange rate policies.[13]

The 30 April 1993 declaration by the IMF interim committee on 'Cooperation for Sustained Global Expansion' reflects the desire for macroeconomic coordination and effective surveillance by the IMF.[14] The declaration assigned industrial countries the principal responsibility for creating the basis of a non-inflationary expansion of the world economy. The interim committee committed the industrial nations to a tripartite economic strategy: fiscal consolidation over the medium term, the adoption of structural policies to improve the functioning of markets, and policies introducing greater flexibility to labour markets to reduce high structural unemployment in Europe. Towards the larger objective of global cooperation, the committee undertook 'to strengthen collaboration with the IMF as the central international monetary institution' and underlined the importance of IMF surveillance over national exchange rate and macroeconomic policies. It also emphasised the need for national authorities to embed their policies in the broader global macroeconomic context. Moreover, the interim committee endorsed the decision by the executive board of the IMF to enhance the surveillance procedures of the IMF, particularly surveillance of regional developments that have the potential to disrupt the international monetary system. The declaration and decision by the executive board represented a significant redirection of the IMF and a strengthening of its role as manager of the international monetary system. The interim committee, in effect, made an effort to shift the attention of the IMF away from the debt crisis and structural balance of payments difficulties of the Third World to the problem of coordinating the macroeconomic and exchange rate policies of the major industrialised economies.[15]

The G-7 remains the most important institution and focal point of macroeconomic and exchange rate policy coordination among the major economic powers in the post-Cold War Atlantic economy. The institutional origins of the

G-7 are found in the informal and largely secretive meetings of the British, French, German and American finance ministers in the so-called Library Group which first met in early 1973. The Library Group was later expanded to include Japan as a permanent member while Italy was an episodic participant. The impetus to form the Library Group was the need for close cooperation among the major finance ministers outside the glare of public and bureaucratic scrutiny to cope with the strains developing and emerging in the international monetary and financial systems as the Bretton Woods agreement began to and finally did collapse. When Valéry Giscard d'Estaing and Helmut Schmidt, two of the finance ministers who were original members of the Library Group, became President of France and Chancellor of Germany, respectively, they persuaded the other leaders of the advanced industrial countries to meet as a group to discuss pressing monetary and economic problems facing the industrialised world in the wake of the oil price rise and the collapse of the international monetary system. The first meeting of the G-5 nations (France, Germany, the United States, Britain and Japan) was held at Rambouillet in 1975. This meeting was conceived of as a one-off affair. Its purpose was to facilitate an informal exchange of ideas between the leaders of the major industrial powers, and the topics of discussion were restricted to the outstanding economic and monetary problems facing the West.

The growth of the G-5 summit after the Rambouillet meeting, and its eventual expansion into the G-7 at the Tokyo economic summit of 1986, created a new institutional feature of the international economic system. It reflected the conviction that the many problems facing the industrialised nations must be solved in concert and that only the heads of state possessed sufficient political heft to commit their governments to a joint course of action. Robert Putnam and Nicholas Bayne have identified three advantages of the summit system for addressing the macroeconomic and exchange rate policy coordination requirements of the major industrialised countries: the G-7 heads of government are uniquely positioned to integrate the various elements of national (economic) policy into a single negotiated package, to broker a compromise between the countervailing demands of domestic and foreign policies, and to commit their national governments to a joint policy initiative that requires a compromise between the interests of the individual country and the broader interests of the group.[16] Yet the prominence that the G-7 has taken on may be explained as a response to the inability of the United States to manage the international system unilaterally and the continued inability of international institutions to rein in the major economic powers in the area of macroeconomic policy and exchange rates. It may also be the case that the G-7 has emerged as a dominant forum for the negotiation of outstanding macroeconomic and exchange rate issues between the major powers because it is best suited to the structural characteristics of the international system. John Kirton, for example, has argued that the G-7 satisfies the criteria of an effective concert and as a consequence it is not only uniquely situated to facilitate the management of the international economy but in fact ought to become the core institution of the post-Cold War security order.[17] The longer-term policy domain of the G-7 and its relationship with the other institutions of the post-Cold War security order is open, but it is quite clear that the G-7 figures prominently in any 'blueprint' for refashioning the international monetary system or facilitating macroeconomic coordination between the major industrial states.[18]

The G-7 process now represents a set of interrelated meetings between heads of state and government at the annual economic summit in July, between the finance ministers and central bank governors three times a year, and between the senior treasury deputies assigned responsibility for G-7 negotiations that meet regularly throughout the year. The G-7 deputies are charged with multilateral surveillance of G-7 economic policies according to a number of 'objective indicators' although no commitments have been entered into with respect to the target ranges for those variables. These indicators – and the subsequent refinements of them – were designed to do more than simply create a basis for comparable national projections of economic performance over a twelve-month period. They were intended to form the basis of mutual adjustment and bargaining over economic policies between the G-7 countries.[19] In the context of multilateral surveillance, the G-7 deputies are also responsible for negotiating coordinated policy responses to economic disequilibria that arise in the G-7 economies. The finance ministers and central bank governors meet at the beginning of the year to establish the baseline of each national economy, the 'benchmark' surveillance session that frames policy discussions and responses over the course of the year. The ministers and central bank governors also meet in a separate caucus during the spring and autumn meetings of the IMF when the economic performance of each country and of the G-7 as a group is assessed. And the annual economic summits, attended by the heads of state and finance ministers, function as a forum for setting the economic agenda, for achieving break-throughs on critical or outstanding economic policy problems (e.g. aid to Russia or concluding the Uruguay round of trade negotiations), and increasingly for establishing a common position on political and strategic problems facing the countries jointly.[20]

The challenges of the post-Cold War international system led the G-7 to announce at the 1994 summit in Naples that a review of international institutions would be undertaken and mechanisms for strengthening macroeconomic and exchange rate cooperation adopted at the 1995 G-7 summit in Halifax, N.S. At the Halifax summit a set of proposals was presented by the G-7 to strengthen institutional cooperation between the IMF and the G-7 to facilitate greater macroeconomic and exchange rate stability. The G-7 acknowledged its primary role of promoting sustained non-inflationary growth, maintaining external balance, and ensuring exchange rate stability. But that task, which requires a greater level of policy coordination, was dependent upon 'enhanced consultation with the IMF'. The IMF role would be restricted, however, to providing a common source of macroeconomic and exchange rate data to the G-7, providing 'sharper' policy advice to G-7 governments, and delivering 'franker messages' to miscreant governments.[21] The fulcrum of political power, however, would appear to remain firmly within the G-7 orbit.

The institutions of the EU aim not only at macroeconomic coordination, but at the more ambitious target of macroeconomic convergence. The primary institutions of macroeconomic convergence in the EU are the Council of Economic and Finance Ministers (ECOFIN) and the Frankfurt-based European Monetary Institute. The EMI replaces the Committee of EC Central Bank Governors and has assumed the tasks of the European Monetary Cooperation Fund (EMCF), which was formerly managed by the Bank for International Settlements (BIS). The EMI is the institutional precursor to the European System of Central Banks (ESCB). The EMI formally began its operations in January 1994, the beginning of the second stage of European economic and monetary union (EMU). The second stage of EMU is intended to strengthen the coordination and surveillance of EU macroeconomic and exchange rate policies. Those two tasks now fall to the EMI, which is designed as a half-way house between a single European central bank system conducting a European monetary policy and the existing system of central banks coordinating (nominally) national monetary policies. The primary goal of the EMI is the coordination of national monetary policies, with the objective of maintaining price stability. Towards that objective, the EMI can issue comments and recommendations about the general orientation of national monetary policies, can submit opinions to either ECOFIN or national governments on any aspect of internal or external monetary affairs, and can make monetary policy recommendations to national central banks. These comments and recommendations are non-binding, but have the effect of establishing a pan-European monetary institution with the competence to speak for the monetary interests of Europe. The political independence of the EMI, a feature of the institutional independence of the anticipated ESCB, is balanced by the continuing role of ECOFIN.

The Maastricht treaty established the principle that national economic policies are of common concern to the EU member states and that those policies are to be coordinated within the council. In December 1993 the Council of Finance Ministers established the 'broad guidelines of the economic policies' of the Union. The EU has committed itself to the twin macroeconomic objectives of price stability and the consolidation of public-sector deficits. To that end, the ECOFIN conducts a biannual, multilateral survey of the EU economies. Whenever a national macroeconomic policy is found to be inconsistent with the guidelines, the council, on the proposal of the Commission, may issue a public recommendation to the deviating country. The recommendation, like those of the EMI, remains non-binding and policy prerogatives remain national in nature. Perhaps the most important task of the ECOFIN will be that of encouraging macroeconomic convergence, particularly in the area of budgetary policy. The ECOFIN now has the prerogative to conduct budgetary surveillance of the EU states. The referent values of budgetary policy are the indicators of convergence established by the treaty, namely a current government deficit limited to 3 per cent of GDP and a gross public-sector debt no larger than 60 per cent of GDP. Whenever the council, as part of its budgetary surveillance procedure, finds that a state exceeds these ratios, it can make budgetary policy recommendations to the offending state. If the council is dissatisfied with the member state response, that recommendation may be made public. Although no other severe sanction against the state is provided for until the third and final stage of EMU, the legal basis of council surveillance is established by a council regulation which defines the three elements of budgetary surveillance (GDP, public-sector debt and public deficit) and provides for the provision of the data to the council.[22]

The problem of macroeconomic coordination: the Atlantic dimension

The emergence of the Deutschmark as the antipolar currency of the dollar and the potential role of the 'Euro' – the rechristened Ecu – as a direct competitor of the dollar (and the yen) in international money markets provides the basis for the potential fragmentation of the Atlantic economy into two trade and currency blocs. The patterns of European (particularly French and German) and American direct foreign investment may reinforce rather than mitigate the increasing regional concentration of European and North American trading patterns. North America and Europe are not symmetrically interdependent. Trade, capital and currency relationships between these two economic groupings do not indicate that the two key currency states of the Atlantic economy, the United States and Germany, have a sustained and unconditional interest in the coordination of macroeconomic policies or in the convergence of economic performance that would contribute to the stabilisation of the Atlantic economic area and beyond.[23]

The Bonn economic summit in 1978, the Carter administration's subsequent belated effort to stabilise the dollar and the creation of the EMS as the basis of monetary stability in Europe were an early effort at macroeconomic and exchange rate coordination in the Atlantic economy.[24] This level of macroeconomic and exchange rate coordination was short-lived, however. The Reagan administration's policies of high real interest rates and growing budget deficits, combined with the monetary machismo of equating a strong dollar with a strong American economy, disrupted international financial markets, crippled the export potential of the United States, and introduced unnecessary and divisive conflicts into bilateral trading relationships, particularly between the United States and two of its most important political and economic partners, Germany and Japan. Consequently, the Germans and other Europeans were compelled in the 1980s to conduct their monetary and exchange rate policies so as to meet the requirements of external balance rather than the requirements of domestic growth and structural unemployment.[25]

The steady rise of the Deutschmark against the dollar between 1981 and 1985 exasperated the federal government and the Bundesbank; both had lost a considerable degree of control over the German economy, particularly the level of interest rates and the value of the Deutschmark. In 1983 the Bundesbank described the Deutschmark as the 'antipolar' currency of the dollar; the value of the Deutschmark became inversely related to the value of the dollar (a relationship reflecting both the openness of the German capital market and the growing reserve currency role of the Deutschmark). Thus the Bundesbank complained that the unfavourable Deutschmark–dollar exchange rate did not reflect economic fundamentals – the large German current account surplus, the consolidation of the West German federal budget, and a modest revival of economic activity.[26] The source of Germany's economic management and policy woes was located in Washington and the defective economic management of the Reagan administration: high interest rates, willingness to let the market establish an equilibrium rate of exchange between the dollar and the Deutschmark, and massive current account and budgetary deficits. When the United States turned to the Federal Republic (and Japan) to correct the overvaluation of the dollar in September 1985, it found a reluctant and suspicious partner in the Federal Republic.[27]

In September 1985 the finance ministers of the G-5 nations met at the Plaza Hotel in New York. They agreed to an orderly appreciation of their currencies against the dollar with the coordinated intervention by their monetary authorities in the foreign exchange markets. The Plaza agreement helped correct the overvaluation of the dollar and paved the way for a coordinated interest rate reduction in 1986, but the West Germans nonetheless resisted American pressure to adopt more expansionary fiscal and monetary policies until the United States made serious cuts in its budget deficit.[28] When the Baker–Miyazawa accord failed to stabilise the dollar–yen rate in early 1987 the dollar continued to decline and occasioned renewed turbulence in the foreign exchange markets which led to the Louvre accord in February 1987.

At the Louvre meeting in February 1987 the major industrial nations agreed to stabilise exchange rates at the existing levels and to intervene in the exchange markets towards that end. But over the course of 1987 the West Germans voiced their concern that the United States would rely upon a depreciating dollar rather than upon corrective domestic economic policies to reverse the American trade deficit.[29] After the October 1987 stock-market crash, the G-7 met in late December and reaffirmed its intention to stabilise exchange rates in accordance with the Louvre accord. The December meeting committed the United States to significant cuts in the budget deficit, the Japanese to expansionary economic policies consistent with a reduction of their trade surplus, and the West Germans to tax cuts and an interest rate reduction. The Bundesbank coordinated an interest rate reduction among the EMS countries, but it provided only limited support for the dollar.[30] The Americans failed to make good their promises of a significant cut in the federal budget deficit despite the

Gramm–Rudman–Hollings legislation.

At successive G-7 meetings of finance ministers and central bank ministers, as well as at the annual economic summits, the United States was reminded that the reduction of American budget deficits was essential for stable exchange rates, lower interest rates and a stable global economy. The G-7 did coordinate interest rate reductions and extensive interventions in the foreign exchange markets to stabilise the dollar–yen–Deutschmark rates; at the Houston summit, the G-7 declared that its cooperation had 'improved the stability of exchange rates by concentrating attention on multilateral surveillance and close coordination of economic polices ...'[31] But in early 1990 the Americans redefined and diluted the definition of successful and meaningful cooperation; it now meant

> the ability of the participants to grasp more fully all the dimensions of their own situation and the situation of others and their ability to frame their own policies in a manner in which the sensitivities to the problems and perspectives of others loom larger rather than smaller.[32]

But by this time a string of broken American promises and the pressures of German unification made even this modest criterion too high a hurdle for the Germans to surmount.

Prior to the 21 January 1991 G-7 meeting, the restrictive monetary policy of the Bundesbank had been criticised by the other members of the G-7. The January communiqué reaffirmed G-7 'support for economic policy coordination' and the need to undertake fiscal and monetary policies that would 'create conditions favourable to lower global interest rates ...'[33] The other members of the G-7 believed that the Germans had agreed to refrain from an interest rate increase at a time when their partners where fighting recession. Yet ten days later the Bundesbank raised two key interest rates, an act that forced partner nations in the EMS to choose between higher interest rates and a deeper recession or a realignment of their currencies' value against the Deutschmark. It also made it more difficult, given the Deutschmark's role in the international monetary system, for the United States to lower its interest rates to moderate the American recession without risking a flight from the dollar.

The German decision to raise interest rates was interpreted as an indication that priority was being given to domestic economic policy needs rather than to Germany's commitment to EMU or to the more general principle of international economic cooperation. In the intervening months, it became clearer that cooperation with the United States was subordinate first to the needs of the domestic economy and then to the requirements of EMU: after the American Federal Reserve had lowered interest rates in an effort to support the weak recovery in August 1991, the Bundesbank raised both the discount and the Lombard rates. The German central bank cited two reasons for its action: first, inflation was running at an intolerable 4.4 per cent; second, the Bundesbank feared that it had lost credibility by accommodating the financing of German unification. The Bundesbank and the Federal Reserve repeated their interest rate duet in December 1991, when the Bundesbank raised the discount and Lombard rates to the highest levels of the post-war period to combat inflation just as the Federal Reserve lowered interest rates to combat recession in the United States.

At the January 1992 G-7 meeting of finance ministers and central bank governors, the Germans arrived in Garden City, N.Y., intent on resisting G-7 pressure to reduce interest rates to aid the recovery of either the French or the Anglo-Saxon economies. The Germans made it clear that a cut in interest rates should not be expected in the near future despite their broad agreement that the global economic recovery needed reinforcement. The Garden City communiqué accepted the persistence of high German interest rates, noting that interest rates could be lowered only after fiscal consolidation, a deceleration of the growth of the money supply, the easing of wage pressures, and the restoration of price stability – in effect it restated Bundesbank conditions for lower interest rates in Germany and Europe. Just like the Americans before them in the 1980s, the Germans were being encouraged to adopt fiscal policies consistent with monetary policies supporting lower interest rates.[34]

American criticism of German fiscal policies set the backdrop to the spring 1992 G-7 meeting. In late April, David Mulford, US Treasury Under Secretary for International Affairs, attributed high interest rates and low growth in Europe to German monetary policy, which in turn reflected Germany's growing and structural fiscal deficits. Mulford identified the problem facing Germany as one of large public-sector debt financed by high real interest rates: the same policy mix the Germans had been criticising and the Americans had been defending for almost a decade. The German response was to describe Mulford's analysis as 'one-sided and partially false'. Moreover, Horst Köhler, treasury state secretary, characterised the American criticism as 'unacceptable' because it violated the principle of G-7 cooperation that 'every country should keep its own house in order'.[35] Finance Minister Waigel arrived at the April meeting unrepentant and unwilling to have German economic policy 'put in the dock', and any hope of lower German interest rates was dashed before the meeting took place when Bundesbank President Helmut Schlesinger ruled out a reduction in interest rates.[36] The G-7 communiqué urged both the United States and Germany to consolidate their budget positions, but urged Germany to pursue policies that would facilitate growth and reminded the United States to refrain from implementing policies that would jeopardise the process of budgetary consolidation. The communiqué also noted the lack of congruence between the high level of real interest rates in Europe and the low levels of investment and economic activity; and as the level of European interest rates could be traced to Frankfurt, the Germans were once again subjected to demands for change in their macroeconomic policy[37] – a change that was not forthcoming until the currency crisis in late summer 1992, when it amounted to an inconsequential reduction of twenty-five basis points in the Lombard rate and fifty basis points in the discount rate.

The Germans met American expectations in early summer 1992 with their public decision to limit the growth in spending to 3 per cent overall and to begin the process of budgetary consolidation because it offered the only prospect of lower German (and European) interest rates. But the German decision was taken strictly for domestic economic management purposes rather than for external reasons, even though it is true that the new budget was brought forward to deflect criticism of German policy at the German-hosted G-7 meeting in Munich. By the time of the Munich summit, the renewal of macroeconomic and exchange rate cooperation in the mid-1980s had been replaced with a sort of macroeconomic 'Sinatra doctrine' ('My way') and exchange rate relationships did not figure in any of the three preceding G-7 communiqués. The United States, Japan and Germany indicated prior to the summit that national economic policy would be dictated by domestic priorities. The Germans restated their unwillingness to lower interest rates despite a reduction in the American discount rate to 3 per cent (a twenty year low) and the federal funds rate to 3.25 per cent (a policy decision taken in response to a jump in unemployment to 7.8 per cent – the highest level since 1984). After the Munich summit, the Bundesbank, preoccupied with bringing inflation down to 2 per cent, raised its discount rate to 8.65 per cent – the highest level since September 1931. A minor foreign exchange crisis began in late July in response to the interest rate differential of 6.50 per cent favouring the Deutschmark against the dollar which was coupled with the 'no' vote in the first Danish referendum on the Maastricht treaty and the real prospect of a French *non* later that summer. The Bundesbank, the Federal Reserve and other G-7 central banks intervened modestly in the foreign exchange markets five times to moderate the dollar's slide between 20 July and the end of August. In addition to driving the dollar to a new low against the Deutschmark, high German interest rates forced a departure of the Italian lira and pound sterling from the ERM, pushed five other currencies to the ERM floor against the Deutschmark, and precipitated a run against the French franc at a time when the French economy was in arguably better shape than that of Germany.

The connection between high German interest rates and the turmoil in foreign exchange markets that persisted after the dramatic withdrawal of sterling and the lira in September 1992 was not lost on any of Germany's partners, even if the connection was lost on the Germans.[38] The Bundesbank was placed in the unenviable position of having to pursue the legally dictated policy objective of stable money and withstand the considerable external pressures for an orderly reduction of German interest rates in support of European exchange rate stability. But the persistent inability of the Bundesbank to control the money supply, persistent high inflation in Germany and the negative fiscal consequences of the recession made it impossible to achieve the necessary reduction in the level of interest rates that would reduce the pressure on the French franc and other ERM currencies, meet the American preference for lower European interest rates to aid the American and global economic recovery, and retain the

Bundesbank's hard-earned reputation for fighting inflation.

The Clinton administration assumed office desirous of rejuvenating the G-7 process, particularly to aid the American recovery with renewed coordination of macroeconomic policies and to avoid the deepening of the European recession, particularly in France and Germany. The first meeting of the G-7 finance ministers and central bank governors after the American election took place in late February 1993. That meeting was portrayed as a meeting to familiarise the Europeans with the Treasury Department Secretary, former Senator Lloyd Bentsen. The Treasury Secretary, who went to London to press the Germans to do more to reduce their high interest levels, enjoyed a greater degree of credibility than his predecessor, Nicholas Brady: the Clinton deficit reduction package, which provided for $500 billion budgetary savings over five years, addressed a long-lived German (and Japanese) complaint about American macroeconomic policy and could consequently be viewed as removing a barrier to the coordinated lowering of interest rates, particularly in Europe. Nonetheless, the United States, Britain and France were unable to extract a promise from the Germans to lower German interest rates substantially – the key to the recovery of the European economy.

More progress was made towards the coordination of macroeconomic policy at the G-7 meeting that coincided with the spring meeting of the IMF in April. At that time, the G-7 adopted a set of mutually reinforcing measures to lower unemployment and foster faster growth. The renewed cooperation efforts on the macroeconomic front were reinforced by the 'Interim Committee Declaration on Cooperation for Sustained Global Expansion'. The declaration committed the industrialised states to continue the policy of fiscal consolidation in the United States and Europe; and it committed Europe, a convenient shorthand for Germany, to pursue a policy of lowering interest rates. Although the movement towards policy coordination was undeniable, the G-7 countries had not entirely abandoned the prerogative of autonomy in macroeconomic policy in terms of either objectives or instruments. The G-7, according to German state secretary Horst Köhler, moved from the Sinatra doctrine to Sinatra-plus.[39]

The German government introduced a fiscal package prior to the Tokyo economic summit in July 1993 that enabled the Bundesbank to lower the discount and Lombard rates for a fifth time since the September crisis, to 6.75 per cent and 8.25 per cent, respectively. This policy move defused criticism of Germany at the summit, but it did not relieve the American or European desire (and demand) for a further, and significant, reduction in the level of German interest rates. The Tokyo summit communiqué did nothing to enhance progress towards macroeconomic coordination; it merely invoked the mantra of pursuing 'prudent macroeconomic policies to promote non-inflationary sustainable growth' and stated the need for fiscal policies that would create the conditions necessary for 'rapid reductions in interest rates'.[40] The G-7 economic declaration had little immediate effect on the Bundesbank: despite the consolidation of the federal budget, the slight improvement in the rate of German inflation, and the persistent pressure on the French franc within the ERM, the Bundesbank declined to lower interest rates at the end of July 1993.

That decision left France with three equally unenviable options: raising interest rates further to continue the *franc fort* policy; devaluing the franc within the ERM; or withdrawing from the ERM altogether and ending any hopes of European monetary union by 1997. In the end, the French were forced to accept a *de facto* devaluation of the franc, albeit after heroic efforts by the Bundesbank to defend the bilateral rate between the franc and Deutschmark: in July 1993 the Bundesbank purchased EMS partner currencies equivalent to almost DM 60 billion, most of which was devoted to supporting the French franc. The EC finance ministers and central bank governors declined to alter the bilateral central rates of exchange and instead agreed to widen the margins of fluctuation within the ERM from the existing bands of ±2.25 per cent or ±6.0 per cent (for Spain and Portugal) to ±15 per cent – a decision that transformed the ERM from a quasi-fixed exchange rate system into a thinly disguised floating exchange rate system with the bilateral central rates of exchange left intact. Germany clearly opted for protecting the internal value of the Deutschmark at the expense of its most important partners in Europe and perhaps at the expense of European monetary union. Ironically, high real interest rates and soaring public-sector deficits in the early 1990s placed the Germans in the position occupied by the United States for most of the 1980s: target of G-7 criticism for implementing an egregiously self-indulgent macroeconomic policy conducted with a callous and self-righteous disregard for its external ramifications.[41]

The difficulties attending macroeconomic coordination to foster growth and the repeated crises in the ERM generated agreement within the G-24 that 'the existing mechanisms of policy coordination' were inadequate and a call on the IMF to 'play a more active role in policy coordination among the industrial countries'. The call to the IMF reflected growing pessimism about the ability of the G-7 to coordinate effectively critical components of their macroeconomic policies, about the institutional inability of the G-7 countries to account for and consider fully the international externalities and feedbacks associated with national economic policy choices, and about the seeming preference of the G-7 countries for national policies indifferent to those externalities and feedbacks. By the end of 1993 the inability of the G-7 to coordinate macroeconomic policy had contributed to a new focus on the necessity of putting in place structural policies at the national level that could generate internal opportunities for growth and employment that would have the beneficial side effect of contributing to global economic growth and stability. The effort to coordinate the traditional objectives of macroeconomic policy – interest rates, exchange rates and fiscal policies – was temporarily removed from the (public) agenda of the G-7.[42]

The inward focus of the G-7 policy prescriptions did not last into 1994 or 1995, when the disability of the dollar threatened price stability and economic growth in Europe and Japan. The decline of the dollar over 1994 and into 1995 set the agenda of successive meetings not only of the G-7 but of the IMF as well. On 4 February 1994 the Federal Reserve raised the federal funds rate by twenty-five basis points, from 3.0 per cent to 3.25 per cent, and that decision was followed two weeks later by the Bundesbank with a fifty basis point reduction in the discount rate to 5.25 per cent, the first reduction since the unexpected fifty basis point reduction in the discount and Lombard rates in October 1993. According to the New York Federal Reserve, the combination of German economic developments in early 1994, particularly a surge in the growth of M3, and the rise in the American federal funds rate and subsequent decline in the German discount rate, created the market expectation that any further cuts in any of the key German interest rates would be dependent upon increases in the key American interest rates.[43] Prior to the G-7 finance ministers' and central bank governors' meeting in April 1994, the Bundesbank continued its policy of cautiously lowering its key interest rates: the discount and Lombard rates were reduced by an additional twenty-five basis points. And just as the Germans lowered their interest rates the Federal Reserve moved in the opposite direction: the federal funds rate was increased to 3.75 per cent on 18 April. The reduction in the German discount rate to 5 per cent represented a drop of 3.65 per cent since the post-war high of 8.65 per cent in July 1992; and the interest rate differential favouring the Deutschmark against the dollar dropped from 6.50 per cent to 2.35 per cent. At the April G-7 meeting, Secretary Bentsen made a statement on behalf of the G-7 which emphasised the progress made towards fulfilling the cooperative global strategy established at the first G-7 meeting with the new Clinton administration. Bentsen noted the progress made by the United States in cutting its budget deficit with the five-year, $500 billion deficit reduction programme and the halving of the fiscal deficit-to-GDP ratio expected for fiscal 1995. He also welcomed the interest rate cuts in Europe (Germany) that would support not only renewed economic growth but the lowering of Europe's double-digit unemployment.[44] Scepticism about the fruits of the meeting were met with a spirited, if not entirely convincing, defence by Philippe Maystadt, chair of the IMF interim committee. Maystadt argued that the importance of Bentsen's statement lay in the consensus between German finance minister Theo Waigel and Bundesbank president Hans Tietmeyer that there was still room for interest rate reductions in European and German money markets.

Despite the upbeat message of the G-7, the precipitous slide of the dollar resumed in early May 1994 and continued throughout June. For the first fifteen months of the Clinton administration there had been nonchalance about the rate of exchange between the dollar and its two competitor currencies, the yen and the Deutschmark. In the earliest days of the Clinton administration, it appeared that American policy favoured a decline in the dollar–yen rate as a means of establishing equilibrium in the bilateral trade balance and of leveraging the Japanese in ongoing trade negotiations to open the Japanese market to American products. The decline of the dollar to a six-month low on 4 May against the Deutschmark prompted the coordinated intervention of eighteen central banks in the foreign exchange markets to counter 'disorderly conditions' in the foreign exchange markets. The level of intervention reached around $3 billion, with the United States intervening that day to the tune of $1.25 billion, of which $750 million was against the Deutschmark and $500 million against the yen. Both Secretary Bentsen and Bundesbank president Hans Tietmeyer issued statements seeking to return calm to the markets and shore up the dollar's value: Secretary Bentsen assured the foreign exchange markets that the Clinton administration saw 'no advantage in an undervalued currency' and Bundesbank president Tietmeyer complained that '[t]oo strong an appreciation of the D-Mark, against the dollar, for example, is not in the interests of our economy.'[45] And the Bundesbank, fearing for the economic recovery in Germany and the rest of Europe, made good on the public musings by Hans-Jürgen Koebnik of the Bundesbank that a reduction of fifty basis points could be expected no later than the end of June. The Bundesbank acted more quickly than that: on 11 May the discount rate was reduced to 4.5 per cent and the Lombard rate to 6.0 per cent. The Federal Reserve mirrored the Bundesbank decision a week later by increasing the federal funds rate to 4.25 per cent, further narrowing the interest rate differential in favour of the Deutschmark. Nonetheless, the dollar came under renewed attack in mid-June. Public statements by Secretary Bentsen and Federal Reserve chairman Alan Greenspan on 22 June, in combination with concerted intervention by sixteen other central banks in the foreign exchange markets on 24 June temporarily alleviated the pressure on the doliar.

By the time of the G-7 economic summit in Naples the dollar had fallen to a post-war low against the yen and remained weak against the Deutschmark. The Germans went to the Naples summit unwilling to allow the meeting to be dominated or captured by the weakness of the dollar, which had fallen to a fourteen month low against the Deutschmark the week before the meeting. Helmut Kohl's G-7 sherpa, Gert Haller, publicly stated that there was no reason to be excited about the fall of the dollar because it had no 'significant effect on European exchange rates'. German *sang-froid* reflected, in part, the positive impact a rising Deutschmark would have on the effort to return to non-inflationary growth within Germany and, in part, the nominal impact the rising mark would have on the German trade balance so long as European cross-rates with the Deutschmark were not substantially affected. It also reflected the German position that the problem with the dollar was in large measure a reflection of inconsistent American economic policies, particularly with respect to the desired level of the dollar against the yen and the Deutschmark, and the low American savings rate that made the United States dependent upon capital imports sensitive to short-term interest rates. Consequently, the Germans did not believe that the solution to the dollar's problem was to be found in concerted intervention in the foreign exchange markets.[46]

The German government announced before the summit, therefore, that it was not particularly eager to bail the dollar out, particularly since the dollar's decline appeared to have been manufactured by political and economic policies that were not only outside the control of the German government but self-inflicted. German unwillingness to support the dollar was coupled with a statement by US President Clinton that the markets were undervaluing the dollar and his administration had no interest in a joint effort to prop the dollar up.[47] The results of the Naples summit corresponded to American and German preferences. The communiqué failed not only to suggest that the G-7 had reached a consensus on the appropriate level of the dollar against the yen or the mark but to commit the G-7 to coordinate its intervention in the foreign exchange markets to prevent 'disorderly market conditions'. The meeting also failed to produce agreement to a concerted interest rate strategy that would relieve pressure on the dollar. In fact the communiqué failed to mention exchange rates at all. It only contained the request that the finance ministers of the G-7 seek to enhance the 'ongoing process of multilateral surveillance and policy cooperation'.[48] Coordination became, once again, too ambitious an objective for the G-7.

In the aftermath of the G-7 meeting, President Clinton spent most of his time assuring the markets that the United States would not use the exchange rate as an instrument of trade policy and that his administration was not pursuing a policy of benign neglect of the dollar. However, it was also the case that the administration viewed a downward floating dollar as preferable to higher interest rates in the United States. The dollar promptly began its downward descent and hit a twenty-month low against the mark and a post-war low against the yen. The continuing decline of the dollar led to a concerted effort within the Clinton administration to 'articulate a clear preference for a stronger dollar' and to emphasise that the decline of the dollar was out of line with the fundamentals of the American economy. Secretary Bentsen stated on 14 July, the day after the dollar hit its post-war low against the yen, that the administration would 'work towards a stronger dollar'; Federal Reserve chair Alan Greenspan, in his Humphrey–Hawkins testimony before the Senate Banking Committee on 20 July, commented that 'any evidences of weakness in [the dollar] are neither good for the international financial system nor good for the American economy'; and Under Secretary of the Treasury Lawrence Summers told the Congress on 21 July that 'The Administration believes that a strengthening of the dollar against the yen and the mark would have important economic benefits for the United States ... we believe that a renewed decline of the dollar would be counterproductive to global recovery.'[49] These statements helped bolster the dollar by the end of July, although its decline was renewed *after* the Federal Reserve had announced a fifty basis point increase in the federal funds and discount rates in mid-August. The dollar declined as the expectation set in that there was little room for a further increase in the US and perhaps even less room for a decline in the German rates.

The emphasis on purely domestic responses to the global problems of exchange rate instability, sustainable non-inflationary growth and job creation was reinforced by the autumn meeting of the IMF. At that meeting, the interim committee signed off on the Madrid 'Declaration on Cooperation to Strengthen Global Expansion'. The interim committee of the IMF outlined three policy areas where the industrialised countries could improve their economic performance and contribute to sustainable non-inflationary growth: structural reforms, the strengthening of fiscal consolidation, and more vigilant monetary policies that anticipated rather than reacted to inflationary pressures. Each of these three policy recommendations was domestic in nature, required no explicit coordination, and neglected to outline policy recommendations in the area for which the IMF has statutory responsibility, the guardianship of the international monetary system. While it is true that the Madrid declaration outlined policy guidelines that would strengthen the economic fundamentals of the international monetary system, the topics of exchange rate coordination and even the coordination of interest rates were left unaddressed.[50]

The dollar resumed its slide against the yen and mark in November. The US Treasury intervened to support the dollar against the mark and yen to the tune of $2.6 billion over a two-day period. Secretary Bentsen made a forceful statement ending any doubt that the Clinton administration preferred a weak dollar to resolve its trading dispute with Japan. He stated that the downward trend of the dollar was 'inconsistent with the fundamentals of the American economy' and that 'continuation of recent foreign exchange trends would be counterproductive for the United States and the world economy'. The United States was supported in its efforts to reverse the slide of the dollar by the Bank of Japan, which coordinated its intervention in the foreign exchange markets to reverse the decline of the dollar. The president of the Bundesbank offered only tepid words of support for the American effort, and the Bundesbank refrained from participating in the coordinated intervention in the foreign exchange markets to support the dollar.[51] The Federal Reserve bolstered the dollar in mid-November when it raised the federal funds rate by seventy-five basis points to 5.5 per cent, the largest single increase in the rate since 1981. The promise of coordinated exchange rate and interest rate policies did not survive the first half of 1994: by the end of the year, the Germans were refusing to coordinate intervention with the United States to halt the slide of the dollar against the mark despite the robustness of the American economy; and despite six increases in the discount and federal funds rates over 1994, the Bundesbank held its interest rates steady from April 1994 into early 1995.

The decision by the Federal Reserve was directed at domestic economic conditions, namely concern that the American economy was growing too rapidly, but it had the external effect of contributing to exchange rate stability: it narrowed the interest rate differential between the federal funds rate and the Lombard rate to fifty basis points in favour of the mark against the dollar – a shift of 6 per cent in favour of the dollar since July 1992. The German hope in early 1994 that the G-7 had moved from the Sinatra doctrine to Sinatra-plus was premature nonetheless, a judgement informed by the tensions within the

G-7 not only over American efforts to coordinate intervention in the exchange markets to support the dollar in the spring and summer but over the Mexican bail-out early in 1995.

The currency crisis brought about by the Zedillo government's decision to float the Mexican peso and the peso's rapid decline against the dollar not only caused further pressure on the dollar against the yen and Deutschmark and created an investors' panic in all the large emerging market countries, but underlined the inability of the G-7 countries to coordinate either intervention in the foreign currency markets or mutually reinforcing macroeconomic policies. Moreover, it laid bare European inability to view economic disturbances outside the compass of Europe as critical to European welfare and European unwillingness to embrace a joint leadership role with the United States in the management of the global economy.

The Mexican peso declined from a target rate of 4.00 to the dollar on 20 December 1994 to 5.57 against the dollar by 4 January 1995 – a cumulative decline of 39.25 per cent. The precipitous drop of the peso not only created a financial crisis within Mexico (by the first week of January 1995 the dollar-denominated Mexican Brady bonds had experienced a 23 per cent decline, while the stock market experienced a 30 per cent decline).[52] The impact upon the stock markets of the emerging Asian markets was palpable: decline in the value of equity markets ranged from a low of around 8 per cent on the Jakarta market to a high of 13 per cent on the Manila market; currency markets were likewise affected, with a marked decline not only in the currencies of emerging markets linked to the dollar but also in weaker European currencies linked to the Deutschmark, including the Italian lira, Spanish peseta and the Portuguese escudo. The Clinton administration responded on 12 January with a $40 billion loan guarantee to finance the restructuring of Mexico's dollar-denominated debt. The liquidity crisis facing the Zedillo government was caused in large part by monetary and fiscal policies that were inconsistent with the targeted rate of exchange between the peso and the dollar, by a large current account deficit financed by short-term capital inflows, and by the rapid devaluation of the peso, which made it all but impossible for the government to refinance the $29.5 billion Tesebono debt (dollar-denominated bonds) that was falling due in 1995. The difficulty of refinancing its short-term debt was illustrated by the 140 per cent decline in the demand for Tesobonos against the previous week in mid-January despite interest rates that ranged from 21.4 per cent to 26.7 per cent.[53] The Clinton administration viewed the Mexican crisis as one that not only affected the macroeconomic welfare of the United States, owing to Mexico's role as the third largest trading partner of the United States, but also threatened to inundate the United States with economic refugees and to undermine the American policy of expanding hemispheric free trade via the NAFTA agreement.[54]

The $40 billion American loan guarantee to Mexico and the signing of a letter of intent with the IMF on 27 January 1995 worth $7.76 billion bolstered investor confidence in the management of the Mexican economy and aided the refinancing of outstanding dollar-denominated debt. However, delays in the Congress and continuing turmoil in the foreign exchange markets led the Clinton administration to announce an alternative $50 billion loan package that had a multilateral nature and bypassed the American Congress. The Clinton administration offered Mexico $20 billion of US credits in the form of currency swaps and guarantees drawn from the Exchange Equalisation Fund of the Treasury, which was available to the President and beyond Congressional purview. The US credits were bolstered by an additional $17.76 billion from the IMF – the largest stand-by credit ever extended by the IMF – which included the $7.76 billion stand-by agreement and an additional $10 billion channelled by the IMF to Mexico from the central banks and treasuries of other member states; by a doubling of the $5 billion line of credit from the Bank for International Settlements to $10 billion; and by a $3 billion contribution from commercial banks which failed to materialise at the end of March.[55] Although the financial package enabled the Mexican government to restructure its debt – by early March the Zedillo administration had reduced its dollar-denominated debt burden by nearly 40 per cent, from $29.5 to $17.8 billion – the peso continued its downward spiral to over seven pesos to the dollar.[56]

The IMF decision to extend special access to Mexico – the $17.76 billion was equal to 688 per cent of Mexico's quota, almost double the normal ceiling – was neither unanimous nor frictionless. Within the IMF, the governments of six European countries – Belgium, Germany, the Netherlands, Norway, Switzerland and the United Kingdom – abstained during the formal vote to approve the IMF loan to Mexico; the executive directors of those countries, who represented more than thirty-four countries in Europe and central Asia, objected to the package as 'a *fait accompli* with minimal consultation'. Pique was particularly pronounced in the British and German cases, driven in part by an inadequate level of consultation by the United States and in part by scepticism of the American and IMF claim that the Mexican crisis either represented or could have become a systemic crisis. Neither believed that the IMF package was the appropriate policy response for bailing out either the Mexican government which had mismanaged the economy or, more important, imprudent American banks. At the G-7 meeting held in Toronto by the finance ministers and central bankers, agreement was reached to support the rescue package designed by the Clinton administration, but the Germans in particular were unhappy with the lack of consultation and the fear that they had created a precedent for bailing out other emerging market countries at great cost (and little benefit) to Germany. For the Germans the lesson drawn from the Mexican crisis was fourfold: before a country pegs its currency, it should have a compatible and consistent macroeconomic programme in place; countries should be aware of the risks attending large external debt linked with another currency; international surveillance of economies should be intensified; and the prospect of moral hazard suggests that the international community should not create additional financing mechanisms in anticipation of future liquidity crises like that experienced by Mexico. Although the G-7, including Germany, agreed in October 1995 to the creation of a $26 billion fund to cope with a Mexico-style financial crisis in the future, the three remaining lessons are consistent with the German demand that the interpretation of the Maastricht agreement on economic and monetary union should be strict and suggest that the prospect for the eastward expansion of the EU may stumble on the macroeconomic criteria of the Maastricht treaty.[57]

The fundamental problem underlying the resentments and acrimony animating the negotiations between the United States and its European partners is found in the relative weight and importance given to the perimeter of the Atlantic community in the western hemisphere as opposed to the weight and importance given to the perimeter nations of the Atlantic community in the eastern hemisphere. The fears and concerns attending the Clinton administration response to the Mexican crisis are very nearly the same as those preoccupying the Europeans, particularly the Germans, in their approach to the economic dislocations of the CEE nations: support of the transition to market-orientated economies, the preservation of regional economic and political stability, and the nurturing of regional trade preferences.[58] The success of the G-7 and the IMF – the provision of a $50 billion package that contributed to the short-term resolution of the Mexican liquidity crisis – should not overshadow the more ominous implications of the episode for future cooperation between Europe and the United States, namely, that the interests of these two actors diverge not only in perceptions of economic propriety and preference, but on a geo-economical basis reflecting cultural affinities and biases, patterns of trade and investment, and calculations of political and societal interest.

The Mexican crisis also contributed to the continuing slide of the dollar against the yen and the Deutschmark, although the underlying causes of the decline must be located in the confluence of the decade-long twin trade and budget deficits, an inward-looking Federal Reserve Board and the suspicion created by the early Clinton administration that a strong dollar was not a policy priority. Coinciding with the Mexican financial crisis was renewed concern by the Federal Reserve with the potential for future inflationary impulses in the United States owing to the high growth rates registered in 1994 and anticipated for 1995. The Federal Reserve raised the discount rate by fifty basis points to 5.25 per cent and the federal funds rate from 5.5 per cent to 6 per cent. The dollar came under renewed downward pressure nonetheless by the middle of February 1995 in response to the defeat of the Balanced Budget Amendment and the announcement that the trade imbalance for 1994 was over $166 billion, by uncertainty about the dedication of the Clinton administration to supporting the dollar with appropriate macroeconomic policies, by the fear that the United States would bear the entire cost of the Mexican bail-out, and by the expectation that the interest rate differential between dollar and Deutschmark-denominated assets would narrow or remain stable. These five developments conspired to drive up the value of the Deutschmark against both the dollar and most other European currencies. When the dollar and other European currencies fell to all-time lows against the Deutschmark and yen in early March, there was a notable lack of central intervention in the foreign exchange markets to defend a target range for the dollar when the coordinated intervention of fourteen central banks on 3 March failed to reverse the dollar's decline. Whereas the Bank of Japan continued to enter into foreign exchange markets to support the dollar, the Bundesbank declined to do so. The lack of intervention by the Bundesbank or the Federal Reserve created the impression either that American officials were indifferent to the value of the dollar or that both central banks discounted coordinated intervention as an effective mechanism for reversing the decline of the dollar.[59]

The inability or unwillingness to coordinate intervention in the foreign exchange markets to support the dollar, and the other ERM currencies that were under pressure owing to the rise of the Deutschmark against the dollar, produced a coordinated effort to support the dollar verbally: Bundesbank president Tietmeyer announced his expectation that a correction of the dollar-Deutschmark rate would occur sooner rather than later, Federal Reserve Board chairman Greenspan described the dollar's weakness as 'both unwelcome and troublesome', and both Treasury Secretary Rubin and Under Secretary Summers reaffirmed the Clinton administration's position that a 'strong dollar was in America's national interest'.[60] The Bundesbank finally took action in late March when it cut the discount rate to 4 per cent, left the Lombard rate unchanged and lowered the securities repurchase agreements to 4.5 per cent from 4.85 per cent. The interest rate cut, taken largely for the purpose of lessening pressure on the French and Belgian francs, had a limited effect on the downward pressures facing the dollar and the peripheral European currencies like the Italian lira and Swedish krona. The negligible impact of the German interest rate cut was amplified by the Bundesbank president, who stated, 'I do not believe that our decision can significantly change currency markets' – a view widely shared by both market participants and observers.[61] The Bundesbank's actions were driven by concern that its European partner countries should not deviate from the non-inflationary path prescribed by the Maastricht treaty, by unwillingness to jeopardise the hard-won credibility of the Bundesbank or the 'hardness' of the Deutschmark and by the decades-long frustration with American macroeconomic policies.

Policy coordination suffered a double default during this period when Japan, Germany and the United States were either unable or unwilling to coordinate intervention in the foreign exchange markets despite the high levels of intervention undertaken by the Federal Reserve, the Bank of Japan and other European central banks except the Bundesbank in early 1995, and when the Bundesbank and Bank of Japan cut key interest rates within two weeks of each other without seeking to leverage the changes by coordinating the timing or the size of the interest rate changes or by seeking an additional increase in the American short-term interest rate structure.[62] Just as the changes in the

German, Japanese and American interest rates that occurred between February and April had no appreciable impact on the relative values of the dollar, yen and Deutschmark, intervention in the foreign exchange markets was likewise ineffective.

Coordinated intervention on the foreign exchange markets in early April did little to influence the value of the dollar against the yen and Deutschmark. The Federal Reserve, which purchased between $1 billion and $2 billion worth of Deutschmark and yen on 3 April, coordinated its intervention with that of the Bank of Japan, and there was coordinated intervention on the foreign exchange markets by the Bundesbank, the Federal Reserve and the Bank of Japan on 5 April. The belated tripolar exchange rate intervention did little to buoy the dollar. By mid-April the dollar had fallen to an historical low against the yen ($1 : ¥79.75) and was hovering around its historical low against the Deutschmark ($1 : DM 1.34). It became a commonplace assumption in the market that the Bundesbank had once again become sceptical of concerted intervention and had reverted to its previous belief that it would neither slow nor reverse the decline of the dollar. Market scepticism also hindered the efforts of the Japanese and American central banks to halt the slide of the dollar – scepticism supported by the routine intervention of the Bank of Japan, which robbed it of an ability to alter market expectations and by the assumption that the American Treasury Secretary's experience as the chief currency trader at Goldman Sachs left him unconvinced of the administration's ability to massage the price of the dollar.[63]

The decline of the dollar below the psychological barrier of ¥80 generated blunt German criticisms of American macroeconomic policy. Chancellor Kohl, in anticipation of the spring meeting of the IMF interim committee and the G-7 finance ministers, described American policies as 'unacceptable' and urged the Clinton administration to take more active steps to reduce the American budget deficit, a policy problem intentionally left by the Clinton administration to the Republican majority in the Congress in anticipation of the 1996 presidential election. Unhappiness with American domestic economic policy also became the German rationale for not participating in coordinated intervention in support of the dollar: without appropriate fiscal and monetary policies in place, the Germans were unwilling to support the dollar with coordinated interventions in the foreign exchange markets. Bundesbank president Tietmeyer went so far as to state on record that the ability of central banks to intervene in markets to influence bilateral rates of exchange was limited and that central banks should focus on 'stability orientated domestic policies.'[64]

In the days leading up to the G-7 meeting it became clear that many central bank governors and finance ministers had lost any residual enthusiasm for coordinated intervention in foreign exchange markets and had adopted a very modest view of what central banks could achieve, individually or collectively. Germany, the IMF and Japan called for a rise in American interest rates prior to the meeting, although France and Japan also indicated their desire for a more coordinated response to rescue the declining dollar. The Japanese position was driven by the threat posed to Japanese export prospects by a rising dollar; and the French position was informed by the franc's weakened position within the exchange rate mechanism of the EMS – any strengthening of the Deutschmark against the dollar was immediately translated into weakness of the French franc as well. The Japanese proposal that the G-7 discuss the establishment of formal target zones for the yen, dollar and Deutschmark had no takers prior to the meeting; the other non-North American members simply emphasised that the problem of the dollar was linked with the fiscal mismanagement of the American economy, a point made not only by Bundesbank president Tietmeyer but by Alan Greenspan, the chairman of the Federal Reserve.[65] But the Clinton administration went to the meeting without feeling the need to coordinate an interest rate rise in the United States with a corresponding decline in Japan or Germany or unilaterally to adjust domestic macroeconomic policy to support the dollar. President Clinton stated after the meeting that the United States could not 'do itself any good to spark a recession here at home by raising interest rates further'. And the German position was that the G-7 could not be expected to take exchange rate decisions. Rather the German finance minister placed the onus of responsibility on the individual economic policies of the G-7 member states, particularly the United States and Japan. In the German view, it was the responsibility of the Japanese to boost consumption to reduce their large trade surpluses and America's responsibility was to reverse its lax attitude towards the dollar as well as its massive budget and trade deficits.[66]

The G-7 communiqué issued at the end of the meeting reflected the general consensus that an 'orderly reversal' of trends in the foreign exchange markets was desirable; it included what was initially interpreted as an innocuous commitment to 'strengthen their efforts … to continue to cooperate closely in exchange markets'. The commitment undertaken at the April G-7 meeting was reaffirmed at the Halifax G-7 summit; and there was concerted intervention on the foreign exchange markets in late May which strengthened the dollar and was preceded by legislative progress towards a deficit reduction package in the House of Representatives.[67]

The dollar received a major boost in August 1995 with the coordinated intervention in the foreign exchange markets by the Bank of Japan, the Bundesbank, the Swiss National Bank and the Federal Reserve. The intervention was a temporary success: it pushed the dollar to a six-month high against both the Deutschmark and the yen. The success of the intervention was attributed to heavy central bank intervention in a thin foreign exchange market as well as to the clear message sent by the central banks of the major currencies, particularly the recalcitrant Bundesbank, that they were willing to lend their prestige and financial resources to supporting an undervalued dollar. The concerted intervention in the foreign exchange markets was supported at the end of August with a fifty basis point reduction in the German discount and Lombard rates to a six-year low of 3.5 per cent and 5.5 per cent, respectively, and the reduction of the Japanese discount rate to 0.50 per cent in early September. This renewed effort to reverse the decline of the dollar reflected not only coordination of the monetary and intervention policies of the G-3 countries but, perhaps more important, a confluence of self-interest. The precipitous decline of the dollar against the yen threatened the competitiveness of Japanese exports not only on the important North American market but along the Pacific rim as well. German willingness to intervene reflected concern over the strain a falling dollar would put upon the exchange mechanism of the EMS, particularly upon the cross-rate of the Deutschmark and the French franc.

The eagerness of the Japanese to intervene in support of a target rate between the yen and the dollar has not been reciprocated by their American counterparts; and the Bundesbank has been prepared, it would seem, to intervene only *in extremis*. The ability of the G-3 central banks to correct overvaluation of the dollar with a combination of monetary cooperation and concerted exchange market intervention does not promise the continued willingness of the Bundesbank, in particular, to cooperate unconditionally. The Bundesbank remains sceptical, not only of concerted intervention, but of the notion that central banks possess sufficient knowledge to defend a target rate between the dollar and Deutschmark.[68]

The Mexican financial crisis revealed the divergent geo-economical interests of the United States and the major European countries, particularly the United Kingdom and Germany. The unabated decline of the dollar against the yen and Deutschmark from January 1993 to May 1995, which was arrested only when it appeared that the Republican Congress was going to produce a credible balanced budget programme in May 1995, indicated not only the inward calibration of American macroeconomic interests but the mutual indifference of the United States and Germany to one another's economic preferences. The pattern of macroeconomic and exchange rate interaction between 1990 and late 1995 demonstrated that the United States and Germany adopted increasingly parochial definitions of their economic interests and economic responsibilities; and that, despite the renewal of concerted monetary policy and exchange rate intervention in August 1995, the overall pattern of interaction suggests sustained indifference, if not conflict, in the future regardless of the institutional configuration managing this dimension of the security equation in the post-Cold War world.

Macroeconomic policy convergence in the European Union

The agreement at Maastricht in December 1991 to abandon the national control of currencies, a key element of national sovereignty, was located in the need to complement the integration taking place in the real sector of Europe's national economies and to ensure European economic and monetary autonomy by providing a mechanism for counterbalancing the macroeconomic policies of the United States and the instability of the dollar. The precursor to European economic and monetary union (EMU), the exchange rate mechanism (ERM) of the European Monetary System (EMS), had the initial objective of creating a 'zone of monetary stability' in Europe to buttress European–American economic cooperation and to serve as a hedge against its failure in the late 1970s. In addition to exchange rate stability among the European currencies, the EMS also had the objective of laying the foundations of EMU: price stability, policy stability, and economic convergence among the EMS member states. The EMS enjoyed considerable political and technical success between 1979 and 1992. Politically, two developments had taken place: first, national elites slowly accepted that anti-inflationary economic policies were the best means of ensuring long-term economic growth and employment; second, national elites made a commitment to stable exchange rates in Europe and adopted domestic macroeconomic policies consistent with that objective. Technically, the ERM has allowed the Germans to establish the parameters of European macroeconomic policy. The anti-inflationary credibility of the Deutsche Bundesbank and the size of the German economy make the Deutschmark the 'anchor' currency of the ERM. Consequently, German macroeconomic policy and the Deutschmark function as benchmarks for the other European currencies and economic policies.[69] Thus the monetary authorities of EMS countries have been forced to orientate their monetary policies to those of the Bundesbank to prevent realignments within the EMS. German and European enthusiasm for the EMS, despite the setbacks of 1992 and 1993, reflects a combination of political will and economic necessity. The high level of financial and economic interdependence within the European economy and the high level of economic openness of the individual national economies suggests that the individual and collective welfare of the Europeans would be best served by stable rates of exchange between the European currencies or by a single European currency. The political will to pursue EMU reflects dedication to the European project, particularly in France and Germany, and the assumption that the political union of Europe will follow rather than precede economic and monetary union. Nonetheless, the prerequisites of monetary union, policy and economic convergence, have yet to be met – a failure underlined by the European currency crisis of 1992, an event described by the Bank for International Settlements as the 'most severe and widespread foreign exchange market crisis since the breakdown of Bretton Woods';[70] by the exchange rate crisis in the summer of 1993 that significantly widened the band of fluctuation between the ERM currencies; by the devaluation of the peseta and escudo in 1995; and by renewed Bundesbank scepticism over the timing and likely membership of EMU.

Before and after Maastricht the German chancellor, finance minister and central bank assured the German public that during the transition to full monetary union neither the statutory obligation of the Bundesbank to target price stability nor its political independence would be jeopardised. Both the German government and the Bundesbank jealously guard the Bundesbank's domestic monetary autonomy and its informal role as the manager of Europe's money.[71] Prior to and during the negotiations leading to the Maastricht treaty on EMU, the German government and the Bundesbank established six general conditions for German participation in European monetary union, some of which have been met: the internal market programme is virtually complete; price stability has been accepted by the major central banks as the sole objective of any European central bank; and the future European central bank will be federal in structure. But some of them still dominate the debate over EMU within the EU: the political independence of the future European central bank from national and Community institutions; the necessity of binding restrictions on the monetary financing of national or Community budgets; and parallel progress on the convergence of economic policies and performance.[72]

Notwithstanding the adoption of the German blueprint for EMU and the commercial benefits of a single European currency, Germans remain uneasy at the prospect of bidding farewell to either the Deutschmark or the Bundesbank. This uneasiness may be traced to a number of factors. First, the symbolic value the Deutschmark holds for the Germans should be neither underestimated nor disparaged. The post-war German economic miracle, which the Deutschmark has come to symbolise, served a double function for the Germans: it enhanced their standard of living beyond that of all but a few countries and it served as a source of pride in a country which had very little to be proud of. The Deutschmark has become a national symbol of German success and hard work, particularly since economic success was the back door through which the Germans regained legitimacy and a sense of redemption in the international community. The psychological importance of the national currency as a source or symbol of national identity is not restricted to the Germans, however. The British, Danes and Austrians, in particular, are likewise unwilling to abandon their national currency or the symbolic sovereignty vested in it. For the Austrians and Danes, the unwillingness to abandon the schilling and kroner reflects a desire to underline their cultural and political independence of Germany; for the British, the abandonment of the pound sterling would signify a symbolic abandonment of the monarchy and Britain's pretensions to great-power status.

Second, the Deutschmark has also had a very real significance for Germans: the hyperinflation of the inter-war period and the cigarette economy of the immediate post-war period have made Germans particularly sensitive to the importance of sound money and suspicious of any policy that has the potential to threaten it. The German economy was not perceived to be particularly threatened by EMU prior to German unification; arguably the ERM promoted inflation-averse central bankers and finance ministries throughout Europe. The anchor role of the Deutschmark in the EMS has had a salutary effect upon Germany's most important economic partners without threatening German price stability. But the Germans fear that the success of the EMS in creating a more inflation-averse Europe will not necessarily survive the transition to a European central bank. The political benefits of EMU – the realisation of the European project and the final resolution of the 'German problem' – were thrown into doubt, paradoxically, with the economic consequences of German unification. Unification altered German calculations; unification demonstrated the real fragility of the Deutschmark, demonstrated the susceptibility of even a government as practised in the art of fiscal prudence as the German government to fiscal profligacy, and demonstrated the susceptibility of a bank as independent and dedicated to price stability as the Bundesbank to political pressure in the management of money.

The political rationale for EMU has flowed from the internal progression of the EU: the objective of an 'ever greater union' among the European states requires the pooling of monetary sovereignty as a complement to the pooling of political sovereignty. It has also flowed from the preoccupation with creating a 'zone of monetary stability' in Europe that would perform the double task of insulating the European economy from external disturbances, particularly wayward American macroeconomic and exchange rate policies, and providing the Europeans with a monetary profile commensurate with their economic, military and strategic importance. These political imperatives of monetary union, however, cannot withstand the economic barriers to a single currency that are identified by the theory of the optimum currency area, a body of theory which has established a set of criteria for identifying the most appropriate or optimum geo-economical area that could be served by a single currency. The theory of the optimum currency area allows us to ask and answer tentatively several questions. Does the structure of the national economies of the EU conform to the criteria of an optimum currency area? Does a 'two-speed Europe' make economic sense and consequently political sense? Should the CEE nations seek membership of the EU by the year 2000 if a two-speed Europe is precluded?

Whether a geo-economical area in fact constitutes an optimum currency area is dependent upon whether it meets four criteria: a high level of factor mobility across national boundaries; a high level of openness and intra-regional trade within the geo-economical area; the symmetrical impact of external shocks on the national economies within the geo-economical area; and whether the group of states have highly diversified economies.[73] There is little consensus as to whether the EU constitutes an optimum currency area. Barry Eichengreen, for example, argues that the EU does not constitute an optimum currency area, owing to low levels of factor mobility.[74] And while it is true that labour mobility in Europe faces linguistic and cultural barriers that are not present, for example, in the United States, it is also the case that the legal inhibitions on labour mobility (e.g. mutual recognition of qualifications) have been significantly reduced. And restrictions on the mobility of capital have been removed within the EU. Moreover, the member states of the EU – with the notable exceptions of Greece and Portugal – would also appear to meet the other criteria of an optimum currency area: the economies of the EU states are highly open, as is the level of intraregional trade; and the national economies are highly diversified. Tamim Bayoumi has found that the member states of the

EU have experienced 'relatively symmetric supply shocks' and others have found that shocks tend to be industry-specific rather than nation-specific.[75] And even the most sceptical economists assume that at least France, Germany, Austria and the Benelux countries fully meet the criteria of an optimum currency area.[76] On balance, it would be reasonable to assume that the benefits of an optimum currency union could be captured by the EU.

The European Commission has outlined the four major benefits of a single currency: the reduction of transaction costs associated with multiple currencies as well as the elimination of exchange risk for intra-EU trade; the assurance of an inflation-averse European economy with the establishment of a politically independent European central bank; enhanced surveillance and discipline over the budgetary policies of the EU member states; and considerable international advantages, including seigneurage gains as well as the enhanced ability of the EU to protect its interests in international coordination negotiations with the United States and Japan. These benefits of monetary union, which are not contested, are offset by a long list of disadvantages, the least trivial of which include the loss of nominal sovereignty of most EU member states over the price of money and the exchange rate, the introduction of budgetary constraints on EU member states that may adversely affect the ability of the state to make good on the social contract, and the necessity of meeting the convergence criteria, which may temporarily raise the level of unemployment and depress the level of output in individual EU countries.[77]

Within the EU only three countries can be said to wield any effective sovereignty over their monetary and exchange rate policies: France, Germany and the United Kingdom. The other nations of the EU, particularly those in northern Europe, have more to gain politically from monetary union than they would lose: with the creation of an independent single European central bank the loss of sovereignty would be compensated by effective participation in the making of European monetary policy rather than simply reacting to the policy decisions of the Bundesbank. The loss of sovereignty that would be incurred by the states participating in EMU would also be compensated by the greater balance that would be introduced into the emerging tripolar world. EMU would not only create the initial objective of the EMS, a zone of monetary stability in Europe, but would also enable Europe to bargain as an equal with the United States and Japan over questions of international monetary and exchange rate policies.

The balance of costs and benefits of monetary union in Europe is unclear; it is difficult to make an overwhelming case for either on strictly economic grounds. The political advantages of EMU derive largely from the enhanced role Europe could play in the international economy and a heightened level of insulation from the vagaries of American macroeconomic and exchange rate policies. The political disadvantages of EMU are derived from the intra-EU political costs of abandoning national sovereignty, regardless of how illusory and nominal it may be, a fear that EMU is just a euphemism for a formalised

Deutschmark zone, and that a non-inclusive EMU – a two-speed Europe – could undermine the EU itself. Yet the argument could also be put that the relative heterogeneity of the fifteen-member EU, combined with the prospect of successful applications for membership by any number of CEE states, suggests that a two-speed Europe should be viewed as an opportunity to be embraced rather than an option to be avoided at all costs. The argument in favour of a two-speed Europe in the medium term is located in the inability of the fifteen EU states to meet the convergence criteria of the Maastricht treaty as well as the political desirability of binding the CEE states to the EU and the economic arguments against CEE state membership of EMU.

The Maastricht treaty specified five convergence criteria that each state must meet if it is to join EMU: inflation must be within 1.5 per cent of the average of the three EC countries with the lowest rates of inflation; long-term interest rates must be within 2 per cent of the three-country average; national budget deficits cannot exceed 3 per cent of GDP; total public debt cannot exceed 60 per cent of GDP; and national currencies must be free from realignment within the EMS for two years.[78] Until September 1992 the EMS fostered greater exchange rate stability among the states participating in the ERM[79] and it encouraged a greater degree of economic convergence in the Community, particularly with respect to price stability: in the period 1974–78 the gap between the lowest-inflation country (Germany) and the highest (Italy) was 11.6 per cent; in 1988 the gap between the lowest (Netherlands) and highest (Portugal) inflation countries had narrowed to 8.7 per cent; and the projected gap for 1996 between the lowest (Germany) and the highest (Italy) will close to 3.0 per cent.[80] The reduction in the gap between the highest and lowest levels of inflation obscures a more important development: the average of the lowest three nations' inflation rates increased from 1.1 per cent in 1988 to 3.2 per cent in 1994 (see Tables 2 and 3). Thus policy convergence in the area of price stability has had the unsettling affect of ratcheting the acceptable level of inflation upwards rather than downwards. Yet the number of countries meeting the inflation convergence criterion increased: only three countries qualified in 1988, while ten qualified in 1994 (including Austria, Finland and Sweden). The number of states meeting the other financial criterion, long-term interest rates, rose from three in 1988 (Germany, the Netherlands and Belgium) to ten in 1994 (France, Germany, the UK, Belgium, Denmark, Ireland, Luxembourg, the Netherlands, Austria and Finland). Consequently, in 1994 a total of ten countries met both the inflation and the interest rate convergence criteria, a substantial improvement over 1988.

Progress towards fiscal convergence has not been as noteworthy. Unlike monetary policy, which was indirectly coordinated via the ERM, the Maastricht treaty established fiscal criteria without providing a mechanism for the coordination of fiscal policies.[81] In 1988, only four countries had central government budgetary deficits under the 3 per cent ceiling (France, Germany, the United Kingdom and Denmark). That number dropped to two countries in 1994

Table 2 Maastricht convergence criteria, 1988

Country	CPI	Central government budget deficit	Public debt	Long-term interest rates
France	2.7	-1.8	47.2	9.2
Germany	1.3	-2.1	44.1	6.1
Italy	5.1	-10.9	99.3	10.8
UK	4.9	1.1	50.3	9.4
Belgium	1.2	-6.9	132.4	7.8
Denmark	4.8	-0.5	65.6	9.9
Greece	13.5	-14.4	80.4	n.a.
Ireland	2.2	-5.2	110.1	9.5
Netherlands	0.9	-5.2	77.7	6.1
Portugal	9.6	-5.4	75.2	13.9
Spain	4.8	-3.3	42.9	11.7
Maastricht criteria	2.6	-3.0	60%	8.67

Table 3 Maastricht criteria, 1994

Country	CPI	Central government budget deficit	Public debt	Long-term interest rates
France	2.2	−5.6	48.5	7.35
Germany	2.9	−2.8	50.1	6.67
Italy	4.6	−9.2	124.4	10.57
UK	3.8	−7.4	52.5	8.05
Belgium	2.4	−5.6	136.2	7.76
Denmark	1.9	−4.2	75.6	7.41
Greece	10.9	−13.3	113.6	20.50
Ireland	2.3	−3.8	90.9	8.19
Luxembourg	2.3	–	7.0	6.38
Netherlands	2.7	−3.9	78.3	7.20
Portugal	4.9	−5.4	69.5	10.83
Spain	4.8	−7.1	62.2	9.69
Austria	2.9	−3.0	64.5	6.69
Finland	1.1	−9.5	60.1	5.25
Sweden	2.6	−11.5	79.1	9.41
Maastricht criteria	3.2	−3.0	60.0	8.4

(Austria and Germany). The performance of EU countries in consolidating and reducing total public debt has worsened. Not only has the number of countries meeting the criterion declined from four in 1988 (France, Germany, Spain and the United Kingdom) to three in 1994 (France, Germany and the United Kingdom), but with the exception of the United Kingdom, Ireland and Portugal every country in the EU has experienced an increase in the level of public debt.[82]

The progress towards fiscal and financial convergence is counter-indicative: the financial indicators suggest that the majority of EU member states should qualify for EMU by the 1999 deadline specified in the Maastricht treaty; the fiscal indicators suggest that only Austria and Germany will have qualified for EMU. The projections for 1996 on two of the four indicators, inflation and central government debt, reinforce the pattern established between 1988 and 1994: a fiscally profligate Europe exists with a Europe that is increasingly anti-inflationary. Even on a weighted basis, which would carry a downward bias in the level of fiscal excess owing to the fiscal rectitude of France, the United Kingdom and Germany, the convergence indicators point to a similarly disappointing conclusion: there has been progress on the financial indicators, but there has been a gradual deterioration in the fiscal performance of the EU member states (see Table 4).

Table 4 Maastricht criteria, EU on a weighted basis, 1986–95

Year	CPI	Central government budget deficit	Public debt	Long-term Interest rates
1986	3.5	−4.8	60.0	9.2
1988	3.6	−3.7	61.0	9.4
1990	5.6	−4.0	60.3	11.1
1991	5.5	−4.4	61.8	10.4
1992	4.4	−5.0	63.4	9.7
1993	3.8	−6.5	67.5	7.8
1994	3.5	−6.1	71.0	8.4
1995*	2.9	−4.8	72.1	9.4

*Projected.

The Maastricht treaty also provided that a state would be eligible to proceed to stage 3 only if, in the two years preceding the onset of EMU, its currency was neither devalued nor moved outside the 2.25 per cent margin of fluctuation of the ERM. The target year of 1999 looks increasingly unrealistic on this criterion alone. In September 1992 the Italian lira and the British pound were forced to leave the ERM and have not yet returned; in May 1993 the Irish punt was devalued; in September 1993 the margin of fluctuation was expanded to 15 per cent to prevent the devaluation of the French franc; and the Spanish peseta and Portuguese escudo have been devalued thrice, most recently in March 1995. The German demand for a strict interpretation of the Maastricht treaty would imply, consequently, that monetary union is also dependent upon a return to the 2.25 per cent margins of fluctuation by 1997 at the latest.

The preparation of the CEE states for eventual EU membership has concentrated primarily on the real sector of the economy (see Chapter 5). An unspoken and largely unaddressed issue facing the EU and the CEE states is the problem of macroeconomic convergence. There is no apparent rationale for CEE membership of EMU. The CEE states meet none of the economic criteria of an optimal monetary area, and it would appear that the premature abandonment of the nominal sovereignty they possess over monetary and exchange rate policies would deny those governments an important tool of macroeconomic adjustment. Moreover, the CEE states cannot realistically meet the convergence criteria established by the Maastricht agreement by the turn of the century; and currency convertibility, let alone currency stability, will continue to be problematic.[83]

It appears increasingly unlikely that a sufficient number of the present ERM countries will meet the convergence criteria by 1999. There is no chance that the convergence criteria of EMU will be relaxed. In September 1995 Germany found itself as the source and at the centre of two diplomatic flaps: the first was initiated when Finance Minister Waigel expressed public scepticism about the prospects for Italian and Belgian charter membership of EMU; the second occurred when Bundesbank president Tietmeyer suggested that Germany would declare which countries were qualified to participate in EMU. At the EU Valencia Council of Finance Ministers meeting in early October 1995, Germany was also able to extract a commitment to a strict interpretation of the Maastricht criteria, particularly the fiscal criteria, in exchange for German acceptance of the Maastricht timetable.[84] Just as the British have held on to their opt-out option from monetary union, the Germans have jealously guarded their right to interpret the exact meaning of the Maastricht convergence criteria, exercise a unit veto on matters of substance (the location of the eventual European central bank) and symbol (the name of the eventual European currency) and act as the gatekeeper between the ERM and EMU. Those three prerogatives suggest that Germany will either choose to consolidate the role now played by the Bundesbank as Europe's central bank and forestall the transition to EMU or it will embrace a two-speed Europe to reap the political and economic benefits of a common currency without forgoing the political commitment to the European periphery, particularly the Visegrad nations.

Conclusion

The major institutions of macroeconomic and exchange rate management embrace and enforce consistent and mutually reinforcing norms. The macroeconomic policy preferences of the IMF, the G-7 and the EU reflect a consensus within the Atlantic macroeconomy, shared not only by those international institutions but by national central banks and finance ministries as well, that monetary policy should target non-inflationary growth and that fiscal rectitude is preferable to fiscal laxity. These macroeconomic preferences have been conjoined with greater dependence upon market forces to allocate resources efficiently within national economies and between them. Structural policies removing impediments to the market have increased factor mobility within and between the nations of the Atlantic economy. Greater capital mobility, which has become a fixture of the Atlantic economy in the 1990s, has had two consequences for the nations of Europe and North America: it has increased the efficiency of capital markets and national economies; and it has made even less effective the nominal monetary sovereignty enjoyed by the majority of the nations of the Atlantic economy.

The growing openness of the economies of the Atlantic area has progressively reduced the ability of any individual government to control national macroeconomic aggregates. The EU has gone the furthest in establishing the criteria for macroeconomic convergence in the Atlantic area. The convergence criteria of the Maastricht treaty have created a set of macroeconomic norms that have gained widespread currency throughout Europe; and arguably the convergence criteria have indirectly influenced the North American macroeconomic policy debates. The norms of the EU are likely to become the norms of the Atlantic area. The norms of fiscal rectitude and monetary propriety established by the Maastricht treaty have been embraced not only by the member states of the EU but by the prospective members of the Union. The International Monetary Fund, in its stand-by arrangements with the nations of central and eastern Europe as well as the republics of the former Soviet Union, has contributed to the adoption and enforcement of the Maastricht norms.

The legitimacy accorded the Maastricht norms within Europe and the norms of fiscal rectitude and monetary propriety within the larger Atlantic economy face the problems of enforcement (and free riding) and coordination. The IMF and the G-7, for example, can impose these macroeconomic norms only on countries that approach either institution as a supplicant for balance of payments support. Consequently, the IMF and the G-7 have considerable leverage over the CEE nations, particularly when conformity with those norms is an implicit criterion for membership of the EU. Those states already in the EU, such as Italy or Belgium, have the option of challenging the Maastricht norms of fiscal rectitude. The United States still has the option of ignoring the interests of the Europeans or changing the rules unilaterally. Perhaps most tellingly, the most important institution of the Atlantic economy, the foreign exchange market, can discipline national policy-makers. With the integration of international financial markets, states have largely lost control over monetary policy; it is increasing subject to the calculations of gain and loss of individual economic agents. The financial norms of Maastricht have been enforced by the foreign exchange market and the dedication to a quasi-fixed exchange rate. Fiscal policy still offers states a greater degree of latitude; the market is less capable of reining in fiscal irresponsibility because it is simply factored in as a part of inflationary expectations. The inability of the market to discipline fiscal deficits directly helps explain how the decade-long fiscal irresponsibility of the United States could persist and why there has been less success in creating fiscal convergence within the EU.

The problems of coordinating macroeconomic policy within the Atlantic economy are not amenable to an institutional fix. A strengthening of G-7 or IMF surveillance over the macroeconomic policies of the major Atlantic economies will not eliminate differences of interest which may only reflect different stages of the business cycle or political disabilities foreclosing the mutual adjustment of economies regardless of how beneficial that adjustment might be in terms of welfare maximisation. Within the European context, the problem of macroeconomic coordination has been solved by the monetary dominance of the Bundesbank and the fiscal criteria embedded in the Maastricht treaty. So long as the prospect of EMU remains an alluring one, the fiscal criteria will be largely self-enforcing if enforced at all. The difficulty of enforcing the fiscal criteria is made all the more difficult by the constant reinterpretation of what Maastricht actually means and Germany's *penchant* for *ad hoc* additions to the criteria for membership, the most recent example being Finance Minister Waigel's proposal for a 'stability pact' that would penalise states exceeding the 3 per cent budget deficit with pyrrhic fines.

A fundamental assumption of this book is that a peaceful and stable pan-European security order is contingent upon the successful and permanent transition to democracy and the market economy in central and eastern Europe. The transition requires, at a minimum, a stable if not robust macroeconomic environment. High levels of economic growth, which will make the political and economic dislocations of the transition less burdensome and stressful to the social fabric, depend upon rising levels of trade between the two halves of Europe and sustained capital flows to central and eastern Europe. The successful completion of the marketisation process and the transition to a functioning and stable democracy are explicit membership criteria for both NATO and the EU. The ability of the Atlantic states to expand the zone of security eastwards, therefore, depends upon domestic economic and political developments that are extremely sensitive to the macroeconomic environment. Yet it is also the case that the provision of that macroeconomic environment cannot be guaranteed, nor do the nations of the Atlantic economy make macroeconomic decisions upon the basis of these important security considerations. The narrow pursuit of national advantage in the conduct of macroeconomic policy, while it can lead to minor welfare losses for the North American and EU states, could jeopardise the prospects for a stable European security order.

The CEE states, which have acknowledged the legitimacy of the Maastricht norms for the conduct of macroeconomic policy, cannot be expected to fulfil them by 1999. It is unlikely that the majority of the EU states will fulfil either the fiscal criteria or the exchange rate criterion. The CEE states began to make the transition to convertible currencies only in 1995; it seems unlikely that Poland or Hungary will succeed where Britain, Italy and Spain have failed.

Another option facing these nations is a 'Big Bang' whereby they would simply adopt the Deutschmark as the national currency or as a parallel currency. While such a step would help solve most of the problems associated with meeting the Maastricht criteria, it would undoubtedly unleash as severe an economic contraction as that experienced in the early 1990s. While the experiment would prove a narrow economic success, the subsequent economic and social dislocation could reverse the democratisation process and disqualify those states from both NATO and the EU.

The best institutional solution to the macroeconomic dimension of security in post-Cold War Europe is located in the continued efforts to coordinate macroeconomic policy within the Atlantic economy, while acknowledging the difficulty of doing so, and in the embrace of a 'two-speed' Europe that is divided between the countries that have met the Maastricht criteria and those that aspire to do so. This solution would protect the integrity of the Maastricht criteria, create a stable macroeconomic core at the centre of Europe, provide a point of orientation for nations along the European periphery, and foster greater political balance in the Atlantic economy that could facilitate greater cooperation on macroeconomic and exchange rate policies between the United States and the EU.

Notes

1. W. Max Corden, 'Fiscal Policies, Current Accounts and Real Exchange Rates: In Search of a Logic of International Policy Coordination,' *Weltwirtschaftliches Archiv*, vol. 122, no. 3 (1986), p. 430.
2. For a theoretical explication of the transmission of economic disturbances in open economies see Michael Mussa, 'Macroeconomic Interdependence and the Exchange Rate Regime,' in Rudiger Dornbusch and Jacob A. Frenkel (eds.), *International Economic Policy* (Baltimore: Johns Hopkins University Press, 1979), pp. 160–204; and Jacob A. Frenkel and Michael Mussa, 'Monetary and Fiscal Policies in an Open Economy,' *American Economic Review*, vol. 70 (May 1980), pp. 374–81. On the distinction between *de facto* and *de jure* control over policy instruments and control over policy outcomes see Ralph Bryant, *Money and Monetary Policy in Interdependent Nations* (Washington, DC: Brookings Institution, 1980), pp. 135–206; and Assar Lindbeck, 'Economic Dependence and Interdependence in the Industrialized World,' in *From Marshall Plan to Global Independence* (Paris: OECD, 1978), pp. 59–86.
3. The importance of the integration of capital markets as a structural constraint on the macroeconomic policy choices of the nations of the Atlantic economy has become increasingly noted. See Michael Webb, 'International Economic Structures, Government Interests, and International Coordination of Macroeconomic Adjustment Policies,' *International Organization*, vol. 45 (1991), pp. 309–42; 'Understanding Patterns of Macroeconomic Policy Co-ordination in the Post-war Period,' in Richard Stubbs and Geoffrey R. D. Underhill (eds), *Political Economy and the Changing Global Order* (New York: St Martin's Press, 1994), pp. 176–89; and David Andrews, 'Capital Mobility and State Autonomy: toward a Structural Theory of International Monetary Relations,' *International Studies Quarterly*, vol. 38, no. 2 (June 1994), pp. 193–218.
4. See James Sperling, 'America, NATO, and West German Foreign Economic Policies,

1949–89,' in Emil J. Kirchner and James Sperling (eds.), *The Federal Republic of Germany and NATO: Forty Years After* (London: Macmillan, 1992), pp. 168–72.

5   The coordination of macroeconomic policy is distinct from mere cooperation (which entails the sharing of information between national authorities), policy harmonisation (which reflects an ambition to achieve a greater degree of uniformity in economic structure across national boundaries), and convergence (which aims for uniformity of economic targets across national boundaries). See Joceyln Horne and Paul R. Masson, 'Scope and Limits of International Economic Cooperation and Policy Coordination,' *IMF Staff Papers*, vol. 35 (June 1988), pp. 259–96.

6   Macroeconomic policy coordination may be defined as 'the agreement by two or more countries to a cooperative set of policy changes, where neither would wish to take the policy change on its own, but where each expects the package to leave it better off relative to [where] each sets its policies as taking the other's as given.' See Günter Grosser, 'Empirical Evidence of Effects of Policy Coordination among Major Industrial Countries since the Rambouillet Summit of 1975,' in Wilfried Guth (ed.), *Economic Policy Cooperation* (Washington, DC: IMF, 1988), p. 110.

7   Atish R. Ghosh and Paul R. Masson, 'International Policy Coordination with Model Uncertainty,' *IMF Staff Papers*, vol. 35 (June 1988), pp. 230–58.

8   Patrick J. Kehoe, 'Policy Cooperation among Benevolent Governments may be Undesirable,' *Review of Economic Studies*, vol 56 (April 1989), pp. 289–96; Kenneth Rogoff, 'Can International Monetary Cooperation be Counterproductive?' *Journal of International Economics*, vol. 18, no. 1 (May 1985), pp. 199–217; and M. Stephen Weatherford, 'The International Economy as a Constraint on US Macroeconomic Policy-making,' *International Organization*, vol. 42, no. 4 (autumn 1988), pp. 605–39.

9   Wendy Dobson, *Economic Policy Coordination: Requiem or Prologue?* (Washington, DC: Institute for International Economics, 1991), pp. 26–35.

10 Roland Vaubel, 'Coordination or Competition among National Macro-economic Policies?' in Fritz Machlup, Gerhard Fels and Hubertus Mueller-Groeling (eds), *Reflections on a Troubled World Economy: Essays in Honour of Herbert Giersch* (London: Macmillan, 1983); 'International Collusion or Competition for Macroeconomic Policy Coordination: a Restatement,' *Recherches Economiques de Louvain*, vol. 51, no. 3/4 (1985), pp. 223–40; Alfred Steinherr, 'Convergence and Coordination of Macroeconomic Policies: some Basic Issues,' *European Economy*, vol. 20 (July 1984), pp. 69–110; and Matthew Canzoneri and Jo Anna Gray, 'Monetary Policy Games and the Consequences of Noncooperative Behavior,' *International Economic Review*, vol. 26, no. 3 (October 1985), pp. 547–64.

11 Ralph Byrant, 'Intergovernmental Coordination of Economic Policies: an Interim Stocktaking,' in *International Monetary Cooperation: Essays in Honor of Henry C. Wallich*, Essays in International Finance 169 (Princeton: Princeton University, 1987), pp. 4–15; Gilles Oudiz and Jeffery Sachs, 'Macroeconomic Policy Coordination among the Industrialized Economies,' *Brookings Papers on Economic Activity* 1 (1984), pp. 1–64; and Jeffery A. Frankel and Katherine Rockett, 'International Macroeconomic Policy Coordination when Policymakers do not agree on the True Model,' *American Economic Review*, vol. 78, no. 3 (June 1988), pp. 318–40.

12 Koichi Hamada, 'A Strategic Analysis of Monetary Interdependence,' *Journal of Political Economy*, vol. 84, no. 4 (1976), pp. 677–700; *The Political Economy of International Monetary Interdependence* (Cambridge, MA: MIT Press, 1979); Ronald I. McKinnon, 'Monetary and Exchange Rate Policies for International Financial Stability: a Proposal,' *Journal of Economic Perspectives*, vol. 1, no. 1 (winter 1988); and Adries S. Brandsma and J. R. Pijers, 'Coordinated Strategies for Economic Cooperation between Europe and the United States,' *Weltwirtschaftliches Archiv*, vol. 121, no. 4 (1985), pp. 661–81.

13 For a fuller discussion of the IMF role in surveillance see IMF, *Annual Report 1993*

(Washington, DC: IMF, 1993), pp. 24–31; and *Annual Report 1994* (Washington, DC: IMF, 1994), pp. 31–40. The principles and procedures guiding surveillance are found in IMF, *Annual Report 1977* (Washington, DC: IMF, 1977), pp. 107–9. On the roles played by the IMF in the context of the G-7 see Wendy Dobson, *Economic Policy Coordination: Requiem or Prologue?* (Washington, DC: Institute for International Economics, 1991), p. 31; Morris Goldstein and Peter Isard, 'Mechanisms for Promoting Global Monetary Stability,' in Morris Goldstein, Peter Isard, Paul R. Masson and Mark P. Taylor, *Policy Issues in the Evolving International Monetary System* (Washington, DC: IMF, 1992), pp. 28–31; and Manuel Guitián, *Rules and Discretion in International Economic Policy* (Washington, DC: IMF, 1992), p. 11.

14 'Interim Committee Declaration on Cooperation for Sustained Global Expansion,' 30 April 1993, reprinted in IMF, *Annual Report 1993*, p. 160.

15 'Interim Committee Declaration,' p. 161 and Executive Board decision no. 10273-(93/15), 29 January 1993, reprinted in *Annual Report 1993*, p. 141; and *Financial Times*, 4 May 1993, p. 6.

16 Robert D. Putnam and Nicholas Bayne, *Hanging Together: Cooperation and Conflict in the Seven Power Summits* (Cambridge, MA: Harvard University Press, 1987), pp. 29–32. For a discussion of the origins of the G-5 summit in the Library Group see Robert D. Putnam, 'The Western Economic Summits: a Political Interpretation,' in Cesare Merlini (ed.), *Economic Summits and Western Decision-making* (London: Croom Helm, 1984), pp. 43–89.

17 John Kirton, 'The Seven Power Summit as a New Security Institution,' in David Dewitt, David Haglund and John Kirton (eds), *Building a New Global Order* (Oxford: Oxford University Press, 1993), pp. 335–57; 'Contemporary Concert Diplomacy: the Seven Power Summit and the Management of International Order,' paper delivered at the London meeting of the International Studies Association, 1989. See also G. John Ikenberry, 'Salvaging the G-7,' *Foreign Affairs*, vol. 72, no. 2 (spring 1993), pp. 132–9.

18 See for example John Williamson and C. Randall Henning, 'Managing the Monetary System,' in Peter Kenen (ed.), *Managing the World Economy* (Washington, DC: Institute for International Economics, 1994), pp. 102–7.

19 See Jeffrey A. Frankel, 'International Nominal Targeting (INT): a Proposal for Monetary Policy Coordination in the 1990s,' *The World Economy* vol. 13, no. 2 (June 1990), p. 265.

20 This discussion has been drawn from Dobson, *Economic Policy Coordination*, pp. 26–49.

21 *IMF Survey*, 3 July 1995, p. 202.

22 See Deutsche Bundesbank, 'The second stage of European economic and monetary union,' *Monthly Report*, vol. 46, no. 1 (January 1994), pp. 23–9; and Daniel Gros and Niels Thygesen, *European Monetary Integration: from the European Monetary System to European Monetary Union* (London: Longman, 1992), pp. 343–66.

23 For a discussion of the structural characteristics of German and American investment and trading patterns see James Sperling, 'The Atlantic Economy after German Unification,' *German Politics*, vol. 1, no. 2 (August 1992), pp. 201–7; and 'A Unified Germany, a Single European Economic Space, and the Prospects for an Atlantic Economy,' in Carl Lankowski (ed.), *Germany and the European Community: Beyond Hegemony and Containment?* (New York: St Martin's Press, 1993), pp. 181–9.

24 For an extended discussion of the Bonn summit see Robert D. Putnam and C. Randall Henning, 'The Bonn Summit of 1978: a Case Study in Coordination,' in Richard N. Cooper, Barry Eichengreen, Gerald Holthãm, Robert D. Putnam, and C. Randall Henning, *Can Nations Agree? Issues in International Economic Cooperation* (Washington, DC: Brookings Institution, 1989).

25 Sachverständigenrat, 'Wirtschaftsentscheidungen im Sommer 1985,' *Sondergutachten vom 23. Juni 1985*, section 16, reprinted in Sachverständigenrat, *Jahresgutachten*

1985/1986 (Bonn, 1985).
26. Deutsche Bundesbank, *Report of the Deutsche Bundesbank for the Year 1983* (Frankfurt: Deutsche Bundesbank, 1984), pp. 24, 28, 51, 66.
27. For an extended discussion of German–American economic cooperation over the course of the post-war period see James Sperling, 'America, NATO, and West German Foreign Economic Policy, 1949–89,' in Emil Kirchner and James Sperling, (eds), *The Federal Republic of Germany and NATO: Forty Years After* (London: Macmillan, 1992), pp. 157–93; and 'The Atlantic Economy after German Unification: Cooperation or the Rise of "Fortress Europe?"', *German Politics*, vol. 1, no. 2 (August 1992), pp. 200–22.
28. Sachverständigenrat, 'Wirtschaftspolitische Entscheidung im Sommer 1985,' *Sondergutachten vom 23 Juni 1985*, reprinted in *Jahresgutachten 1985/86* (Bonn: 1986), section 12; Finance Minister Gerhard Stoltenberg, 'Statement,' *Summary Proceedings* (Washington, DC: IMF, 1986), p. 103.
29. Finance Minister Gerhard Stoltenberg, 'Aufgabe und Ziele wirtschaftlicher Mitwirkung,' 10 March 1987, *Bulletin*, 36 (12 March 1987), pp. 308–10.
30. Stephen H. Axilrod, 'Treasury and Federal Reserve Foreign Exchange Operations,' *Federal Reserve Bulletin*, vol. 73 (August–October 1987), pp. 48–53; and (November 1987–January 1988), pp. 54–9.
31. US Department of State, 'Houston Economic Declaration,' *Selected Documents*, 39 (Washington, DC: GPO, 1990), section 7.
32. E. Gerald Corrigan, 'Reflections on the 1980s,' *Federal Reserve Bank of New York, Annual Report* (New York: FRBNY, 1990), p. 14.
33. *New York Times*, 22 January 1991, p. C1.
34. *Financial Times*, 27 January 1992, pp. 1 and 2; 24 January 1992, p. 2; and Peter Norman, 'Economic Weight-watchers,' 24 January 1992, p. 13.
35. *Financial Times*, 25–6 April 1992, p. 2.
36. *Financial Times*, 27 April 1992, p. 1.
37. 'Group of Seven Statement ...,' 26 April 1992, *IMF Survey* (11 May 1992), pp. 148–9; *Financial Times*, 28 April 1992, pp. 6, 14.
38. At the annual meeting of the International Monetary Fund, Finance Minister Waigel stated that 'the turbulences on the exchange markets ... were not the result of the stability-orientated policy in Germany'. Finance Minster Waigel, 'Statement by the Alternative Governor for the Fund for Germany,' *Summary Proceedings: Annual Meeting, 1992* (Washington, DC: IMF, 1993), p. 74.
39. Quoted by Peter Norman in 'From Sinatra to Sinatra-plus,' *Financial Times*, 4 May 1993.
40. 'Extracts from the Group of Seven economic communiqué,' *Financial Times*, 10/11 July 1993, p. 2.
41. For this argument see James Sperling, 'German Foreign Policy after Unification: the End of Cheque Book Diplomacy?' *West European Politics*, vol. 17, no. 1 (January 1994), pp. 73–97. In the Bundesbank version of the July currency crisis, the central bank stated that '[f]or domestic reasons, there were strict limits to any relaxation of German monetary policy ... ' The limits of monetary policy were established by 'sustained monetary growth' and 'persistent inflationary pressures' driven by 'high financial deficits of public authorities'. See Deutsche Bundesbank, 'The recent Monetary Policy Decisions and Developments in the European Monetary System,' *Monthly Report*, vol. 45, no. 8 (August 1993), pp. 19–27. The Bundesbank president Helmut Schlesinger rejected any suggestion that German interest rates were too high or any connection between high German interest rates, German unification and a low European growth rate. *Financial Times*, 27 September 1993, p. 2.
42. *IMF Survey*, vol. 22, no. 20 (25 October 1993), p. 333.
43. FRBNY, 'Foreign Exchange Operations of the Treasury and the Federal Reserve. Febru-

ary–April 1994,' *FRBNY Quarterly Review*, vol. 19, no. 1 (spring 1994), p. 73.
44 Secretary of the Treasury Lloyd Bentsen, statement on behalf of the G-7, 25 April 1995. Reprinted in *IMF Survey*, vol. 23, no. 9 (2 May 1994), p. 139.
45 Cited by Christopher Parkes, 'Strengthening D-Mark rattles the Bundesbank,' *Financial Times*, 5 May 1994, p. 1; and Federal Reserve Board of New York, 'Treasury and Federal Reserve Foreign Exchange Operations. May–June 1994,' photocopy, n.d.
46 *Financial Times*, 5 July 1994, p. 1; and 7 July 1994, p. 1.
47 R. W. Appel, Jr, 'Unclimbed Summit,' *New York Times*, 11 July 1994, p. A4.
48 'Wirtschaftsgipfel Neapel,' 9 July 1994, *Bulletin*, 67 (15 July 1994), p. 633.
49 FRBNY, 'Treasury and Federal Reserve Foreign Exchange Operations. July–September 1994,' photocopy, n.d., pp. 2–3.
50 'Madrid Declaration on Cooperation to Strengthen Global Expansion,' *IMF Survey*, vol. 23, no. 19 (17 October 1994), pp. 320–1.
51 Bundesbank president Tietmeyer stated, 'I welcome the fact that the American monetary authorities have clearly expressed their interest in a strong dollar.' FRBNY, 'Treasury and Federal Reserve Foreign Exchange Operations. October–December 1994', photocopy, n.d., pp. 2–3; and George Graham, 'Fed steps in to back dollar,' *Financial Times*, 3 November 1994, p. 1.
52 FRBNY, 'Treasury and Federal Reserve Foreign Exchange Operations. October–December 1994,' n.d., p. 8–9; *Economist*, 7–13 January 1995, p. 59.
53 Stephen Fidler, 'A clearer view now of Mexico's debt troubles,' *Financial Times*, 14/15 January 1995, p. 3; Stephen Fidler and Ted Bardacke, 'Three critical mistakes along a trail to trouble,' *Financial Times*, 27 January 1995, p. 4; *Economist*, 21–7 January 1995, p. 73; and 28 January–3 February 1995, pp. 68–9.
54 Under Secretary of the Treasury Lawrence H. Summers, 'United States Support for Mexico,' 3 March 1995, *Treasury News*, RR-126, pp. 2–3.
55 *Financial Times*, 1 February 1995, p. 1; and 23 March 1995, p. 1; *IMF Survey*, vol. 24, no. 3 (6 February 1995), p. 33; and vol. 24, no. 4 (20 February 1995), pp. 54–5; and Under Secretary of the Treasury Lawrence H. Summers, *Treasury News*, 3 March 1995, RR-126, pp. 4–5.
56 Treasury Secretary Robert E. Rubin, Senate Banking Committee, *Treasury News*, RR-143, 10 March 1995, pp. 1–5; *Financial Times*, 23 March 1995, p. 1.
57 *Financial Times*, 9 October 1995, p. 1.
58 On US policy objectives in the Mexican bail-out see the remarks of Deputy Secretary of the Treasury Lawrence H. Summers, 'After the Storm. Latin American Finance: a Progress Report,' reprinted in *Treasury News*, 29 September 1995, RR-609, pp. 2–6.
59 Susan Phillips, a Federal Reserve Board governor, stated, for example, 'Certainly the dollar is something that we look at, but bear in mind that the United States has a very large domestic economy and I think that domestic economic considerations in many ways are certainly primary.' Philip Gawith, 'Dollar mugged – but nobody seems to care,' *Financial Times*, 7 March 1995, p. 3. See also FRBNY, 'Treasury and Federal Reserve Foreign Exchange Operations. January–March 1995,' n.d., pp. 6–7.
60 To this chorus could be added similar statements supporting the bilateral rates of exchange between the Deutschmark and the major European currencies, notably the Italian lira and the French franc. *Financial Times*, 9 March 1995, p. 2; 10 March 1995, p. 1.
61 Andrew Fisher and Philip Gawith, 'German rates cut by half a point,' *Financial Times*, 31 March 1995, p. 1; and Andrew Fisher, 'Countering the rise of the D-Mark,' *Financial Times*, 31 March 1995, p. 2.
62 This argument was put by Michael Mussa, chief economist of the IMF. See Robert Chote, 'IMF urges US rate rise to bolster dollar,' *Financial Times*, 24 April 1995, p. 1.
63 William Dawkins and Gerard Baker, 'Japan cuts main rate as package fails to impress,'

Financial Times, 15/16 April 1995, p. 1; Philip Gawith and George Graham, 'Dollar hits low despite action,' *Financial Times*, 4 April 1995, p. 1; and Philip Gawith, 'Why intervention by central banks failed to save the dollar,' *Financial Times*, 29/30 April 1995.

64 Andrew Fisher, 'Kohl urges US to back dollar,' *Financial Times*, 21 April 1995, p. 1.

65 For a critique of American fiscal policy see interview of Bundesbank president Tietmeyer with Nathaniel C. Nash in the *New York Times*, 8 May 1995, p. C2; for a similar critique of budgetary policy see statements by Federal Reserve chairman Greenspan in Keith Bradsher, 'Greenspan says weak dollar is caused by federal deficits,' *New York Times*, 17 May 1995, p. C2.

66 'Let's all now wring our hands,' *Economist*, 19 April–5 May 1995, p. 80; Paul Lewis, 'An Eclipse for the Group of Seven,' *New York Times*, 1 May 1995, p. C2; Peter Norman, George Graham and Robert Chote, 'G7 ministers focus on dollar fall,' *Financial Times*, 26 April 1995, p. 2..

67 See FRBNY, 'Treasury and Federal Reserve Foreign Exchange Operations. April–June 1995,' n.d., pp. 5–7.

68 In a recent comment published by the Deutsche Bundesbank, the bank concluded that 'there is no empirical basis for reliably quantifying the extent of possible market misalignments or, conversely, the fundamental "equilibrium levels" which should be aimed at. The proposals for "target zones" and "reference areas" for the system of exchange rates between the world's major currencies … .are thus based on very shaky foundations …' See Deutsche Bundesbank, 'Overall Determinants of the Trends in the real External Value of the Deutsche Mark,' *Monthly Report*, vol. 47, no. 8 (August 1995), p. 30.

69 Deutsche Bundesbank, 'Exchange Rate Movements within the European Monetary System: Experience after Ten Years,' *Monthly Report*, vol. 41, no. 11 (November 1989), pp. 30ff; Horst Ungerer, Jouko Hauvonen, Augsto Lopez-Claros and Thomas Mayer, *The European Monetary System: Developments and Perspectives*, Occasional Paper 73 (Washington, DC: IMF, 1990).

70 For an overview of the currency crisis, see Bank for International Settlements, *Sixty-Third Annual Report* (Basle: BIS, 1993), p. 200.

71 Chancellor Kohl, 'Regierungserklärung des Bundeskanzlers vor dem Deutschen Bundestag,' 22 November 1990, *Bulletin*, 136 (23 November 1990), p. 1407; Deutsche Bundesbank, *Annual Report of the Deutsche Bundesbank for the Year 1989*, pp. 5–6; and Chancellor Kohl, 'Erklärung der Bundesregierung,' 4 February 1988, *Bulletin*, 20 (5 February 1988), p. 163. The German preference for managing Europe's money alone was demonstrated in late June 1993 when Finance Minister Waigel cancelled the meeting of the Franco–German economic and finance council after the French economics minister, Edmond Alphandéry, had suggested that Germany and France should coordinate a reduction in European interest rates. *Financial Times*, 1 July 1993, p. 2.

72 Deutsche Bundesbank, 'Statement by the Deutsche Bundesbank on the Establishment of an Economic and Monetary Union in Europe,' *Monthly Report*, vol. 42, no. 10 (October 1990), pp. 40–4; Deutsche Bundesbank, *Report of the Deutsche Bundesbank for the Year 1989*, p. 5; 'The First Stage of European Economic and Monetary Union,' *Monthly Report*, vol. 42, no. 7 (July 1990), pp. 29ff; Economics Minister Martin Bangemann, 'Auswirkungen und Perspektiven der Vollendung des Binnenmarktes,' 9 November 1988, *Bulletin*, 149 (10 November 1988), pp. 1339–40; Deutsche Bundesbank, 'Forty Years of the Deutsche Mark,' *Monthly Report*, vol. 40, no. 5 (May 1988), p. 22.

73 These criteria were established by Robert Mundell (factor mobility) in 'A Theory of Optimum Currency Areas,' *American Economic Review*, vol. 51, no. 4 (September 1961), pp. 657–64; by Robert I. McKinnon (level of openness and level of interregional trade) in 'Optimum Currency Areas,' *American Economic Review*, vol. 53, no. 4 (September 1963), pp. 717–25; by Tamim Bayoumi (symmetry of external shocks) in 'The Effect of the ERM on Participating Economies,' *IMF Staff Papers*, vol. 39, no. 2 (June 1992),

pp. 330–56; and by Peter Kenen (diversification of economies) in 'The Theory of Optimum Currency Areas: an Eclectic View,' in Robert A. Mundell and Alexander Swoboda (eds), *Monetary Problems in the International Economy* (Chicago: University of Chicago Press, 1969).

74   Barry Eichengreen, 'One Money for Europe? Lessons from US Currency Union,' *Economic Policy*, vol. 10 (1990), pp. 117–87.
75   Tamim Bayoumi, 'The Effect of the ERM on Participating Economies,' *IMF Staff Papers*, vol. 39, no. 2 (June 1992), p. 354; and literature cited in Gros and Thygesen, *European Monetary Integration*, pp. 235–6.
76   'EEA Meeting focuses on Transition Economies, European Integration,' *IMF Survey*, vol. 24, no. 19 (October 1995), p. 302.
77   On the benefits and the costs of EMU see Commission of the European Communities, 'One Market, one Money: an Evaluation of the potential Benefits and Costs of forming an Economic and Monetary Union,' Study of the Directorate-General for Economic and Financial Affairs, *European Economy* (October 1990), p. 11; Hervé Carré and Karen H. Johnson, 'Progress toward a European Monetary Union,' *Federal Reserve Bulletin*, vol. 77, no. 10 (October 1990), p. 773–4; Daniel Gros, 'Paradigms for the Monetary Union of Europe,' *Journal of Common Market Studies*, vol. 27, no. 3 (March 1989), p. 229; Klaus Gretschmann, 'EMU: Thoughtful Wish or Wishful Thinking?' in Klaus Gretschmann (ed.), *Economic and Monetary Union: Implications for National Policy-makers* (Maastricht: European Institute of Public Administration, 1993), pp. 16–17; and Gros and Thygesen, *European Monetary Integration*, pp. 247–55.
78   For an excellent and concise overview of the Maastricht agreement see Bank of England, 'The Maastricht Agreement on Economic and Monetary Union,' *Quarterly Bulletin*, vol. 32, no. 1 (February 1992), p. 64–8. For studies examining progress towards economic convergence and exchange rate stability by the EMS countries see Horst Ungerer, with Owen Evans and Peter Nyberg, *The European Monetary System: the Experience, 1979–82*, Occasional Paper 19 (Washington, DC: IMF, May 1983); Horst Ungerer, Owen Evans, Thomas Mayer and Philip Young, *The European Monetary System: Recent Developments*, Occasional Paper 48 (Washington, DC: IMF, December 1986); and Ungerer et al., *The European Monetary System*.
79   Deutsche Bundesbank, 'Exchange Rate Movements within the European Monetary System: Experience after Ten Years,' *Monthly Report*, p. 35.
80   *Ibid.*, pp. 30ff; for 1993 figures, BIS, *Sixty-third Annual Report*, p. 29.
81   This distinction between what is to be coordinated and how policies are to be coordinated is found in Alexander K. Swoboda, 'Policy Conflict, Inconsistent Goals, and the Co-ordination of Economic Policies,' in Harry G. Johnson and Alexander K. Swoboda (eds), *The Economics of Common Currencies* (London: Allen & Unwin, 1973), p. 134. See also Paul R. Masson and Mark P. Taylor, 'Fiscal Policy within Common Currency Areas,' *Journal of Common Market Studies*, vol. 31, no. 1 (March 1993), pp. 29–44.
82   The increase in indebtedness has been significant in some cases: German public debt increased by 13.6 per cent; Denmark's by 15.2 per cent; and Spain's by 44.9 per cent.
83   The difficulty of these states meeting the convergence criteria is evident from the available statistics (see Table 5).

Table 5 Maastricht criteria, Visegrad countries, 1994

Country	CPI	Central government budget deficit	Public debt*	Long-term interest rates
Czech Republic	10.1	-1.1	27.0	13.1
Hungary	18.8	-5.4	67.0	27.4
Poland	33.25	-4.8	60.0	32.8
Slovakia	13.36	-7.2	28.0	14.56

*Hard-currency debt/GDP.

84 Examples of 'weak' interpretations of the fiscal criteria, see Commission of the European Communities, 'The Maastricht Conclusions on EMU: Six Points,' Brussels, February 1992, JDX/ndc; and Michael Artis, 'The Maastricht Road to Monetary Union,' *Journal of Common Market Studies*, vol. 30, no. 3 (September 1992), pp. 306–7.

5

The economic dimension of security
Binding trade ties

The treatment of trade as a security issue for industrial nations was limited to two general cases during the post-war period. The first and most sustained security concern was the sale or transfer of military or dual-use technologies to Warsaw Pact member states. This security concern was addressed during the post-war period with COCOM, a multilateral institution whose member states included the majority of the industrial nations of the West and which worked reasonably well during the post-war period. The end of the Cold War led to the dissolution of COCOM and its proposed replacement with the New Forum, a follow-on multilateral institution for controlling the sale of military and dual-use technologies. The membership of the New Forum would eventually include the former member states of the Warsaw Pact as well as the membership of COCOM.[1] Two changes have occurred in this security dimension of trade: first, the former member states of the Warsaw Pact are now viewed as potential security partners of the NATO states. The concern with the transfer of military or dual-use technologies persists, but the developing nations outside Europe are the targets of control.[2] Second, the transfer of dual-use technologies to central and eastern Europe is seen as yet another means of aiding the transition to the market economy and as a mechanism for integrating the CEE states into the broader global economy. The transfer of technology to those countries is no longer treated as a potential threat to the military security of the NATO states.

The second general security concern linked with trade was located in the vulnerability arising from too great a dependence upon foreign suppliers of critical raw materials, intermediate goods or finished goods.[3] Trade vulnerability – the fear of market domination by foreign suppliers in critical sectors of the real economy, and the potential loss of technological dominance – remains a salient security concern for the United States, the EU and Japan. This category of threat, however, has been attenuated by significant changes in the international economy. Commodity cartels, particularly in oil, have failed to set the price or fix the quantity of raw materials available on the international market. Dependence upon the foreign supply of intermediate or finished goods no longer poses a credible threat to the security of the industrial countries: the sources of industrial country supply are dispersed within the OECD, much of the merchandise trade registered by industrial countries is intra-industry and increasingly intra-firm, and the deregulation of national markets reduces both the incentives and the opportunities for the restriction of trade for political advantage between the major poles of economic power, particularly in the European security space.

These traditional security concerns revolving around trade do not preoccupy the nations in transition: these nations are not defending technological pre-eminence; and although their dependence upon the industrial nations for the supply of intermediate and finished goods is great, it does not provide the EU, Japan or the United States with any effective leverage over the internal or external policies of these nations. Moreover, if the industrial countries were to use trade as a negative instrument of statecraft, it would simply retard the process of transition within the targeted country and possibly destabilise the entire region.

Yet trade remains a part of the post-Cold War security problematique in Europe. The security dimension of trade flows from the palpable and non-contestable welfare benefits attributed to free trade in standard economics textbooks: trade contributes to the more efficient allocation of resources within and between national economies, to greater levels of consumption at lower prices, to economic growth and development, and potentially, to a higher level of employment.[4] The stability of the European political space is partially dependent upon the ability of the CEE countries to exploit market opportunities in the west, and thereby make successful and permanent the transition to the market economy and democracy. Thus the welfare benefits of trade provide the nations in transition with a compelling rationale for participation as full members of the GATT/WTO trading regime and for seeking preferential access to the market of the EU.

If the importance of trade to the pan-European security order were limited to the welfare benefits and support of the transition process in central and eastern Europe, the discussion could be brought to a close. Any such closure would be premature, however. The benefits of trade reach beyond the narrow economic benefits attributed to freer trade. Freer trade with the west also provides a mechanism for a market-driven restructuring of these nations' economies; it enables these countries to discover and exploit the complementary nature of the economies of the two halves of Europe.[5] Consequently, unimpeded trade provides a non-intrusive mechanism for achieving the task of economic transition. Trade delegates the task of economic transition to individual economic agents without entailing the political costs and engendering the political resentments of direct intervention in the economy by western advisers, bankers and political authorities. Concomitantly, larger volumes of trade between the two halves of Europe should carry the advantage of lowering the cost of aiding the transition to the market. Trade will enable the CEE nations to earn the hard currency necessary to retool their economies, and subsequently lessen the burden on Western budgets by reducing these nations' dependence upon Western aid from either bilateral or multilateral donors. Thus the security importance of freer trade between eastern and western Europe is located in the contribution it can make to systemic stability via its support of the successful transition to the market and the stabilisation of democracy – a concern expressed in a joint statement by the managing director of the IMF, the president of the World Bank and the director-general of the General Agreement on Tariffs and Trade (GATT) in late 1993.[6]

The security dimension of trade also emerges in the debate between the Anglo-Saxon and Continental schools of political economy. The Anglo-Saxon school strongly suggests that trade contributes to the comity of nations. More generally, writers from Adam Smith to John Stuart Mill to John Hobson have held that free trade and the web of interdependences created by free trade generate positive externalities that contribute to stability, prosperity, peace and amity between states in an anarchical international system. There is also a significant thread of the Continental tradition, embodied in the works of J. G. Fichte and Friedrich List, which holds trade to be a source of international mischief and the pretext for or cause of war. A third approach, however, holds that free trade should be treated as an externality produced by the structure of power in the international system; that the openness of the trading system reflects the polarity of the international system. Joanne Gowa extends the argument of Kenneth Waltz: just as a bipolar system is the most stable politically and strategically, a bipolar system of power is most likely to support free trade. Just as the prospects for peace are diminished by multipolarity, so are the prospects for stable free-trade coalitions. The rationale for this argument is located in the limited opportunities for exit from an alliance in a bipolar system, the inability of coalition members to impose an optimum tariff upon the dominant state, and the interest of the dominant coalition partner in its allies obtaining the benefits of free trade to strengthen the coalition overall.[7] In other words, post-war bipolarity created a structural incentive for the nations of NATO to adhere to a liberal trading system because it would maximise their aggregate economic output, which in turn would sustain or enhance their relative position of power. While Gowa's argument that a bipolar distribution of power privileges free trade is plausible, as is the alternative argument that system-wide free trade is dependent upon hegemony, it does not necessarily follow that free trade will collapse in the absence of either. If trade relations are a function of the structure of power, then the post-Cold War European security space should be characterised by preferential or regional trading agreements. As a consequence, the expectations of both the Anglo-Saxon and the Continental schools will be met: the decay of multilateral free trade will loosen the bonds that have entwined the security interests of North America and Europe; regional trading arrangements will inevitably engender conflict between North America and Europe.

Thus the contemporary security problem associated with trade arises out of the structural characteristics of the post-Cold War system: it is neither strictly bipolar nor multipolar. It remains an open question whether free trade will generate the externalities of stability and amity attributed to it by the Anglo-Saxon school. Or whether the uneasy accommodation of military-political bipolarity with economic multipolarity will rob the GATT/WTO of its (military) security externality and facilitate the reversion of the international system to the dynamic of self-destructive protectionism as it did in the 1930s.

The contemporary pattern of trade in the economic space encompassing the European security area does not augur well for the continued openness of the international trading system. The structural characteristics of trade on both the import and the export ledgers suggest at least a tripartite cleavage in the international trading system formed by a European bloc, an American bloc and an Asian bloc. The prospects for an American bloc have improved with the relative success of the North American Free Trade Agreement signed by Canada, Mexico, and the United States, with the potential extension of the agreement in the near term to Chile, the progress towards a South American free trade area anchored by Mercursor, and the rhetorical commitment by the United States and echoed throughout the Americas to an American free trade area by 2005. The prospects for a self-contained Asian bloc appear less favourable, but have improved with the success of the Associaton of South East Asian Nations (ASEAN) and its extension to Vietnam, the sustained economic growth of China, Taiwan and South Korea, and the role of Japan as the world's number two trading and economic power. The pattern of trade within and between these putative blocs does not foreordain the creation of exclusionary and antagonistic trading blocs, particularly in the case of Asia. But the potential does exist for a European bloc in opposition to an Asian Pacific bloc, a development supported by American enthusiasm for the Asia Pacific Economic Cooperation (APEC) forum. Agreement has been reached in principle to transform APEC into a pan-Pacific free-trade area by 2020, a development that could direct American attention and aspirations in the areas of trade and investment to Asia at the expense of Europe, perhaps extending into the sphere of military security as well.[8]

Yet it is the European bloc which remains the most fully formed and institutionally elaborated of the three identifiable regions. It has at its core the EU, which now encompasses all the nations of western Europe, with the exception of Norway, Switzerland, Malta and Cyprus; it foresees the eventual membership of the Visegrad nations (the Czech Republic, Slovakia, Poland and Hungary) as well as Rumania, Bulgaria, Slovenia and the Baltics; it will undoubtedly form a customs union (as in the case of Turkey) with the peripheral states of a widened EU; and it may even agree to a free-trade area with the CIS (or Russian Federation). The European bloc may also be buttressed along the southern periphery by the establishment of a free-trade area encompassing the littoral states of the

Mediterranean Sea as well as the successful creation of a free-trade area encompassing the member states of the Black Sea Cooperation Council.[9] Taken together, a European bloc could encompass the economic space extending from Ireland to Siberia along an east–west axis and the arctic circle beyond the Mediterranean Sea along a north–south axis.

The potential fragmentation of the international economy along these potential geo-economic fault lines in the post-Cold War world may be the result of regionalism, where political agency creates a preferential trading area for a group of politically privileged partners; or of regionalisation, the integration of national economies owing to 'natural locational phenomenon leading to closer economic ties within a region';[10] or some combination of the two. There is a large body of economic theory that foresees the regionalisation of the global economy. Regionalisation is driven by a large number of variables traditionally ignored by mainstream economists, including geographical propinquity, *per capita* GNP, and 'close ties of sentiment and interest arising out of ethnological, or cultural, or historical political affiliations'.[11] Paul Krugman has focused on two overlooked economic variables – economies of scale and transport costs – that may not only drive regionalisation but suggest that the transition to the market and the opening of the CEE markets to competition from EU (and North American) goods may permanently place those nations in an inferior position within the EU in terms of technological sophistication, range of products produced, and national income.[12]

The final destination of the pan-European trading system will reflect some combination of political choice and economic destiny. The political choices facing the nations of the European security space are already embedded in a large number of regional, bilateral and multilateral arrangements governing trade between the prosperous and impoverished halves of Europe. What is incontrovertible, however, is that trade is one of the primary and most efficient transmission belts of economic growth and development. Trade is an impartial instrument for restructuring economies malformed by the allocation of labour and scarce capital by political diktat rather than by the market for over fifty years. Unimpeded trade between the nations of eastern and western Europe, as well as trade between the CEE, is critical to the successful and timely transition to the market economy and embrace of democracy. The creation of a dense web of trade interdependences between the nations of western, central and eastern Europe contributes to greater amity within the European security space and consequently makes easier and more likely the construction of a comprehensive and inclusive set of security institutions. Trade interdependence can create a basis for political trust – an externality supporting cooperation in other areas impinging directly upon or requiring the sacrifice or pooling of national sovereignty. Enhanced trade between the two halves of Europe also carries with it, however, the potential for premature demands for participation in military security institutions such as NATO or the WEU; for the creation of the anomaly that, within the narrow confines of the European political space, close trade ties are not paralleled by membership or participation in one of the leading institutions of military security, namely NATO or the WEU; or for the 'natural' regionalisation of the European economy that leads to the alienation or dissociation of Europe and the United States.

The institutions of trade

Trade relations between the three components of the pan-European security area – North America, industrialised Europe, and Europe in transition – are embedded in a complex web of trade arrangements and agreements, but have become infected by a number of 'isms' reducing the welfare and security benefits of trade. Multilateralism increasingly competes with regionalism, bilateralism, and unilateralism. The proliferating bilateral and regional trading arrangements within Europe compete with the multilateral framework embodied in the GATT and WTO frameworks that bind Europe and North America. The regionalisation of the European economy, a development aided and sustained by geography, economic complementarity and a shared culture, has been reinforced by a conscious policy of regionalism by the EU and the willing cooperation of the CEE states. Three sets of trading agreements are facilitating the regionalisation of the European economy: the bilateral trade agreements between the EU and the other former member states of the Council for Mutual Economic Cooperation (CMEA) – the now defunct regime that regulated trade between the Warsaw Pact member states; the EU accession strategy for the CEE nations; and the trading arrangements between the nations in transition.

The trading identity of Europe was progressively expanded in the 1980s with the opening of talks between the EC and the EFTA to create a single European economic space; the EC Single European Act, which mandated the creation of a single internal market by 1992; and the EC–CMEA Joint Declaration of 25 June 1988 which aimed to include the CEE nations in the anticipated European economic space. The Single European Act deepened the integration of the EU. Generally, the Act removed the remaining non-tariff barriers to trade within the Community, erected a common regulatory environment, and deepened the market integration of the national economies by liberalising the movement of goods, services, capital and labour within the Community. The progress towards the Single European Act acted consequently as a magnet on the EFTA countries to align their market legislation with that of the Community. As early as 1989 the EFTA nations had expressed an interest in conforming to the legislation associated with the provisions of the Act, and they suggested the expansion and deepening of the institutional forums for EC–EFTA discussions on a broad array of economic and monetary issues, including trade. An EC–EFTA agreement to form a European Economic Area (EEA) was signed on 2 May 1992 and came into force on 1 January 1993. The treaty, which established a set of common political and legal institutions and provided for the free movement of goods, services, capital and labour, aimed at reducing barriers to competition within the nineteen country grouping. While the EEA agreement fell short of creating a customs union between the EC and EFTA countries, it created a free-trade area substantially free of non-tariff barriers to trade outside the agricultural sector. The EEA required the EFTA nations to adopt approximately 14,000 Community laws and directives.[13] The regionalisation of the western European economy was effectively institutionalised by the beginning of 1993; it was consolidated with the accession of Austria, Sweden and Finland to the EU in 1995.

At the January 1990 CMEA meeting in Sofia, the nations of the CMEA agreed to conduct trade at world prices and to clear trading balances in convertible currencies. This decision heralded the collapse of the Soviet-dominated bilateral trading system that had complemented the Warsaw Pact military alliance over the course of the Cold War.[14] The unilateral decision by the Soviet Union to withdraw from the CMEA payments system beginning in 1991 left the CEE states at a double disadvantage: it robbed them of preferential access to their primary market, the former Soviet Union; and it removed one of the struts supporting the post-war development of their economies – oil and natural gas imports subsidised by the Soviet Union.[15] EC inroads into central and eastern Europe preceded the collapse of the CMEA in 1991. As early as November 1989 the EC began the process of removing quantitative restrictions on manufactured goods imported from Hungary and Poland. By the beginning of 1991 the EC had lifted the majority of its quantitative restrictions on 'non-sensitive industrial products' imported from eastern and central Europe, but in those sectors where the CEE countries possessed a comparative advantage – agriculture, steel and textiles – quantitative restrictions remained in force. The improved market access agreements, which included the extension of the EC Generalised System of Preferences,[16] were superseded at the beginning of 1992 by the Europe Agreements signed between the Community and the Visegrad countries, Bulgaria and Romania. The Europe Agreements were declared at the Copenhagen summit of 1993 to be the first step towards membership of the EU. A second tier of preferential trading agreements was the EU free-trade agreements signed with Slovenia and the Baltic states; and the third-tier agreements were the Trade and Cooperation agreements signed with the Soviet Union in 1989. The agreement with the Russian Federation served as the contractual basis of trade pending the negotiation of the commercial clauses of the Partnership and Cooperation agreements signed with the Russian Federation, Ukraine, Belarus and Moldova and under negotiation with other successor states of the former Soviet Union.[17]

The preamble to the Europe Agreements acknowledged their role as the preparatory stage for the accession of the CEE states to the EU. The liberalisation of trade between the EU and the Visegrad nations (and subsequently Bulgaria and Romania) was expected to fulfil a number of political objectives, ranging from supporting and consolidating democracy in those countries to enhancing security and stability in Europe. The Europe Agreements created a free trade regime between the EU and the individual CEE countries across a broad spectrum of industrial goods, although it excluded agricultural goods from the agreement and retained quantitative restrictions for a broad array of 'sensitive' industrial goods. The agreements anticipated a gradual and asymmetrical transition to free trade in industrial goods between the EU and these countries over a ten-year period. Although the CEE states were allowed a ten-year transition period, the EU initially offered to abolish all tariff and non-tariff barriers to trade over five years, subsequently shortened to three years. Free trade was achieved by 1995 for the Visegrad countries and by 1996 for Bulgaria and Romania. The quotas on textiles and clothing are to be eliminated by 1998 for the Visegrad countries and by 1999 for Bulgaria and Romania. Until that time the quotas for textiles and clothing were 'significantly enlarged'. The increase in quotas and slack demand in western Europe resulted in the rate of quota utilisation for the Europe Agreement countries falling between a high of 67 per cent (Bulgaria) and a low of 30 per cent (Hungary) in 1994. The Europe Agreements also provided for the eventual elimination of tariffs on steel after a six-year period, immediately eliminated the quantitative restrictions on steel exports to the EU, and scheduled the phased reduction of the existing voluntary export restraints on steel.[18] Within the first three years of the Europe Agreements, zero tariffs were to be applied on 50–60 per cent of the Visegrad nations' exports to the EU. It is also the case, however, that with those products where the Visegrad countries have a clear comparative advantage, those goods classified as 'sensitive', the pace of liberalisation is slowest and alternative forms of protection most readily given.[19]

The Copenhagen Council of Ministers' summit in 1993 announced the EU decision to establish the criteria for the accession of the CEE states. The accession criteria included the consolidation of democracy and democratic institutions, the observance of human rights, the recognition and protection of minorities, a functioning market economy, the ability to withstand competition from the members of the EU, and ability to fulfil the convergence criteria of economic and monetary union enumerated in the Maastricht treaty.[20] The accession strategy of the Community, as elaborated at the Copenhagen summit, was to be facilitated by the accelerated opening of the EU market to CEE goods. The purpose of enhanced trade was located not in the welfare gains of trade, but in the political benefits of consolidating democracy and the market economy as well as supporting the political and military security of the European region. The number of countries eligible for accession was expanded by the Corfu summit in June 1994: Slovenia as well as the Baltic states were cited as candidates for Europe Agreements, the initial hurdle of accession to the EU. At the Essen Council meeting in December 1994 the EU declared that the essential preparatory step towards accession was the conformity of the Europe Agreement countries with the internal market programme of the EU; it outlined a series of meetings between the EU and the prospective applicants for accession.[21]

The strategy for conforming to the internal market presented at Essen was superseded by the Commission White Paper outlining a strategy for integrating the Europe Agreement countries into the internal market of the Union.[22] The White Paper identifies the necessary 'legislation and regulatory systems, standards and certification methods compatible with those of the European Union'.[23] The goal of the White Paper is the alignment of the Europe Agreement countries with 'internal market rules and practices ... and to safeguard their efforts to complete the process of economic transition and achieve macro-economic stability'.[24] The White Paper established a legislative agenda that would enable the Association countries to meet the obligations of the internal market to ensure the free movement of persons, goods, capital and services. The EU intention was to provide a legislative road map for these nations to facilitate conformity with the internal market and aid the integration of the Europe Agreement economies into the EU economy.[25] The sequencing of the legislative agenda adopted by the Europe Agreement countries distinguishes key measures from the total legislative *acquis* in a specific area of the internal market programme. The key measures are those that establish the legislative framework laws setting out the fundamental principles of the internal market. The adoption of the key measures and of the legislative *acquis* relevant to the internal market has been described as indicative – the priority, sequencing and speed of adoption of legislation for each component of the internal market is left to the individual state – but the condition of accession is legislative conformity with the EU, namely the adoption of the *acquis communautaire*.[26]

The reorientation of the CEE economies towards western Europe, the deepening of trade relations with the EU and the promise of EU membership outlined by the accession strategy in 1995 have generated what Richard Baldwin has called 'spoke-and-hub bilateralism'. Trade between the EU (the hub) and the individual CEE states (the spokes) inhibits trade between the central and eastern Europeans, to the detriment of those nations' economies, and provides a barrier not only to rapid economic growth but to the development of 'natural' trading relations between contiguous countries of similar culture, levels of income and product mix – the variables identified by others as generating the natural integration of national economies. Baldwin identifies several economic mechanisms which drive the marginalisation of these economies and strengthens the market position of the EU countries at their expense: trade diversion from more efficient suppliers in the United States or Japan; investment-deterring effects which lead to lower levels of investment in the CEE economies and increase investment in EU countries to exploit both the EU and the CEE markets; and the concentration of industry in the EU, which would permanently retard the economic development of the CEE states.[27] The failure of the CEE countries to proceed along a dual path of market integration with the EU and the other CEE countries simultaneously reflects a combination of political choice and economic necessity.

Bilateral trade flows between the CEE states were low prior to 1989. Trade flows were determined by administrative diktat rather than by the exploitation of comparative advantage. The CEE economies were orientated towards the Soviet Union; the composition of trade reflected the 'socialist division of labour'. The CEE countries exported industrial products to the Soviet Union in exchange for (subsidised) raw materials and energy. Moreover, intra-CEE trade could not provide the nations with what they needed most: hard currency and high-quality investment and industrial goods could be found only in the industrialised West.[28]

The decision to effect the reorientation of these nations' economies to the EU also reflected the political calculation that it would best secure closer levels of cooperation between the EU and the individual CEE countries. The integration of the real sectors of these nations' economies was perceived to produce a number of beneficial side effects. First, it would provide much needed markets for CEE industrial goods following the collapse of CMEA and the loss of each country's most important market, the Soviet Union. Second, market integration with the EU would create the much desired political distance between the CEE countries and the former Soviet Union by enhancing the quality and breadth of relations between the central and eastern Europeans and the western Europeans. Third, closer trade relations would facilitate closer political relations and advance the political aspiration to be a part of the democratic society of states and an integral part of the European project. Fourth, closer relations between the EU and the CEE states facilitated by trade could eventually be translated into closer military cooperation. And, finally, the CEE nations had no desire to duplicate the CMEA trading system for fear of replicating or perpetuating economic or political dependence upon the Soviet Union or Russian Federation.

Progress has also been made towards the multilateralisation of CEE trading relations. The most important step towards the multilateralisation of CEE trading relations was the signing of the Central European Free Trade Association (CEFTA) agreement in December 1992 and the establishment of the East European Clearing Union (EECU) in February 1993.[29] CEFTA was established to facilitate intra-regional trade as well as to allow the EU to treat the CEFTA states as a customs union, thereby simplifying rules of origin for these nations' exports to the EU. The CEFTA agreement envisioned a free-trade area in industrial goods after a five-year period ending in 1998. Perhaps more important than the CEFTA treaty, however, was the EECU, which established ten clearing banks operating in Bulgaria, the Czech Republic, Hungary, Poland and Russia. The EECU is a computerised clearing system that facilitates the multilateralisation of trade and the clearing of hard-currency balances.[30]

The Black Sea Economic Cooperation (BSEC) is another prominent regional economic grouping that includes Turkey, six former Soviet republics (Russia, Ukraine, Georgia, Moldova, Azerbaijan, Armenia), Romania, Bulgaria, Greece and Albania. The BSEC is a nascent trading group that reflects the Turkish calculation that its claim to EU membership may be bolstered by providing leadership along the southern periphery of the European continent. It affords an opportunity for developing a strategic relationship with Russia, thereby lessening dependence upon the United States, and furthers the Turkish objective of becoming the entrepot for energy and raw materials exports from the former Soviet republics to the west. The BSEC falls far short of forming a free-trade area, but it does form the political basis for creating and consolidating a potential market of 400 million people rich in natural resources and for stabilising the southern flank of the EU.[31]

The expansion of trade in the post-war western economies and the subsequent economic growth and interdependence of those economies may be attributed in no small part to the successful GATT trade agreements that successively liberalised trade on a multilateral basis. The United States and to a lesser extent the European powers, in particular Germany and the United Kingdom, were proponents of the progressive liberalisation of the international economy based upon the principles of the GATT. However, the origins of the GATT can be attributed to American hegemony and British support in the immediate post-war period; the success of the GATT in liberalisaing trade up to and including the Kennedy round of trade negotiations (1962–67) may be attributed to American hegemony; and the success of the Tokyo (1973–79) and the conclusion of the Uruguay rounds (1986–94) may be attributed to an American-led oligopoly comprised of the EU, Canada and Japan.[32] Trade liberalisation on a multilateral basis was part of the post-war economic dogma that the United States adopted and then externalised to promote peace and prosperity in the international system, particularly in western Europe. The multilateral trading system has been under attack by four contending approaches to securing the benefits of trade: regionalism, plurilateralism, bilateralism and unilateralism.

Of the major trading powers, the United States has relied most heavily upon the threat and resort to unilateral trade measures to resolve conflicts with its trading partners or to correct bilateral trade imbalances. The American preference for unilateral measures was evident in the failed Burke–Hartke Bill of 1971 and the restrictive measures of the 1974 trade Act, and became palpable with the Section 301 provision of the 1988 Omnibus Trade Act, the administrative extension of modified Super 301 provisions in 1994 by the Clinton administration, and the inclusion of a watered-down version of Section 301 in the enabling legislation ratifying the Uruguay round.[33] Section 301 required the United States Special Trade Representative to report annually on those countries engaging in unfair trading practices and to propose retaliatory action to enhance market access. It provided and continues to provide the US government with a mechanism outside the GATT framework for punishing nations the United States deems protectionist.

Bilateral threats to the multilateral trading system are evident in the trading policies of a large number of industrialised countries. In the recent past the Americans, Japanese and Europeans have fashioned voluntary export restraint agreements (VERs) and orderly marketing agreements (OMAs) with each other to manage politically sensitive trade (e.g. the automotive and steel sectors) or have imposed them on others (e.g. the Europe Agreement provisions in textiles and agriculture). Other forms of bilateralism include the Structural Impediment Initiative (SII) between Japan and the United States, the objective of which was the opening of the Japanese market to American goods in specific sectors of the economy, and the Market Access Fact Finding talks (MAFF), which were designed to explore ways of increasing American exports to the Federal Republic of Germany. Likewise, the series of free-trade agreements between the EU and EFTA represent further bilateral exceptions to the spirit of multilateralism embodied in the GATT.

The plurilateralism of the international trading system, manifested by the Quad talks between Japan, the EU, the United States and Canada, reflects a structural characteristic of the international economy: no trade agreement that can lay any claim to being global or meaningful is possible without prior agreement between these major trading blocs. The successful conclusion of the Uruguay round was made possible by the Blair House agreement between the United States and the EU on agricultural export and production subsidies; and by the agreement within the Quad framework prior to the Tokyo G-7 summit on the depth and breadth of tariff cuts on industrial products.

The final feature of the international trading system eroding its multilateral quality is the growth of regionalism, a development sanctioned ironically enough by Article XXIV of the GATT. Regionalism, particularly the creation of a single European economic space in the European context and the trend towards the creation of a free-trade area in the Americas (possibly encompassing the entire Asian Pacific area) also reflects a structural change in the post-Cold War trading environment: the United States now possesses the option of pursuing a regional free-trading option, something which was precluded in the American context owing to the development strategies of the Latin American countries and the exigencies of the Cold War.

The GATT/WTO regime, which has provided and will provide the legal and institutional basis for a liberal multilateral trading regime, embodies a number of principles:[34]

1. Trade barriers should take the form of tariffs rather than quantitative restrictions. The flow of goods and services should be determined by the market according to fixed rules rather than fixed quantities; managed trade with quantitative targets is to be eschewed.
2. Preferential or discriminatory trading arrangements are generally inferior to the non-discriminatory application of trading rules.
3. Reciprocity, the granting of mutual and balanced trade concessions, is the preferred method of reducing barriers to trade; states superior in political or economic strength should also refrain from extracting concessions from weaker trading partners.
4. There should be transparency in the application of law and in the creation

of barriers to trade.
5   States should settle trade disputes through consultation and conciliation, and should have recourse to an impartial trade dispute settlement mechanism.

The Uruguay round, which was concluded in 1994, reinforced these principles but the GATT member states also agreed to establish a World Trade Organisation (WTO) to 'provide a common institutional framework for the conduct of trade relations among its Members'.[35] The WTO was assigned five tasks: to administer and implement the current Multilateral Trade Agreements and Plurilateral Trade Agreements;[36] to provide a continuous forum for the negotiation of multilateral trade relations; to administer the dispute settlement mechanism provided for in the Dispute Settlement Understanding (DSU); to administer the Trade Policy Review Mechanism, an exercise that will regularly examine member countries' trade practices and policies; and to achieve greater coherence in international economic policy-making by fostering cooperation between the WTO, the IMF and the IBRD.[37] All these functions could strengthen the multilateral trading system and protect the liberalisation of trade that began in 1947. The multilateral quality of the international trading system was reinforced by two facets of the GATT 1994 trade agreement: membership of the WTO carries with it the obligation to accept all the Uruguay round multilateral agreements, an obligation that would considerably reduce if not eliminate the free-rider problem in international trade; and the establishment of a dispute settlement procedure could inhibit bilateralism in the international trading system.

Critical to the success of the WTO and the multilateral character of the global trading system, however, is the success of the dispute settlement mechanism established with the DSU, particularly the ability of the WTO to resolve trade disputes between the primary trading nations – the United States, Japan and the EU. Most important, the DSU corrected the defects that plagued the dispute settlement process agreed to at the Tokyo round of trade negotiations. The DSU provided a single unified dispute settlement procedure; created a standard procedural method for bringing a complaint before the WTO; established a dispute settlement body that can automatically establish a dispute panel, adopt panel and appellate reports, and authorise retaliation when a panel report is not implemented or the parties fail to reach a satisfactory compensation agreement; provided for cross-retaliation – for the implementation of trade restrictions in a sector other than the one in dispute; and, finally, strengthened the multilateral character of the global trading system by prohibiting states from acting unilaterally to resolve a trade dispute.[38] The WTO charter also contributed to the liberalisation of the international trading system owing to the institutional incorporation of the 'new' trading issues into the post-Uruguay trading system. The WTO charter provides for the creation of a Council for Trade in Goods, which is responsible for monitoring the 1994 GATT multilateral trade agreement; a Council for Trade in Services, which is responsible for monitoring the General Agreement on Trade in Services (GATS); and a Council for Trade-related Aspects of Intellectual Property Rights (TRIPS), which is responsible for monitoring the agreement on TRIPS.

Yet GATT 1994 retained Article XXIV of the GATT, which governs the creation of preferential trading blocs in the international economy. Article XXIV stipulates that preferential trade agreements – free-trade areas or customs unions – may be concluded, providing they meet three criteria: trade barriers are eliminated on substantially all trade between the contracting parties; the agreement does not create barriers to trade that are higher or more restrictive than existing barriers to trade; and interim arrangements preceding the establishment of a free-trade area must be completed within a reasonable period of time. The rules governing the creation of free trade areas or customs unions are considered by many to be at odds with a multilateral trading system; and some have suggested that Article XXIV be substantially reformed to reduce the risk to multilateralism posed by the creation of trading blocs. The Uruguay round, however, left Article XXIV untouched; and the language guiding regional liberalisation in the GATS conformed with Article XXIV and thereby ensured the conformity (and laxity) of the service sector with the real sector in free-trade areas and customs unions.[39]

The strengthening of the multilateral trading system with the conclusion of the Uruguay round and the establishment of the WTO has yet to prove itself. The establishment of the WTO has created an institutional basis for the protection and advocacy of a liberal trading order on a global basis. The bilateralism and unilateralism that have characterised trade since the late 1970s should be suppressed by the creation of councils for the management of specific sectors of the international economy, a dispute settlement mechanism that provides an escape from bilateralism and unilateralism, agreements inhibiting the duration and application of anti-dumping and countervailing duties, and the agreement to phase out existing voluntary export restraints. It is also the case, however, that the real challenge to a multilateral trading system that encompasses both North America and Europe remains: the regionalism sanctioned by Article XXIV of the GATT and the progressive regionalisation of the European and North American segments of the Atlantic economy.

Trends in the trading system

The future trends of the international trading system are circumscribed by the Uruguay round achievements, the regional trading agreements struck between the EU and the CEE states as well as the North American experiment with free-trade agreements and the emerging structure of trade within the Atlantic economy.

The conflicts of the Uruguay round put to rest for the time being the deepest cleavage within the Atlantic economy, agricultural trade. The Uruguay round of trade negotiations, stretching from the Punta del Est declaration in 1986 to the conclusion of the round with the formal signing of the agreement at Marrakesh in April 1994, was pocked with long-lived and intense conflicts-between the United States (supported by the Cairns group of agricultural producers) and the EC over the reform of the rules governing trade in agricultural products. The talks were suspended in December 1990 when the United States and the EC were unable to reach an agreement on agricultural trade. An agreement on agriculture was not forthcoming until November 1992, when the EC and the United States were able to reach agreement not only on the issue of European subsidies for soya bean production but on a broader package on agricultural trade issues that enabled the Uruguay round negotiations to resume. The resolution of the agricultural dispute, which had threatened not only the Uruguay round but Germany's relations with its most important partners, France and the United States, provided the basis for the Tokyo G-7 agreement in 1993 on industrial tariffs and paved the way for the conclusion of the negotiations in December 1993.

The Uruguay round strengthened the multilateralisation of international trade, particularly between the industrial economies. The Uruguay round not only liberalised trade in areas previously exempted by the GATT (e.g. agriculture) or subject to restrictive trade agreements (e.g. Multi-fibre Agreement) outside the GATT, but liberalised trade in new areas such as trade-related intellectual property, trade-related investment measures and trade in services. Moreover, the Uruguay round produced even lower tariff levels between the industrialised and developing nations. Industrial economies' tariffs on industrial goods were reduced by 39 per cent on a trade-weighted basis, from 6.3 per cent, agreed at the Tokyo round, to 3.9 per cent, agreed at the Uruguay Round; and the percentage of duty-free imports increased from 20 per cent to 44 per cent on a trade-weighted basis. The zeroing out of tariffs was agreed for steel, construction and agricultural machinery, furniture, paper, toys, medical equipment, drugs, beer and liquor; agreement was also reached to reduce substantially tariffs on chemicals and electronics. The liberalisation of industrial countries' goods was matched by the Visegrad countries: these nations reduced tariffs by 30 per cent, on a trade-weighted average, and their tariff levels declined from 8.6 per cent to 6.0 per cent. The percentage of industrial goods entering duty-free, however, remains low at 16 per cent.[40]

Increased market access was also promised in the textile and clothing sector. The Agreement on Textiles and Clothing mandates the phasing out of the Multi-fibre Agreement within a ten-year period. The agreement specifies that the quotas will be eliminated within a ten-year period in three stages, but that quotas must be reduced by 50 per cent at the beginning of the seventh year. The Uruguay Agreement also provided for the elimination of grey-area measures that include voluntary export restraints, orderly marketing agreements and industry-to-industry agreements. The Agreement on Safeguards provides for the elimination of voluntary export restraints and other non-tariff barriers to trade within a four-year period; and those grey-area restraints not eliminated have to be applied to a product category rather than to the source of supply. The Agreement on Safeguards, then, has the potential to reduce significantly the bilateralism of the international trading system by eradicating the chief instruments of bilateral trade relations, non-tariff barriers to trade.[41]

Although agreements on trade-related intellectual property rights and trade-related investment measures were reached for the first time in a GATT trading round, the effect of the agreements on trade within the Atlantic economy appears to be limited. Both these agreements were aimed at increasing market access in the emerging markets of Latin America and Asia rather than at resolving any outstanding dispute between the industrial countries of the Atlantic economy.[42] The United States also established as one of its objectives for the Uruguay round the liberalisation of trade in services, a sector which accounts for an increasingly large share of American GDP. In the American view, the liberalisation of services was a natural complement to the liberalisation of financial markets in the OECD economies. The GATS was a broad framework agreement that had three core obligations: unconditional most-favoured-nation treatment; increased market access; and national treatment for foreign firms supplying services. The GATS was not signed until July 1994 and the United States remains a non-signatory to the agreement. The United States, dissatisfied with the residual protection offered to the service sectors in the emerging markets of Latin America and Asia, reserved for itself the right to discriminate against countries which did not extend national treatment to American service-sector firms. Despite the short-term absence of the United States from the GATS, the service sector has become a part of the competence of the WTO, and conflicts over market access in services have become subject to negotiation and resolution within that forum. Nonetheless, the impact of this agreement on the Atlantic economy is limited in corrosive effect: the integration of the service sector and reciprocal market access have been guaranteed by the American decision to allow European firms to operate in the United States on the basis of national treatment, by the free access offered to the American service sector by the EU, and by the accession strategy adopted by the CEE states which allows American firms unfettered access to those markets as well.[43]

The Uruguay round was nearly derailed by the dispute over agricultural trade between the United States, supported by the fourteen-country Cairns group, and the EU. Agricultural trade had previously been excluded from the GATT trade rounds. The exclusion of agriculture reflected American deference to the European process of integration, which was largely dependent upon the Common Agricultural Policy (CAP) and the fundamental bargain struck between Germany and France that it represented, and the American government's desire to have a free hand in the provision of subsidies for American agricultural exports. Yet the United States held the success of the Uruguay round hostage to the liberalisation of agricultural trade.[44] An agreement on agriculture required (and eventually produced) a reduction of internal support measures, lower tariffs and a reduction in export subsidies; in other words, it required a refashioning of the CAP. While the French accused the United States of blackmail over the establishment of a linkage between the success of the Uruguay round and the liberalisation of agricultural trade, the French subsequently held the trade round hostage to their demand that the Blair House agreement, the EC–US agreement on agricultural trade struck in November 1992, must be renegotiated.[45] In the end the Blair House agreement was left largely intact and served as the basis of the agreement on agricultural trade.[46]

The liberalisation of agricultural trade should reduce the potential for conflict within the Atlantic economy for three reasons. First, the agreement is results – rather than policy – orientated. The agreement on quantity reductions in the level of subsidisation and the increased level of market access provides a basis for future negotiations and should reduce the prospect of new trade conflicts in the agricultural area. Second, the integration into the GATT agreement of the Blair House 'peace clause', which prohibits unilateral action by either the United States or the EU to resolve outstanding agricultural trade disputes, provides another measure bolstering the multilateralism of the global trading system in general and of the Atlantic economy in particular. It removes a long-lived source of tension and conflict between the United States and the Europeans. Third, the integration of agricultural trade into the GATT directs conflicts between the US and the EU to the dispute settlement mechanism of the WTO.[47]

GATT 1994 and the WTO have broadened the shallow integration of the global and Atlantic economies. The reduction of tariff barriers to trade, the movement towards duty-free trade in industrial goods among the OECD countries, and the tariffication of non-tariff barriers to trade, particularly in agriculture, enhance the welfare benefits of trade and promise a greater intertwining of national markets. There is a simultaneous movement towards the deep integration of the regions comprising the global and Atlantic economy. Deep integration – the harmonisation of national competition policies and the free movement of goods, services, labour and capital – is the objective of the Single European Act and the convergence criteria of monetary union; and the deep integration of the European economy is being expanded with the accession of Sweden, Austria and Finland to the EU and the accession strategy adopted by the CEE countries as detailed by the 1995 Commission White Paper.

The European economy had undergone a number of changes between 1989 and the conclusion of the Uruguay round. Among the most important changes has been the precipitous decline in the level of inter-CMEA trade between 1989 and 1993. Trade in most of the former CMEA states, particularly those in central and eastern Europe, experienced a double-digit decline in the level of exports and imports which contributed to the negative growth experienced by these countries (see Table 6). Second, the CEE nations have experienced a pronounced shift in the direction of trade. There has been a marked decline in the level of trade between the 'spokes' of the post-Cold War European trading system. The reorientation of these nations' trading structures reflects both economic necessity and political choice. Import demand has been reorientated towards the nations of the industrialised west because only those nations can supply the CEE nations with the goods necessary to restructure and modernise their economies; and export efforts have been aimed at the industrialised west because only those nations can provide the hard currency required to buy Western goods.[48] While all the CEE states have restructured their trade, the wide variation between them reflects the integration of those countries into the Western trading system prior to the collapse of CMEA and the relative success of the national programmes of economic reform. The most radical shifts in the structure of trade occurred in the former Czechoslovakia, where the export share held by CMEA Europe declined from 52.7 per cent in 1989 to 25.5 per cent in 1993 and the OECD export share rose from 36 per cent to 63.3 per cent; in Hungary, where the export share for CMEA Europe fell from 41.5 per cent in 1989 to 27.1 per cent in 1993, while the OECD export share rose from 40.4 per cent to 66 per cent; and in Poland, where the export share held by CMEA Europe fell from 34.8 per cent in 1989 to 19.8 per cent in 1983, while the OECD export share rose from 47.9 per cent to 64 per cent (see Table 8).[49] And, third, the European economy has steadily progressed towards the creation of a closed trading bloc.[50] Sixty-eight per cent of EU exports went to Europe in 1993, while 66.34 per cent of EU imports originated within Europe. The Americas and the Pacific rim countries accounted for only 11.03 per cent and 9.22 per cent, respectively, of EU exports; and only 10.98 per cent and 11.71 per cent, respectively, of EU imports (see Table 7).

Germany, the anchor and motor of the European economy, exhibits a greater level of export concentration in Europe than does the EU: Europe accounts for 73.16 per cent of German exports (and 62.70 per cent of German imports). German exports to and imports from the Americas and the Pacific rim are of the same order: the Americas account for 10.93 per cent of German exports (and 9.41 per cent of German imports); and the Pacific rim accounts for 10.83 per cent of German exports (and 14.75 per cent of German imports) (see Table 9). The concentration of German and EU trade far exceeds the concentration of American trade. American exports are fairly equally distributed between the primary regions of the global economy: Europe takes 25.76 per cent, the Americas take 38.43 per cent and the Pacific rim takes 30.11 per cent of American exports. American imports, on the other hand, are somewhat more heavily concentrated: the Pacific rim provides 42.46 per cent, the Americas provide 31.74 per cent and Europe provides 20.52 per cent (see Table 10). The potential for a corrosive cleavage in the Atlantic economy stemming from varied levels of trade concentration is likely only if the trading world is treated as bipolar with a Europe anchored by Germany and a Pacific rim anchored by the United States and Japan. In that case, the level of export concentration for the United States would rise to 68.54 per cent for a broadly defined Pacific rim (Asia and the

Americas), while the import concentration would rise to 74.2 per cent (see Table 11). The deliberate evolution of a new bipolarity, however, would violate the security and economic interests of the United States as well as of the members of the EU, particularly the United Kingdom and the Netherlands.

Table 6 Annual percentage change in intra-CMEA trade, 1989-93

Country	1989	1990	1991	1992	1993
Bulgaria					
X	−18.4	−25.3	−16.3	4.1	−32.5
M	−21.0	−44.0	−19.3	256.9	70.0
Czechoslovakia					
X	−7.8	−30.5	−18.4	−25.3	−
M	−4.3	−20.3	−26.3	−4.7	−
Hungary					
X	−11.2	−18.2	−30.8	18.5	−13.2
M	−15.3	−21.9	−6.6	29.4	16.5
Poland					
X	−14.6	−27.3	−14.8	−22.6	35.9
M	−37.8	−31.5	42.7	−27.3	18.3
Romania					
X	−9.0	−44.0	−37.1	−10.6	−9.0
M	2.1	−16.7	−58.8	2.2	1.2

Source: IMF, *Direction of Trade Statistics Yearbook* (Washington, DC: IMF, 1994).

Table 7 Regional concentration of trade in 1993, EU (%)

Region/bloc	EU exports to	EU imports from
EU	55.93	53.56
EFTA	6.79	7.94
North America*	8.87	8.96
South America	2.13	2.02
Pacific rim	9.22	11.71
Developing Europe	5.78	4.84

*US, Canada, Mexico.
Sources: IMF, *Direction of Trade Statistics Yearbook* (Washington, DC: IMF, 1994); authors' own calculations.

Table 8 Geographical distribution of trade, 1989 and 1993 (%)

Country	Exports 1989	Exports 1993	Imports 1989	Imports 1993
Bulgaria				
OECD	26.3	54.4	53.4	37.3
EU	19.5	42.9	36.2	29.8
Developing Europe*	31.5	15.8	21.4	49.8
Czechoslovakia†				
OECD	36.0	63.3	38.6	62.1
EU	25.6	53.8	28.6	48.8
DE	52.7	25.5	51.2	31.7
Czech Republic				
OECD		62.4		65.7
EU		49.3		47.0
DE		32.3		32.0
Slovak Republic				
OECD		45.4		47.5
EU		34.6		34.2
DE		53.7		52.1
Hungary				
OECD	40.4	66.0	46.4	64.8
EU	24.9	45.8	28.5	40.1
DE	41.5	27.1	37.8	29.8
Poland				
OECD	47.9	64.0	52.6	71.9
EU	32.0	53.0	33.8	56.4
DE	34.8	19.8	32.3	14.0
Romania				
OECD	38.4	39.3	12.3	51.0
EU	26.6	33.5	6.7	44.3
DE	40.4	22.5	52.5	23.0

* Developing Europe includes all the former member-states of the CMEA as well as the underdeveloped nations of western Europe, including Turkey, Malta and Cyprus.
† Czechoslovakian statistics end in 1992 and are replaced by those for the Czech Republic and Slovakia.
Source: IMF, *Direction of Trade Statistics Yearbook* (Washington, DC, 1994).

Table 9 Regional concentration of trade in 1993, Germany (%)

Region/bloc	German exports to	German imports from
EU	47.78	41.01
EFTA	15.95	13.85
North America	9.12	7.44
South America	1.81	1.97
Pacific rim	10.83	14.75
Developing Europe	9.43	7.93

Sources: IMF, *Direction of Trade Statistics Yearbook* (Washington, DC: IMF, 1994); authors' own calculations.

Table 10 Regional concentration of trade in 1993, United States (%)

Region/bloc	US exports to	US imports from
EU	20.86	16.81
EFTA	2.73	2.71
North America	30.51	25.59
South America	7.92	6.15
Pacific rim	30.11	42.46
Developing Europe	2.17	1.00

Sources: IMF, *Direction of Trade Statistics Yearbook* (Washington, DC: IMF, 1994); authors' own calculations.

Table 11 Bloc concentration of US, German and EU Exports, 1993 (%)

Exporter	Americas	Europe	Pacific rim
US	38.43	25.76	30.11
Germany	10.93	73.16	10.83
EU	11.00	68.50	9.22

Sources: IMF, *Direction of Trade Statistics Yearbook* (Washington, DC: IMF, 1994); authors' own calculations.

Membership of a European trading bloc is in the interests of the CEE states. The nations in transition are heavily dependent upon the European market for both exports and imports. These nations' export dependence on the western European market possesses an important political dimension: whereas these nations face a large number of geographically dispersed suppliers providing a wide range of relatively homogeneous goods, the export markets for their goods are much more difficult to establish, the loss of an export market is neither easily nor rapidly replaced, and market access is subject to political manipulation. These nations are overwhelmingly dependent upon European export markets: for example, almost 94 per cent of Latvian exports go to Europe; 91.34 per cent of Czech exports go to Europe; and 79.95 per cent of Polish exports go to Europe (see Table 12).

Table 12 Export concentration ratio of selected former member states of CMEA, 1993 (%)

Country	North America	OECD Europe	Developing Europe
Bulgaria	7.30	46.00	15.70
Czech Republic	2.47	59.06	32.28
Hungary	4.60	60.12	27.12
Poland	3.18	60.17	19.78
Romania	1.80	36.10	22.50
Slovakia	1.84	43.40	53.65
Estonia	1.98	49.00	45.30
Latvia	2.40	89.70	4.20
Lithuania	1.30	84.40	9.00
Belarus	5.20	42.27	39.80
Russia	6.60	66.40	4.10
Ukraine	7.56	42.85	14.65

Sources: IMF, *Direction of Trade Statistics Yearbook* (Washington, DC: IMF, 1994); authors' own calculations.

The fact that the majority of CEE exports are destined for OECD Europe would suggest that these nations adopt as a minimalist strategy a free-trade or customs union agreement with the EU, and, as a maximalist strategy, membership in the EU. Membership of or close association with the EU would deliver most of the benefits normally attributed to a regional trading arrangement.[51] First, it would deliver the economic benefits associated with a preferential trading agreement, including security of market access. Second, preferential trading arrangements like the Europe Agreements establish the trading rules of the game, which can be used to bolster domestic economic and political reforms. Third, participation in a European preferential trading bloc can enhance the bargaining power of the weaker European states with the stronger and yield a more favourable division of the gains from trade or at a minimum reduce the incentives of the stronger countries to act as rent-seekers in their trading relations with the weaker.[52] Fourth, mutual membership within a preferential trading zone will reduce both the incentives and the opportunities for the larger European powers to transfer their adjustment problems on to the weaker European nations via structural adjustment policies. And fifth, both the minimalist and the maximalist strategies of economic integration with the EU promise to yield non-economic dividends, particularly the ability to translate mutual economic gain into the language of common political and strategic interests in

Europe. Although the CEE nations as well as the successor states to the Soviet Union account for a small fraction of total EU trade, the role played by the EU as a source of supply and as a market for those nations' goods is very large.

Political power in trade relations flows from the ability of one partner to affect the terms of trade of the other – for example, through the imposition of an optimal tariff or an export tax, or from the ability to alter markedly the level of economic activity by the closing of the national market. There are two methods of identifying the level of concentration in trade: the concentration ratio and the Herfindahl–Hirschman index. The concentration ratio is measured by determining the market share of the top five or six countries. When a concentration ratio exceeds 55 per cent it is assumed that market power can be exercised by those five or six states. What the concentration ratio does not convey, however, is how that market power is dispersed within the group. The dispersion of market power is described by the Herfindahl–Hirschman index. The Herfindahl–Hirschman index is derived by squaring the market shares held by the trading partners of the target country, summing the squares of market share, and finding the square root of that sum. The upper limit of the Herfindahl–Hirschman index is 100 (a condition of monopoly or monopsony) and the lower limit will approach zero (perfect competition).[53] The Herfindahl–Hirschman index has been calculated for those countries with a Europe Agreement, the three Baltic states, three successor states to the Soviet Union (Belarus, Russia and Ukraine) and the United Kingdom. A Herfindahl–Hirschman index of 42.4 or higher indicates a high potential for manipulation or dependence; an index number under 31.6 indicates the absence of either. An index between 31.6 and 42.4 is considered a grey area, but does indicate a level of market concentration that may be susceptible to political manipulation. The critical index number is that attached to export dependence: the ability to manipulate access to critical markets or to alter unilaterally the terms of trade can be translated into an instrument of political influence.[54]

In 1938, the year prior to the commencement of the Second World War and the last peacetime year in which the German commercial strategy of creating a web of dependencies between itself and its CEE neighbours was not enforced by occupation, two trends are identifiable in the structure of trade of those nations. First, the export indices were greater than the import indices, with the exception of Romania and Lithuania. Second, the export indices of Bulgaria, Hungary, Estonia, Latvia and Lithuania exceeded or met the hurdle of 42.4; only Czechoslovakia and the United Kingdom, the country with the lowest trade indices in 1939, had a clearly dispersed structure of trade. The indices for this same group of nations tell a different story in 1993. First, the indices for Bulgaria, Hungary, Romania, Estonia, Latvia and Lithuania are lower than in 1939. Second, the indices for Bulgaria, Romania and the United Kingdom suggest a diffuse structure of trade. And third, and perhaps most significantly, import concentration exceeds export concentration for Bulgaria, Hungary, Romania, Estonia, Latvia, Lithuania, Belarus, Russia and Ukraine (see Table 13).

Table 13 Herfindahl–Hirschman trade concentration ratios, 1938 and 1993

Country		1938	1993
Bulgaria			
	X	60.3	23.9
	M	54.0	25.3
Czech Republic			
	X	26.0	39.8
	M	26.0	38.5
Hungary			
	X	48.2	34.6
	M	44.5	35.1
Poland			
	X	33.2	36.5
	M	30.3	35.4
Romania			
	X	33.2	27.5
	M	42.1	29.1
Slovakia			
	X	–	59.4
	M	–	57.8
Estonia			
	X	47.4	35.0
	M	38.5	37.1
Latvia			
	X	55.0	35.2
	M	38.5	37.1
Lithuania			
	X	41.5	36.2
	M	48.9	42.4
Belarus			
	X	–	48.7
	M	–	50.3
Russia			
	X	–	31.2
	M	–	33.2
Ukraine			
	X	–	33.8
	M	–	37.0
UK			
	X	21.8	27.42
	M	19.6	25.25

Sources: for 1939, Albert O. Hirschman, *National Power and the Structure of Foreign Trade* (Berkeley: University of California Press, 1949), pp. 102-3; for 1993, authors' own calculations.

The Herfindahl–Hirschman index for these nations suggests, then, that the trade vulnerability of these countries is not as great as that of the commercial satellites of National Socialist Germany, but that they are nonetheless dependent upon a few major European national markets for exports and imports.[55]

The European area generally meets the formal criteria of a successful trading bloc: similar levels of *per capita* GNP, geographical propinquity, compatible trading rules and commitment to a regional political identity.[56] The question that remains, however, is whether Europe forms an 'optimal area of jurisdiction'.[57] Can Europe provide the public goods necessary to maximise the benefits of free trade and an integrated market on a regional basis without undermining the WTO effort to maximise free trade on a global basis? It would seem that the EU and the accession strategy adopted by the EU and accepted by the candidate countries would answer that question in the affirmative; there is not necessarily a conflict between regional liberalisation and the progressive multilateral liberalisation of global trade. Michael Mussa has suggested that the foreign policy community should avoid falling into the trap of what he calls 'hysterical multilateralism'; and there appears to be a consensus that regional solutions are not necessarily opposed to global free trade and may actually support progress towards that objective.[58] The questions that remain, however, are the following. Is there sufficient coalescence between the optimal areas of jurisdiction in trade and money? Is the emerging European economic space contiguous with the proposed European political area anchored by the EU?

Conclusion

The treatment of trade as an element of the security order is problematic. There is no particularly compelling logic leading to the conclusion that the presence or absence of trade ties between the states of Europe would either enhance or degrade regional or systemic security. As noted in the introduction to this chapter, there are two competing schools of thought which lead to opposite conclusions about the pacific consequences of international trade. In the contemporary international system, however, where there is growing openness of national economies, where the gossamer boundaries between national economies suggest the pooling of sovereignty to manage better a common economic space, and where there is a political premium on the creation of 'an ever closer union', the explicit exclusion of peripheral nations from a protected market like the EU carries a political charge not always evident in matters of trade. The security dimension of trade is also generated by the peculiar circumstance of the post-Cold War world: the nations on the periphery of the Atlantic economy have set a political and security patina on their economic relations with the industrialised countries. Just as the macroeconomy creates the framework conditions for the transition to the market economy and the support of democratisation, trade (along with investment) is the engine of growth that will consolidate those transitions. If the CEE states are denied markets for their goods, economic growth will remain slack and the ability of their governments to make good their reform efforts handicapped. Trade is yet another mechanism for creating the environmental conditions for a stable and prosperous pan-European security order. In this respect, trade is a pillar of the European security order and must be considered as such until the transitions to the market and democracy are consolidated and irreversible.

The trends in the Atlantic economic area are counter-indicative. The structure of trade of the EU countries indicates closure of the European market – an increasing proportion of trade is carried on within the European market rather than outside it. The CEE states are overwhelmingly dependent upon the western European market, not only as the primary source of supply but as the primary destination of their exports. This trend towards the regionalisation of trade is not evident in the case of the United States – its trade is more or less evenly divided between the Americas, the Pacific rim, and Europe. This development creates the potential for a divergence of interest, yet the volume of trade between the industrial nations of North America and Europe suggests a continuing community of interest.

The problem facing the Atlantic trading system is located not so much in the structure of trade as in the conscious policies of regionalism practised by both the Europeans and the North Americans. The EU efforts to expand trade with the states of the former Soviet bloc have created a trading caste system. The most privileged trading partners of the EU are the states that have signed Europe Agreements, the first step towards EU membership. The second group of states, standing outside the charmed circle of potential members, are those that have signed free-trade agreements with the EU or will sign customs union agreements. This latter group, which includes Turkey, is consigned to a trade purgatory that hints at future membership without any guarantee of it. The third group of countries, which are comprised of the republics of the former Soviet Union, are those that have signed Trade and Cooperation Agreements with the EU. These states are drawn into the EU trading orbit without any prospect of EU membership. This trend towards regionalism on a pan-European basis may become a source of conflict between the EU and the United States. However, it is also the case that the United States is pursuing its own regionalism in the context of the Americas as well as the Pacific rim. The potential for the dissociation of the states of the Atlantic trading system may be blunted by the renewed interest in an Atlantic Free Trade Area. This solution to the political problem of regionalism and the process of regionalisation has been long favoured by the United Kingdom and has recently found favour in Germany.

A real political problem that may plague the Atlantic trading system is the emergence of 'spoke-and-hub bilateralism'. The economic problem associated with this development for the CEE states, particularly the welfare losses associated with not trading with countries of similar economic development and *per capita* GDP, are well documented. The political problems are not. The absence of intense trade ties between these countries suggests atrophied political relations and works against the acknowledgement of a community of interest. Yet the persistence of 'hub-and-spoke bilateralism' is unlikely, for a number of reasons. First, its emergence undoubtedly reflected the efforts of national authorities in the CEE states to embed their national economies in the global market economy and to create a community of interest with the Atlantic nations as insurance against a revanchist Russian Federation. Second, investment capital and the hard currency necessary to finance imports strongly suggested the orientation of trade relations with the industrialised Western states. Third, the scarcely suppressed desire to join the Western clubs suggested a national strategy of engendering closer ties with the EU states in particular. And finally, the free-trade agreement in place between the Visegrad states should contribute to the multilateralisation of CEE trade.

Trade also poses a danger to the security order if it encourages the progressive dissociation or even fragmentation of the two pillars of the Atlantic economy. The creation or perception of a Fortress Europe could be accompanied by a Pacific reorientation by the United States. Such a development, were it to occur, would certainly degrade the security relationship not only between the United States and the Europe but within Europe itself. The self-interest of the major players, particularly the United States, Germany, France and the United Kingdom, counsels against that development. The recently concluded GATT agreement and the creation of the WTO also suggest that multilateralism is not a spent force in the Atlantic economy.

The extension of the Maastricht norms in the European macroeconomy have been paralleled by the extension of the Single European Act norms to the real sector of the European economy. The accession strategy outlined by the EU, although it is described as indicative, requires the conformity of the prospective members to the *acquis communautaire*. The intention of those nations to adopt the norms of the Act for the real sector of the economy reinforces the normative congruence of the real and monetary sectors of the European economy. The normative congruence of the European economy does not suggest, however, that there will be contiguity of economic and political boundaries in post-Cold War Europe. There will be two core political and economic boundaries of Europe: the EU and the Russian Federation, particularly its links with Belarus and Ukraine. Many states will fall outside either grouping. Some states will be stranded, like Turkey and Albania, while others will elect to remain nominally independent, like Norway and Switzerland. Yet the EU is uniquely placed to establish and enforce the norms governing economic activity in the European security space.

Notes

1. See Michael Mastanduno, *Economic Containment: COCOM and the Politics of East–West Trade* (Ithaca: Cornell University Press, 1992); and Nancy Dunne, 'Cocom: demise of yet one more Cold War warrior,' *Financial Times*, 31 March 1994.
2. See James Sperling, David Louscher and Michael Salomone, 'A Reconceptualisation of the Arms Transfer Problem,' *Defence Analysis*, vol. 11, no. 3 (December 1995), pp. 293–311.
3. See Wayne Sandholtz *et al.* (eds), *The Highest Stakes: the Economic Foundations of the Next Security System* (Oxford: Oxford University Press, 1992); and Robert O. Keohane and Joseph P. Nye, *Power and Interdependence: World Politics in Transition* (Boston, MA: Little Brown, 1977).
4. See Richard E. Caves and Ronald W. Jones, *World Trade and Payments: an Introduction*, second edition (Boston, MA: Little Brown, 1977), pp. 12–28.
5. This point was made in 1989 by the Deutsche Bundesbank, 'Recent Trends in External Transactions with the Centrally Planned Economies,' *Monthly Report*, vol. 41, no. 7 (July 1989), pp. 19–24.
6. They stated: 'Failure to conclude [the Uruguay] Round ... could also put at risk the new democracies in Eastern Europe and the countries of the former Soviet Union, for which economic reform and assimilation into the global economic system are vital to political stability and economic growth.' *IMF Survey*, vol. 22, no. 19 (11 October 1993), p. 308.
7. Joanne Gowa, 'Bipolarity, Multipolarity, and Free Trade,' *American Political Science Review*, vol. 83, no. 4 (December 1989), pp. 1249–53.
8. See statements of Treasury Secretary Robert E. Rubin, Los Angeles World Affairs Council, 13 April 1995, *Treasury News*, RR-205, p. 2; and of Treasury Under Secretary Lawrence H. Summers, American Business Council, 21 September 1994, *Treasury News*, LB-1098, pp. 9–11.
9. The EU announced the intention of forming a free-trade area with the littoral states of the Mediterranean by 2010 in June 1995. See 'Europäischer Rat in Cannes,' 26/27 June 1995, *Bulletin des Presse- und Informationsamtes der Bundesregierung*, 62 (8 August 1995), p. 613.
10. This distinction is drawn from Detlef Lorenz, 'Economic Geography and the Political Economy of Regionalization: the Example of Western Europe,' *American Economic Review*, vol. 82, no. 2 (May 1992), p. 85. See also Richard E. Baldwin, *Towards an Integrated Europe* (London: CEPR, 1994), chapter 3; and Alexis Jacquemin and André Sapir, 'Europe post-1992: Internal and External Liberalization,' *American Economic Review*, vol. 81, no. 2 (May 1991), pp. 168–9.
11. See Andreas Predöhl, *Aussenwirtschaft*, second edition (Göttingen: Vandenhoeck & Ruprecht, 1971); Paul Krugman, *Geography and Trade* (Cambridge, MA: MIT Press, 1991); and Jacob Viner, *The Customs Union Issue* (New York: Carnegie Endowment for International Peace, 1950), p. 18–19, cited in Jacquemin and Sapir, 'Europe post-1992,' p. 168.
12. If Paul Krugman and Richard Baldwin are correct, the anticipated investment boom driven by economic growth in central and eastern Europe is as likely to occur in Germany and Austria as in the nations in transition. See Krugman, *Geography and Trade*, pp. 96–8; and Richard E. Baldwin, *Towards an Integrated Europe* (London: Centre for Economic Policy Research, 1994), pp. 134–5.
13. See Rory O'Donnell and Anna Murphy, 'The relevance of the European Union and European integration to the world trade regime,' *International Journal*, vol. XLIX (summer 1994), pp. 535–67; Paolo Cecchini, *The European Challenge, 1992: the Benefits of a Single Market* (Aldershot: Gower, 1988); Seamus O'Cleireacain, 'Europe 1992 and Gaps in the EC's Common Commercial Policy,' *Journal of Common Market Studies*, vol.

28, no. 3 (March 1990), pp. 201–18; Banca d'Italia, 'Recent Trade Agreements concluded by the EC with EFTA and certain Countries in Central and Eastern Europe,' *Economic Bulletin*, vol. 14 (February 1992), pp. 58–9; L. Alan Winters, 'The Welfare and Policy Implications of the International Trade Consequences of "1992",' *American Economic Review*, vol. 82, no. 2 (May 1992), pp. 104–8; Dale L. Smith and Jürgen Wanke, 'Completing the Single European Market: an Analysis of the Impact on the Member States,' *American Journal of Political Science*, vol. 37, no. 2 (May 1993), p. 530–1; and James Sperling, 'A Unified Germany, a Single European Economic Space, and the Prospects for the Atlantic Economy,' in Carl Lankowski (ed.), *Germany and the European Community: Beyond Hegemony and Containment?* (New York: St Martin's Press, 1993), pp. 179–216.

14 For an overview of the CMEA system see Thomas Baylis, *The West and Eastern Europe: Economic Statecraft and Political Change* (Westport: Praeger, 1994), pp. 89ff.

15 Economic Commission for Europe, *Economic Survey of Europe in 1990–1991* (New York: UN, 1991), p. 78; Peter B. Kenen, 'Transitional Arrangements for Trade and Payments among the CMEA Countries,' *IMF Staff Papers*, vol. 28, no. 2 (June 1991), pp. 235–8; and Michael Bleaney, 'Some Trade Policy Issues in the Transition to a Market Economy in Eastern Europe,' *The World Economy*, vol. 13, no. 2 (June 1990), pp. 251–5.

16 The GSP provided for duty-free quotas on a range of industrial exports and the application of preferential tariffs on a further quota of exports. Most-favoured-nation tariffs are applied to any exports in excess of the quotas.

17 Commission of the European Communities, *Towards Greater Economic Integration: the European Union's Financial Assistance and Trade Policy for Central and Eastern Europe and the Countries of the Commonwealth of Independent States* (Brussels: EC, 1995); and Economic Commission for Europe, *Economic Survey of Europe in 1992–1993* (Geneva: UN, 1993), table 4.2.1.

18 Economic Commission for Europe, *Economic Survey of Europe in 1991–1992*, pp. 187–8; Banca d'Italia, 'Recent Trade Agreements,' pp. 59–60; and Commission of the European Communities, *Towards Greater Economic Integration*, p. 15.

19 Banca d'Italia, 'Recent trade agreements,' p. 60. In November 1992 anti-dumping duties were imposed on steel exports from Czechoslovakia, Poland and Hungary far in excess of the tariff reductions extended in the Europe Agreements. 'Dumping duties anger E. Europeans,' *Financial Times*, 20 November 1992, p. 11.

20 'Europäischer Rat in Kopenhagen,' *Bulletin*, 60 (8 July 1993), p. 632.

21 Beginning in 1995, there would be an annual meeting of the heads of state at the same time as the EU summit; semi-annual meetings of the foreign ministers; annual meetings of economic, finance and agricultural ministers; and semi-annual meetings of justice and/or interior ministers. 'Anhang IV. Bericht des Rates an den Europäischen Rat Essen über die Strategie zur Vorbereitung des Beitritts der assoziierten MOEL. Schlussfolgerungen des Vorsitzes. Europäischer Rat in Essen,' *Bulletin*, 118 (19 December 1994), pp. 118–19.

22 Commission of the European Communities, *White Paper. Preparation of the Associated Countries of Central and Eastern Europe for Integration into the Internal Market of the Union*, COM (95) 163 final, 3 May 1995.

23 *Ibid.*, para. 1.6.

24 *Ibid.*, para. 2.5.

25 *Ibid.*, paras 4.4, 4.5 and 6.3.

26 Commission of the European Communities, *White Paper. Preparation of the Associated Countries of Central and Eastern Europe for Integration into the Internal Market of the Union. Annex.* COM (96) 163 final/2, p. viii.

27 Baldwin, *Towards an Integrated Europe*, pp. 130–5.

28 Peter B. Kenen, 'Transitional Arrangements for Trade and Payments among the CMEA

Countries,' *IMF Staff Papers*, vol. 38, no. 2 (June 1991), pp. 239–48.
29 The original CEFTA member states were the Visegrad countries. Slovenia subsequently joined in September 1995 and membership is anticipated for Bulgaria, Romania and the Baltics. *Economist*, 16–22 September 1995, p. 60.
30 The nations in transition farther to the east are also tied together by a large number of free-trade and economic cooperation agreements. There have been two sets of agreements that have sought to re-establish trading ties between the former Soviet republics, the Baltic Free Trade Agreement (1994) and bilateral trading agreements between the Russian Republic and the other CIS republics. The Baltic Free Trade Agreement between Estonia, Latvia and Lithuania came into force in 1994. The 1993 Minsk summit of the CIS envisioned a 'common economic space' facilitating the free movement of persons, goods, services, capital and labour; and the Russia–Belarus treaty on economic union may provide the basis of a reintegrated economy encompassing most of the political space once occupied by the Soviet Union. Economic Commission for Europe, *Economic Survey of Europe 1993–1994* (Geneva: UN, 1994), p. 156; and Leyla Boulton, 'Two-track CIS emerges from Minsk conference,' *Financial Times*, 23/24 January 1993, p. 2; 'Three into one might go,' *Financial Times*, 13 July 1994, p. 17; and John Lloyd, 'Russia begins to choose between Union and empire,' *Financial Times*, 18 April 1994, p. 2.
31 John Murray Brown, 'Black Sea Economic Cooperation: All trading together,' *Financial Times*, 25 November 1993, p. IV; 'Economics binds those whom Politics divides,' *Financial Times*, 10 July 1992, p. 6; and Leyla Boulton, 'Slow Embrace of Former Rivals,' *Financial Times*, 8 September 1992, p. 6; and European Bank for Reconstruction and Development, *Annual Economic Review, 1992* (London: EBRD, 1993), p. 28.
32 For a thematic treatment of the progression from hegemon to oligopsonist see Robert E. Baldwin, 'US Trade Policy: Recent Changes and Future US Interests,' *American Economic Review*, vol. 79, no. 2 (May 1989), pp. 128. For detailed discussions of the Kennedy round see Kenneth Dam, *The GATT: the Law and International Economic Organization* (Chicago: University of Chicago Press, 1970); for the Tokyo round see Gilbert R. Winham, *International Trade and the Tokyo Round Negotiation* (Princeton: Princeton University Press, 1986); and for the Uruguay round see OECD, *OECD Documents. The New World Trading System: Readings* (Paris: OECD, 1994).
33 Nancy Dunne, 'Not so Super 301 after all,' *Financial Times*, 6 October 1994, p. 6.
34 This list is drawn from Jagdish Bhagwati, 'Multilateralism at Risk. The GATT is Dead. Long live the GATT,' *The World Economy*, vol. 13, no. 2 (June 1990), p. 150. For an extensive cataloguing of the principles, norms and rules of the GATT trading system see Jock A. Finlayson and Mark W. Zacher, 'The GATT and the Regulation of Trade Barriers: Regime Dynamics and Functions,' in Stephen D. Krasner (ed.), *International Regimes* (Ithaca: Cornell University Press, 1982), pp. 273–314.
35 *Agreement Establishing the World Trade Organization*, 15 April 1994, Article II, para. 1.
36 There are thirteen multilateral agreements on trade in goods. These agreements include the General Agreement on Tariffs and Trade 1994 and separate Agreements on Agriculture; on the Application of Sanitary and Phytosanitary Measures; on Textiles and Clothing; on Technical Barriers to Trade; on Trade-related Barriers to Investment Measures; on Reshipment Inspection; on Rules of Origin; on Import Licensing Procedures; on Subsidies and Countervailing Measures; on Safeguards; on the Implementation of Article VI of the GATT 1994; and on the Implementation of Article VII of the GATT 1994. There are four Plurilateral Trade Agreements: on Trade in Civil Aircraft; on Government Procurement; regarding Bovine Meat; and the International Dairy Agreement.
37 *Agreement Establishing the World Trade Organization*, Article III, paras 1–5.
38 On the dispute settlement understanding see Jeanne J. Grimmett, 'World Trade Organization: Institutional Issues and Dispute Settlement,' *CRS Report for Congress*, (Wash-

ington, DC: Congressional Research Service, 1994); and John Jackson, 'Dispute Settlement Procedures,' *The New World Trading System: Readings* (Paris: OECD, 1994), pp. 117–25.

39 George D. Halliday, 'GATT and Regional Free Trade Agreements,' *CRS Report for Congress* (Washington, DC: Congressional Research Service, 1993); John H. Jackson, 'Regional Trade Blocs and the GATT,' *The World Economy*, vol. 16, no. 2 (March 1992), pp. 121–31; Bernard Hoekman, 'General Agreement on Trade in Services,' in *The New World Trading System: Readings* (Paris: OECD, 1994), pp. 181–2.

40 For tariff data see Anwarul Hoda, 'Trade Liberalisation,' in *The New World Trading System: Readings* (Paris: OECD, 1994), pp. 47–54; and Edward Rappaport, 'Uruguay Round: Industry Issues,' *CRS Issues Brief* (Washington, DC: CRS, 1994), pp. 1–2.

41 The Agreement on Technical Barriers to Trade and the Agreement on Sanitary and Phytosanitary Measures were developed to minimise the (un)intentional barriers to trade created by technical and/or health standards. For a discussion of these agreements see John H. Jackson, 'Managing the Trading System: the World Trade Organization and the post-Uruguay Round GATT Agenda,' in Peter B. Kenen (ed.), *Managing the World Economy: Fifty Years after Bretton Woods* (Washington, DC: Institute for International Economies, 1994), pp. 131–51; and Hoda, 'Trade Liberalisation,' pp. 43–5.

42 Jonathan Startup, 'An Agenda for International Investment,' in *The New World Trading System: Readings* (Paris: OECD, 1994), pp. 189–91. The inclusion of intellectual property rights in the Uruguay round reflected American dissatisfaction with developing countries' unwillingness to enter into negotiations in the existing property rights forum, the World Intellectual Property Organisation, located in Geneva, and was made possible by the willingness of the United States to entertain developing country demands for the reform of the rules governing trade in textiles and agricultural products. Frances Williams, 'GATT joins Battle for Right to Protect,' *Financial Times*, 7 July 1994, p. 7.

43 Paul Lewis, 'Global Services Pact Concluded: Goods News and Bad for the US,' *New York Times*, 29 July 1995, p. 17; and 'Trade Accord without US set in Geneva,' *New York Times*, 27 July 1995, p. C1; and Bernard Hoekman, 'General Agreement on Trade in Services,' in *The New World Trading System* (Paris: OECD, 1994), pp. 177–83.

44 Carla Hills, the US Trade Representative, stated in September 1990 that the United States would allow the Uruguay round to fail rather than yield on agriculture to the EC. *Economist*, 22–8 September 1990.

45 The Blair House agreement provided for a 21 per cent reduction in the volume of agricultural export subsidies over a six-year period; the value of subsidised exports to be cut by 36 per cent; the level of internal supports to be cut by 20 per cent; the limitation of EC oilseed production; and a six-year 'peace clause' on outstanding agricultural disputes between the US and EC. David Gardner, 'Hopes rising that Deal can be Saved,' *Financial Times*, 20 September 1993, p. 3.

46 The agreement had four key elements. First, market access was improved with the tariffication of non-tariff measures which were then to be cut by 36 per cent, and a minimum access clause which guaranteed 3 per cent of domestic consumption, rising to 5 per cent, to foreign suppliers. Second, export competition was improved with the reduction of export subsidies by 36 per cent in value and the reduction of subsidised exports by 21 per cent in volume. Third, the level of domestic support was to be reduced by 20 per cent exclusive of so-called 'green box' measures. And, finally, barriers to trade in agricultural goods were also lowered, owing the agreement on sanitary and phytosanitary import barriers; the agreement specified that the sanitary and phytosanitary standards should be scientifically based to preclude their use as a non-tariff barrier to trade.

47 The discussion of the agricultural agreement was based on Stefan Tangermann, 'An

Assessment of the Agreement on Agriculture,' pp. 143–51; Kym Anderson, 'Implementation of the Agreement on Agriculture,' pp. 153–62; and Dale E. Hathaway, 'New World Order in Agricultural Trade,' in *The New World Trading System: Readings*, pp. 167–9.

48 Helen B. Junz, 'Integration of Eastern Europe into the World Trading System,' *American Economic Review*, vol. 81, no. 2 (May 1991), pp. 176–80; and Thomas A. Baylis, *The West and Eastern Europe*, pp. 89–102.

49 The rate of growth in CEE exports to the EU between 1989 and 1994 was 219 per cent in the former Czechoslovakia; 135 per cent in Poland; 103.3 per cent in Bulgaria; 88.8 per cent in Hungary; -4.5 per cent in Romania. The rate of change during the same period for the former Soviet Union was 47.3 per cent. Commission of the European Communities, *Towards Greater Economic Integration*, pp. 11 and 18

50 See Bank of England, 'The Advent of Trading Blocs,' *Bank of England Quarterly Bulletin*, vol. 30, no. 3 (August 1990), pp. 372–3.

51 The generic benefits associated with regional trading arrangements are drawn from Clinton Shiells, 'Regional Trading Blocs: Trade Creating or Diverting?' *Finance and Development*, vol. 32, no. 1 (March 1995), pp. 30–2.

52 There is a considerable body of literature arguing that larger states have an incentive to impose optimal tariffs on smaller states while refraining from imposing such tariffs on each other. See John A. C. Conybeare, *Trade Wars* (New York: Columbia University Press, 1987); and Kenneth Rogoff, 'Bargaining and International Policy Cooperation,' *American Economic Review*, vol. 80, no. 2 (May 1990), pp. 139–42.

53 'The Herfindahl–Hirschman index,' *Federal Reserve Bulletin*, vol. 79, no. 3 (March 1993), pp. 188–9.

54 Albert O. Hirschman, *National Power and the Structure of Foreign Trade* (Berkeley: University of California Press, 1969), pp. 98–116.

55 Germany is the primary export market for the Czech Republic, Hungary, Poland, Romania and Russia, and an important export market for the others. In addition to Germany, the CEE countries, as well as the successor states to the Soviet Union, have close trading ties with France, Italy, the United Kingdom, the Netherlands, Finland or Russia.

56 Jeffrey J. Schott, 'Trading Blocs and the World Trading System,' *The World Economy*, vol. 14, no. 1 (March 1991), p. 2.

57 Richard N. Cooper, 'Worldwide versus Regional Integration: is there an Optimum Size of the Integration Area?' in Fritz Machlup (ed.), *Economic Integration: Worldwide, Regional, Sectoral* (London: Macmillan, 1976), p. 49, quoted in Lorenz, 'Economic Geography and the Example of Western Europe,' p. 85.

58 Michael Mussa, 'Making the Practical Case for Freer Trade,' *American Economic Review*, vol. 83, no. 2 (May 1993), p. 375; and 'Trade Liberalization is linked to Global Prosperity,' *IMF Survey*, vol. 24, no. 10 (22 May 1995), p. 157–8.

6

The economic dimension of security
Financing the transition

The CEE nations as well as the newly independent states of the former Soviet Union have undertaken an ambitious plan of transforming their economies and polities in conformity with the liberal capitalist model. The task facing the western Europeans and the United States is not the relatively simple one that faced the United States in the immediate post-war period, namely the economic reconstruction of war-ravaged states. Rather, the western Europeans and the United States face the less tractable problem of recasting the economies and polities of eastern and central Europe in their own image. The transition to a market-driven and entrepreneurial economy requires large and sustained capital inflows. But capital inflows to the CEE states have been offset by sustained capital outflows reflecting not only the uncertainty of individual economic agents about the pace and final destination of economic and political reform, but the need to service external hard currency debt, the majority of which was incurred prior to 1989.

The Western states seek the integration of the CEE states and the newly independent states of the former Soviet Union into the global economy. These nations, taken together, represent a potential market of 500 million inhabitants with similar tastes and complementary economies. The recasting of these states promises to create a new and large and market for the goods and services produced by the industrialised states of western Europe and North America. And underlying this economic calculation is the political calculation that such recasting is the requisite foundation of a secure, peaceful and integrated pan-European security area. But this potential market and anticipated security externality will not be realised for the states of the Atlantic economy unless the programme of economic and political reform is successfully completed in the east.[1]

The failure of that programme could have any number of consequences for the European security order. Firstly, it could lead to the reassertion of a Russian zone of influence that would not only divide Europe once again into two antagonistic blocs but rob the social democracies of western Europe and a deficit-ridden United States of the 'peace dividend' promised by the end of the Cold War. Yet economic and political collapse need not result in a reassertion of Russian power in the heart of Europe. It could lead instead to the mass migration of immiserised eastern and central Europeans to the wealthier states of western Europe. Such a development would sorely test the social fabric of those societies and possibly undermine the economic and political progress they have enjoyed since the end of the Second World War. A third potential consequence of economic and political collapse would be the spread of ethnic or religious conflict from the former Yugoslavia to its neighbours or the intensification of the conflicts between ethnic Russians and the indigenous populations of the newly independent states of the former Soviet Union.

The process of correcting the malformation of the CEE economies is handicapped by the budget deficits of the industrialised West, which limit the level of financial aid that can be made available to their governments, and the sovereign debt overhang of the reforming east, the repayment of which stakes a privileged claim to domestic savings and export earnings.[2] The budget deficits of the industrialised West have compromised the ability to provide aid on a scale similar to the European Recovery Programme (ERP) that accelerated the reconstruction of western Europe after the Second World War: whereas ERP disbursements were equal to an annual average of 1.875 per cent of American GNP between 1948 and 1951, all the G-24 aid both to the CEE states and to the former Soviet Union is equal to an annual average of 0.60 per cent of American GNP between 1990 and 1994.[3] The external debt obligations of the reforming east, which were carried over from the communist regimes and assumed by the newly established democratic governments, were a drag on the process of economic reform. Debt service requirements have sustained an outflow of capital from the struggling east, where it is most desperately needed, to Western commercial banks and creditor governments. The fragile process of transition and the geopolitical position and importance of the CEE states to the security of the Atlantic area suggest that the debt service obligations of those nations must be treated as something more than the relatively simple problem of protecting the balance sheets of commercial banks. Nor can sovereign debt be viewed simply as the distributional problem of shifting the burden of default on to western taxpayers to cover officially guaranteed loans. Rather, it represents a key element of the pan-European security order even though it neither portends the onset of war nor corresponds to traditional conceptualisations of security.

The stability and solvency of the international financial system are the commonly identified connection between sovereign debt default and national security.[4] Sovereign default by any of the CEE states would fall far short of disrupting the international financial system. But sovereign default could lead to the stagnation of economic and political reform in central and eastern Europe. The stability of the European security order is threatened not only by the inability (debt default) or unwillingness (debt repudiation) of these states to service their external debts, but by the economic consequences of servicing external debt with domestic savings. Either debt default or debt repudiation would lower the overall level of investment in these economies because both foreign and domestic investors would have disincentives to invest and incentives to disinvest. Sovereign debt overhang has reduced the ability of these states to finance the economic transition and has placed five kinds of strain on the emerging and fragile democratic political fabric. First, high sovereign indebtedness limits the ability of firms and governments to borrow on international capital markets – the spectre of default dissuades lending by both commercial banks and Western governments. Second, high sovereign indebtedness raises the price of capital. Consequently, higher interest rates limit the ability of governments and the incentive for individual economic agents to invest in the domestic economy. Third, domestic and foreign investors, in calculating the real rate of return on the investment, will be forced to require a higher nominal rate of return to compensate for the near certainty of higher future taxes to service external debt. A fourth consequence of debt overhang is lower incentives to pursue economic reform by the fledgling democratic governments: the political costs of economic reform and servicing external debt are borne exclusively by the national governments, whereas the lion's share of the economic gains from economic reform are enjoyed by the creditor banks and governments.[5] A final consequence for these economies is the use of scarce domestic savings to service external debt rather than to finance the transition to a market economy and accelerate economic growth.

The cumulative economic consequences of debt overhang for the CEE states are slower economic growth and a more difficult transition to a sustainable market economy. The cumulative security consequences of debt overhang range from a return to (involuntary) economic autarky, which would preclude the Western objective of an economically integrated Europe, to the resurgence of authoritarian governments supported by widespread resentment of the West. If Western governments wish to build the future European security order upon a firm foundation, a delicate balance must be struck between guaranteeing that the CEE governments service their external debt and ensuring that the debt service burden neither undermines the transition to the market economy nor destabilises these fledgling democracies.

The institutions of debt

The management of the debt problem facing the CEE and the ex-Soviet states, as well as Portugal and Turkey in the West, is facilitated by the post-war institutions of the debt regime: the IMF, the World Bank, the Paris Club, the London Club and ancillary support institutions (e.g. the BIS and the OECD). One of the most important institutions of debt relief is the Paris Club. The Paris Club, which has met on an *ad hoc* basis since 1956, when a number of creditor governments met to reschedule supplier credits to Argentina, meets only when a debtor country submits a formal request to the French government for debt relief. Paris Club negotiations only reschedule officially guaranteed debt; they do not consider debt held by international financial institutions, by non-bank private creditors or by commercial banks. Paris Club negotiations are intended to restore the debtor nation's external creditworthiness, to allow it voluntary access to international markets, and to give the government a respite to introduce credible domestic macroeconomic policies to restore internal and external balance.[6]

The Paris Club has no legal charter and lacks a formal organisational forum. It didn't acquire a secretariat until 1980, when one was provided by the French Treasury. Its membership is not fixed, because the participation of a creditor country in Paris Club negotiations is determined by a creditor country's level of exposure to the debtor country. The parties to multilateral debt relief negotiations within the Paris Club framework include the creditor countries, the IMF, the World Bank and the debtor government. Despite the absence of any permanent institutional character, the Paris Club is governed by a set of well defined principles and operating procedures. There are five primary principles guiding Paris Club negotiations. The first is imminent default. Imminent default, which protects creditors from frivolous requests for debt relief, allows a debtor government to petition for debt relief only when failure to do so would force the country into default.[7] Default is considered imminent when two conditions are met: the debtor country is in substantial arrears to its creditors and the IMF identifies a financing gap between foreign exchange uses and sources. The second principle is conditionality. Paris Club creditors require debtors to have in place a high conditionality stand-by agreement with the IMF. This requirement reflects the underlying assumption that the inability to service existing debt reflects a poorly managed domestic economy. In this way, the Paris Club effectively employs the IMF as an agent of the creditors that ensures both debtor compliance with the stand-by arrangement and the servicing of official debt.[8]

Burden-sharing, the third principle, has three parts: first, it obligates the debtor to ensure that each creditor country participating in the Paris Club negotiation receives treatment no less favourable than that which it may accord to any other creditor country; second, it obligates the debtor country to negotiate debt relief on similar terms with other non-participating creditor countries; third, it obligates the debtor to secure comparable treatment with external private creditors.[9] The burden-sharing principle provides the basis for creditor country cooperation and it ensures that commercial bankers do not receive an indirect subsidy by negotiating a less forgiving rescheduling agreement with sovereign debtors. A fourth principle of the Paris Club is non-discrimination; creditors are to treat equally all debtor nations with similar debt service problems, economic circumstances, or ability to pay. Although the debt relief innovations that have been put in place since 1988 have honoured this principle, it is also the case that it has been violated to serve the foreign policy objectives of the primary creditors, as in the cases of Poland and Egypt in the early 1990s. The final principle of the Paris Club is the desire to preserve the *ad hoc* character of debt relief negotiations. This preference for the *status quo* reflects the creditor countries' calculation that the Paris Club places the debtor government at a distinct disadvantage: it provides a mechanism for ensuring comparable treatment of creditors; the negotiation process operates in such a way that it 'makes creditor initial offers ... the basis for negotiations'[10] and the absence of a legal framework provides creditors a forum that provides flexibility in the granting of debt relief.

The Paris Club negotiation produces an *ad referendum* framework agreement between the debtor and represented creditor countries. Following the signing of an 'agreed minute', the debt rescheduling is implemented after the signing of bilateral agreements between each of the creditor governments with the debtor government. The standard terms of Paris Club agreements have been non-discriminatory: the terms set are indifferent to the level of indebtedness or income level of the country seeking relief. And the terms of the debt relief were unvarying prior to the 1980s: a consolidation period ranging from one to three years depending upon the terms of the IMF stand-by or structural adjustment agreement; up to 100 per cent of principal and interest, as well as arrears, were eligible for rescheduling; and the interest rate charged on the consolidated debt was market-based.[11] These standard terms were viewed as inadequate by the mid-1980s. This change of view reflected the realisation that the problem facing many indebted nations was not a temporary payments imbalance and a liquidity shortage, but a problem of sovereign solvency and economic development. Consequently, the Paris Club introduced a number of innovations in debt relief which combine debt restructuring with debt reduction, below market-level interest rates, and extended repayment periods with generous grace periods.

The terms of Paris Club agreements evolved in response to the debt crisis of the 1980s. At the June 1988 Toronto economic summit, the G-7 took the first major step in revising the terms of Paris Club agreements. The "Toronto terms" provided that restructured concessional debt would have a twenty-five-year repayment schedule with a grace-period of fourteen years. At a subsequent G-7 finance ministers' meeting in Berlin, it was agreed that, for non-concessional debt, official creditors could choose from a menu of terms ranging from partial cancellation of one-third of the debt combined with extended grace and repayment periods (eight and fourteen years, respectively) to extending exceptionally longer maturities (up to twenty-five years for repayment after a fourteen-year grace period) in combination with concessional interest rates. These terms were improved in December 1991 with the so-called "enhanced Toronto terms" which allowed creditors to choose from one of three options: first, to reduce by 50 per cent the present value of the consolidated debt with a twenty-three-year repayment schedule and six years' grace period; second, to apply a concessional interest rate that lowered the present value of the consolidated debt by 50 per cent with a twenty-three-year repayment schedule and no grace period; or third, to apply a market-based interest rate on the consolidated debt with a fourteen-year grace period and a twenty-five-year repayment schedule.[12] The process of political and economic restructuring in central and eastern Europe has been significantly eased by these innovations in Paris Club debt relief. The innovations have been matched by the commercial banks in the other major institution of debt, the London Club.

The London Club serves the same function for commercial banks as the Paris Club for sovereign creditors. The London Club meets to reschedule or refinance uninsured commercial credit extended to sovereign borrowers. The London Club, like the Paris Club, has neither a legal nor an institutional basis; it even lacks a secretariat. The membership of the London Club is non-exclusionary – there are no *de minimis* commercial bank creditors. When a state seeks the restructuring of commercial bank debt, it must seek an agreement with all its commercial bank creditors. The actual negotiation between the commercial banks and the debtor country is streamlined, however: commercial banks with limited exposure are represented by the commercial banks with the largest exposure to the debtor country. The major creditor banks form the steering committee empowered to conduct the negotiations and the meetings are led by the committee chairs. The committee chairs, in turn, represent the group of national banks that have the largest exposure to the debtor country. Unlike a Paris Club negotiation, which normally takes one or two days to complete, a London Club agreement takes several months of negotiation between the creditors and the debtors, and – equally important – between creditors with different levels of exposure and (dis)incentives to reschedule.[13]

London Club negotiations are normally set in motion when a country is in substantial arrears to commercial creditors and has agreed to a high conditionality IMF stand-by agreement, although commercial banks have pre-emptively rescheduled sovereign debt before these conditions are met.[14] The commercial bankers are willing to negotiate not only the rescheduling of debt, but the refinancing of debt. The preference of commercial bankers for refinancing debt reflects the desire to sustain the fiction that the debts in arrears have been retired, rather than acknowledge that the debt has been rescheduled or that interest arrears have been consolidated.[15] Consequently, the normal precondition of a London Club agreement is the payment of interest in arrears. The IMF's role, as in the case of the Paris Club, is to ensure that the debtor country is prepared to undertake the necessary domestic macroeconomic reforms to restore internal and external balance; and to provide IMF credit, enabling the debtor to resume its debt service obligations.

There are a number of identifiable principles that define a London Club negotiation. A core principle of the London Club is the duty of a government to service its debt regardless of the legitimacy of the regime that contracted it. Commercial banks have accepted the proposition that sovereign debtors may occasionally have a need to reschedule or refinance their debt, but have rejected any presumptive right of sovereign debtors to do so. They likewise reject the notion that a sovereign debtor can unilaterally impose new terms on debt service agreements.[16] The second principle is that negotiations are taken on a 'case by case' basis. The London Club seeks a close fit between the economic situation of the debtor country and the terms of the rescheduling or refinancing agreement.[17] Thirdly, the London Club requires the debtor government to adopt an IMF high-conditionality programme, which demonstrates a commitment to sound macroeconomic policies and provides a reasonable chance that debt service will resume on a regular basis. Burden-sharing is not as problematic as in the case of the Paris Club negotiations, because commercial bank loans are based on the LIBOR (London InterBank Offer Rate) plus some risk premium. There is little agreement, however, on the extent to which preceding Paris Club agreements establish the terms of a London Club negotiation. Despite the Paris Club requirement that commercial creditors should not receive more favourable terms in a debt rescheduling agreement, it appears that official creditors do 'subsidise' the commercial creditors by offering lower interest rates as well as longer grace periods and repayment schedules.

The terms of a London Club negotiation vary from debtor to debtor, the more so with the introduction of the debt and debt service reduction (DDSR) agreements which offer commercial banks a menu of debt reduction instruments in combination with IMF and World Bank financing. Every London Club agreement imposes a number of common conditions on debtors: it provides for the economic working party representing the banks to monitor debtor conformity with the IMF programme; it requires equal treatment for all creditors; it provides for the suspension of the agreement in 'exceptional' circumstances; and it may explicitly link future debt negotiations with the performance of the debtor with the IMF programme.[18]

London Club terms evolved in tandem with the changes that took place in the Paris Club, both of which were driven by the deliberations of the G-7 in response to the severity of the debt crisis throughout the 1980s. The innovations within the Paris and London Clubs were usually mooted by an American Treasury Secretary, most prominently Secretaries James Baker and Nicholas Brady. The first innovation in the treatment of commercial bank debt was in 1985 with the introduction of multi-year refinancing agreements which extended the consolidation period beyond the usual twelve to twenty-four months. The Baker plan, which sought to increase the commercial bank financing of highly indebted nations, failed because commercial banks were unwilling to lend additional sums of money to bad credit risks. The proposals of Secretary Brady fundamentally changed the basis of the relationship between commercial banks and sovereign debtors: it proposed that commercial banks should either agree to debt forgiveness or supply new money to resolve the debt crisis. The Brady plan sought to reduce the debt overhang facing highly indebted middle income countries by 20–5 per cent as well as to reduce their debt service by 30 per cent.

The Brady plan imposed obligations upon the debtor nations and provided incentives for the commercial banks. The key proposals of the Brady plan included a commitment on the part of the debtor nations to adopt 'sound economic policies' that would increase the attractiveness of the domestic economy to foreign investors and reverse capital flight; the provision of timely support by the IMF and World Bank for the economic policies of the debtor nations, including a commitment to finance debt and debt service reduction transactions; and a commitment by commercial banks to provide support via debt and debt reduction agreements and new lending. The IMF agreed to set aside 25 per cent of a stand-by arrangement for the reduction of debt stocks; and up to 30 per cent of quota would be provided for interest support in connection with a DDSR agreement. These funds were conditional: the debtor country had to have a Fund-supported adjustment programme on track and the debt reduction operations were to be 'market-based and involve substantial discounts'.[19] In addition to the IMF funds made available to support DDSR transactions, the World Bank pledged that it would lend 25 per cent of its structural adjustment loans for debt reduction and a further 15 per cent for debt service reduction.[20]

The Brady plan expected commercial banks, for their part, to agree upon a uniform level of debt reduction on a present value basis or the provision of new funds to finance debt reduction. The route to achieving this general objective was left relatively open: the Brady plan acknowledged that diverging commercial bank interests, which reflected different levels of country exposure, different tax and provisioning laws and different bank supervision requirements, would make a uniform debt reduction agreement all but impossible. The Brady plan introduced the notion of a menu of debt-reduction instruments that would correspond to individual commercial bank interests, enabling a debtor country to enjoy a comprehensive debt and debt service reduction agreement.[21] The Brady plan provided both liquidity relief and debt reduction.

The IMF has been a key supporting actor in the global debt regime. The IMF plays a key role in the lead-up to either a Paris or a London Club negotiation. Prior to the initiation of debt negotiation in either club, the IMF is responsible for providing critical macroeconomic and debt information to the creditors as well as assessing the amount of financing necessary for the projected debt relief. The IMF also plays the important role of providing the "seal of approval" necessary to assure official and commercial creditors that debt relief will yield the desired outcome: the resumption and continuation of debt service into the future.[22] Creditors assume that the acceptance of an IMF programme of economic adjustment is the best guarantor of that outcome, despite the poor track record of most countries seeking debt relief.

IMF stand-by arrangements include a detailed adjustment programme that outlines a set of macroeconomic policy targets as well as 'policy understandings' over the medium term. Moreover, negotiations between the IMF and the debtor nation allow the IMF to advise creditors on the economic prospects of the debtor nation and to judge the debtor nation's commitment to adjustment and consequent ability to service debt – key elements of the *ad referendum* framework agreement produced by a Paris Club negotiation as well as a London Club agreement. Yet the IMF will release funds only to nations engaged in a debt relief negotiation which have attained satisfactory 'financing assurances', i.e. creditor assurances that the financing gap between debt service needs and IMF funds will be met by new creditor financing. The conditionality of an IMF programme and the complementary financing assurances contribute to the re-establishment of a debtor nation's creditworthiness and allow the IMF to claim that it functions as a mechanism for mobilising new funds for debtor nations on the international credit market.

The IMF debt strategy in the 1990s has been designed to achieve three objectives with regard to the debtor nation: to re-establish external balance; to assure access to voluntary commercial and official capital flows; and to re-establish a satisfactory level of economic growth consistent with the (presumed) need for structural adjustment. The IMF facilitates the realisation of these broad objectives by ensuring the implementation of a growth-orientated adjustment programme that also initiates a programme of structural reform, by securing access to official, multilateral and private sources of financing, and by maintaining a favourable external economic environment.[23] The new debt strategy, concretised by the implementation of DDSR agreements with commercial and official creditors, has also altered the IMF's time frame. Whereas the IMF viewed the imminent default of official loans and interest arrears to commercial creditors as a short-term problem requiring an equally short-term solution, a high level of indebtedness is now viewed not only as a structural problem but as a problem of sovereign solvency in need of a medium-term cure. One consequence of this recognition has been the implementation of medium-term adjustment programmes that last for three or four years rather than the once favoured twelve- to eighteen-month programmes. Another change has been the move away from charging market rates of interest for Fund credit and the willingness to engage in concessional lending to the poorest and most highly indebted nations.

There are several Fund facilities from which a member state can borrow in support of a debt relief agreement. The most common source of finance, a stand-by arrangement, is a drawing on the IMF by the debtor in excess of its reserve and first credit tranche in the Fund.[24] The hallmark of a stand-by agreement is the high level of conditionality attached to the loan: the IMF commits the debtor government to adopt a set of macroeconomic policies and meet a set of performance criteria that range from instituting an 'adequate public expenditure management system' to effecting when necessary a real devaluation of the exchange rate or adopting monetary policies that support domestic investment and external balance. Conformity with the performance criteria and policy targets is assured – at least in theory – by the phased disbursement of Fund credit, which is conditional upon the success of the borrowing member in meeting the terms of the stand-by arrangement.

Debtor states can also draw on the extended Fund facility (EFF), which was established in response to the oil price rise in 1974; and the enhanced structural adjustment facility (ESAF), which is available only to a few of the CEE states – notably Albania – and the states along the southern periphery of the Russian Federation. When a state draws on the EFF, it must present the Fund with a programme outlining the objectives and policies it will pursue to re-establish external equilibrium and to update that programme annually over a three- to four-year period. The EEF enables a Fund member in balance of payments difficulties, or seeking to placate its creditors in a debt negotiation, to draw 68 per cent of quota on an annual basis and 300 per cent of quota on a cumulative basis.[25] The ESAF, a concessional lending facility, supports macroeconomic adjustment and structural reform in low-income states. Drawings on this facility are accompanied by a medium-term policy framework paper developed and updated on an annual basis in a three-way consultation between the IMF, the World Bank and the member state. Drawings on the ESAF can reach 255 per cent of quota, disbursed over a three- or four-year period.[26]

The three sources of IMF finance that support debt reschedulings within either the Paris or the London Club – the stand-by agreements, the ESAF and the EFF – carry varying levels of conditionality. There are two generic categories of conditions: performance criteria and policy understandings. Policy understandings are a set of timetabled policy actions agreed to by the debtor nation. Performance criteria are the specific macroeconomic targets to which the debtor nation is committed in exchange for access to Fund resources. If a state fails to meet the macroeconomic targets or fails to implement the policy understanding, the Fund can either suspend disbursements of Fund credit or waive the criteria. Stand-by arrangements and ESAF drawings have quite explicit macroeconomic targets and commitments to structural reform. Generally, stand-by arrangements with the former Soviet and CEE states have specified a broad set of policy elements addressing price liberalisation, tight financial policies, a reduction of central government budget deficits, a 'reasonably' independent central bank, the liberalisation of trade and payments, and progress towards currency convertibility.[27]

Although the Paris and London Clubs both require that a high-conditionality IMF stand-by loan is in place prior to the initiation of negotiations with a debtor nation, it is also the case that the IMF exercises some leverage over commercial creditors. The IMF, particularly in the case of London Club negotiations, had a long-standing policy of requiring debtor states to reach agreement with commercial creditors before drawing on Fund resources to finance the debt restructuring. The IMF insisted that funds would be disbursed only if satisfactory financing assurances were reached. Without those financing assurances, the IMF was unwilling either to provide additional funds or to undertake the role of surveillance, both of which would threaten near certain default and potentially repudiation. The objective of the financing assurance was threefold: to ensure that the adjustment programme was adequately financed; to assure that the level of financing was consistent with a return to balance of payments equilibrium and an ability to repay the Fund; and to restore orderly relations between the creditors (official and private) and the debtor state.

The IMF increased its leverage when it undertook to change its policy on financing assurances in the early 1990s. The Fund will now conclude an arrangement before a financing package is worked out between private creditors and the debtor country if two conditions are met: first, that concluding the arrangement will enhance the prospects of the success of the adjustment programme; and second, that the negotiations between the creditors and debtor promises a viable financing package that will return the debtor to external equilibrium. This change provided that the disbursement of Fund resources would no longer be hostage to commercial bankers holding out for the harshest possible terms on the debt restructuring.[28] Despite the considerable leverage possessed by the IMF over both creditor and debtor countries, the Fund also seeks to avoid playing a direct role in London Club negotiations, a role it does play in Paris Club negotiations. The centrality of the IMF to the successful conclusion of debt negotiations in either the London or the Paris Club is assumed by the principals, although some analysts are less convinced than others.[29]

The World Bank's role in Paris and London Club negotiations remains secondary to that played by the IMF. It plays a prominent role only under one of two circumstances: when it assists the IMF in the drawing up of a policy framework paper in connection with an ESAF arrangement; or when the World Bank grants a structural adjustment loan. Despite the clear demarcation of responsibilities between the World Bank (structural adjustment) and the IMF (macroeconomic policy), there has been increasing collaboration between the two organisations and a blurring of roles. This development is most evident in the drawing up of policy framework papers supporting debt and debt service reduction programmes under the aegis of the ESAF arrangements.[30] The increasing coordination of World Bank and Fund advice has also led to the problem of cross-conditionality. World Bank disbursement of structural adjustment loans has become contingent upon a member-country reaching a stand-by arrangement with the Fund. The structural loan programme of the World Bank, which was designed to disburse funds more quickly to states undergoing a process of structural adjustment, has effectively been made subject to the onerous demands of IMF stabilisation programmes. The IMF and World Bank have demonstrated a steady convergence of policy preferences, and this convergence of policy preferences has led to each institution requiring the same economic conditions to be met before a loan from either institution is sanctioned.[31]

The debt profile of the CEE countries and the Russian Federation

The absolute level of debt in central and eastern Europe and the former Soviet Union is not alarming when taken in the aggregate, especially when compared with the nations of Latin America and the Caribbean. Total debt stocks for eastern Europe and the former Soviet Union totalled $192 billion in 1994, compared with a figure of $437 billion for Latin America and the Caribbean. This relatively modest level of indebtedness obscures, however, a sharp upward trend in its growth rate: debt increased by 62.4 per cent between 1989 and 1994. With the exception of the former Yugoslavia, where the total debt stock has declined by 40.7 per cent, the CEE states and the Russian Federation have increased their total stock of debt – sometimes substantially.[32] The composition of debt as between commercial and official creditors for these nations, however, is similar to the Latin American case. Of the $137.71 billion of long-term debt held by the nations of eastern Europe and the former Soviet Union in 1990, 33.76 per cent ($46.5 billion) was owed to official creditors and 66.24 per cent ($91.22 billion) to private creditors. The mix of official and private debt varies significantly by country: Poland, Romania and the former Yugoslavia are predominantly indebted to official creditors, whereas the remaining states are overwhelming indebted to private creditors (see Table 14). These two different groups of states face different incentives and opportunities in managing their indebtedness. States carrying a large proportion of commercial debt are less likely to default: a loss of creditworthiness would preclude access to international capital markets and would raise the cost of future borrowing. Those states carrying a large proportion of official debt, on the other hand, are less constrained and have greater leverage with their creditors. Loans made for political purposes can be similarly forgiven for political purposes since the cost of debt default or restructuring is shifted more easily on to creditor-state taxpayers: taxpayers are less likely to be concerned with the financial ramifications of debt forgiveness than are commercial bank stockholders.[33] The importance of the transition to the market economy and the causal connection made by Western elites between the success of that transition and the stability of the European state system as well as the survival of the democratisation process abetted Polish efforts, for example, to reduce the country's official and commercial debt substantially.

Table 14 Long-term debt, by creditor, 1990

Debtor	Official ($ billion)	Commerical ($ billion)	Official (%)	Commercial (%)
Bulgaria	0.664	8.900	6.90	93.10
Czech Republic	0.370	5.129	6.75	93.25
Hungary	2.715	15.285	15.08	84.92
Poland	27.744	11.541	70.62	29.38
Romania	0.190	0.340	35.85	64.15
Russian Federation	6.197	41.504	12.99	87.01
Former Yugoslavia	7.539	9.307	44.75	55.24
Total	45.414	92.006	33.05	66.95

Source: World Bank.

More important than the absolute level or composition of debt, however, is the ability of a state to service it. On that measure the CEE states and the Russian Federation threatened neither the stability of the international financial system nor a general debt repudiation. The World Bank has employed four indebtedness ratios to determine the severity of a state's overall indebtedness: debt-to-GNP (EDT/GNP), debt-to-exports (EDT/XGS), debt service payments (interest and principal)-to-exports (TDS/XGS) and interest payments-to-exports (INT/XGS). A state is considered highly indebted if three of the four ratios exceed the critical values of 165 per cent for EDT/XGS, 30 per cent for EDT/GNP, 18 per cent for TDS/XGS and 12 per cent for INT/XGS. It is clear that, on a regional basis, central and eastern Europe and the former Soviet Union do not have a particularly severe level of indebtedness, particularly compared with Africa and Latin America (see Table 15). It is also the case, however,

Table 15 Regional debt ratios, 1992 (%)

Ratio	All developing countries	Africa	Latin America	Eastern Europe and Russian Federation
EDT/XGS	166.7	239.2	258.4	130.62
EDT/GNP	37.7	71.8	41.8	22.42
TDS/XGS	17.6	15.8	27.9	8.9
INT/XGS	7.4	7.6	12.0	3.6

Source: World Bank.

that a casual examination of Table 16 reveals an unfavourable trend for two measures of indebtedness, the debt-to-exports and debt-to-GNP ratios. Yet the deterioration in these two debt ratios for the CEE states and the Russian Federation is not surprising, given the collapse of output and the trade after 1989. On a national basis, only a few of the CEE states – Bulgaria, Poland and Albania – and the Russian Federation may be considered seriously indebted. The Russian Federation, while not exceeding the critical values for three of the four indebtedness ratios, exceeded the critical values for the debt-to-export (176.8 per cent) and debt service-to-export ratios (68.5 per cent) in 1990 and bumped up against the interest payments-to-exports ratio (10.5 per cent). The other CEE states are considered to be moderately to less indebted; and the NIS states are classified as less indebted.[34] Bulgaria, Poland and the Russian Federation had significant arrears in the early 1990s and each state has subsequently negotiated debt reduction agreements within the Paris and London Club frameworks between 1991 and 1995.[35]

Table 16 Debt indicators for eastern Europe and the Russian Federation, 1989–93 (%)

Ratio	1989	1990	1991	1992	1993
EDT/XGS	93.0	106.5	157.0	161.5	173.0
EDT/GNP	18.3	19.2	22.5	24.9	28.0
TDS/XGS	14.4	15.5	20.7	11.0	11.2
INT/XGS	5.2	5.5	7.3	4.5	5.2

Source: World Bank.

Rudiger Dornbusch has identified four factors capable of triggering a debt crisis: an increase in real interest rates facing debtors, which increases the debt service requirements of the existing stock of debt; a deterioration of the current account that reflects either a worsening of the terms of trade, poor macroeconomic performance or dampened demand for exports; an increase in world inflation that increases nominal interest rates and consequently creates difficulties in servicing debt; and a fear of overexposure that leads creditors to resist the refinancing of existing debt.[36] The indebted CEE states and the former Soviet Union have faced a difficult and hostile world macroeconomy. Although there was no significant increase in world inflation between 1989 and 1992, real interest rates peaked in Germany in 1992, although there was a decline in American interest rates over the same period. For many of the CEE states as well as the Russian Federation Germany was an important creditor, and the appropriate benchmark interest rates in the early 1990s were those on Deutschmark-denominated debt.[37]

There was also a collapse in output in these nations as they grappled with the twin challenges of making the transition to the market economy and coping with the collapse of the CMEA trading system. Bulgaria, Romania and the Russian Federation all experienced a severe contraction in the growth of trade between 1989 and 1992; only Hungary experienced significant positive growth.[38] This trend also reflected the collapse in output in all the economies in transition.[39] The downturn in the eastern portion of the European economy was reinforced by anaemic GDP growth as well as low and declining levels of domestic demand in the industrialised countries, particularly in the EU.[40] The terms of trade of these nations have significantly worsened, a trend driven in large part by the collapse of trade between the CMEA countries, the loss of subsidised raw materials, particularly oil imported from the Russian Federation, and the progressive real devaluations of national currencies.[41] Finally, commercial banks reduced their exposure to the region, despite its manifest financing needs: the level of commercial financing fell from $58.523 billion in 1989 to $47.344 billion in 1992, a 20.98 per cent decline.[42] It is clear that in 1989 the medium-term outlook for the seriously indebted CEE nations was not favourable. Real interest rates were rising and growth rates remained below the

OECD benchmark of 3 per cent, the rate of growth considered necessary for autonomous resolution of the debt crisis. These unfavourable macroeconomic variables were complemented by a limited ability to earn hard currency owing to some significant restrictions on CEE and Russian exports, particularly in the agricultural sector.[43] Taken together, it came as no surprise that some of the former member states of CMEA should either default or declare debt moratoria, as occurred in the cases of Bulgaria, Poland and the Russian Federation.

Three tests of the debt regime: Bulgaria, Poland and Russia

Bulgaria, Poland and the Russian Federation are three countries that have undertaken successful Paris and London Club negotiations since 1989. Bulgaria and Poland are interesting cases, owing to the distribution of their total long-term debt between commercial and official creditors. Over 90 per cent of Bulgarian debt was owed to commercial creditors, just as over 70 per cent of Polish debt was owed to official creditors. The terms of the negotiations reflected not only the privileged position of Poland in the geopolitical calculations of Western creditors, particularly the United States and Germany, but the ability of creditor states to offer more generous terms than commercial banks. The Russian Federation is an interesting case owing to the centrality of Russian participation in the future European security order, the high level of Russian indebtedness to commercial banks and official creditors, and the burden on the Russian Federation owing to its willingness to assume Soviet debt, a decision that left the other successor states to the Soviet Union relatively debt free.

Bulgaria
Bulgaria's importance in post-Cold War Europe derives in part from its geographical location along the border of the former Yugoslavia and a general fear that an unsuccessful transition to the market economy and democracy in Bulgaria could provide fertile ground for the extension of that country's civil war into Europe. By the end of the first quarter of 1990 Bulgaria had experienced a solvency crisis driven by a 26 per cent decline in the level of trade with hard-currency countries, the inability of Iraq to service its $1.2 billion debt to Bulgaria, and the maturity of $3.4 billion of medium and long-term debt without any chance of new credits or the roll-over of maturities by Western commercial banks. As a consequence, the Bulgarian Foreign Trade Bank declared a moratorium on principal payments in March 1990 and a moratorium on interest payments later in June. The declared moratorium on interest and principal payments not only denied Bulgaria access to commercial finance until 1994, it led commercial banks to reconsider their exposure in central and eastern Europe as a whole.

Commercial banks granted Bulgaria a postponement of scheduled payments contingent upon an IMF stand-by credit. A twelve-month stand-by credit with the IMF did not materialise until 15 March 1991. The Bulgarian government sought IMF financing worth $634 million in the autumn of 1990. The stand-by agreement announced in March 1991 provided a less generous financial package of $480.5 million, of which $399.1 million was part of a stand-by package and $81.4 million was contingency financing. The provision of this stand-by credit paved the way for a Paris Club agreement on 17 April 1991. At that time, $554 million of Bulgaria's external debt to official creditors was consolidated, including arrears, on standard Paris Club terms, although the grace period was 6.6 years rather than the normal five years.[44] Bulgaria met the performance criteria contained in the first stand-by agreement and in April 1992 successfully concluded yet another stand-by deal which laid the foundations of a second Paris Club agreement and negotiations for a DDSR agreement with the London Club. The 20 April 1992 stand-by agreement was designed to support the 1992 financial and economic programme of the Bulgarian government. The second stand-by agreement obligated the Bulgarian government to reduce monthly inflation by 2 per cent by the end of 1992, to conduct monetary policies consistent with the inflation target, to contain the deterioration of output to 4 per cent per annum, to liberalise prices further, and to restrain the expansion of bank credit to 3 per cent of GDP.[45] As it turned out, the Bulgarian performance did not meet all the performance criteria established by the Fund: inflation dropped only to 5 per cent a month (80 per cent in 1992), the contraction of output was 14.5 per cent of GDP and the budgetary deficit was 6.9 per cent of GDP.[46]

The April 1992 stand-by credit had raised hopes that a three-year programme could be established with the IMF before the expiry of the second stand-by agreement in March 1993. That hoped was dashed in November 1992 when a coalition formed by the former communist party and the party representing Bulgaria's Turkish minority successfully brought down the government of Filip Dimitrov in a vote of no confidence. The ensuing political crisis put the talks with the IMF on hold and led to the cancellation of the November meeting with the London Club. Prior to the political crisis of November, however, Bulgaria announced its intention of resuming debt service payments of $10 million per month beginning in September – an amount equal to approximately a quarter of its interest arrears – in the hope of repairing relations with its creditors.[47] Despite the November political crisis, a further $256 million of debt service payments due in April 1993 were rescheduled.

The London Club negotiations were deadlocked after the postponement of debt service in late 1992: the commercial banks initially offered a 38 per cent reduction in external debt while Bulgaria demanded a 70 per cent buy-back of existing debt at $0.10 on the dollar with the remaining debt exchanged for bonds. The Bulgarian counter-proposal was that the bonds should be either thirty-year collateralised par bonds with a twelve-month rolling interest guarantee or discount bonds at $0.20 on the dollar. The eventual London Club agreement finalised in July 1994 rescheduled $6.2 billion of principal and $1.9 billion of interest arrears.[48] It reduced Bulgaria's commercial debt by 50 per cent. But the finalisation of the agreement was contingent upon another stand-by arrangement with the IMF and sufficient financing to enable Bulgaria to make the initial projected payment of $715 million at the signing of the agreement – a figure in excess of Bulgaria's hard-currency reserves of $600 million.

In May 1994 Bulgaria and the IMF reached agreement on new credits worth $259 million. The credit was composed of a twelve-month $97 million stand-by credit and $162 million as the first drawing of a systemic transformation facility (STF) credit. A second disbursement of $162 million was contingent upon progress towards meeting the objectives of the financial and economic programme. In addition to supporting Bulgaria's 1994 economic and financial programme, the STF credit was to facilitate a DDSR agreement with the London Club. These IMF credits, in conjunction with G-24/EU grants of $325 million, enabled Bulgaria to make the initial $715 million payment to London Club creditors without depleting its hard-currency reserves. In early September 1994 the IMF augmented the amount of credit available to Bulgaria under the April 1994 stand-by arrangement by $102 million to replenish international reserves in connection with the London Club agreement.[49]

Poland

Poland introduced a radical stabilisation programme in early 1990 as a part of an IMF stand-by agreement. This agreement, which was designed to support the restructuring of the Polish economy, also facilitated the first rescheduling of Polish external debt with official creditors in the 1990s and provided a $300 million structural adjustment loan from the World Bank.[50] The Paris Club agreement, which postponed $6 billion of interest and principal due from the beginning of 1990 to March 1991, was preceded by the June 1989 London Club agreement to defer until 1991 the principal due between May 1989 and December 1990. Poland failed to service fully its debt for 1990, paying only $460 million in interest payments out of a total $3.9 billion due.[51] The default was married to the suspension of the IMF stand-by agreement reached in February 1990 – the Polish government had failed to meet the performance criteria established by the IMF.[52]

The renewed efforts in 1991 to negotiate a solution to the Polish debt crisis was complicated by the absence of an IMF-sanctioned economic and financial programme for the medium term and by the gap between contrary expectations over the amount of debt forgiveness Poland would enjoy. The Polish government had sought an 80 per cent reduction in the level of external debt, a position looked upon favourably by the United States and rejected by other members of the G-7.[53] The G-7 reached a consensus in early 1991 that Poland could be offered the Toronto terms reserved for the poorest African nations, namely a one-third reduction level of debt. A Paris Club accord was conditioned upon a new stand-by arrangement with the IMF. In February 1991,

Poland and the IMF signed a draft accord that provided a $2.487 billion financing package that included a three-year EFF arrangement ($1.665 billion). The IMF accepted the Polish request that 25 per cent of the EFF credit should be set aside for a debt reduction operation within the context of the expected Paris Club accord. The performance targets of the stand-by agreement included: a reduction in the level of inflation from 250 per cent in 1990 to 36 per cent in 1991 to single-digit inflation in 1993; a fiscal deficit of no more than 0.6 per cent of GDP in 1991; the liberalisation of prices, of the exchange system and of capital controls; and a series of initiatives supporting the transformation of the economic system.[54]

In March 1991 the Paris Club and Poland reached a far-reaching and extraordinary agreement: the official creditors of the Paris Club granted Poland a 50 per cent reduction in its external debt in net present value terms. The reduction was scheduled to take place in two stages, the second stage conditional upon the satisfactory performance of the three-year economic programme for 1991–93. The agreement promised a 30 per cent reduction for 1991–94. The Paris Club agreement consolidated $30.5 billion of Polish official debt. Polish interest payments were reduced by 46.67 per cent in present value terms and the interest accruing between 1991 and 1994 was reduced by 80 per cent. The second stage reduction of principal was conditional upon the performance criteria of the three-year EFF arrangement being met. Poland enjoyed a six-year grace period on principal repayments and a twelve-maturity ending in 2009. The agreement also provided for voluntary debt swaps between Poland and its creditors up to the higher of 10 per cent of the remaining debt or $20 million.[55] The agreement had a salutary affect on Polish debt service obligations: the ratio of principal and interest payments to exports of goods and services dropped from 56 per cent in 1989 to 9 per cent in 1992; the ratio of total outstanding debt to the export of goods and services fell from 457 per cent to 301 per cent. The agreement also bound Poland to seek comparable treatment from its commercial creditors in any London Club negotiation – a clause preventing agreement until July 1994.

The three-year EFF arrangement was suspended in 1992, the budget performance target not having been met for 1991. The Polish government eventually negotiated a new $655 million stand-by agreement at the end of 1992. It achieved three objectives. First, it restored the opportunity to take advantage of the second stage reduction of the Paris Club agreement. Second, the new stand-by agreement was required to restart the long-suspended London Club negotiations that would dispose of Poland's $13.3billion commercial debt. And third, it released $750 million in World Bank structural adjustment loans.[56] The stand-by agreement established new and less disciplined performance targets, provided for a 25 per cent set-aside of the new credit for debt reduction operations, and held open the possibility of an augmentation of the credit to finance a debt reduction agreement with the London Club of commercial bank creditors.[57] In February 1994 the IMF approved the Polish budget for 1994–95, certified Poland as having met the terms of the 1993 stand-by agreement, and paved the way for the second stage reduction in Poland's official debt.

Poland faced a double bind in its negotiations with the London Club. First, Poland had to seek agreement with the commercial bank creditors on comparable terms with the Paris Club creditors or risk invalidating the conditions of its debt reduction agreement. Second, Poland was constrained by the amount of debt service it could undertake if it were to remain within the budgetary performance target of the March 1993 stand-by and not jeopardise the additional 20 per cent reduction in its official debt in 1994. The negotiations between Poland and its commercial bank creditors were broken off in June 1991 when the commercial banks demanded repayment of 25 per cent of the interest due, about $2.6 billion, as a condition of further talks. Poland refused and negotiations remained in abeyance until June 1993. The London Club negotiations also floundered on the terms the 360 creditor banks were willing to offer and the terms that Poland demanded. The banks offered Poland the standard 35 per cent reduction normally associated with a Brady-type DDSR agreement, a reduction that was partially driven by a fear of setting a precedent with Poland that would inevitably be carried over into the ongoing negotiations with Bulgaria and the Russian Federation.[58]

When the London Club commercial bank creditors met the Polish government in June 1993 the commercial banks offered Poland an 8 per cent effective reduction in the level of debt. The offer was quickly refused, since acceptance would have violated the terms of both the Paris Club agreement and the IMF stabilisation programme.[59] The German commercial banks, Poland's largest creditors, were unwilling to make any significant improvements on their offer to the Polish government. Poland also faced a bind in so far as 60 per cent of Polish debt was denominated in Deutschmarks. Consequently, tight monetary conditions in Germany meant that little relief was forthcoming from the decline in interest rates on dollar-denominated assets. As a consequence, neither the commercial banks nor the Polish government had much of an incentive to strike a quick bargain, particularly as Poland faced a potential debt service burden of over $8 billion in 2007 and Polish debt was selling on the secondary market at around 27 per cent of face value.[60]

The gap between what Poland would accept and what the commercial banks would offer was eventually narrowed and a London Club agreement was signed in March 1994. It reduced the present value of Polish debt by 42.5 per cent and provided for a thirty-year repayment schedule that allowed Poland to service its debt out of export earnings rather than central government budgetary expenditure. Approximately 26 per cent of Polish debt was subject to a Polish buy-back at $0.41 on the dollar, 55 per cent of Polish debt was discounted by 45 per cent, and the remaining debt was either restructured as par bonds (no debt forgiveness, but a sub-market interest rate) or as interest arrears bonds.[61] The buy-back of Polish commercial debt was financed by a $791 million stand-by credit from the IMF, Polish reserves and World Bank loans of $500 million.

The IMF augmented the August stand-by credit in October with an additional $221 million. This credit was granted for the sole purpose of enabling the Polish government to set aside $202 million to finance the DDSR operation with the commercial banks. The agreement allowed Poland to lower its debt service obligations by $300 million on an annual basis for the remainder of the 1990s; it also provided the basis of Poland's return to international capital markets in June 1995, when it received an investment grade rating from Moody's.[62] These Paris Club and London Club DDSR agreements eased Poland's transition to the market economy in two ways: by removing the stigma attached to default, so that Poland regained access to global credit markets and an investment grade credit rating which has lowered the cost of capital for the Polish economy; and by reducing Poland's stock of debt and debt service obligations, so that more capital is available for financing the transition to the market economy.

The Russian Federation
The transformation of the Soviet Union from a highly creditworthy borrower in 1985 to a potential candidate for debt default by 1991 can be traced to the conflation of three developments that have reduced the hard currency available to service the debt: the contraction of the Soviet economy, the unwillingness of Western commercial banks to roll credits over and the effort to reduce their exposure, and falling oil production that contributed to a sharp deterioration in the current account.[63] One consequence of *perestroika*, the loss of central control over the management of debt, had helped cause Soviet debt to balloon from $29 billion in 1985 to $59.4 billion in 1990 and the debt service to hard-currency exports ratio to increase from 20 per cent in 1985 to 68.5 per cent in 1990.

The uncertainty over Soviet debt was compounded by the unsuccessful August 1991 *coup* and the internal debate over the assignment of Soviet debt among the successor states to the Soviet Union. The failed August *coup* left commercial bankers more unwilling than they had previously been to extend new credits. In 1991, it was estimated, between 1989 and 1991 commercial banks reduced their exposure to the Soviet Union by $19.7 billion (from $37.2 billion to $17.5 billion). That decline in commercial lending was compensated for by Western governments, whose exposure rose to $30.4 billion from $12.2 billion over the same period.[64] The confluence of political crisis triggered by the August *coup*, the uncertain reordering of relations between the republics of the former Soviet Union and the collapse of trade and production in the former Soviet Union created a widespread expectation of default and the inevitable need to restructure Soviet debt.

The G-7, negotiating on behalf of the Paris Club, and the former Soviet republics reached agreement in October 1991 on the disposition and allocation of the existing debt of the former Soviet Union among the successor republics. The memorandum of understanding[65] between the G-7 and the successor states to the Soviet Union provided that the successor republics would be 'jointly and severally responsible' for former Soviet Union debt, a provision designed to protect Western creditors against the likely default of the smaller and poorer republics. The memorandum paved the way for an agreement on Soviet official debt in November 1991.[66] The November agreement deferred payments on principal from December 1991 to December 1992, extended short-term loans and guarantees to banks and suppliers by G-7 governments, and provided a $1 billion bridging loan from the BIS via a gold swap.[67] The deferral was conditional upon 'satisfactory progress' towards a macroeconomic stabilisation programme in consultation with the IMF and the punctual servicing of non-deferred debt service due. The G-7 also pledged its support in aiding the Soviet Union to gain comparable treatment for the $140 billion of former Soviet Union claims on the developing world – claims that have not yet been successfully pressed by the Russian Federation or received much support from the G-7.[68]

The memorandum did not allocate Soviet debt or assets among the successor states of the Soviet Union. An initial agreement was reached by the majority of the successor republics in December 1991 with the signing of the Treaty on the Assignment of Foreign Debt and Assets of the USSR. The treaty fixed each republic's share of debt-service obligations: it allocated 61.3 per cent of Soviet debt to the Russian Federation, 16.4 per cent to Ukraine and less than 4 per cent to each of the other ten successor republics. The debt-to-exports ratio of all the successor states except the Russian Federation, Ukraine and Belarus indicated inability to service that debt.[69] The background to the drawn-out Paris and London Club negotiations with the Russian Federation was shaped by the difficult intra-republic negotiations between Ukraine and Russia throughout 1992 and early 1993, and by the deteriorating political and economic conditions in the Russian Federation itself.

Ukraine signed the memorandum only in March 1992 after significant pressure from the G-7, the German government's explicit threat in February 1992 to block the IMF membership of any successor state not signing the memorandum, and the EU decision to freeze the $150 million line of credit extended to Ukraine. But in July 1992, the Russian Federation initiated negotiations with the other successor republics on two options for managing the external debt and liabilities of the former Soviet Union over the long term: the 'zero option', which provided that the Russian Federation would assume each republic's share of assets and liabilities of the former Soviet Union, and an interim protocol that authorised the Russian Federation to manage each republic's share of external liabilities and assets until a final agreement could be negotiated. The Russian Federation signed 'zero option' agreements with Armenia, Azerbaijan, Belarus, Kazakhstan, the Kyrgyz Republic, Moldova, Tajikistan, Turkmenistan and Uzbekistan.[70] Ukraine rejected the 'zero option' in October, but endorsed Russia's sole right to negotiate with Western creditors and to represent Ukraine in Paris Club negotiations. This so-called November protocol was renounced by Ukraine in January 1993. The Russian government consequently called off its scheduled January talks with the Paris Club, which in turn forestalled the beginning of London Club negotiations.[71] The secretary-general of the Paris Club, Jean-Claude Trichet, intervened in March and Ukraine provisionally agreed to the 'zero option'. In exchange for Ukrainian cooperation the Paris Club agreed to postpone any debt service due from Ukraine pending a final agreement between Ukraine and the Russian Federation on the external debt and assets of the former Soviet Union.[72]

The political difficulties and uncertainties created by the dispute between the Russian Federation and Ukraine only reinforced an already intolerable economic situation. The macroeconomic condition steadily worsened: inflation rose from 97.2 per cent in 1991 to 1,354 per cent in 1992; interest rates remained grossly negative; the net material product contracted by 11 per cent in 1991 and by 20 per cent in 1992; credit expanded at a rate of 127 per cent in 1991 and of 803 per cent in 1992; the value of the rouble began its precipitous and sustained decline against the dollar; and Russian currency reserves dropped by almost 40 per cent, from $14.7 billion to $8.87 billion. These pressures were worsened by a large-scale capital flight of approximately $15 billion to $19 billion in 1991 and 1992 – a figure equal to the debt service requirement of $15.6 billion for 1992.[73]

The Russian Federation presented the IMF with a shadow programme for economic reform in early March 1992. The programme and Russian membership of the IMF were approved on 30 March 1992. Both developments paved the way for a multilateral aid programme designed to relieve the $18 billion financing gap projected by the IMF and to reach a comprehensive rescheduling of Russian debt. The IMF approved a stand-by credit of $1.04 billion in August 1992, which was supplemented by a World Bank loan of $600 million to finance hard-currency imports. The primary performance indicators of the stand-by agreement were the containment of inflation to 10 per cent a month for the remainder of 1992; the reduction of the budget deficit for the second half of 1992 to 5 per cent of GDP; a limit on the growth of new central bank credit to Rb 700 billion; and the implementation of an interest rate policy that would produce positive interest rates and support the external value of the rouble.[74]

The August stand-by agreement, which was a part of an earlier agreement reached in June, included an unorthodox debt rescheduling provision: the rescheduling of debt was in place before a letter of intent was signed with the IMF. Yet the conditionality requirement was preserved: the debt deal was to be revoked if the Russian government failed to sign a letter of intent with the IMF before the autumn.[75] At the Munich economic summit, the G-7 governments mooted a rescheduling over ten years of both principal and interest payments falling due in the autumn of 1992 with a three- to five-year grace period. But the G-7 offer was contingent upon the ability of the Russian Federation to meet the performance targets of the IMF stand-by agreement, the successful completion of debt rescheduling negotiations within the Paris Club, and the ability to strike a similar deal with the commercial bankers in the London Club – the Russian government eventually fell short on all three.

Paris Club negotiations were complicated by three sets of factors. First, the Russian government was unable to service debt not deferred in late 1991 and early 1992 and it budgeted only $2 billion for projected debt service obligations of $10 billion. Second, the financial disabilities of the Russian government were compounded by conflicts of interest between the major creditors in the Paris Club. The United States and the United Kingdom favoured a liberal treatment of Russian debt. The United States, which had a minimal exposure to Russia, favoured granting the Russians some degree of debt forgiveness. The German government, on the other hand, with the largest exposure to the Russia, preferred to strike a Paris Club agreement on standard terms.[76] German intransigence was also driven by a knot of financial claims and counter-claims between Germany and Russia flowing from the forty-year Russian stay in eastern Germany. The claims were settled at the end of 1992 only after both sides had agreed that their mutual financial claims cancelled one another out, and after the German government had consented to make an additional payment of DM 550 million ($343.9 million) to relocate Russian soldiers withdrawing from Germany, to defer until the year 2000 payments on the outstanding Russian transferable rouble debt of $11.2 billion, and not to block a Paris Club agreement to reschedule $16 billion of Russian debt.[77] And third, the Russian Federation failed to meet the macroeconomic performance targets of the August 1992 stand-by agreement, which carried the potential penalty of nullifying any agreement with either the Paris or the London Club. The difficulty the Russian government faced in managing the transition to the market economy, its poor macroeconomic performance, its inability to service more than a fraction of its official debt obligations and the conflicts of interest between the creditor countries made a Paris Club agreement an essential contribution to the stabilisation of the Russian economy and polity, but nonetheless difficult to reach.

The wrangling among the creditors, however, was overshadowed by the declared inability of the Russian government to make its projected debt service payments of $20 billion in 1993.[78] The intractability of the debt issue was increasingly tied to the problem of alleviating the economic difficulties that compounded the political problems facing President Yeltsin. Prior to the summit between Presidents Boris Yeltsin and Bill Clinton in Vancouver, the Paris Club and the Russian government agreed to consolidate $15 billion of the $20 billion due in 1993. The Paris Club arrangement was made without an IMF stand-by agreement in place, although it stipulated that the agreement would lapse should the Russian government fail to secure a stand-by agreement by October 1993.[79]

The first step towards a second IMF stand-by credit was taken in June 1993 when the IMF extended a $1.506 billion credit to the Russian Federation under the new STF. Credits drawn on the STF lack the strict conditionality attached to stand-by credits, because the facility was designed as a temporary lending window that would ease the transition to the market economy for the CEE nations as well as the former Soviet Union. But the STF came with some strings attached. It committed the Russian government to a number of performance targets: a reduction in the rate of inflation from a monthly rate of 20–5 per cent over the first three months of 1993 to low single digits by the end of the year and a reduction in the budget deficit to 10 per cent of GDP. The overall objective of the IMF programme was the elimination of (hyper)inflationary expectations in Russia and the stabilisation of the rouble.[80]

Despite the progress towards economic stabilisation, the G-7 states were increasingly frustrated with the Russian government in its negotiations over a rescheduling of its official debt: the requisite bilateral agreements between Russia and the individual Paris Club creditor countries to activate the rescheduling agreement were few and far between. Russia remained in arrears to many G-7 countries, including the United States, and was unable to conclude a stand-by credit by the October deadline stipulated in the April agreement. Consequently the April agreement lapsed and the G-7 faced the prospect of negotiating a new rescheduling agreement for the $21 billion Russia owed its creditors in 1994. The difficulty of reaching a Paris Club agreement was made worse with the defeat of the reformist parties in the parliamentary elections.[81]

The G-7 established two conditions that the Russian government had to meet before it would enter into a new round of Paris Club rescheduling negotiations: first, the Russian government was given until April 1994 to secure a second $1.5 billion tranche drawn on the STF and a $4.1 billion stand-by from the IMF; second, there had to be some evidence that inflation and the government budget were stabilised.[82] At the end of March the IMF and Russia concluded the negotiations over the economic and financial plan for 1994 that served as the basis of the second $1.5 billion credit for Russia under the STF. The performance criteria stipulated in the agreement for 1994 included the reduction of the monthly rate of inflation to 7 per cent by the end of year, the contraction of the economy by no more than 10 per cent of GDP, a budget deficit limited to 'around' 7 per cent of GDP, and a monetary policy consistent with the inflation target. The IMF concluded that the second STF credit and progress towards macroeconomic stabilisation – a decline in inflation from 1,353 per cent in 1992 to 896 per cent in 1993 and the reduction of the budget deficit from 18.2 per cent of GDP in 1991 to 8 per cent of GDP in 1993 – laid the basis of a successful application for a new stand-by arrangement. Yet a critical barrier to the success of the Russian stabilisation programme was located in the need for further financing from the international community, particularly debt relief.[83]

Although the debt service due in 1994 was estimated to be almost $21 billion, the Paris Club and the Russian government were able to reschedule only $7 billion of the debt falling due in 1994. This agreement fell far short of alleviating the debt service burden facing the Russian government.[84] Prior to the Naples G-7 summit, the Russians called on the Western nations to fashion a long-term resolution of the debt service difficulties experienced by Russia (and the other states in transition) and again requested G-7 help in collecting some of the $140 billion owed the Soviet Union by its former client states.[85] No debt relief was forthcoming at the Naples summit and the climate for further G-7 aid worsened throughout 1994. The progress made towards the stabilisation of the Russian economy by late summer 1994 – the budget deficit was kept to under 10 per cent of GDP and the monthly inflation rate dropped to 8 per cent by August – was tempered by concern over a rapid expansion of credit in July and August that augured ill for a continuing downward trend in inflation. Moreover, the Russians resisted the IMF demand that inflation should be brought down to a monthly rate of 1 per cent by the end of 1995 as a condition of a stand-by agreement.[86] At the October 1994 annual meeting of the IMF in Madrid a provisional agreement with the Paris Club was reached to reschedule the debt due in 1994. This agreement did not alleviate the tension between the G-7 and Russia over the lack of progress towards the stabilisation of the economy. And that tension was aggravated by the Russian suggestion at the Madrid conference that Russian debt should receive the same treatment as German debt after the Second World War in the 1950s London Agreement; by the appointment of Oleg Davydov, the former trade minister who advocated debt forgiveness by the G-7, as the chief Russian debt negotiator in the Paris and London Club negotiations; and by the divisive internal debate over the desirability and feasibility of the 1995 budget proposed by Prime Minister Viktor Chernomyrdin's government that met the criteria specified by the IMF but lacked support in the Duma. These internal developments and the rebuff by the IMF cast into question not only additional Western financial support but a quick resolution of the debt crisis.[87] By the end of December a monthly inflation rate of 12 per cent had significantly overshot the STF target of 7 per cent and the divisive budget proposed by the Chernomyrdin government exceeded the budgetary ceiling demanded by the IMF.[88]

The Russian government failed to meet the performance criteria outlined in the STF for 1994: the annual inflation rate was 302 per cent; the central government budget deficit was almost 11 per cent of GDP; monetary policy was insufficiently restrictive; and international reserves fell. Despite the poor showing of the Russian economy, the IMF and the Russian government put together yet another stabilisation programme in April 1995 that was supported with a $6.8 billion stand-by credit. The performance criteria of the stand-by placed a heavy burden on the Yeltsin government: it required a rapid decrease in the rate of monthly inflation to 1 per cent; net credit to the central government was limited to 3 per cent of GDP for 1995 and the net credit to banks was reduced to zero; and the central government budget deficit was nearly halved to 6 per cent of GDP. The IMF, in response to the consistent inability of the Russian Federation to meet the performance criteria of either the STF credits or the first stand-by credit, stipulated that the disbursement of the new stand-by credit would be divided into monthly instalments pending progress towards meeting the performance criteria. The IMF stand-by then cleared the way in June 1995 for a rescheduling of $6.4 billion of Russian debt service due in 1994; and the Paris Club agreed in November 1995 to seek a 'global accord' on the outstanding

$130 billion debt owed by Russia to Western creditors.[89]

The Russian government unilaterally applied the November 1991 agreement with the G-7 on commercial debt in early December 1991. The unilateral declaration of a moratorium on payments of principal reflected not only the inability of the Russian government to service the debt but the contractual obligation to seek comparable treatment from its commercial creditors. The short-term solution to the problem of Soviet debt default was to roll over the interest and principal due on a ninety-day basis. This solution persisted until November 1995.[90] The principles guiding the London Club negotiations, which were unilaterally announced to the Russians by the coordinating committee of commercial bankers, formed a barrier to the completion of a London Club agreement. The commercial bankers insisted that the terms of the rescheduling should be 'realistic enough to be accepted by the markets', consistent with the financial abilities of the Russian government and not bound by a comparable treatment clause of a Paris Club agreement.[91]

The difficulties facing the Paris Club creditors in securing a credible stabilisation programme and the dim prospects of the Duma endorsing an economic policy stringent enough to satisfy the IMF also contributed to the lack of progress in rescheduling the $32.5 billion debt owed to the commercial banks in 1995. An agreement with the commercial bankers was also held up until November 1995 owing to the Russian government's unwillingness to accede to the commercial bankers' condition that Russia must surrender sovereign immunity, which would have given the banks the legal right to seize Russian assets in the event of default. Neither side was under particular pressure to strike an agreement: rolling over the debt allowed the Russians not to service it and thereby save scarce foreign exchange; and the commercial bankers, many of whom had taken charges against future earnings in the event of default, assumed that the future financing needs of Russia would work to their advantage in any negotiation. In the end, a compromise was reached: the commercial banks dropped their demand for the Russians to suspend sovereign immunity and accepted that the Vneshekonombank assumed legal liability for the debt; in return, the Russian government issued a statement committing itself to honour its payment obligations. This compromise, a part of the framework agreement initialled at the Madrid IMF conference in October 1994, formed the basis of the November 1995 agreement to reschedule $32.5 billion of commercial debt.[92]

Conclusion

The transitions to the market economy and to democracy in the CEE states and the former Soviet Union are incomplete and imperfect. The transition to the market was impeded by the burden of debt facing some of those nations, particularly Albania, Poland, Hungary, and the Russian Federation. But the primary impediment was the difficulty of the task itself. The transition to the market and democracy requires a recasting of society rather than the simple reconstruction of economies disrupted by war or natural disaster. The discipline of the market and the ambiguities of democratic politics are neither easily exported nor easily absorbed. Moreover, correcting the malformation of those nations' economies requires sustained and vast capital inflows over a decade or more.

The financial resources required over ten years to recast their economies have been estimated in respect of meeting two economic targets: GDP growth of 4–7 per cent over a ten-year period and raising productivity to western European levels. For six CEE countries (Bulgaria, the Czech Republic, Hungary, Poland, Romania and Slovakia), the lowest estimated investment requirement to sustain GDP growth of 4–7 per cent was $75 billion annually; and the lowest estimated investment requirement to achieve western European productivity levels was $180 billion annually. Similar estimates for the former Soviet Union were $106 billion and $1,164 billion on an annual basis, respectively.[93] Total gross capital inflows and G-24 aid delivered only $61.038 billion to the CEE states between 1990 and 1994. This aid amounts to only $12.267 billion on an annual basis, or only 16.35 per cent of the investment requirements for a 4–7 per cent growth rate and 6.82 per cent of the requirement for western European productivity levels (see Table 17).

Table 17 Investment flows and G-24 aid to selected CEE states, 1990–94 ($ million)

Country	Gross investment	Net investment*	G-24 aid†	Total
Czech Republic+	3,217	(2,884)	2,257	5,474
Estonia	811	(362)	673	1,484
Hungary	10,319	(10,524)	10,656	20,975
Poland	-5,483	(-11,618)	27,194	21,711
Romania	2,457	(2,457)	5,787	8,244
Slovakia+	1,094	(-153)	933	2,027
Slovenia	793	(14)	630	1,423
Total	13,208	(4,488)	47,830	61,038

* not included in total column.
† Excludes international financial institutions
+ 1993–94.
Sources: European Commission; International Monetary Fund.

The international financial market is the most important institution of the post-Cold War order. The marketisation, and indirectly the democratisation, process depends upon voluntary financial transfers to support economic growth. Yet the market has failed to deliver. The capital flows into central and eastern Europe have been modest at best (see Table 17). Aggregate gross investment (the sum of investment inflows) in seven CEE states (the Czech Republic, Estonia, Hungary, Poland, Romania, Slovakia and Slovenia) between 1990 and 1994 was only $13.208 billion. On a national basis, Poland experienced disinvestment of $5.483 billion and Hungary enjoyed the favour of the market with a capital inflow of $10.319 billion. These seven countries have received, on average, direct foreign and portfolio investment of only $2.64 billion annually. This sum is equal to only 3.5 per cent of the lowest estimated capital requirements for a growth rate of 4–7 per cent, and 1.46 per cent of the lowest estimated capital requirement to achieve Western productivity levels. The net capital inflow paints a worse picture. Net investment (the balance of investment inflows and outflows) in the same countries between 1990 and 1994 was a meagre $4.488 billion. This represents an annual net inflow of $888 million, which is only 0.87 per cent of the lowest capital requirement for a 4–7 per cent growth rate and only 0.20 per cent of the lowest capital requirement necessary to achieve Western productivity levels.

In comparative perspective, these capital inflows are quite dismal: gross foreign investment in Denmark, Ireland and the Netherlands was $136 billion between 1990 and 1995. Ireland, with a GNP larger than Hungary's but smaller than Poland's, had gross foreign investment of $17 billion, a figure which exceeds the gross foreign investment in the seven CEE countries for which there are reliable statistics. As a share of GNP, however, investment in the CEE states compares favourably with the advanced industrial states of Europe. The GNP share of direct foreign and portfolio investment for the four Visegrad countries ranges from 19.04 per cent in Hungary to 2.35 per cent in Poland, while the corresponding figure for industrialised Europe ranges from 4.64 per cent in France to 9.9 per cent in Germany (see Table 18).[94]

Table 18 Direct foreign and portfolio investment as a share of GNP for selected CEE and industrialised countries, 1993 (%)

Country	GDP share
Czech Republic	10.00
Estonia	9.87
Hungary	19.04
Poland	2.34
Romania	0.09
Slovakia	6.48
Slovenia	1.07
Denmark	7.79
France	4.64
Germany	9.90
Ireland	0.03
Netherlands	6.63
UK	7.94

Sources: International Monetary Fund; authors' own calculations.

At the onset of the democratisation and marketisation process the ERP was the dominant historical parallel employed by Western politicians to generate domestic political support for the anticipated financial transfers necessary to aid the erstwhile apostates of capitalism and liberal democracy. G-24 aid has both fallen short and exceeded the ERP along three measures of comparison. The first point of comparison is the distribution between grants and loans. On a conservative measure, 77.42 per cent of Marshall Aid was in the form of grants, while the remaining 22.58 per cent was split between loans and conditional aid. The distribution between the grant and non-grant components of the ERP is very nearly reversed in the case of G-24 aid to the CEE states: 29.80 per cent of the aid came in the form of a grant, while the remaining 70.20 per cent was non-grant aid. Second, total ERP transfers accounted for a limited share of the 1949 GNP of the major European states: they ranged from a high of 23.1 per cent of Dutch GNP to a low of 5.9 per cent of West German GNP. G-24 aid, on the other hand, has accounted for a much larger share of 1990 CEE states' GNP: it ranges from a high of 55.24 per cent of Polish GNP to a low of 9.86 per cent of Czech GNP (see Tables 19 and 20). And on an unweighted basis G-24 aid to the Visegrad states is equal to 31 per cent of 1990 GNP.

Table 19 ERP aid as a share of 1949 GNP of recipient countries (%)

Country	Share of GNP
France	11.5
Italy	9.6
Netherlands	23.1
UK	7.5
West Germany	5.9

Source: Alan Milward, *The Reconstruction of Western Europe, 1949–51* (Berkeley: University of California Press, 1984), p. 97, table 16.

Table 20 G-24 aid as a share of 1990 GNP of recipient countries (%)

Country	Share of GNP
Czech Republic*	9.86
Hungary	43.25
Poland	55.24
Slovakia*	12.57
Romania	34.15

*1993 GNP.

Sources: European Commission, *Overview of G–24 Assistance, 1990–1994*, (Brussels: European Commisson, February 1995); authors' calculations.

The most glaring difference between the ERP and the G-24 aid programme has been in the level of sacrifice of the donor countries. Between 1948 and 1951 the Marshall Plan absorbed 1.875 per cent of American GNP on average, and it consumed 2.5 per cent of American GDP in 1949. In contrast, total G-24 aid to the CEE states and the former Soviet Union between 1990 and 1994 represented a transfer of resources equal to only 1.74 per cent of the aggregate 1993 GNP of the United States, France, Germany, Italy and the United Kingdom; and total G-24 aid is only equal to 0.69 per cent of the aggregate American GNP between 1990 and 1994. G-24 aid to the CEE states is roughly 40 per cent the size of the peace dividend indicated by the decline in aggregate defence spending by the NATO countries between 1990 and 1994. In that respect, the peace dividend was far from consumed by the task of recasting Europe. But G-24 aid was only 3 per cent of the aggregate defence spending of the NATO countries between 1990 and 1994.[95] A case could be made that the NATO states continue to over-invest in the wrong kind of security and consequently run the risk of allowing the CEE states to fail in their efforts to achieve the transition.

Total G-24 aid to the CEE states amounts to $98.61 billion. The share of aid held by the three primary categories of donors – international financial institutions and regional investment banks, the EU and its member states, and the United States – suggests that the United States has failed to pull its weight. The international financial institutions, primarily the regional investment banks (EIB and EBRD), the IMF, and the World Bank and the International Financial Corporation, have contributed 29.48 per cent of G-24 aid ($29.08 billion); the EU has provided 11.23 per cent of G-24 aid ($11.07 billion); the EU member states have provided 35.92 per cent of G-24 aid ($35.41 billion); and the United States has contributed 12.82 per cent of G-24 aid ($12.64 billion). Forty-eight per cent of total G-24 aid is supplied on a bilateral basis. This large share of bilateral aid inevitably raises questions about burden sharing. A traditional indicator of burden shirking (or free riding) is the ratio of national financial effort to relative GDP share. That indicator would suggest that the United States is free-riding; it should have contributed 44.4 per cent (its share of alliance GDP) of the bilateral aid (or $21.33 billion). Germany has provided a leadership role in the granting of aid to the CEE states and the former Soviet Union. Germany contributed 15.04 per cent of the total G-24 aid to the CEE states and 43.6 per cent of the total G-24 aid to the former Soviet Union although a large share of that aid was dedicated to encouraging the timely withdrawal of Soviet troops from the former German Democratic Republic.

It is clear that the G-24 states have been unable (or unwilling) to meet the investment needs of the CEE states and the former Soviet Union. Part of the problem reflects disputes over relative responsibility for financing the transition – in the US Congress, in particular, there is a scarcely repressed belief that it is somehow Europe's problem. And part of the problem may be located in the efforts of the western European states to meet the Maastricht fiscal criteria and the American effort to redress over a decade of fiscal malfeasance by the Reagan and Bush administrations. Yet the level of aid and investment as a share of 1990 GNP suggests that more aid or capital might have been redundant without greater Western control over the management of those economies. Seeking greater direct control over those national economies, however, could only engender political resentment against the Western states and transgress our own preference for the development of responsible democratic governance. The relative ineffectiveness of G-24 aid and capital flows (as compared with the ERP experience) also counsels lowered expectations about the speed and constancy of the forced marketisation of those economies. The eastern German case demonstrates the difficulty of transforming a command economy to a market economy, of sustaining economic growth and employment, and of making productivity gains. The German government transferred $294.02 billion to the former GDR between 1991 and 1993, a figure exceeding the $222.17 billion transferred to the states in transition between 1990 and 1994. Those German government transfers represented around 5 per cent of GNP on an annual basis, a figure that far surpasses the anaemic efforts of the G-24 as a whole.

The formal international institutions aiding the transition to the market – particularly the regional investment banks, the international financial institutions, and the Paris and London Clubs – cannot be said to have failed the states in transition, although the performance of the EBRD has not met its original promise and the debt overhang facing the CEE countries could have been resolved with greater dispatch and on more generous terms. The failure has been a political one. Western governments have been unwilling to commit sufficient resources to support the marketisation and democratisation processes, despite the importance of those two processes to the foreign policy agendas of the major European states and to the stability of the European order. The failure to devote sufficient resources to the task at hand reflects the irony of the immediate post-Cold War world: at a time when the economic instruments of statecraft are the most effective and essential to the stability of the European security order, the major states lack the fiscal wherewithal to exploit that opportunity.

Notes

1 See comments of Lawrence H. Summers, Under Secretary for International Affairs, US Treasury Department, 'Russian Reform at a Critical Juncture: the Role of Western Support,' *Treasury News*, LB 640 (Washington, DC: Department of the Treasury, 8 February 1994), p. 1; and Kenneth Clarke, UK Chancellor of the Exchequer, 'Modern Tasks for the Money Men,' *Financial Times*, 20 July 1994, p. 12.
2 Lawrence H. Summers, 'Multilateral Assistance for Russia and the other States of the Former Soviet Union,' *Treasury News*, LB 377 (Washington, DC: Department of the Treasury, 21 September 1993), p. 1.
3 ERP figures drawn from Alan Milward, *The Reconstruction of Western Europe, 1945–1951* (Berkeley: University of California Press, 1984), p. 94; figures for aid to the

CEE states and former Soviet Union drawn from European Commission, G-24 Coordination Unit, *Overview of G-24 Assistance, 1990–1994*, Brussels, 24 February 1995, WD 300. Calculations by authors.
4 See, for example, Jeffery Sachs, 'Conditionality, Debt Relief, and the Developing Country Debt Crisis,' in Jeffery Sachs (ed.), *Developing Country Debt and the World Economy* (Chicago: University of Chicago Press, 1989), p. 276; and Stephan Haggard and Robert Kaufman, 'The Politics of Stabilization and Structural Adjustment,' in Sachs, *Developing Country Debt*, p. 264.
5 Sachs, 'Conditionality,' p. 277; Eduardo Borensztein and Peter J. Montiel, 'Savings, Investment, and Growth in Eastern Europe,' *IMF Working Paper* (Washington, DC: IMF, June 1991), pp. 21–5; and Ishac Diwan and Fernando Saldanha, 'Long-term Prospects in Eastern Europe: the Role of External Finance in an Era of Change,' *Working Papers* (Washington, DC: World Bank, June 1991), pp. 19–25.
6 Christine A. Kearney, 'The Creditor Clubs: Paris and London,' in Thomas J. Biersteker (ed.), *Dealing with Debt: International Financial Negotiations and Adjustment Bargaining* (Boulder: Westview Press, 1993), p. 63.
7 Alexis Rieffel, 'The Role of the Paris Club in Managing Debt Problems,' *Essays in International Finance* 161 (Princeton: Department of Economics, Princeton University: December 1985), p. 5.
8 Charles Lipson, 'International Debt and International Institutions,' in Miles Kahler (ed.), *The Politics of International Debt* (Ithaca: Cornell University Press, 1986), p. 222; and Matthew Martin, *The Crumbling Facade of African Debt Negotiations: No Winners* (New York: St Martin's Press, 1991), pp. 97–8.
9 'Agreed Minute on Poland's External Debt,' 27 April 1981, photocopy.
10 Martin, *The Crumbling Facade of African Debt Negotiations*, p. 113.
11 World Bank, *World Debt Tables, 1992–93. External Finance for Developing Countries* 1, *Analysis and Summary Tables* (Washington, DC: World Bank, 1993), p. 73.
12 For a general discussion of the changes that have taken place in the terms offered by the Paris Club see World Bank, *World Debt Tables*, 1, pp. 75–79; *World Debt Tables, 1993–1994. External Finance for Developing Countries* 1. *Analysis and Summary Tables* (Washington, DC: World Bank, 1994), pp. 46–7; Thomas Klein, 'Innovations in Debt Relief, ' *Finance and Development*, vol. 29, no. 1 (March 1992), pp. 42–3; and IMF, *Annual Report, 1995* (IMF: Washington, DC: 1995), pp. 31–3.
13 The different incentive structures commercial banks face reflect levels of exposure, domestic legal restraints, and taxation and accounting laws. See Charles Lipson, 'Bankers' Dilemmas: Private Cooperation in Rescheduling Sovereign Debts,' *World Politics*, vol. 38, no. 1 (October 1985), pp. 200–25; and 'The International Organization of Third World Debt,' *International Organization*, vol. 35, no. 4 (autumn 1981), pp. 603–32.
14 Rieffel, 'The Role of the Paris Club in Managing Debt Problems,' p. 22.
15 Lipson, 'The International Organization of Third World Debt,' p. 620.
16 Lipson, 'Bankers' Dilemmas,' p. 225.
17 Martin, *The Crumbling Facade of African Debt Negotiations*, pp. 167–8.
18 'Draft Protocol of London Club Arrangement with Poland,' 6 May 1981 (Frankfurt: Dresdner Bank).
19 International Monetary Fund, *Annual Report, 1989* (IMF: Washington, DC: 1989), pp. 24–5; and 'Supplement on the IMF', *IMF Survey*, October 1993, p. 23.
20 Both the IMF and World Bank pledged $10 billion each to DDSR operations; Japan pledged another $10 billion. 'Sisters in the Wood: a Survey of the IMF and World Bank,' *Economist*, 12 October, 1991, p. 19.
21 The initial debt reduction instruments were debt–equity swaps, debt securitisation, debt cash buy-backs, debt-for-goods swaps, debt-for-nature swaps; debt-to-local-debt

swap and informal conversions. To that list have been added: interest reduction bonds (par bonds); principal reduction bonds (discount bond); front-loaded interest reduction bonds; debt conversion bonds; and new money bonds.

22 Susan M. Schadler, 'Developing Countries and the Evolving Role of the IMF,' *IMF Survey*, vol. 23, no. 14 (11 July 1994), p. 224.
23 International Monetary Fund, *IMF Annual Report, 1989* (Washington, DC: IMF, 1989), p. 23.
24 Access to the Fund is based upon the subscription quota of a state for membership in the Fund. The quota is divided into five tranches. The first tranche, designated the reserve tranche, is represented by the IMF holdings of the state's currency in excess of its quota in the General Resources Account. The four other tranches, or credit tranches, are equal to 25 per cent of a member's quota. A first credit tranche drawing lacks any conditionality other than that the state should be making 'reasonable efforts to overcome its balance of payments difficulties'. Any subsequent drawings on the IMF – on the second, third or fourth credit tranche – are conditional upon the implementation of macroeconomic and structural policies that provide some assurance that the member will return to a balance of payments equilibrium; in this case, the ability to service its debt. A stand-by arrangement accompanies any drawing upon the upper credit tranches. IMF, *Annual Report 1992* (Washington, DC: IMF, 1992), p. 49.
25 For an analysis of the EFF see Stephen Haggard, 'The politics of adjustment,' *International Organization*, vol. 39, no. 3 (summer 1985), pp. 503–34.
26 For an analysis of the ESAF see Susan Schadler, Franek Rozwadowski, Siddharth Tiwari and David O. Robinson, *Economic Adjustment in Low-income Countries: Experience under the Structural Adjustment Facility*, IMF Occasional Paper 106 (Washington, DC: IMF, 1993).
27 'Common Themes characterize IMF Assistance to Economies in Transition,' *IMF Survey*, vol. 23, no. 8 (18 April 1994), pp. 114–15.
28 IMF, *IMF Annual Report, 1990* (Washington, DC: IMF, 1990), p. 30.
29 Compare Jeffery Sachs's scepticism of the claim that the IMF is better able to enforce conditionality than commercial creditors with Charles Lipson's argument that the IMF is uniquely positioned to enforce conditionality. See Jeffery Sachs, 'Conditionality, Debt Relief, and the Debt Crisis,' pp. 278ff; and Charles Lipson, *Standing Guard: Protecting Foreign Capital in the Nineteenth and Twentieth Centuries* (Berkeley: University of California Press, 1985), pp. 93.
30 For a discussion of the content of a policy framework paper see IMF, *Annual Report, 1992* (Washington, DC: IMF, 1992), pp. 54–5.
31 On the problem of cross-conditionality see World Bank, *Annual Report, 1993* (Washington, DC: World Bank, 1993); Richard E. Feinberg, 'The Changing Relationship between the World Bank and the International Monetary Fund,' *International Organization*, vol. 42, no. 3 (summer 1988), pp. 552–6; and Hiroyuki Hino, 'IMF–World Bank Collaboration,' *Finance and Development*, 23 (September 1986), pp. 10–14.
32 The increase in debt ranges from 54.3 per cent (Russian Federation) to a low of 5.0 per cent (Poland).
33 For a discussion of the political variables affecting the terms of debt reduction see Haggard and Kaufman, 'The Politics of Stabilization and Structural Adjustment,' pp. 263–74.
34 The CEE states do not compare all that unfavourably with Brazil and Mexico, two states at the centre of the debt crisis in the 1980s. See Table 21.
35 The arrears on interest and principal were significant for all three countries. See Table 22.
36 Rudiger Dornbusch, 'Debt Problems and the World Macroeconomy,' in Sachs, *Developing Country Debt and the World Economy*, p. 301.

Table 21 Debt ratios for selected individual countries in transition and for Mexico and Brazil, 1991–93 average (%)

Country	EDT/XGS	EDT/GNP	TDS/XGS	INT/XGS
Albania	230	n.a.	2	1
Bulgaria	277	122	7	5
Czech Republic	64	2	11	4
Hungary	193	67	37	14
Poland	311	60	9	5
Romania	65	13	6	3
Russian Federation	152	19	12	4
Slovakia	44	28	8	2
Former Yugoslavia	102	23	14	7
Brazil	307	28	24	9
Mexico	189	37	30	12

Source: World Bank.

Table 22 Arrears, 1990–91 ($ billion)

Country	Interest	Principal	Total
Bulgaria	1.021	4.072	4.073
Poland	14.539	10.745	25.284
Russian Federation	5.869	1.522	7.391

Source: World Bank.

37 The high real interest rates on Deutschmark-denominated debt (see Table 23) had the effect of leading to a decrease in the share of debt denominated in Deutschemarks (from 26.9 per cent in 1990 to 18 per cent in 1993) and a rise in the share of debt denominated in dollars (from 30.7 per cent in 1990 to 45.6 per cent in 1993). World Bank, *World Debt Tables, 1994–95*, p. 248.

Table 23 Real short–term interest rates, 1986–93 (%)

Country	1986	1987	1988	1989	1990	1991	1992	1993
US	3.3	2.7	2.8	3.5	3.2	2.0	0.5	0.2
FRG	1.3	2.1	2.8	4.7	5.4	4.7	4.0	2.4

Sources: IMF; authors' own calculations.

38 See Table 24.
39 See Table 25.
40 See Tables 26 and 27.
41 Dani Rodrik estimates that the impact of the Russian trade shock resulted in a GDP decline equal to 3.46 per cent for Poland, 7.82 per cent for Hungary and -7.46 per cent for Czechoslovakia. See Dani Rodrik, 'Making Sense of the Soviet Trade Shock in Eastern Europe: a Framework and some Estimates,' in Mario I. Blejer, Guillermo A. Calvo, Fabrizio Coricelli and Alan H. Gelb (eds), *Eastern Europe in Transition: from Recession to Growth?* World Bank Discussion Papers 196 (Washington, DC: World Bank, 1993), pp. 64–85; and European Bank for Reconstruction and Development, *EBRD Economic Review. Annual Economic Report* (London: EBRD, September 1993), pp. 70–1.
42 See World Bank, *World Debt Tables, 1993–94*, p. 227.

Table 24 Trade growth, 1989–92 (%)

Country	Bulgaria	Czech Republic	Hungary	Poland	Romania	Russian Federation
	−52.4	−2.2	12.4	0.9	−32.0	−46.8

Source: EBRD.

Table 25 National GDP growth rates, 1990–92 (%)

Country	1990	1991	1992	1989–92
Bulgaria	−9.1	−11.7	−5.6	−9.0
Czech Republic	−0.4	−15.9	−8.5	−5.8
Hungary	−4.3	−11.9	−4.4	−4.8
Poland	−11.6	−7.6	1.0	−4.6
Romania	−7.4	−15.1	−15.4	−10.6
Russian Federation	−3.6	−12.9	−18.5	−7.2
Former Yugoslavia	−7.5	−17.0	−34.0	−13.0

Source: IMF and EBRD.

Table 26 Regional GDP growth rates, 1990–94 (%)

Region	1990	1991	1992	1993	1994
World	2.2	0.6	1.7	2.2	3.2
Industrial countries	2.3	0.5	1.7	1.1	2.2
EU	3.0	0.8	1.1	−0.2	1.6
Countries in transition	−3.5	−12.0	−15.4	−10.2	−1.1
Central Europe	−7.1	−12.6	−9.1	−1.8	1.9
Former Soviet Union	−2.3	−11.8	−17.8	−13.7	−2.4

Sources: IMF; EBRD.

Table 27 Real total domestic demand, 1988–94 (%)

Economy	1988	1989	1990	1991	1992	1993	1994
G-7	4.5	3.0	2.0	0.1	1.8	1.5	2.4
EU	5.0	3.7	2.9	1.4	1.2	−0.7	1.4
FRG	3.6	2.9	5.2	3.6	1.5	−2.3	0.9

Source: IMF.

43 See European Bank for Reconstruction and Development, 'Export Access to Western Markets: Recent Issues and Developments,' *EBRD Economic Review. Current Economic Issues* (London: European Bank for Reconstruction and Development, July 1993), pp. 17–27; and Economic Commission for Europe, *Economic Survey of Europe in 1991–1992* (New York: UN, 1992), pp. 187ff. The convertible currency balances of these nations have fluctuated between surplus and deficit without any noticeable trend (see Table 28).

44 IMF, *Annual Report, 1992* (Washington, DC: IMF, 1992), p. 98, table 11.7; and Economic Commission for Europe, *Economic Survey of Europe in 1992–1993* (New York: UN, 1993), p. 246.

45 Bank for International Settlements, *Sixty-second Annual Report, 1 April 1991–31 March 1992* (Basle: BIS, June 1992), p. 65; and *IMF Survey*, 27 April 1992, p. 135.

Table 28 Convertible currency current account balances, 1990–93 ($ million)

Country	1990	1991	1992	1993
Bulgaria	−1,152	−887	−250	−1,500
Czechoslovakia	−1,104	356	226	n.a.
Hungary	127	267	324	−200
Poland	716	−1,359	−269	−600
Romania	−1,650	−1,369	−944	−1,100
Russian Federation	−4,500	−3,400	−3,200	n.a.
Former Yugoslavia	−2,664	−1,092	n.a.	n.a.

Source: Economic Commmission for Europe.

46 EBRD, *Annual Economic Report 1992* (London: EBRD, 1993), p. 74; and *Quarterly Economic Review*, April 1993, p. 77ff.
47 *Financial Times*, 2 September 1992, p. 2; 3 November 1992, p. 2; and 17 November 1992, p. 2.
48 The debt was restructured in the following way: 60.5 per cent was restructured as collateralised discount bonds, 27.1 per cent was restructured as front-loaded interest reduction bonds; and the remaining 12.4 per cent of the debt was subject to a Bulgarian buy-back. *IMF Survey*, 2 May 1994, p. 147; and *Financial Times*, 30 June 1994, p. 2.
49 *IMF Survey*, 26 September 1994, p. 298.
50 World Bank, *Jahresbericht 1991* (Washington, DC: World Bank, 1991), p. 136.
51 World Bank, *World Debt Tables, 1993–94*, p. 110; and Economic Commission for Europe, *Economic Survey of Europe in 1990–1991* (New York: UN, 1991), p. 106.
52 The consumer price index declined only to 249 per cent rather than the expected 94 per cent; the economy contracted by 12 per cent rather than 5 per cent; and the expansion of credit was 122 per cent rather than the target of 87 per cent. The suspension of the stand-by meant that the Polish government was to draw on only three of the four credit tranches. For an analysis of the Polish government's macroeconomic performance between 1989 and 1991 see Michael Bruno, 'Stabilization and Reform in Eastern Europe: Preliminary Evaluation,' in Blejer *et al.*, *Eastern Europe in Transition*, p. 20; and IMF, *Annual Report, 1990* (Washington, DC: IMF, 1990), p. 38.
53 The American government believed that a DDSR agreement with Poland was an 'important pillar' of Polish economic policy and prospects. See comments of Treasury Secretary Nicholas Brady, 'The International Debt Situation: Progress and Perspective,' remarks made at the afternoon session of the Interim Committee of the International Monetary Fund, 29 April 1991, *Treasury News*, NB–1245, p. 3.
54 *IMF Survey*, 29 April 1991, p. 139.
55 In the American case, the agreement immediately reduced Polish debt from $3,672.7 billion to $2,079.9 billion, and reduced it further to $1,228.6 billion in 1994. See *Agreement between the Government of the United States of America and the Government of the Republic of Poland regarding the Reduction and Reorganization of certain Debts owed to, guaranteed by, or insured by the Government of the United States and its Agencies*, 17 July 1991.
56 EBRD, *Quarterly Economic Review*, 30 September 1992, p. 38. The World Bank provided Poland with a $450 million structural adjustment loan to facilitate enterprise and financial-sector adjustment and a sector adjustment loan worth $300 million to aid the restructuring of agriculture. World Bank, *Annual Report, 1993* (Washington, DC: World Bank, 1994), pp. 13, 129 n. 10.
57 BIS, *Sixty-third Annual Report, 1 April 1992–31 March 1993* (Basle: BIS, 1993), pp. 46–7; *IMF Survey*, 22 March 1993, p. 92; EBRD, *Annual Report, 1992* (London: EBRD, 1993),

p. 63.
58 Anthony Robinson, 'Agreement would help,' *Financial Times*, 17 June 1993, *Financial Times* Survey of Poland, p. ii; and 'Poland ready for Deal on $12bn Commercial Debt,' *Financial Times*, 16 July 1993, p. 3.
59 Christopher Bobinski and Anthony Robinson, 'Warsaw ready to revive Talks with Creditors,' *Financial Times*, 27 July 1993, p. 2; and Robinson, 'Poland ready for Deal on $12bn Commercial Debt,' p. 3.
60 Salomon Brothers, *Emerging Markets*, 19 February 1993. The Polish ministry of finance calculated that Polish debt service would rise from around $2 billion in 1995 to $4 billion in 2000 to just over $8 billion in 2007.
61 Conner Middelmann, 'Poland set to enter Virtuous Circle,' *Financial Times*, 8 August 1994, p. 20.
62 Only the Czech Republic has a higher credit rating than Poland; Hungary, which has serviced its debt, has been granted only a sub-investment grade rating. *IMF Survey*, 14 November 1994, pp. 367–8; *Financial Times*, 2 June 1995, p. 1.
63 BIS, *Sixty-second Annual Report*, p. 65; World Bank, *World Debt Tables, 1992–93*, pp. 29–30; *IMF Survey*, 6 January 1992, p. 7.
64 *New York Times*, 19 August 1991, p. A1; 16 October 1991, p. A1.
65 The full title of the agreement is the *Memorandum of Understanding on the Debt to Foreign Creditors of the Union of Soviet Socialist Republics and its Successors*.
66 Economic Commission for Europe, *Economic Survey of Europe in 1991–1992*, p. 177.
67 *New York Times*, 20 November 1991, p. A1; and World Bank, *World Debt Tables, 1992–93*, pp. 33 and 37.
68 'G-7 Ministers finalize Debt Agreement with Soviet Union and Republics,' *IMF Survey*, 2 December 1991. This agreement was formalised in a Paris Club setting on 4 January 1992 with the '*Agreement on the Deferral of the Debt of the Union of Soviet Socialist Republics and its Successors to Foreign Creditors*.'
69 The Russian Federation, Ukraine, Belarus, Kazakhstan, Georgia, Kyrgystan, Armenia and Tajikistan signed the *Memorandum of Understanding* and the *Treaty on the Assignment of Foreign Debt*. Uzbekistan and Azerbaijan signed neither treaty; and Moldova and Tajikistan signed the *Memorandum*. The three Baltic States, Lithuania, Latvia and Estonia, refused to accept any responsibility or liability for the debt of the former Soviet Union – a position not challenged by the former Soviet Union's creditors. *World Debt Tables, 1992–93*, p. 37.
70 *Financial Times*, 24 January 1992, p. 2; 5 February 1992, p. 12; 10 February 1992, p. 1; and 26 February 1992. For details of revised debt management arrangement see *World Debt Tables, 1992–93*, p. 37.
71 *Financial Times*, 6 January 1993, p. 2; 14 January 1993, p. 2.
72 *Economist*, 3 April 1993, p. 75. The agreement between Ukraine and the Russian Federation provided that Ukraine and Russia would share space in the embassies of the former Soviet Union and that the Danube and Black Sea merchant fleets would be divided between the two states. *Financial Times*, 31 March 1993, p. 18; World Bank, *World Debt Tables, 1993–94*, p. 138.
73 *Financial Times*, 26 February 1992; EBRD, 'Current Economic Issues,' *EBRD Economic Review*, July 1993, pp. 112–16, 164; *Economic Survey of Europe in 1991–1992*, p. 113; and *Economic Survey of Europe in 1992–1993*, p. 247.
74 *IMF Survey*, 17 August 1992, p. 267; EBRD, *Quarterly Economic Review*, September 1992, p. 68; Leyla Boulton and Dmitry Volkov, 'Russia seeks Debt Deal with G7,' *Financial Times*, 25 August 1992, p. 2. Lawrence H. Summers, 'Multilateral Assistance for Russia and the other States of the former Soviet Union,' 7 September 1993, *Treasury News*, LP–345, p. 6; David C. Mulford, 'Statement before the Committee on Banking, Finance and Urban Affairs Subcommittee on International Development, Finance,

Trade and Monetary Policy, 29 April 1992,' *Treasury News*, NB–1777, p. 2.
75   Leyla Boulton, 'West to back Yeltsin with Deal on Debts,' *Financial Times*, 30 June 1992, p. 2.
76   Germany held approximately 40 per cent of Russian debt, while the American share is in single figures. The German unwillingness to consider debt forgiveness in the Russian case derived from Germany's status as the largest contributor of Western aid to Russia and the position of German commercial banks as the largest single Russian creditors. Germany wanted to avoid extending to Russia the terms extended to Poland on its debt in 1990. Moreover, the German government did not want to burden its domestic commercial banks with a Paris Club agreement that would force the Russian government to seek and commercial banks to extend comparable terms on $21.9 billion of debt owed to German banks, a sum dwarfing that owed to American banks ($500 million). The next five largest commercial creditors of the Russian Federation were France ($5.6 billion), Japan ($4.5 billion), Italy ($4.4 billion), Austria ($3.5 billion) and the United Kingdom ($3.4 billion). *New York Times*, 21 August 1991, p. C1; *Financial Times*, 20 October 1992, p. 2; 23 September 1992, p. 4; 31 March 1993, p. 18.
77   *Financial Times*, 15 December 1992, p. 2; 17 December 1992, p. 1; 18 December 1992, p. 2.
78   *Financial Times*, 9 September 1992, p. 5; 10 September 1992, p. 2.
79   Lawrence H. Summers, 'Strengthening Russian Economic Reform,' *Treasury News*, LB–436, p. 4; *Financial Times*, 31 December 1993, p. 2.
80   *IMF Survey*, 12 July 1993, p. 220–1; IMF *Annual Report 1994*, p. 114. In June 1993 the World Bank granted a rehabilitation loan of $610 million to boost Siberian oil production, increase Russian hard-currency earnings and subsequently ease the financing gap of the Russian Federation. World Bank, *Annual Report, 1993*, p. 153.
81   *Financial Times*, 31 December 1993.
82   Quentin Peel, 'G-7 ties Russian debt to accord with IMF,' *Financial Times*, 28 February 1994, p. 2.
83   *IMF Survey*, 2 May 1994, p. 148–50; 4 April 1994, p. 98–9. Interim Committee of the Board of Governors of the IMF, 'Communiqué', *IMF Survey*, 2 May 1994, p. 135.
84   *Financial Times*, 18 May 1994, p. 2; 6 June 1994, p. 3.
85   *Financial Times*, 9/10 July 1994, p. 2.
86   *Financial Times*, 4 October 1994, p. 2.
87   *Financial Times*, 3 October 1994, p. 5; and 8 November 1994, p. 3.
88   *Financial Times*, 6 December 1992, p. 3; and 7 December 1994, p. 2.
89   *IMF Survey*, 17 April 1995, pp. 125–6; IMF, *Annual Report, 1995* (Washington, DC: IMF, 1994), p. 104; *Financial Times*, 15 November 1995, p. 2. In April 1996 agreement was reached between the Russian Federation and the Paris Club to reschedule more than $40 billion of official debt. The agreement was reached when Russia signed a $10.1 billion three-year stand-by arrangement with the IMF. John Thornhill, 'Russia agrees $40 bn Paris Club Debt Deal,' *Financial Times*, 30 April 1996, p. 2.
90   *New York Times*, 5 December 1991, p. A5; World Bank, *World Debt Tables, 1992–93*, p. 33; and *World Debt Tables, 1994–1995*, p. 95–6.
91   *Financial Times*, 16 December 1992, p. 2.
92   'The bankers' beanfeast,' *Economist*, 2 October 1993, p. 83; *Financial Times*, 6 October 1994, p. 1; 8 October 1994, p. 2; *World Debt Tables, 1993–1994*, p. 139; *Financial Times*, 17 November 1995, p. 1.
93   A summary of studies estimating the investment requirements of the states in transition is to be found in EBRD, *Annual Economic Outlook* (London: EBRD, September 1993), pp. 82–4.
94   Direct foreign and portfolio investment in Ireland was only 0.03 per cent of GNP. The vast majority of investment in Ireland is classified as 'other' by the IMF.

95 Total G-24 aid comes to $220.83 billion ($122.23 billion to the former Soviet Union and $98.6 billion to the CEE states). That figures is 5.48 times the peace dividend, but only 9.06 per cent of total NATO defence expenditure.

7

The economic dimension of security
Financing environmental security

The cost of cleaning up the environment of eastern and central Europe as well as the former Soviet Union is subject to debate, but it is clear that the sums are not insubstantial. It has been estimated, for example, that the cost of cleaning up the Polish environment will fall within the range of $200 billion to $400 billion over a ten- to twenty-year period; the cost of cleaning up the former Czechoslovakia will be at least $355 billion over a fifteen-year period, the cost of cleaning up the environment of the Russian Federation around $1,000 billion, and the cost of cleaning up the former German Democratic Republic has been estimated at $249–308 billion over a ten-year period. The expectation of the World Bank is that the cost of environmental clean-up in eastern and central Europe will amount to between 2–3 per cent of GNP for a twenty-year period.[1]

The environmental dimension of the new pan-European security order derives its importance from three variables. First, the cost of cleaning up the environmental damage done to the CEE nations as well as the newly independent states of the former Soviet Union competes with the scarce financial resources necessary to restructure and transform of those nations' economies – processes critical to the evolution of a pan-European security order. Second, the environmental damage is in many cases irreversible and portends both environmental migration within those countries and, more problematically, environmental refugees inundating the western European states and triggering civil and societal conflicts driven by ethnic and wealth distribution conflicts. And, third, the heavy reliance upon nuclear energy by the former Warsaw Pact states combined with dependence upon poorly designed and constructed nuclear reactors poses the deadly threat of cross-border radiation poisoning that could conceivably engulf the European continent.

In this chapter, we make the case for including environmental security as an essential element of the post-Cold War security architecture; examine the environmental security framework that has emerged within the major security institutions of the post-Cold War security order as well as the institutions implementing environmental security, particularly the European regional investment banks; and assess the success of North America and Europe in resolving the environmental security threat posed by cross-border radiation poisoning emanating from central and eastern Europe.

The importance of environmental security

Even though there is a large and growing literature seeking to integrate cross-border pollution, resource conflicts and environmental degradation into the security framework,[2] there is no commonly accepted definition or conceptualisation of environmental security. Some authors, like Daniel Deudney, argue that the environment should not be considered as a part of the post-Cold War security equation; some, like John Mearsheimer, refuse to dignify the contention with a response, and others, like Barry Buzan, view environmental security as a concept for the future.[3] Four arguments can be marshalled against the concept of environmental security. The first is that since the concept of national security has been traditionally and usefully defined as security from purposive and organised violence, the concept of environmental security violates the concept of security since environmental degradation is neither purposive nor entails organised violence. The second argument revolves around the observation that there is 'nothing distinctly national about the causes, harm or solution' of environmental degradation, whereas security, traditionally defined, has distinctly national characteristics. The third argument revolves around the level of intention. Deudney argues that the 'threats to environmental well-being involve greatly differing degrees of intention'. In contrast to threats to national security, the threat posed by environmental degradation is not highly organised, not violent and has no specific political objective. Environmental threats are derived from externalities attending other (largely economic) activities. And the fourth argument made by Deudney is that the organisations protecting national security and environmental security are fundamentally different. These objections to the concept of environmental security are misplaced; they represent too narrow and parochial a conception of security, particularly for post-Cold War Europe.[4]

The traditional understanding of national security focuses exclusively upon the notion of state security at the expense of systemic security and societal security. A case can (and will) be made that the appropriate concern of the analyst coping with the security problem posed by environmental degradation is at the systemic level, the societal level as well as at the level of the state. The stability of the post-Cold War European security order depends upon the successful societal transition of the former member states of the Warsaw Pact, namely the transition to the market economy and competitive multi-party democracies. The unabated and conscious degradation of the environment could upend the stability of the system owing to its disruptive effect on the process of either economic or political transition – an effect that could set in motion equally disruptive migratory pressures and could initiate violent group-identity conflicts undermining civil order and perhaps the legitimacy of existing state institutions.[5]

The degradation of the environment, particularly cross-border pollution contributing to the depletion of the ozone layer or the build-up of greenhouse gases, does lack a specific national cause or solution and the harm caused is diffused throughout the international system. Thus not all cross-border pollution can be usefully treated as a security problem, even though the consequences of that type of pollution can be nonetheless devastating and represent a distant threat to the security of a society or state. It is also the case, however, that much cross-border pollution has a specific national cause, inflicts harm on a limited number of neigbouring states, and is susceptible to national albeit cooperative solutions. Nuclear reactor failure throughout eastern and central Europe and the former Soviet Union, heavy metal pollution, and the discharge of industrial wastes into seas and rivers, all fall into this category of environmental degradation; these sources of cross-border pollution pose a specific rather than a diffuse environmental threat. In other words, this category of environmental degradation poses what can be called a 'local public bad'[6] susceptible to political conflict and cooperation between states – not unlike traditional security concerns.

Unlike the threat posed by a concentration of enemy forces at the national frontier, the security problem posed by environmental degradation or the threat of it lacks the same level of intent. Yet it is also true that some environmental abuse – for example, the heavy metal pollution of the Kola peninsula and the continued operation of ageing and defectively designed nuclear reactors in Bulgaria, Ukraine, Lithuania, Slovakia and elsewhere – can be held to represent a 'depraved indifference' to the consequences of the externalities associated with those activities generating cross-border pollution or its threat. It is clearly the case that some potential externalities generated by economic activity – cross-border radiation poisoning flowing from the use of defective nuclear reactors to produce electricity – pose a significant risk to neighbouring states that is functionally equivalent to the risk posed by the massing of armies on a state's borders.

Yet it is true that the organisations that protect states from violence differ greatly from those protecting states from cross-border environmental degradation. The difference in the organisations designed to resolve environmental and military conflicts and their methods of conflict resolution do not, however, bear directly on whether or not environmental security is a valid or useful concept. It does point to the different institutional requirements facing the resolution of the different dimensions of security in the post-Cold War European security order.

Mindful of the neo-realist critique of environmental security by authors like Deudney, Thomas Homer-Dixon and Jon Trolldalen have recast the environmental security issue in terms of viewing environmental scarcity as a source of violent conflict between states. Both authors focus on conflicts of interest derived from environmental change that can escalate into violence. While Trolldalen is concerned primarily with the resolution of environmental conflicts before war does erupt, Homer-Dixon restricts his analysis to environmental change that precipitates '*acute* national and international conflict ... a conflict involving a substantial probability of violence' and considers the sources and processes of such conflicts.[7] Homer-Dixon argues that environmental change yields three sources of conflict: scarcity disputes between countries (e.g. competition over common water sources), group identity conflicts driven by environmentally induced migratory pressures, and relative deprivation conflicts triggering the disruption of social and political institutions. Environmental change triggers these conflicts – and the attendant probability of inter-state violence – owing to environmentally driven economic decline and population displacement. Others, like Peter Gleick, identify an environmental security agenda that follows the fairly traditional concern with assuring access to and control over strategic raw materials in addition to the more recent concern with the manipulation of the environment to achieve political or military advantage. While these dimensions of environmental security are meaningful in the contemporary international system, particularly in the Third World, their salience for the European security order is minimal.[8] The one dimension of environmental security that has salience for the contemporary European security order is the abuse of the regional commons that either starkly reduces the quality of life or jeopardises life itself – security threats that do not necessarily portend or generate violent conflict between states, but are likely to generate environmental refugees or environmentally motivated migration and widen the gap between 'state capacity and demands on the state ... [that] erodes the state's legitimacy'.[9]

The most relevant contribution of these analysts, in addition to the generation of useful taxonomies of environmental conflict, is the discussion of the impact that environmental degradation can have upon the ability of the state to cope with the threat caused by environmental change – an insight of particular relevance given the importance and fragility of the transition to multi-party democracy and the free market in the eastern portion of Europe for the future stability of the pan-European security order. As noted, environmental degradation can spur environmental migration or create environmental refugees. Such a shift of population within a state can strain the economic capacity of a political system or generate violent ethnic conflicts within multinational societies. Either development has the secondary consequence of straining the legitimacy of the state. The restoration of political order in a state under siege can lead to the formation of what Homer-Dixon calls 'hard regimes' which are defined as regimes which are 'authoritarian, intolerant of opposition, and militarized'.[10] This development, were it to occur in the European context, would undermine one of the bases of the European security order – the peaceful transition towards the market economy and multi-party democracy in the east – and reintroduce the security dilemma to Europe. Mass migration from eastern to western Europe driven by environmental degradation would promise a lowering of living standards in the west and generate political resentment towards those seeking relief from a degraded environment. An anticipated inevitable lowering of living standards, probable ethnic or group identity conflicts and strain on state capacity to cope with the side effects of migration would have one of two effects on western European governments. First, it could lower the quality of democracy owing to measures taken to mitigate the effects of accepting environmental refugees/migrants; or, second, it could reinforce the economic wall dividing Europe with an environmental wall supported by the remilitarisation of Europe's borders on a national or EU basis. In either case there would be a degradation of the national security of the states affected, increased insecurity of national societies, and a general lowering of the systemic security of the European space.

Environmental degradation can be held to be a security threat only if the threat posed to national, societal or systemic security is one of high intensity. The intensity of a threat, and hence the usefulness of treating it as a security threat, is determined by five variables: the specificity of the threat, the closeness of the threat in time and in space, the high probability of the threat being realised, and the seriousness of consequences the threat will have for the state, society or system.[11] There are a large number of environmental threats facing the nations of Europe today, ranging from concern over the proliferation of greenhouse gases to destruction of the ozone to the cross-border pollution of water and air. Many of these threats to the environment fail to meet the criteria that transform a critical policy concern into a security concern: most are diffuse in terms of the source of the problem, the threat is not close in terms of time and space, and the probability of the threat turning into reality, while almost certain, is mitigated by intense scientific debate over the consequences of continuing pollution and the ability to employ abatement technology successfully. There is at least one environmental threat, however, that meets the criteria of high intensity: cross-border nuclear radiation poisoning emanating from eastern Europe and the Russian Federation that threatens national, societal and systemic security on a pan-European scale.

The expansion of the security agenda to include an environmental dimension in post-Cold War Europe reflects not only Cold War security institutions seeking additional or legitimising missions, but a growing sense of vulnerability to the consequences of cross-border pollution and the ability to move towards the abatement of that pollution.[12] The elements of the environmental security framework have been outlined by the major institutions of the post-Cold War security order – NATO, OSCE and the EU.

The frameworks of environmental security cooperation in Europe

Cooperation on environmental issues within NATO have taken place within the Committee on the Challenges of Modern Society (CCMS), a programme proposed by US President Richard Nixon in April 1969. The CCMS was highlighted in the May 1989 declaration of the North Atlantic Council when the gathered heads of state formally established environmental degradation as a security concern, as stated in Article 2 of the North Atlantic Treaty. The role played by environmental degradation in the security calculus of the NATO nations became increasingly prominent in subsequent NATO communiqués and declarations by the heads of state. But, perhaps more important, common environmental problems facing the nations of western and eastern Europe were transformed into a basis for demonstrating the importance of cooperation in post-Cold War Europe to resolve common problems and for staking out another issue facilitating cooperation between the OSCE and NATO.[13] The ecological dimension of security was reinforced at the 1991 Copenhagen NATO meeting. Cooperation in the environmental sector was defined as a part of the 'evolving security partnership' between the nations of western and eastern Europe. The participation of CEE states in the CCMS, particularly in NATO environmental programmes, was one of the first formal institutional linkages between the former member states of the Warsaw Pact and the NATO countries.[14] At the Copenhagen meeting the NATO ministers issued a statement outlining the core security functions of NATO in post-Cold War Europe, but no mention was made of the environmental dimension of security. But the environmental dimension of security was subsequently included in the alliance's 'New Strategic Concept' in November 1991. The New Strategic Concept committed NATO to the adoption of a broad approach to security, including the environmental dimension, which contributed to 'cooperation and dialogue' with the former member states of the Warsaw Pact necessary to fulfil the broader security objectives of the alliance.[15]

In conformity with the redefinition of security outlined in the New Strategic Concept, the NACC affirmed at its December 1991 meeting that 'security is today based on a broad concept that encompasses more than ever political, economic, social and environmental aspects as well as defence' and promised 'enhanced participation of liaison partners in NATO's "Third Dimension" scientific and environmental programmes.'[16] The NATO alliance also committed itself to financing the anticipated cooperation in the 'Third Dimension' of security in March 1992 and the NACC agreed, within the framework of successive 'Work Plans' detailing NACC activities, and under the aegis of the CCMS for execution, to undertake pilot studies of defence-related environmental issues, including cross-border pollution.[17] Perhaps more important, by the end of 1994 the NACC partner countries had formally defined environmental degradation as an integral element of the security dimension of economic development.[18]

With the collapse of the political-military wall separating eastern and western Europe, the CSCE has also been able to play a more important role in creating the framework conditions for environmental cooperation on a pan-European basis. The emphasis and focus of the CSCE had been primarily on the security and human rights 'baskets' until 1989. At the Vienna meeting in January 1989 significant attention was paid to the environmental dimension of the European security space. A common commitment was made to the elaboration of national measures to protect the environment and to facilitate closer international cooperation, particularly in the areas of airborne cross-border pollution and the protection of international waterways and seas. The Vienna meeting also announced a CSCE meeting devoted to environmental questions in late 1989. The Sofia meeting of the CSCE failed to produce a final document, owing to the objections of Romania, but the conference marked an important step in the relationship between OSCE and NATO: OSCE had become the preferred institutional forum for the discussion of pan-European environmental protection – the German environment minister, Klaus Töpfer, remarked at the end of the meeting that it was the first step towards 'the creation of a "European House" with a strong environmental dimension'.[19]

The Bonn CSCE meeting in April 1990 elevated environmental cooperation between the nations of Europe to an essential element of the future Europe. The member states acknowledged the growing importance of environmental conditions in shaping and conditioning economic cooperation, but also noted the security dimension of cross-border pollution – particularly in the case of nuclear and chemical accidents. Moreover, the opportunity was taken to link the transformation of the CEE economies with the prospect of reversing the environmental degradation found in those nations.[20] The new-found emphasis on 'basket two' economic and environmental concerns was carried over into the Charter of Paris, signed in November 1990. In this document the member states acknowledged the necessity of creating 'common obligations and objectives' for the European environment. It also established in a rudimentary form the notion of burden-sharing in the environmental task facing Europe; it suggested that countries lacking the resources or technologies to combat environmental degradation could count upon those who had them to tackle common environmental problems.[21]

The environmental agenda of the CSCE had been expanded by the time of the Helsinki meeting in 1992. It established the principle that the member states were individually and jointly responsibility for achieving their goals for the European environment. For the first time, the CSCE also established 'the polluter pays' and 'the consumer pays' principles at the European level – in other words, that the environmental externalities should be captured in the price charged to consumers for the good and that the producer of the pollution should pay for environmental degradation. But, more important, the document focused on the environmental threat posed by civilian nuclear energy; it called on the member states to adopt IAEA guidelines and to raise the level of nuclear safety found in European nuclear power stations. It also noted that where a technical solution was not feasible, unsafe nuclear facilities should be decommissioned and replaced with environmentally friendly power stations that improved energy efficiency.[22] The Budapest meeting of the OSCE in December 1994 restated the environmental principles of the previous final documents, but focused upon the important regional cooperation in managing common environment problems, the importance of international institutions for ensuring adherence to environmental standards of the OSCE region, and the continued role of the IAEA in safeguarding and enhancing the safety of civilian nuclear reactors in the region.[23]

The EU has also been active in the environmental field. The EU decided to adopt its first environmental programme in 1972 and since that time has produced five environmental programmes, the most recent being completed in March 1992. Until the Single European Act, however, the EU had no formal responsibility for environmental policy; the actions of the Community had been taken on the basis of what Nigel Haigh calls a 'generous interpretation of the treaty' backed by favourable decisions of the European Court of Justice.[24] The Single European Act expanded the policy-making powers of the EU to include an explicitly environmental brief. It provided that the Community had responsibility for preserving, protecting and promoting the quality of the European environment. Community action was to be based on three interlocking principles: environmental policy should be aimed at preventing environmental damage rather than addressing its effects; environmental policy should aim to make the polluter pay for his activities; and environmental policy should seek to correct environmental degradation at the source of pollution. These three principles, in addition to the principle of burden-sharing made explicit in the fifth Action Programme, have shaped the EU's environmental policy not just internally but with its CEE partners.

The fifth Action Programme of the EU, published on 27 March 1992, provided an environmental blueprint for the Community between 1992 and 1997. The programme, in addition to examining the tasks and objectives of the EU's environmental policy, took into account the changes that had taken place in the international system; viz the collapse of the political wall that had prevented environmental cooperation but failed to prevent cross-border pollution. The fifth Action Programme embodied the environmental principle laid down in the Maastricht treaty – 'the promotion of sustainable growth respecting the environment' – and the Maastricht requirement that environmental policy should promote measures at the 'international level to deal with regional or worldwide environmental problems'.[25] The policy objectives of the programme also sought to guarantee an international dimension: Community policy should contribute to the solution of regional and global environmental problems; the Community should play a leading role in promoting environmental cooperation; and the Community should establish an 'inextricable link' between the internal and external dimensions of Community environmental policy.[26] Three principles were to animate EU environmental policy: sustainable development (economic growth should not come at the cost of mortgaging the environmental future), preventive and precautionary action (environmental action can be taken without conclusive scientific proof) and shared responsibility (burden-sharing of costs). These principles and the policies of the EU were to be realised not only with respect to internal environmental policy measures, but extended to eastern and central Europe within the 'framework of their co-operation and association agreements'.[27]

The consequences of environmental degradation in eastern Europe served as a major source of concern in the fifth Action Programme. The Community took cognisance of the tension between the costs and difficulty of making the transition to the market economy and competitive multi-party democracy in the CEE countries while at the same time undertaking not only the abatement of future pollution but the cleaning up of the pollution generated by over forty years of economic and environmental mismanagement. The EU also reiterated the declaration on the environment made in Dublin in June 1990: the Community adopted the position that it 'must use more effectively its position of moral, economic and political authority to advance international efforts to solve global problem ...'. Nonetheless, the targets of EU environmental policy remain cast in terms quite distant from security considerations, and policy objectives remain tied to the Community's concept of sustainable development, with the exception of the discussion of chemical and nuclear accidents, where the language of security, although it remains opaque, is discernible. The security dimension of the environment is couched in terms of the impact environmental issues could have upon the security dimension of international relations, rather than as a distinct concept driving policy. In the discussion of nuclear safety and radiation protection, for example, the Community's attention was focused upon the consequences of the Chernobyl nuclear accident for the member states. It suggested that the Community should 'provide leadership in the field of nuclear safety' and increase the level of regional cooperation on environmental issues, particularly cross-border radiation pollution.[28] Yet the overall concern of the Community in eastern and central Europe was the severe environmental degradation in the eastern portion of the European continent. The Community assigned priority to environmental cooperation with the CEE nations in order to abate polluting industries, to create a set of framework conditions – 'a closer convergence of environmental policies' – that would inhibit investment strategies in Europe that took advantage of slack environmental policy enforcement and facilitated dumping. The Community assigned environmental policy a weight equal to that attributed to the economic and political transformation of central and eastern Europe. It has used the association agreements signed with most of the CEE nations to provide a mechanism for addressing common environmental problems and for providing the basis for the long-term transition of those nations to an environmental policy regime whose key elements and standards are established by the EU.[29]

An important document that established the basis of a pan-European environmental framework was produced by the April 1993 Lucerne meeting of the European environment ministers. The ministers issued a declaration that committed the participating states to seek the 'convergence of environmental quality and policies in Europe'.[30] The Lucerne meeting endorsed an environmental action programme (EAP) for the CEE nations. The EAP had three pillars: the integration of environmental criteria into investment and development strategies to ensure sustainable development; the creation of a viable administrative and legal infrastructure to ensure compliance with environmental regulations; and the provision of the necessary finance to provide immediate relief from the most pressing environmental stresses and sources of cross-border pollution. Unlike the fifth Action Programme of the Community, the EAP detected a fundamental compatibility, rather than a tension or trade-off, between the tasks of restructuring the CEE economies and cleaning up the environment. The principle of burden-sharing also permeates the Lucerne document: the central and eastern Europeans were assigned primary responsibility for undertaking the appropriate policy and institutional reforms necessary to arrest and then reverse environmental degradation, while the nations of western Europe and the EU would assume responsibility for providing the finance. Moreover, the western European ministers demanded and gained the agreement of their CEE counterparts that environmental standards would be strictly applied in the granting of assistance by their governments and by international financial institutions. The second principle animating European environmental cooperation is a modified 'polluter pays' principle: the western European environmental ministers accepted that the special circumstances facing the central and eastern Europeans suggested that the principle should be interpreted liberally owing to the special financial and political burdens facing the nations in transition. This modified 'polluter pays' principle was joined by adherence to the principle of burden sharing, which calls for assistance for countries unable to meet the costs of critical environmental policy objectives from their wealthier European neighbours.[31]

Another important document contributing to the creation of a pan-European environmental area is the 'Environmental Standards and Legislation in Western and Eastern Europe: Towards Harmonisation', a joint initiative of the EBRD and the EU Commission. This document states categorically that for the CEE nations to attain the greatest level of cooperation with the nations of the OECD, it is imperative for them to harmonise their environmental standards with those obtaining in the West, particularly in the EU. This conclusion was driven by the express objective of many CEE states of eventually joining the EU. The EBRD and the Commission stated that environmental harmonisation is therefore 'the single most important driving force of the harmonisation process and sets a clear target of what should be harmonised ...'. Economic and environmental rationales were also offered to support the harmonisation of these nations' environmental legislation with that of the EU. Economic considerations focused on the prospect of stringent environmental standards for these nations' exports to western Europe; and the environmental rationale was located in the sorry state of the CEE environment.[32]

The United Nations Environmental Programme (UNEP), established in 1972, has been described as a 'dwarf agency' of the UN system.[33] Nonetheless its influence has been phenomenal in setting the outlines of the environmental debate on a global basis. The UNEP established the viability of the concept of 'sustainable development' with the 1987 Brundtland Commission report, a concept which has served as the basis of environmental policy for post-Cold War Europe. The limitations of the UNEP as an effective institution for implementing policy are well documented, but its influence exceeds its material and institutional resources.[34] In addition to placing international environmental issues on the agendas of national governments, the UNEP was instrumental in establishing in 1980 the Committee of International Development Institutions on the Environment (CIDIE), which pledged the signatory international financial institutions to impart a significant environmental component into their lending activities – an environmental component that has become marked in the lending activities of the major multilateral lending banks servicing Europe. The CIDIE was suspected of introducing a 'new conditionality' to development lending that was resisted earlier by the nations of the Third World in the application of the Brundtland report to UNEP activities: the UNEP's governing council agreed that the requirements of sustainable development did 'not imply in any way encroachment upon national sovereignty'.[35] Yet that 'new conditionality' has become part and parcel of the new lending regime for the European security space.

The Earth Summit in Rio de Janeiro produced the Rio Declaration on the Environment and Development, *Agenda 21*, and a new institution, the United Nations Commission on Sustainable Development. The Rio Declaration sustains many of the principles embraced by NATO, OSCE and the EU. The declaration provides for the joint and common responsibility of nations for the international environment and the pursuit of sustainable development – akin to the principles of joint responsibility (principle 7). The declaration also embraces the precautionary approach in coping with environmental threats of a national or international nature (principle 15). It embraces the 'polluter pays' principle (principle 16). And it sanctions investments that shift the environmental burden from one country to another (principle 14).[36] *Agenda 21*, the blueprint for the global environment until the year 2000, pays special attention to the environmental tasks facing the CEE states. It acknowledges that the financial and economic resources necessary to reverse the environmental degradation of eastern and central Europe are potentially in conflict with the task of economic and political transition, a process causing 'considerable social and political tension'.[37] Yet *Agenda 21* did not provide for the uniform application of environmental standards across national boundaries; rather it allowed for differing environmental standards, reflecting disparate levels of economic development.[38] This sliding scale of environmental rectitude has not found favour in the European case: the western European states expect the CEE states to adopt the full environmental standards of the EU. The Rio programme also emphasised the collateral economic requirements of the successful implementation of appropriate and desirable environmental policies for the CEE states (as well as the Third World): easing the debt burden, supplying adequate development finance, the lowering of barriers to trade by the wealthy governments, and macroeconomic policies supporting sustainable growth.[39]

Agenda 21 also paid close attention to the requirements of implementing the programme. There were two critical requirements: finance and the institutionalisation of environmental cooperation. The issue of finance created particular difficulties for the nations attending the conference. It was estimated that the cost of implementing the programme in the developing countries would amount to an annual sum of $600 billion between 1993 and 2000. The G-7 nations rejected the demand for the creation of a 'Green Fund' to be administered by the Sustainable Development Commission established at Rio, and instead offered marginal increases in available environmental aid, specifically the renewing of the Global Environmental Facility that would continue to be administered by the World Bank.[40] The problem of institutionalising environmental cooperation resulted in a patchwork of institutions centred in the UN. Environmental responsibilities were parcelled out to the newly created Commission on Sustainable Development, the primary task of which is monitoring progress towards fulfiling the *Agenda 21* action plan; to a strengthened UNEP, particularly in the area of establishing international environmental standards and the promotion of environmental cooperation at the global and regional levels; and to regional and sub-regional organisations, particularly regional development banks, in creating a dense network of environmental cooperation consistent with the objectives of sustainable development.[41]

The European institutions implementing environmental security

The patchwork of conventions and treaties monitoring the environment, while impressive in their scope and objectives, are largely dependent upon voluntary compliance or the provision of side payments to encourage recalcitrant or impoverished nations to meet their obligations. This is particularly true in the case of the European environmental space.[42] The primary mechanism for encouraging the CEE nations – as well as the poorer states of the EU – is the setting aside of financial resources dedicated to EU environmental objectives or of embedding environmental criteria into the decision-making process of regional investment banks and other development funds. The European regional investment banks – the Nordic Investment Bank (NIB), the Nordic Environment Finance Corporation (NEFCO), the EIB and the EBRD – are playing an important role in extending western European environmental standards eastward and meeting the broader objective of establishing a pan-European environmental space.

The NIB is an investment bank established by the Nordic countries in 1975 with the objective of providing a source of finance that would support investment projects with an expressly 'Nordic interest.' Until the end of the Cold War the NIB limited its environmental loans to investment in the Nordic countries (Sweden, Denmark, Finland, Iceland and Norway), but expanded environmental lending to the nations of the Baltic region because it represented a 'Nordic interest' owing to the inability of pollution to respect national borders and the level of pollution flowing into the Baltic from Poland, the Baltic states and the Russian Federation. The rise in environmental lending was facilitated by a change in the lending criteria of the bank: the environment was designated an element of the Nordic interest. This expanded definition of the Nordic interest corresponded to the end of the Cold War, reflecting the necessity of cooperating with the littoral states of the Baltic to address a common environmental threat as well as the new-found ability to do so on Nordic terms. The changed external context and the redefinition of the Nordic interest facilitated the dramatic increase in environmental lending between 1989 and 1990, when the share of environmental lending rose from 1 per cent of total loans in 1989 to 20 per cent in 1990; the total of environmental loans reached a cumulative amount of $1.138 billion between 1990 and 1994.[43]

Another category of loan that addresses the environmental interests of the Nordic countries is the project investment loan. Such loans are made to nations other than the Nordic countries, but retain the criterion of creditworthiness on the part of the borrowing nation as well as requiring the loan to have a Nordic interest. The NIB is also enabled to grant environmental protection loans under this category to the CEE nations – it provides yet another means of furthering the environmental agenda of the Nordic nations with their neighbours. The ceiling for the project investment loans was set in 1990 at $1.423 billion. Despite concern about the environmental degradation of the Baltic Sea, the CEE states captured only 11 per cent of the project investment loans granted by the NIB between 1990 and 1993.[44]

The Nordic countries also responded to the environmental opportunity presented by the end of the Cold War with the creation of the Nordic Environment Finance Corporation. NEFCO was designed to address the 'Nordic environmental interest' in central and eastern Europe.[45] NEFCO investments target the abatement of cross-border pollution via the supply of environmental technology to CEE nations. The initial capital of NEFCO was set at $51 million and participation was limited to 25–35 per cent of a project's cost. Loans and credit guarantees under this fund were required to meet three lending criteria: the project must involve a 'significant Nordic environmental impact', it must be technically and commercially feasible, and it must involve the production or use of environmental technology.[46] By the end of 1993 NEFCO had dedicated $25.6 million to twenty-five environmental projects in central and eastern Europe.[47]

The Baltic Sea study co-sponsored by the NIB, EBRD, EIB and World Bank produced an action programme for redressing the stress on the Baltic Sea caused by 130 environmental 'hot spots'. These sources of pollution were estimated to require a fifteen-year investment programme of $25.6 billion. The vast majority of the environmental hot spots threatening the Baltic are to be found in Poland, the Baltic states and the Russian Federation; they range from radioactive waste outside St Petersburg to emissions from Estonia's oil shale power stations in Narva to abating a million cubic metres of the hazardous waste that has accumulated in the eastern Baltic. The level of environmental degradation in the Baltic led to the creation of a third source of environmental financing, the Baltic Investment Programme (BIP). The BIP was created jointly in March 1992 by the NIB, EBRD and Nordic Project Fund. The loan facility, which was set at $42.7 million, is completely guaranteed by the Nordic countries and is designed to redress the environmental stress on the Baltic Sea emanating from Latvia, Lithuania and Estonia.[48]

The EIB was established in 1958 by the EC as an autonomous investment institution. Its primary purpose was to finance projects within the EC on a non-profit basis. The overarching objectives of the EIB remain regional development in the member states of the EU and the narrowing of the gap between the richer and poor regions of the Community. The criteria driving EIB financing decisions have been both political and financial. The political purpose of EIB loans is to contribute to European integration; the financial criteria require the proposed project to be financially and economically viable. The environment did not play an explicit role in EIB investment decisions until June 1984, when the EIB made the protection of the environment a specific eligibility criterion for its loans, in line with its membership of CIDIE. The environmental criterion established by the EIB has been interpreted as requiring the EIB to assess a specific project's overall impact on the environment and to ensure that the project conforms with existing environmental norms; to finance projects that are aimed at the protection of the environment, including the extension of additional financing to supply anti-pollution measures exceeding existing legislation equal to 10 per cent of the cost of the project; and to disqualify projects from EIB finance on the grounds that the project would be likely to cause 'serious environmental damage'.

The environmental role played by the EIB in the European economy was expanded by a number of provisions of the Maastricht treaty. The first, which calls for 'a high level of protection' of the Community's environment, endorsed the environmental brief assumed by the EIB and expanded its role to include the implementation of EU environmental policy through its lending activities; and the second, which calls for the promotion of 'measures at the international level to deal with regional or worldwide environmental problems', has created a basis for the expanded environmental lending of the EIB outside the EU, particularly in eastern Europe.[49] Thus the EIB plays an important role not only in implementing the objectives of the Maastricht treaty relating to the environment (and economic and social cohesion) within the EU, but in extending EU environmental norms and objectives (e.g. those stated in the fifth Action Programme) to central and eastern Europe.[50]

The underlying criterion of lending outside the EU is simply that the project being financed must promise a 'particular benefit' for the EU. The importance of the economic transition in central and eastern Europe was acted upon early by the EIB: at the end of November 1989 the bank was authorised to grant loans to Hungary and Poland up to Ecu 1 billion; in April 1991 Bulgaria, the Czech and Slovak Republic and Romania were eligible for loans up to Ecu 700 million; and the signing of Europe Agreements in December 1991 with Poland, the Czech and Slovak Republic and Hungary contained financial provisions that set continued access to EIB financing on a long-term basis. By early May 1994 the EIB had been authorised to operate independently in four additional countries, Estonia, Latvia, Lithuania and Albania; its loan and guarantee ceiling was raised to Ecu 3 billion. EIB lending to the republics of the former Soviet Union was made possible by the bank's status as a shareholder in the EBRD and contingent upon EIB–EBRD co-financing of projects. The EIB, like the EBRD, is intended to serve as a source of complementary finance for investments in central and eastern Europe. EIB participation cannot exceed 50 per cent of the total cost of a project, but the bank can participate with other EU budgetary funds, including the Phare programme. Any loan by the EIB to support an investment project in central and eastern Europe must be subject to a project appraisal that includes an environmental impact assessment. EIB participation in a project requires, at a minimum, conformity with the relevant environmental legislation; and the EIB cannot ignore 'internationally set recommendations' in the assessment of the project's environmental impact. In addition to granting project loans, the EIB can also grant 'global loans' to financial intermediaries. Global loans, intended to support project investments between Ecu 15 million and Ecu 20 million, require financial intermediaries to conform with EIB eligibility criteria, including those pertaining to the environment.[51] The third means whereby the EIB can grant environmental loans is via the Edinburgh Lending Facility. The Edinburgh Lending Facility, created in December 1992, is a Ecu 5 billion temporary lending facility, the objective of which is to accelerate the financing of infrastructure projects, particularly those 'connected with trans-European networks'. The EIB was designated manager of the Edinburgh Facility, and in April 1993 the EIB determined that, in addition to the support of trans-European network projects, environmental projects could be supported by the facility in central and eastern Europe 'provided that they further implementation of, or supplement, trans-European networks'.[52]

EIB lending in central and eastern Europe has taken on a new quality in view of the anticipated accession of the CEE nations in the EU.[53] The environmental assessments and loans either to abate pollution or to redress existing environmental degradation underline the importance of the EIB as an agent of externalising western European environmental norms in central and eastern

Europe. The level of EIB lending in central and eastern Europe amounted to Ecu 1,702 million between 1990 and 1993. The EIB has no separate category of environmental loans, yet it is possible to argue that two categories of loan – global loans and loans to the energy sector – have a significant environmental component. Global loans either extend or integrate EU environmental norms into the lending behaviour of CEE financial intermediaries; loans to the energy sector have either a direct (pollution abatement) or an indirect (pollution prevention) impact on the environments of central and eastern Europe.

EIB support of the environment in central and eastern Europe has been limited – at least in terms of projects financed. Between 1990 and 1993 the total lending of the EIB was Ecu 65,376.4 million. The share of the financing captured by the CEE nations was only 2.6 per cent of the total (Ecu 1,702 million). And of that amount, environmental lending to central and eastern Europe amounted to Ecu 650 million, or just under 1 per cent of the total lending of the EIB. Although the level of project finance supplied by the EIB to central and eastern Europe is dwarfed by the level of finance supplied within the EU (93.22 per cent of the total, or Ecu 60,944.1 million), it is also the case that environmental lending within the EU is significantly higher, at Ecu 13,017.2 million, or 19.9 per cent of total EIB lending.[54] The environmental role of the EIB in central and eastern Europe is putative and will expand significantly only as these nations become members of the EU. Until that time, the most likely champion of the environment will be the EBRD.

The purpose of the EBRD was to facilitate the transition to the market economy in central and eastern Europe. Unlike the World Bank, the EBRD was intended to target primarily private-sector investment and to eschew infrastructure projects; in other words, it was designed to function as an investment bank targeting central and eastern European small and medium-sized enterprises.[55] Consequently, one of the criteria constraining EBRD lending was that its investments must meet the normal financial criteria of feasibility. The EBRD also faces the constraint that it must be the lender of last resort; in a sense, the EBRD is there to put its imprimatur on investment projects, thereby catalyzing additional private-sector finance. What is novel about the EBRD, however, is the three additional elements of conditionality that separate the EBRD from the other international financial institutions operating in Europe (or elsewhere). First, the EBRD is charged with the task of fostering 'the transition toward open market-orientated economies in central and eastern Europe' and of promoting 'private and entrepreneurial initiative'; second, the EBRD can operate only in countries successfully making the transition to competitive multi-party democracies; third, EBRD investments must promote 'environmentally sound and sustainable development'.[56] The breaching of the first or second elements of the 'new conditionality' imposed on the countries in transition can result in the suspension of a nation's access to EBRD funds. The third criterion, the necessity for EBRD-sponsored investments to contribute to the sustainable development of CEE nations' economies, is the most novel and perhaps significant responsibility of the EBRD. Yet it remains significant that the EBRD is not charged with the task of environmental restoration, but rather with the integration of environmental criteria into project lending decisions. Moreover, environmental infrastructure loans can be granted only when the loans make a direct contribution to the transition to an open market economy.[57]

The EBRD is the only international financial institution that was created with a responsibility to the environment written into its charter or articles of agreement. The necessity of the environmental lending criterion is located in two factors: first, the degree of environmental degradation in central and eastern Europe is so severe that future economic growth depends upon investments that will contribute to the reversal or stabilisation of the CEE environment; second, it places the bank in the position of deflecting the criticisms directed at other international financial institutions' poor environmental record.[58] Moreover, it has formed a powerful advocate within the institutional framework of post-Cold War Europe, addressing the environmental challenge facing Europe with a built-in mechanism for correcting the environmental consequences of project investment – the compulsory environmental screening of project investments.[59]

The EBRD has developed and applied a series of environmental criteria that shape its lending policies. The starting point of the EBRD treatment of the environment is found in the underlying assumptions about the state of the CEE environment: first, that the source of environmental problems is found in 'inappropriate and distortionary economic policies', and, second, that the solution of such environmental problems is located in the linkage of environmental policies within those countries to the broader framework of structural change. The bank also accepted a comprehensive set of environmental principles that captured not only responsibility for the consequences of pollution but the best methods of abating and preventing pollution in the future. These principles conformed with those of the EU, but the bank also reserved for itself the 'use of more stringent environmental standards in areas which suffer from high levels of pollution or are ecologically fragile'.[60] These principles are not only applied during the process of the project's environmental review, but are a part of the project financing agreement. The EBRD project approval process provides for the inclusion of environmental covenants specifying the environmental conditions of a project; and project financing agreements also provide for environmental supervision. Environmental supervision supplies the EBRD with a sanctioning instrument for ensuring conformity with the environmental conditionality of a project. The supervision process provides the bank with a range of sanctions, including the ability to freeze disbursements, which could have the consequence of halting the project.

The EBRD helped finance 151 projects between 1991 and 1993. EBRD funds committed to those projects amounted to Ecu 3,776.47 million. The types of project financed by the EBRD are categorised as those requiring a full environmental assessment (category A), those requiring a partial environmental assessment (category B) and those requiring no environmental assessment (category C). Each of the categories is divided further into projects that need an environmental audit and those that do not. Over the period 1991 and 1993 forty-three projects, or 28.47 per cent of the total, fell into category A or B and required an environmental audit. Bank lending to those forty-three projects amounted to Ecu 1,253.81 million, or 33.2 per cent of total EBRD financing. The level of environmental lending, however, is understated by these statistics. The EBRD has used two other means to achieve its environmental objectives: the environmental conditionality attached to financial intermediary loans; and the establishment of 'environmental linkage' in its project lending.

The second method of extending western European environmental norms and standards into central and eastern Europe is the use of corporate or financial intermediaries. The EBRD has channelled Ecu 786.56 million, or 25.16 per cent of total EBRD lending between 1990 and 1993, through financial intermediaries to support the transition to the market economy, particularly the fostering of investment in small and medium sized enterprises. The EBRD has supported thirty-eight financial intermediary projects, or 25.15 per cent of the total projects financed by the EBRD. The EBRD has established a set of environmental procedures that guide lending by financial intermediaries, the most remarkable of which are the requirement that both existing and new facilities are subject to environmental audits, that the environmental standards applied by the intermediary match those applied by the EBRD, and that the EBRD can help those intermediaries develop an 'in-house' environmental capacity.[61] The importance of these financial intermediary projects is located in the importance of the banking system to the successful and self-sustaining capacity of the transition to the market economy; its rationale is located in the importance of a developed banking system in a market economy, particularly the role of financial institutions in the mobilisation of financial resources, the creation of a local capital market, and the creation of viable payments systems. The environmental conditionality attached to these project loans has another consequence of some importance: it supports and encourages the internalisation of western European environmental norms in central and eastern Europe.[62]

Three cases in 1993 and early 1994 illustrate the evolution of 'environmental linkage' in the EBRD's lending activities. The EBRD financed the completion of the Hrasdan Unit 5 gas-fired power plant in Armenia in March 1993. The EBRD supplied Ecu 51.45 million of the total investment cost of Ecu 80.48 million. In addition to meeting the financial, political and environmental criteria applied to all the projects it finances, the bank established an additional criterion disconnected from the financial viability of the project; the project would be approved only on two conditions: the restricted reopening of the Medzamor nuclear power plant and the restricted use of heavy fuel oil at the Hrasdan complex. The EBRD's willingness to supply Ecu 40.47 million of the Ecu 56.20 million necessary to finance the Orsha gas-fired combined cycle power plant in Belarus on 9 December 1993 was conditional upon measures being taken to reduce the emissions produced by other power plants. And in 1994 the EBRD announced its willingness to supply DM 412.5 million of the DM 1.3 billion necessary to complete the Mochovce nuclear power plant in Slovakia on condition that Slovakia agreed to shut down the ageing and dangerous nuclear power plant at Bohunice – a condition which eventually proved unacceptable.[63]

Environmental security and nuclear power plants in central and eastern Europe

The threat of a nuclear war on the European continent has been significantly reduced with the end of the Cold War. The diminution of the political threat posed by either the United States or the Russian Federation to the European continent has been reinforced by a reduction in the number of nuclear weapons stationed outside the two military superpowers as well as by the redeployment of those weapons. Yet the threat of a nuclear catastrophe remains an immediate one for all Europeans. The Chernobyl nuclear power plant accident in 1986, where one of the four RMBK nuclear reactors exploded, caused around 8,000 deaths, required the medical treatment of 11 million Ukrainians for radiation exposure, poisoned the environment around Kiev, and contaminated western European agricultural crops and dairy produce. The Cherbobyl accident alerted both elites and publics in western Europe to the scale of the threat posed to the European environment by the nuclear power plants operating in the east, yet it was only with the end of the Cold War that the breadth and severity of that threat became understood. The prospect of nuclear accidents throughout central and eastern Europe meets the criteria of a security threat: the sources of the threat to the states of Europe are specific and identifiable; the source of cross-border radiation poisoning emanating from reactors of Soviet design is close in both time and space to the European states; there is a near certainty that design flaws and operational inadequacies in at least two categories of Soviet-designed reactors still operating throughout the former Soviet bloc will cause major nuclear accidents; and the consequences of a nuclear accident will not only be international, but will degrade societal, state and systemic security in Europe.[64]

Nuclear power generates a large proportion of the electricity used by the CEE economies. The dependence upon nuclear power for electricity generation ranges from a high of approximately 60 per cent in Lithuania to a low of 11.8 per cent in Russia. For the CEE nations that depend upon nuclear power, the share falls between just over 20 per cent in the Czech Republic to just under 50 per cent in Hungary and the Slovak Republic. While it is true that dependence upon nuclear power is significantly higher in several western European countries, particularly France (72.9 per cent) and Belgium (59.9 per cent), it is also the case that Western-designed nuclear reactors are of better design and meet both the IAEA Nuclear Safety Standards (NUSS) codes and guidelines and the

International Nuclear Safety Advisory Group's (INSAG) Basic Safety Principles for Nuclear Power Plants. Nuclear power generation is particularly troublesome in the CEE countries owing to the failure to meet NUSS codes and guidelines, and to the inadequacies of Soviet-designed reactors, particularly the first-generation pressurised water reactors (designated VVER440/230) and the graphite-moderated reactors (designated RMBK). Nuclear power plants with these two categories of reactor are located in the Slovak Republic, Bulgaria, Ukraine, Lithuania and the Russian Federation. Each presents a palpable threat to the European security order.

The IAEA initiated a programme in 1990 to assess and meet the challenges posed by the problem of Soviet-designed reactors. The financial costs of the programme, the first stage of which was the assessment of the most dangerous of the Soviet-designed reactors (VVER 440/230), were met on a voluntary basis by Austria, Germany, the Netherlands, Norway, Spain, Switzerland and the United Kingdom. The United States contributed only technical assistance; the three largest donors, the Netherlands, Spain and the Federal Republic, contributed almost 75 per cent of the $643,000 cost. When the IAEA published the results of the study in 1992 its findings reinforced the widespread opinion of most experts that all ten reactors operating in Russia, Slovakia and Bulgaria should be closed immediately. All ten reactors suffered from a long list of maladies: insufficient containment capability in the event of a nuclear accident; poor instrumentation and control; inadequate emergency cooling systems; lack of redundancy of safety systems and/or non-separation of safety systems; non-separation of operational and safety systems; and insufficient fire protection. These design and safety flaws were compounded, in the case of the Bulgarian nuclear power plant at Kozloduy, by flawed construction and the use of substandard material, by the poor physical state of the power plant, particularly the embrittlement of the pressure vessel; and the inability of the reactors to withstand earthquakes. The RMBK reactors are located only in Ukraine, notably at Chernobyl, in the Russian Federation and in Lithuania, at the Ignalina complex. These reactors were less well understood by Western experts, but they too were found to suffer from serious design flaws which included the lack of a containment system, the limited capacity and redundancy of safety systems, insufficient fire protection, and a limited core cooling system. The considerable design flaws of both the RMBK and VVER 440/230 nuclear reactors are compounded by poorly trained work forces and underdeveloped or non-existent safety procedures and regulatory regimes. The other Soviet-designed reactors operating in central and eastern Europe are not considered to pose the threat of an imminent nuclear accident. The IAEA has concluded that the second-generation VVER 440/213 nuclear reactors could be upgraded to conform with international standards; the third-generation VVER 1000 nuclear reactors have Western-type safety systems and containment.[65]

The recognition of the problem posed by Soviet-designed reactors was manifest with the Chernobyl disaster, but the incentive to redress the problem has become bound up with the broader strategy of integrating the CEE states into the international economy and establishing a broader and more inclusive European security order. The solution to the problem posed by Soviet-designed nuclear reactors faced three problems. First, the nuclear reactors supplied too great a proportion of the electricity generating power of Bulgaria, Lithuania and Slovakia to be simply shut down. The closing of the plants and the subsequent loss of electricity output would threaten progress towards political and economic reform. Second, the total cost of resolving the threat posed by Soviet-designed nuclear reactors was put at around $25 billion: remedying the design flaws and lax operational and safety procedures at the VVER 440 nuclear reactors in the short term was estimated to cost $700 million; the cost of resolving the long-term threat of cross-border radiation poisoning stemming from the ten VVER 440/230 and fifteen RMBK nuclear reactors was estimated at $10 billion; and the construction of non-nuclear power generating plants that would replace the capacity lost by shutting the reactors down was estimated to cost an additional $14 billion. The third problem facing the efforts of governments to meet this environmental threat was the failure of CEE governments to sign the 1963 Vienna Convention on Nuclear Safety, which provides that liability for nuclear accidents shall fall exclusively on plant operators rather than on (Western) nuclear suppliers. This problem dragged on into 1994 until the United States signed special indemnity agreements with Ukraine and Russia which became the basis of a similar agreement with the EU.[66]

Although there are international conventions establishing liability for cross-border damage caused by nuclear accidents, and requiring early notification of nuclear accidents, slow progress has been made towards the creation of a binding international convention establishing an international nuclear safety regime. In other words, progress has been made towards shutting the stable door after the horse has bolted, but little progress has been made towards setting in place a regime that would minimise the prospect of a nuclear accident in the first instance.[67] Yet the EU made an effort as early as 1975 to meet the problem of a regional nuclear safety regime. A Council resolution on the technological problems of nuclear safety recognised the need to assure that a nuclear safety culture extended beyond 'the frontiers not only of Member States but of the community as a whole ...'. The EC resolved at that time to support the 'progressive harmonisation of safety requirements and criteria in order to provide [the Community] with an equivalent and satisfactory degree of protection' from radiation. The effort to establish a single nuclear safety area encompassing Europe was furthered with the Single European Act; and the eastward enlargement of the EU would also spread the regional nuclear safety regime farther to the east. It is also the case, however, that the states that are the most likely entrants into the EU have either nuclear power plants of Western or second-generation Soviet design (Slovenia, Hungary and the Czech Republic) or no nuclear power plants (Poland). Nonetheless, the EU has made it an explicit policy objective to support the establishment of internationally agreed upon safety requirements and the implementation of those requirements in central and eastern Europe.[68]

Additional building blocks of a nuclear safety regime are also in place. In September 1991 negotiations began on the drafting of an international safety convention to standardise the operation and construction of nuclear power plants, and a nuclear protocol to the European Energy Charter has been drafted. The nuclear protocol to the European Energy Charter seeks to establish the 'principles governing the peaceful use of nuclear safety facilities', establish liability and financial responsibility for nuclear accidents, and establish 'principles of responsible nuclear conduct'.[69] The absence of either an effective global or a regional nuclear safety regime combined with an IAEA that is both financially weak (the 1993 budget was only $191 million) and overburdened (it is responsible for monitoring and assessing both the operational safety of nuclear power plants and the proliferation of nuclear weapons) made the initial response to the nuclear safety crisis in central and eastern Europe largely bilateral and *ad hoc*. Moreover, the problem facing Europe is not assuring a high level of operational and design standards in the future, but with coping with the problems derived from the deviation from Western technological standards in the 1970s.

The initial bilateral responses to the nuclear safety crisis in central and eastern Europe were promising, but fell short of the amount of finance necessary to address the problem. In March 1990 the United States and the Soviet Union signed an accord to enhance nuclear safety. The American Congress pledged $7 million for fiscal 1991 to support the programme, which focused on the vulnerable VVER 440/230 reactors at the Novovoronezh nuclear power plant. The United States and the Federal Republic of Germany signed a bilateral accord in May 1991 that promised $400,000 and a team of experts to help the IAEA carry out the review of the VVER 440/230 nuclear reactors, and pledged an additional $2 million to support follow-on measures to the IAEA safety review. France initially took the lead in redressing the safety problems at the Kozloduy site in Bulgaria, while the British Atomic Energy Authority led a multinational safety review of RMBK nuclear reactors in late October 1992. Despite the pressing need to resolve the nuclear safety problem, however, burden-sharing almost immediately became a divisive issue even though the consequences of a nuclear accident met the criteria of a collective bad: cross-border radiation is neither excludable nor divisible. It was the position of the US Department of Energy, for example, that the safety danger posed by Bulgarian reactors was largely a European problem and that the Europeans should consequently provide the financial and technical assistance necessary.[70] Likewise, the German government absorbed the cost of shutting down the four nuclear reactors at the Greifswald nuclear power plant in eastern Germany, but placed a firm limit on its relative contribution to the G-7 nuclear safety programme.

There have been two major multilateral initiatives addressing the problem of nuclear safety in central and eastern Europe. The EU made an early and sustained effort to reduce the risk of a nuclear accident in central and eastern

Europe with the Phare programme and in the former Soviet Union with the Tacis programme. Between 1990 and 1993 the Phare and Tacis programmes committed approximately $400 million to enhancing the safety of Soviet-designed nuclear reactors.[71] The Phare programme provided on-site assistance at the Kozloduy nuclear power station in Bulgaria, at the Bohunice nuclear power station in Slovakia, the Dukovany nuclear power station in the Czech Republic, and the Ignalina nuclear power station in Lithuania. The Tacis programme has aided the decommissioning of RMBK reactors at the Chernobyl nuclear power plant as well as upgrading the safety of the other thirteen RMBK reactors in the western Russian Federation.

EU funds committed to the problem of nuclear safety were considerably enhanced in December 1992 when the Commission proposed that it should be authorised to exhaust the statutory limit on Euratom borrowings to finance the conversion work on nuclear power stations in the Phare and Tacis countries to improve nuclear safety, to complete the construction of nuclear power plants, or to decommission nuclear reactors that could not be upgraded to meet Western safety standards. The authorisation to allow the Commission to tap the Euratom borrowing limit and provide an additional $1.2 billion to complement the Phare and Tacis nuclear safety programmes was not finalised until early 1994. The potentially large loan facility carried with it a number of caveats: Euratom financing of any project would be limited to 50 per cent of the project's cost, the repayment period would be limited to a maximum of twenty years, the interest rate charged by Euratom would be linked closely with market rates, the loans would be guaranteed by the recipient state, project approval would be subject to the approval of the EIB, which would assess the financial viability of the project, and the terms required that each project should 'involve close industrial or commercial cooperation with at least one Community enterprise' – a requirement that only seemed to support the contention of environmental groups that the entire effort to enhance nuclear safety in central and eastern Europe was an elaborate mechanism for supporting Western nuclear power industries.[72]

The other important multilateral source of financing for the upgrading or decommissioning of Soviet-designed reactors is the G-7 Nuclear Safety Fund, which is managed by the EBRD. The G-7 Nuclear Safety Fund was established at the Munich summit in July 1992. At that time the G-7 countries outlined a programme of action that had two overall objectives: financing operational safety improvements at all nuclear power plants and near-term technical improvements at those nuclear power plants posing the greatest danger. The programme's priority was the near-term technical improvements for the VVER 440/230 and RMBK reactors. The G-7 programme of action was designed to finance hardware investment in central and eastern Europe as well as in Ukraine and the Russian Republic. It was designed largely as a complement to the technical studies financed bilaterally or by the EU's Phare and Tacis nuclear safety programmes. The G-7 programme was initially stymied by a conflict of interest between the United States and the western European countries. The latter, particularly France, Germany and the United Kingdom, preferred a multilateral approach to the problem of financing the hardware costs of upgrading or decommissioning Soviet-designed reactors, whereas the United States (and Japan) favoured the establishment of a multilateral mechanism that coordinated bilateral assistance. Prior to the G-7 meeting, the size of the anticipated nuclear safety fund was widely reported to be hovering around $700 to $800 million. However, the Munich summit produced an agreement to create an anaemic $100 million multilateral fund to complement bilateral assistance. The agreement, which established the objectives and priorities of the fund, also provided that the Nuclear Safety Fund would be part of the G-24 coordination mechanism and would be administered by the EBRD. The G-7 eventually agreed in early 1993 to create a nuclear safety fund of $700 million, the amount estimated as the minimum necessary to correct the most dangerous problems at the VVER 440/230 and RMBK nuclear power plants. The negotiations leading to the enlarged fund were led by France and Germany, both of which pledged a total of $80 million over three years to the nuclear safety account. Although the nuclear safety account became effective on 14 April 1993, only two projects had been approved by December 1994: in June 1993 $29 million was dedicated to the Kozloduy nuclear power plant in Bulgaria; and in February 1994 $40 million was dedicated to the Ignalina nuclear power plant in Lithuania. Two other projects have been vetted, one to upgrade four RMBK reactors at the Leningrad complex and the other to redress the problems of four VVER 440/230 nuclear reactors at the Kola and Novovoronezh nuclear power plants in the Russian Federation. The costs of these four projects will nearly exhaust the Nuclear Safety Account: the pledged contributions to the account amount to only $186 million, which is far short of the agreed upon $700 million. The German and French contributions equal 40 per cent of the total pledges made by the fourteen donor countries, and the member states of the EU account for 75 per cent of contributions to the account. The United States and Japan, which possess the two largest economies and face the least risk from nuclear accidents in central and eastern Europe, have contributed 7.3 per cent and 5.8 per cent of the total, respectively.[73]

Conclusion

There are palpable threats to the European environment. It is not clear, however, that these threats to the environment constitute a security threat. Most of the theoretical and empirical work on environmental security has focused on the nations of the developing world. The criteria employed to transform a threat to the environment into an environmental security threat are perhaps excessively narrow, but they nonetheless serve the purpose of maintaining the conceptual integrity of security. One environmental threat that clearly qualifies as a security threat is that posed by nuclear power in the CEE states and the former Soviet Union. The safety flaws of the nuclear reactors, in both design and construction, threaten societal, state and systemic security. A severe nuclear accident like that which occurred at the Chernobyl power plant would cause not only widespread contamination of large tracts of land but death on a large scale. In many of the countries where the reactors are located – for example, Lithuania and Slovakia – the geographical scope of the accident would be large enough to rend the social fabric and produce environmental refugees seeking safety across national borders. Correspondingly, a nuclear accident that threatened societal integrity could also delegitimise the CEE nations' fragile democracies. Thus a nuclear accident could generate the opportunity or demand for authoritarian governments which would have the collateral effect of destabilising systemic security. The re-establishment of an authoritarian government in the Russian Federation or Ukraine would intensify the security dilemma facing the states of the European security area. An uncontrolled flow of environmental refugees in combination with the miscarriage of democracy could easily remilitarise Europe's borders and potentially redivide the European continent.

The environmental dimension of security does not suffer from an institutional deficit. The essential organisational framework is in place. NATO, OSCE and the UN have contributed to the creation of a set of environmental norms which form the basis of environmental cooperation on a global scale. The environmental norms of the EU, as found in the fifth Action Programme, have become the *de facto* norms of the CEE states. The compliance of the CEE states with EU environmental norms is driven in part by the desire to join the EU and in part by the enforcement of those norms by the regional investment banks, particularly the NIB, the EIB and the EBRD. Each investment bank imposes a new conditionality on loans granted to borrowers in the CEE states and the former Soviet Union. Rather than simply imposing a set of financial criteria on loans to the region, these banks have established political-environmental criteria that must be met, namely progress towards marketisation and democratisation and adherence to a set of stringent environmental criteria. The new conditionality will contribute to the minimisation of new environmental degradation but is unlikely to redress the despoilation of the Kola peninsula or the blighting of large portions of Poland, eastern Germany and the Czech Republic, commonly referred to as the Black Triangle

Nuclear safety, or rather the lack of nuclear safety in the CEE states and the former Soviet Union, clearly qualifies as an environmental threat to the European security order. A fairly well developed and highly institutionalised nuclear safety regime exists. The IAEA has established a set of widely accepted nuclear safety standards, INSAG has produced a set of basic safety principles for the operation of nuclear power plants, a nuclear protocol has been added to the European Energy Charter, and negotiations continue towards the conclusion of a nuclear safety convention. There is widespread recognition of the dangers posed by nuclear power plants and a set of well established rules on how to design, construct and maintain such plants. These norms now guide the construction and refitting of nuclear power plants in the CEE states and the former Soviet Union. Yet the problem posed by nuclear power is not so much providing guidelines for the construction of new nuclear power plants as redressing the design, construction and maintenance flaws of the VVER 440/230 and RMBK nuclear reactors.

The nuclear accident at Chernobyl and subsequent studies of the RMBK reactors satisfy most Western experts that these reactors are fundamentally flawed in design, lack even the most rudimentary safety features and are likely to fail again. The EU, which has the largest direct stake in shutting down RMBK reactors, only recently succeeded in extracting a promise from Ukraine that the Chernobyl plant will be closed and stabilised in 1999. Even after agreement had been reached, haggling began almost immediately about the scope of EU aid that would be made available to shut the plant down and to find an alternative source of electricity. Likewise, the problems with the RMBK reactors are duplicated at the nuclear power plants driven by the VVER 440/230 reactors. Slovakia, Bulgaria and the other countries with nuclear power plants driven by VVER 440/230 reactors face a dilemma: the probability of a nuclear accident must be weighed against the certainty that without nuclear-generated electricity the economy will grind to a halt. These countries require a dual strategy: the closure of the nuclear power plants and the creation of alternative generating capacity. This requirement is widely acknowledged. The resolution of the problem is not an institutional one. The EBRD, the EU's Phare and Tacis programmes and the EIB have the institutional experience and expertise to finance the building of alternative generating plants and to close the nuclear power plants most accident-prone. The minimisation of the threat posed by nuclear power, if not its eradication, is located in the absence of political will and financial resources within the G-7, the fear of free riding, and superficially divergent interests.

The travails of the Nuclear Safety Fund best illustrate lack of political will and paucity of financial resources among the G-7. The leaders of the G-7, despite indications of the intensity of the threat posed by the problem of nuclear safety in central and eastern Europe, did not agree to a multilateral solution until July 1992, agreed upon the $700 million figure for the NSF only in early 1993, and the pledged donations allowed only two projects to be approved by December 1994. The preoccupation with free riding (or burden sharing) has also coloured the reaction to the security threat posed by the nuclear power plants. The United States adopted the position that the problem with the Bulgarian reactors was a European problem and the Europeans should consequently pay for its rectification; and Germany has threatened to limit its overall contribution to the NSF to 15 per cent of the total, despite Germany's geographical propinquity to many of the VVER 440/230 reactors. A final obstacle blocking the resolution of the nuclear safety problem is located in the maximalist positions adopted by some western European governments. The EBRD effort to establish a linkage between the financing of the Mochovce nuclear power plant on condition it met Western safety standards with the commitment to decommission the dangerous Bohunice complex is a case in point. This solution would have provided Slovakia with a dependable source of electricity and it promised to decommission one of the most accident prone nuclear power plants in central Europe. Yet the EBRD proposal did not receive the political support of Slovakia's immediate neighbours, particularly Germany and Austria. The Austrians even threatened to resign from the EBRD if the loan were granted. In the end, Slovakia procured a less onerous financing package from the Czechs and Russians. Now neither site will necessarily meet Western safety standards and an opportunity to close a dangerous nuclear power plant was lost.

Geographical space has also created a superficial divergence of interests among the nations of the European security order. National authorities appear to treat distance as the primary indicator of vulnerability to a nuclear accident; it serves as an informal index of the threat posed to the nation. This assessment of risk reflects a narrow definition of national security and ignores the larger contextual consequences of a severe nuclear accident, particularly in one of the CEE states. Environmental security plays a contextual role in the European security order, particularly the interrelated threats to societal, state and systemic security posed by an environmental catastrophe. The inability of the G-7 to grapple successfully with as clear-cut a problem as that of nuclear safety parallels their inability to finance adequately the transitions to democracy and the market. It is the irony of the post-Cold War system that when the economic instruments of statecraft have become the most effective means of addressing the security dilemmas facing the industrialised West, the leading Western states are so financially constrained that they cannot muster the financial resources necessary to prevent a nuclear catastrophe.

Notes

1 See Joanna Spear, 'The environment agenda' in G. Wyn Rees (ed.), *International Politics in Europe: the New Agenda* (London: Routledge, 1993), p.126; Hilary French, *Green Revolutions: Environmental Reconstruction in Eastern Europe and the Soviet Union*, Worldwatch Paper 99 (New York: World Watch Institute, 1991), p. 40; and Martin Kaspar, *The Ecological Reconstruction of Central and Eastern Europe: International and Austrian Contributions* (Vienna: Global 2000 Institute for Environmental Research, 1993), p. 7; Nordic Investment Bank, 'Eastern Europe and the International Lending Agencies' (interview with Willi Wapenhans), *Annual Report, 1990* (Helsinki: NIB, 1991), p. 19.

2 Neville Brown, 'Climate, Ecology, and International Security,' *Survival*, vol. 31, no. 6 (November/December 1989), pp. 519–32; Kent Hugh Butts (ed.), *Environmental Security: a DOD Partnership for Peace* (US Army War College: Strategic Studies Institute Special Report, 1994); Barry Buzan, *People, States and Fear: an Agenda for International Security Studies in the post-Cold War Era* (Boulder: Lynne Rienner, 1991); Peter Gleick, 'Environment and Security: the Clear Connections,' *Bulletin of Atomic Scientists*, April 1991, pp. 17–21; Peter Gleick, 'Water and Conflict: Fresh Water Resources and International Security,' *International Security*, vol. 18, no. 1 (summer 1993), pp. 79–112; Ronnie Lipschutz and John P. Holdren, 'Crossing Borders: Resource Flows, the Global Envi-

ronment, and International Security,' *Bulletin of Peace Proposals*, vol. 21, no. 2 (June 1990), pp. 121–33; Miriam R. Lowi, 'Bridging the Divide: Transboundary Resource Disputes and the Case of West Bank Water,' *International Security*, vol. 18, no. 1 (summer 1993), pp. 113–38; Jessica Tuchman Matthews, 'Redefining Security,' *Foreign Affairs*, vol. 68, no. 2 (spring 1989), pp. 162–77; Norman Myers, 'Environment and Security,' *Foreign Policy*, 74 (spring 1989), pp. 23–41; Joseph J. Romm, *Defining National Security: the Nonmilitary Aspects* (New York: Council on Foreign Relations, 1993); Jon Martin Trolldalen, *International Environmental Conflict Resolution: the Role of the United Nations* (Washington, DC: World Foundation for Environment and Development, 1992); Richard Ullman, 'Redefining Security,' *International Security*, vol. 8, no. 1 (summer 1983); and Ole Wæver, Barry Buzan, Morten Kelstrup and Pierre Lemaitre, *Identity, Migration, and the new Security Agenda in Europe* (London: Pinter, 1993).

3   See Daniel Deudney's 'Environment and Security: Muddled Thinking,' *Bulletin of Atomic Scientists* (April 1991), pp. 22–8 and 'The Case against linking Environmental Degradation and National Security,' *Millennium*, vol. 19, no. 3 (winter 1990), pp. 461–76; and John J. Mearsheimer, 'The False Promise of International Institutions,' *International Security*, vol. 19, no.3 (winter 1994/95), pp. 5–49; and Barry Buzan, *People, States, and Fear*, second edition, (Boulder: Lynne Rienner, 1991), p. 131–44.

4   Deudney, 'Muddled Thinking,' pp. 23–4.

5   Thomas F. Homer-Dixon, 'Environmental Scarcities and Violent Conflict: Evidence from Cases,' *International Security*, vol. 19, no. 1 (summer 1994), p. 20; and 'On the Threshold: Environmental Changes as Causes of Acute Conflict,' *International Security*, vol. 16, no. 2 (autumn 1991), pp. 108–11.

6   For a brief discussion of local public goods see Paul Teske, Mark Schneider, Michael Mintrom and Samuel Best, 'Establishing the Micro Foundations of a Macro Theory: Information, Movers, and the Competitive Local Market for Public Goods,' *American Political Science Review*, vol. 87, no. 3 (September 1993), pp. 702–6.

7   Trolldalen defines an environmental conflict as a 'conflict of interest that arise from the utilization of natural resources in one country which has negative environmental consequences for another country or group of countries'. Trolldalen, *International Environmental Conflict Resolution*, p. 3; Homer-Dixon, 'On the Threshold,' p. 77.

8   Access to and control over resources do not appear at this juncture to be a probable security threat to any European or North American state. It is true, however, that changes in political boundaries, particularly in the former Soviet Union, will have a severe impact on the price and availability of oil and natural gas; access to energy supplies is a matter of financial wherewithal to purchase energy. The one instance where there has been manipulation of the environment with the potential to create political conflict in Europe is the diversion of the Danube along the Slovakian–Hungarian border which threatens Hungarian water supplies.

9   Gleick, 'The Clear Connections,' pp. 19–20; and 'Water and Conflict,' pp. 81–3; quotation drawn from Homer-Dixon, 'Environmental Scarcities and Violent Conflict,' p. 25.

10 Homer-Dixon, 'Environmental Scarcities and Violent Conflict,' p. 36.

11 Buzan, *People, States and Fear*, pp. 134–40.

12 On the expansion of the definition of security concerns see Stanley Hoffmann, 'Security in an Age of Turbulence: Means of Response,' in 'Third World Conflict and International Society' II, *Adelphi Papers*, 167 (London: IISS, 1981), pp. 4–5, cited in Buzan, *People, States and Fear*, pp. 144–5, n. 21.

13 'Declaration of the Heads of State and Government participating in the Meeting of the North Atlantic Council', Brussels, 29–30 May 1989, paras 32 and 35; and 'London Declaration on a Transformed North Atlantic Alliance,' 5–6 July 1990, para. 44.

14 'Partnership with the Countries of Central and Eastern Europe,' 6–7 June 1991, Copenhagen, para. 9; North Atlantic Council, 'Communiqué,' 6–7 June 1991, Copenhagen,

NATO Review, 3 (June 1991), p. 31; and Paul Rambaut, 'Environmental Challenges: the Role of NATO,' *NATO Review*, 2 (April 1992), pp. 24–7. It remains true, however, that the environmental dimension of security was absent from the elucidation of NATO's core security functions in post-Cold War Europe. See 'NATO's Core Security Functions in the new Europe,' 6–7 June 1991, Copenhagen, in *NATO Review*, 3 (June 1991), pp. 30–1.

15 'The Alliance's New Strategic Concept,' 7–8 November 1991, Rome, paras 25, 29 and 30.
16 North Atlantic Cooperation Council, 'Statement on Dialogue, Partnership, and Cooperation,' 20 December 1991, paras 3 and 5.
17 The pilot studies included, but were not restricted to: defence base clean-ups, toxic spills during movements of military goods; cross-border pollution emanating from defence-related installations, and the reuse of contaminated military property. NACC, 'Work Plan for Dialogue, Partnership,and Cooperation, 1993,' 18 December 1992, in *NATO Review*, 1 (February 1993), pp. 30–1; 'Work Plan for Dialogue, Partnership, and Cooperation 1994,' 3 December 1993, in *NATO Review*, 6 (December 1993), p. 32; The first major environmental pilot study initiated within the framework of the NACC work plan was 'Cross-border Environmental Problems emanating from Defence-related Installations and Activities.' This study, initiated in November 1992, focused upon the radiation and chemical pollution of waterways and seas. It targeted the Barents and Kara Seas, the Laptev Sea, the Baltic Sea, the Black Sea, the Bering Strait and the Danube catchment. The information-collecting phase of the project was completed by September 1994 and the next phase will assess the dangers posed to the Barents and Kara Seas by the decommissioning and storage of nuclear reactors. For a discussion of the CCMS and its activities see Deniz Yuksel-Beten, 'CCMS: NATO's Environmental Programme is expanded and opened to the East,' *NATO Review*, 4 (August 1991), pp. 27–32; NATO Scientific Affairs Division, *The Challenges of Modern Society* (Brussels: NATO, November 1992); Jean-Marie Cadiou, 'The Environmental Legacy of the Cold War,' *NATO Review*, 5 (October 1993), pp. 33–5; and 'Meeting on Defence-related Cross-border Environment Problems,' *NATO Review*, 5 (October 1995), p. 33.
18 'Work Plan for Dialogue, Partnership, and Cooperation 1994/95,' 2 December 1994, in *NATO Review*, 6 (December 1994)/7 (January 1995), p. 30.
19 'KSZE-Treffen über Umweltschutz,' *Bulletin*, 120 (7 November 1989), p. 1035.
20 'KSZE-Konferenz über wirtschaftliche Zusammenarbeit in Europa. Dokument der Bonner Konferenz,' 11 April 1990, *Bulletin*, 46 (19 April 1990), p. 360.
21 'Charta von Paris für ein neues Europa. Erklärung des Pariser KSZE-Treffen der Staats- und Regierungschefs,' 24 November 1990, *Bulletin*, 137 (24 November 1990), p. 1413.
22 'Konferenz über Sicherheit und Zusammenarbeit in Europa. Helsinki-Dokument 1992. Herausforderung des Wandels,' 23 July 1992, *Bulletin*, 82 (23 July 1992), pp. 800–1.
23 'Konferenz über Sicherheit und Zusammenarbeit in Europa. Budapester Dokument 1994. Der Weg zu echter Partnershaft in einem neuen Zeitalter,' 6 December 1994, *Bulletin*, 120 (23 December 1994), pp. 1112–13.
24 Nigel Haigh, ' The European Community and International Environmental Policy,' in Andrew Hurrell and Benedict Kingsbury (eds), *The International Politics of the Environment: Actors, Interests, and Institutions* (Oxford: Clarendon Press, 1992), p. 234.
25 Articles 2 and 130r of the Maastricht Treaty. Commission of the European Communities, *Towards Sustainability: a European Community Programme of Policy and Action in relation to the Environment and Sustainable Development*, COM (92) 23 final, II (Brussels: European Community, 27 March 1992), p. 3.
26 Commission of the European Communities, *Proposal for a Resolution of the Council of European Communities on a Community Programme of Policy and Action in relation to the Environment and Sustainable Development*, I (Brussels: 27 March 1992), pp. 1–3.
27 *Ibid.*, p. 6. A fourth principle, subsidiarity, is of importance, but only for internal mat-

ters. Its salience as an element of the European security order will increase as the CEE nations prepare for membership of the EU. On the issue of environmental subsidiarity see Regina S. Axelrod, 'Subsidiarity and Environmental Policy in the European Community,' *International Environmental Affairs*, vol. 6, no. 2 (spring 1994), pp. 115–32.

28   Commission of the European Communities, *Towards Sustainability*, p. 60.
29   'Europäischer Rat in Essen. Schlussfolgerungen des Vorsitzes,' 10 December 1994, *Bulletin*, 118 (19 December 1994), p. 1081; see also statement issued after the Conference of the Environment Ministers of the European Community, Central and Eastern Europe and the Commission, Dublin, 16 June 1990.
30   'Environment for Europe,' Lucerne, 30 April 1993, photocopy, para. 3.
31   *Ibid.*, paras 7, 8, 9.1–4, 17, 18.1–2 and 19.
32   EBRD, 'Harmonisation of Environmental Legislation and Standards,' *Environments in Transition: the Environmental Bulletin of the EBRD*, winter 1993, pp. 1–3.
33   Peter R. Baehr and Leon Gordenker, *The United Nations in the 1990s*, second edition (New York: St Martin's Press, 1994), p. 141.
34   For assessments and descriptions of the UNEP see Andrew Hurrell and Benedict Kingsbury, 'The International Politics of the Environment: an Introduction,' in Andrew Hurrell and Benedict Kingsbury (eds), *The International Politics of the Environment: Actors, Interests, and Institutions* (Oxford: Clarendon Press, 1992), pp. 31–4; Peter S. Thacher, 'The Role of the United Nations,' in Hurrell and Kingsbury, *International Politics of the Environment*, pp. 190–3; Branislav Gosovic, *The Quest for World Environmental Cooperation: the Case of the UN Global Environment Monitoring System* (London: Routledge, 1992), pp. 6–8, 17–18; Lynton Keith Caldwell, *International Environmental Policy: Emergence and Dimensions*, second edition (Durham, NC: Duke University Press, 1990), pp. 71–94; and Trolldalen, *International Environmental Conflict Resolution*, pp. 21–2.
35   Peter S. Thacher, 'The Role of the United Nations,' p. 190.
36   *Rio Declaration on Environment and Development*, principles 10, 14, 15 and 16,
37   *Agenda 21: Programme of Action for Sustainable Development* (New York: UN, 1992), p. 15.
38   *Ibid.*, p. 22.
39   *Ibid.*, p. 19.
40   The increases in western environmental aid were limited to a $2.7 billion increase over a five-year period; the United States promised an additional $150 million; and the EU made no net increase in its environmental aid. See David Lascelles, 'Leaders shy away from Cash Pledges,' *Financial Times*, 15 June 1992, p. 7; 'G-7 states reject "Green Fund" proposed by developing nations,' *Financial Times*, 5 June 1992, p. 16; and 'Brazil steps in as Summit Broker,' *Financial Times*, 6/7 June 1992, p. 2. The $600 billion figure is drawn from *Agenda 21*, p. 251.
41   *Agenda 21*, p. 279.
42   Environmental conventions and agreements that are specific to OECD environmental problems include but are not limited to: the Geneva Convention on Long-range Transboundary Air Pollution (1979); Protocol on the Reduction of Volatile Organic Compounds (1991); Vienna Convention for the Protection of the Ozone Layer (1985); the Montreal Protocol on Substances that Deplete the Ozone Layer (1987); Basle Convention on the Control of Transboundary Movements of Hazardous Wastes and their Disposal (1989); the Nordic Environmental Protection Convention (1974); the Paris Convention on Third Party Liability in the Field of Nuclear Energy (1960); Vienna Convention on Civil Liability for Nuclear Damage (1963); Convention on Early Notification of a Nuclear Accident (1986); Oslo Convention for the Prevention of Marine Pollution by Dumping from Ships and Aircraft (1972); Helsinki Convention on the Protection of the Marine Environment of the Baltic Sea Area (1974); Paris Convention for the Prevention of Marine Pollution from Land-based Sources (1974); Barcelona Convention

for the Protection of the Mediterranean Sea against Pollution (1976); and Convention on the Protection of the Marine Environment of the Baltic Sea Area (1979).
43 It was estimated that if consideration was taken of the environmental criterion applied to NIB loans, that figure would expand to 30 per cent. Nordic Investment Bank, *Annual Report, 1990* (Helsinki: NIB, 1991), pp. 6 and 23 ; and *Annual Report, 1993* (Helsinki: NIB, 1994), p. 26.
44 Table 29 Project investment loans on an annual basis, 1990–93 (SDR million)

Investee	1990	1991	1992	1993
Total	57.0	128.8	123.5	175.8
Eastern Europe	20.4	3.1	29.3	0.0
% share	35.7	2.4	23.8	0

Source: NIB, *Annual Report* (various years).

Table 30 Project investment loans: total outstanding, 1990–93 (SDR million)

Investee	1990	1991	1992	1993
Total	355.00	402.00	459.00	562.16
Eastern Europe	143.42	125.42	133.11	123.67
% share	40.4	31.2	29	22

Source: NIB, *Annual Report* (various years).

45 'Agreement regarding the Establishment of the Nordic Environment Finance Corporation,' Article 1. Eligibility for NEFCO funds was limited to investment projects in the Czech Republic, Slovakia, Hungary, Poland, Estonia, Latvia, Lithuania, Russia, Belarus and Ukraine.
46 'Statutes of the Nordic Environment Finance Corporation,' para. 3. Financial support for feasibility studies of environmental projects is provided by the Nordic Project Fund (NoPEF). NoPEF provides conditional loans for feasibility studies of environmental projects outside the Nordic area in conjunction with project investment loans. The loan is equal to 50 per cent of the cost of the study and is repaid if a Nordic firm wins the contract.
47 NEFCO, *Årsredovilsaning 1993* (Helsinki: NEFCO, 1994), p. 4; and *Årsredovilsaning 1992* (Helsinki: NEFCO, 1993), p. 3.
48 Nordic Investment Bank, *Annual Report, 1992* (Helsinki: NIB, 1993), pp. 40–1; and *Annual Report, 1993* (Helsinki: NIB, 1994), pp. 42–3.
49 EIB, *Loans to Build the European Community* (Luxembourg: EIB, 1990); *Protection of the Environment* (Luxembourg: EIB, 1990), pp. 2–3; *European Investment Bank: the European Community's Financial Institution* (Luxembourg: EIB, 1992), pp. 4–5; and European Commission, 'Fifth Action Programme', p. 71.
50 See comments of Herbert Christie, head of the Economic Research Directorate of the EIB, at Rio Earth Summit, reprinted in *EIB Information*, 73 (September 1992), p. 4.
51 EIB, *Annual Report, 1990* (Luxembourg: EIB, 1991), pp. 18–19; 'Financing in Central and Eastern European Countries: Bulgaria, CSFR, Hungary, Poland, and Romania,' (Luxembourg: EIB, November 1991); *Annual Report, 1991* (Luxembourg: EIB, 1992), p. 21; *Annual Report, 1993* (Luxembourg: EIB, 1994), p. 23; and Christopher Knowles, 'The European Investment Bank' in *Conference on Energy and Environment in European Economies in Transition: Proceedings* (Paris: OECD, 1992), pp. 209–12. For an extended treatment of the EIB's environmental assessment procedures see Carl Lankowski, 'Environmental Impact Review in the European Investment Bank,' paper delivered at the meeting of the International Studies Association, February 1995.

52 The Edinburgh Facility enabled the EIB to increase its share of project finance from 50 per cent to 75 per cent; and from 70 per cent to 90 per cent for cumulative Community financing (i.e. from other Community budgetary sources in addition to EIB funds). The Edinburgh European Council also led to the creation of the European Investment Fund, which targets the financing of major infrastructure projects and of small and medium sized enterprises. Funds disbursed under either the Edinburgh Facility or the European Investment Fund were expected to 'assist implementation of the fifth Community action programme on the environment ...' See EIB, *Annual Report, 1992* (Luxembourg: EIB, 1993), pp. 20–1.
53 See 'Bericht des Rates an den Europäischen Rat Essen über die Strategie zur Vorbereitung des Beitritts der assoziierten MOEL,' 10 December 1994, *Bulletin*, 118 (19 December 1994), pp. 1078 and 1081.
54 EIB, *Annual Report*, p. 115, table Q.
55 See Steven Weber, 'Origins of the European Bank for Reconstruction and Development,' *International Organization*, vol. 48, no. 1 (winter 1994), pp. 19–21; and David Reed, 'The European Bank for Reconstruction and Development: an Environmental Opportunity,' *International Environmental Affairs*, vol. 2, no. 4 (fall 1990), p. 326–8.
56 *Agreement Establishing the European Bank for Reconstruction and Development*, Article 1 and Article 2 (vii).
57 David Reed, 'The European Bank for Reconstruction and Development,' pp. 330–1; Erich Unterwurzacher, 'EBRD's Approach to Energy and Environmental Funding' in *Conference on Energy and Environment*, pp. 213–18.
58 David Reed, 'The European Bank for Reconstruction and Development,' p. 319.
59 The EBRD applied the principles of the UN/ECE Convention on Environmental Impact Assessment in a Transboundary Context in its environmental assessment of investment projects. On the procedure and content of environmental assessments see EBRD, *Environmental Procedures* (London: EBRD, 1992), pp. 25–50.
60 The environmental principles include an emphasis on preventive action, the development and implementation of effective national policies, economic efficiency, polluter-pays, and the assignment of primary responsibility for environmental damage. The EBRD also emphasised the creation of legal instruments and institutions enforcing and guiding environmental policies as well as broad participation in the resolution of competing environmental concerns. See EBRD, 'Environmental Management: the Bank's Policy Approach,' in *Environmental Procedures* (London: EBRD, 1992), annex A, pp. 2–3.
61 EBRD, 'Financial Intermediaries and the Environment,' *Environments in Transition* (winter 1993), pp. 4–5; *Annual Report, 1993* pp. 18–20; *Environmental Procedures*, pp. 8–9. These procedures generally meet the criteria established by David Reed in his analysis of the EBRD's environmental responsibilities and generally exceed those of the International Finance Corporation, the European Investment Bank and the other regional development banks. See David Reed, 'European Bank for Reconstruction and Development,' pp. 334–5; and Raymond F. Mikesell and Larry Williams, *International Banks and the Environment. From Growth to Sustainability: an Unfinished Agenda* (San Francisco: Sierra Club Books), pp. 9–28.
62 Table 31 EBRD environmental lending, 1990–93 (Ecu million)

Type of investment	1991	1992	1993
Project (A/1 or B/1)	14.19	283.36	956.26
Financial intermediary	74.58	194.09	499.89
Total	88.77	477.45	1,455.15

Sources: EBRD, *Annual Report* (various years); authors' own calculations.

63 EBRD, *Annual Report, 1993* (EBRD: London, 1994), pp. 27 and 64–9; and Jane Martinson, 'EBRD at Centre of N-power Row,' *Financial Times*, 16 February 1994, p. 2.

64 For a general discussion of the nuclear accident problem see Oran R. Young, *International Cooperation: Building Regimes for Natural Resources and the Environment* (Ithaca: Cornell University Press, 1989), pp. 146–52.

65 IAEA, *The Safety of WWER-440 Model 230 Nuclear Power Plants* (Vienna: IAEA, 1992); F. Niehaus and L. Lederman, 'International Safety Review of WWER-440/230 Nuclear Power Plants,' *IAEA Bulletin*, vol. 34, no. 2 (1992), pp. 24–31; the prepared statement of William H. Young, Assistant Secretary for Nuclear Energy (US Department of Energy), 'International Commercial Nuclear Reactor Safety,' Committee on Environment and Public Works, US Senate, 25 July 1991, pp. 51–5; IAEA, *IAEA Newsbriefs*, vol. 8, no. 1 (January/February 1993), p. 5; Thomas Halverson, 'Ticking Time Bombs: East Bloc Reactors,' *Bulletin of Atomic Scientists*, vol. 49 (July/August 1993), pp. 43–8; and EBRD, *The Nuclear Safety Account: Central and Eastern Europe and the former Soviet Union* (EBRD: London, December 1994), p. 6.

66 The only two countries that were signatories to the agreement were Poland and Romania, two countries that did not have nuclear power stations at the time. *Financial Times*, 18 February 1994, p. 2; 8 July 1994, p. 2.

67 The director-general of the IAEA began work on such a convention in September 1991. A preliminary outline of a nuclear safety regime may be found in Abel J. González, 'Fundamental principles of protection and safety for nuclear power,' *IAEA Bulletin*, vol. 34. no. 2 (1992), pp. 10–14.

68 'Council Resolution of 22 July 1975 on the Technological Problems of Nuclear Safety,' *Official Journal of the European Communities*, no. C 128, 9 June 1975, p. 24; and L. J. Brinkhorst, 'Nuclear Safety and the European Community: Broadening Perspectives,' *IAEA Bulletin*, vol. 34, no. 2 (1992), pp. 41–3.

69 European Commission, *Phare and Tacis. Nuclear Safety in Central and Eastern Europe: Present and Future Activities* (Brussels: European Commission, April 1993), pp. 11–12.

70 See prepared statement of William H. Young, Assistant Secretary for Nuclear Energy, US Department of Energy, *International Commercial Nuclear Reactor Safety*, 25 July 1991, pp. 51–4; and Halverson, 'Ticking Time Bombs,' p. 45.

71 European Commission, *Phare and Tacis*, pp. 1–8; *Phare Funding, 1990–1994* (Brussels: European Commission, 1995).

72 'Proposal for a Council Decision amending Decision 77/270 Euratom to authorize the Commission to contract Euratom Borrowings in order to contribute to the Financing required for improving the Degree of Efficiency and Safety of Nuclear Power Stations in certain Non-member Countries,' COM (92) 467 final, *Official Journal of the European Communities*, vol. 36 (26 January 1993), pp. 11–12; 'MEPs approve release of Funds for Eastern Europe,' *PTS Newsletter Database* (Brussels: Europe Information Service, 2 February 1994).

73 EBRD, 'The Nuclear Safety Account,' photocopy, June 1993; *The Nuclear Safety Account*, p. 3–11; *New York Times*, 29 January 1993, p. 2A; *Financial Times*, 9 July 1992, p. 2; and 29 January 1993, p. 3.

8

Conclusion
Security architectures and institutional futures

The initial optimism and potential for a radical change of the European security order were promised by the rhetoric of the two major extra-European powers after the unification of Germany. The Bush administration spoke of creating a New World Order that would make good the promises made at San Francisco with the establishment of the UN; and the Soviet Union championed the desire for the creation of a 'common European house' that would accommodate the security interests of all the European states, provide an institutional basis for peace and stability in the European political space, and end the political division of Europe. Neither architecture survived Presidents Bush and Gorbachev. The shape of the post-Cold War security architecture remains undetermined and the debate over the blueprint for that architecture remains vital if muted. The Russian architecture for the Euro-Atlantic security order has shrunk to a preoccupation with the 'near abroad' and the demand that Russia's interests as a great power should not be ignored in the construction of a new security order. Rather than presenting a coherent security architecture, the Russians have only articulated a set of demands that an architecture must meet for its participation. The Clinton administration replaced the Bush administration's rhetoric of a New World Order with the less compelling rhetoric of 'expansion and enlargement'. But both the Bush and the Clinton administrations have, in the end, followed the logic of the Nixon administration's foreign policy: in the face of growing multipolarity, the United States must seek to reduce military commitments in the Euro-Atlantic system without forgoing American influence over the future course of European affairs.

The other major entrants in the architectural competition have been the Federal Republic of Germany, France and the United Kingdom; each state has proposed a security architecture that services the narrow national interest without unduly violating the interests of its most important partners and allies. The architecture on offer by France seeks to achieve European autonomy within the

EU without sacrificing either national autonomy or the American guarantee; the British architecture is preoccupied with sustaining and consolidating the Atlantic connection between Europe and America, at the expense of a common European defence or foreign policy if necessary; and the German architecture seeks a synthesis of the inclusiveness of the common European house promoted by former Foreign Minister Genscher and the Atlanticism that has supported German foreign policy objectives since 1949 without unduly violating French sensibilities.

These security architectures and Russian security requirements will shape the institutional make-up of the Euro-Atlantic security order. But these architectural ambitions may yet be frustrated by the exogenous force of the unsettled structural pressures of the European state system that are beyond the purposeful manipulation of statecraft or contained by the institutionalisation of state preferences. The path that the European security order will eventually follow is indeterminate and uncertain. No path of evolution is yet closed.[1] There are three evolutionary paths that the European security system may follow that can be fruitfully compared with the expectations embedded in the security architectures of these countries.

The Euro-Atlantic security order can follow the path of greater integration, of greater differentiation or of disintegration. The intuitive credibility of each path no doubt reflects a psychological predisposition towards optimism, scepticism and pessimism, respectively. Continued and deepened integration, the path expected by optimists, would continue in both the economic and the military dimensions of security. Deeper economic integration would yield increased economic openness, in particular more intense trade ties and greater financial market integration, and greater cooperation on issues ranging from exchange rate management and macroeconomic policy coordination to common environmental policies. This economic integration would occur simultaneously between the nations of the EU, between the EU and the CEE nations and between Europe and North America. Deeper military integration would include the multinationalisation of NATO forces, NATO's eastward expansion into central and eastern Europe and the Baltic states, the development of an EU common defence policy, and the elaboration of a pan-European security institution, be it within the OSCE or within the context of the NATO PfP programme. Continued and deepened economic and military integration would encourage cooperation in the European security area and ensure a 'doubly safe' security environment.

Another potential path, envisioned perhaps by sceptics, would be that of greater regional differentiation between the nations of the European security space. Greater differentiation could reflect the strengthening of regional economic and military identities that coexists and encourages greater pan-regional integration, a development anticipated, for example, with the 'dumb-bell' concept assigned to the Atlantic economy in the 1960s. Whilst such an option is not precluded, it has become complicated by the prospect of a 'dumb-bell' Europe.

The aspiration of the CEE states – the Baltic states, Poland, the Czech Republic, Slovakia and Hungary – to become members of the EU and WEU, combined with the inevitable deepening of trade ties with the successor states of the former Soviet Union, promise an eastwards reorientation of the EU. That reorientation, driven by calculations of commercial complementarity and strategic interest, could result in the mutual and consensual loosening of the bonds between North America and Europe.

The political and strategic fall-out from such a development could range from benevolent mercantilism, what has been referred to as an 'open regionalism', to benign mercantilism, or 'defensive protectionism'.[2] Open regionalism anticipates the creation of a regional political-strategic identity, of a preferential economic zone buttressed by not-too-discriminatory barriers to trade, the encouragement of cross-regional industrial alliances and the harmonisation of industrial standards. Yet open regionalism, as the name implies, would not actively foster the division of the world into regional economies by vitiating the market mechanism; trade between the regions would be neither encouraged nor discouraged. No effort would be made to reduce the existing levels of economic interdependence. Defensive protectionism, on the other hand, would employ many of the same instruments as open regionalism, but the objective would be the division of the global economy into a set of regional and self-contained economies. In that case, there would be a vitiation of the market mechanism – trade would be managed according to political diktat rather than responding to market-dictated opportunities and constraints – and the existing levels of global financial, commercial and monetary interdependences would be replaced with a set of regional interdependences. The seamlessness of the global economy would be replaced by a series of loosely confederated regional economies. Either of these mercantilisms might be driven by concern with restoring the governability of national economies and the protection of the welfare gains already gleaned from freer trade in the post-war period. Moreover, neither form of regionalism would necessarily unleash the destructively competitive forces associated with the mercantilism of the 1930s;[3] neither would rekindle or deepen the security dilemma facing European states. Both leave open the possibility that the gentle regionalisation of economic relations could be complemented by pan-regional security institutions.

The final path, anticipated by pessimists, would be the disintegration of the global economic system. Disintegration would imply the conscious reversal of the level of economic openness between the North American and European pillars of the Atlantic economy. In the milder form, a 'malevolent mercantilism' would simply result in intense regional economic competition characterised by trade barriers severely limiting the possibility of trade, by the reintroduction of protected or segmented capital markets, and perhaps even by the reintroduction of exchange controls. The process of economic closure would be sharpened by a regional preoccupation with the hierarchy of prestige in the international system, by the pursuit of technological dominance, and by the creation and support of regional champions in those industries competing for dominance along the technological frontier. Economic capacity and technological advantage would be assessed and prized not from the perspective of maximising welfare but from the perspective of maximising relative power.

The 'strong' version of disintegration simply reduces the size of the economic unit from a regional constellation to the national economy. Disintegration of the global economy into robust and highly competitive, if not antagonistic, blocs or national economies would reintroduce the security dilemma into the European security space. Moreover, it would upend the existing institutional solutions to the security dilemma states face today: disintegration, in either its national or its regional manifestation, runs against the logic of collective defence or a permanent alliance system. It favours what has been the historically disastrous dependence of states upon self-help and shifting alliances.

In this conclusion we sketch the security architectures on offer by the major powers and seek to discern points of tangency, opposition and parallelism in the various architectures; seek to place those architectures along the continuum of security system outcomes; and consider the impact on those architectures of the European Stability Pact, the agenda of the EU intergovernmental conference in 1996, and the criteria governing the expansion of NATO. We then return to the institutional issues raised in the introduction. Does the emerging European security order demonstrate the characteristics of regime congruence and interdependence? What lessons can be drawn about the institutional configurations within the institutional clusters defining the security problematique in post-Cold War Europe? Must there be a parallel construction of the economic and military institutions of the European security order?

The security architectures of the great powers: Great Britain

The British contribution to the architectural debate is a conservative one and emerged only after a period of considerable confusion and uncertainty.[4] The British have fought an essentially rearguard action not only against their partners in the EU, particularly France and Germany, but against the United States as well. The Thatcher and Major governments have been recalcitrant participants in any effort to strengthen a European defence identity; in fact, it could be argued that British participation in the WEU is designed to prevent its institutional subordination to the EU and to perpetuate its subordination to NATO. For the British government, the security environment facing Europe and the United Kingdom today suggests a strategy not dissimilar from that adopted during the course of the Cold War: the United Kingdom plays a decisive security role within Europe and in the wider world, but that role must always be played in tandem with the United States. The British concern has been that of fashioning a mechanism for linking the security of the United States with that of Europe and the United Kingdom in particular. In the British view, which has remained largely unchanged since the founding of NATO, 'the best and most effective way to organise the defence of Western Europe is through NATO and in close alliance with the United States'.[5] Thus British support for the creation of a European security and defence identity is driven by the narrow instrumental objective of preventing the United States from withdrawing from Europe over corrosive burden-sharing debates and to extend British influence over the security policies of its major European allies, particularly France and Germany. The WEU, therefore, is limited to achieving a 'sensible sythesis between the European and transatlantic dimensions to the security of Europe'.[6]

The British preference for the security *status quo* reflects a conservative estimate of the security threats facing the United Kingdom in the post-Cold War world and the leverage gained by Britain with the current institutional arrangements. The primary threat to the security of Europe and the United Kingdom remains the Russian Federation; as the pre-eminent European military power, only the Russian Federation has the combined conventional and nuclear forces capable of posing a threat to the military security of the United Kingdom. There is also recognition, however, of the threats to European stability that arise from the inability to integrate the western, central and eastern portions of the European continent. There is in the United Kingdom, as in Germany and France, recognition of the potential destabilising consequences of a failure in central and eastern Europe to become prosperous members of a common European undertaking. The British solution is to extend those states security: their independence and integrity are deemed essential to British security interests. The threats to those nations derive from two sources: internal disorder and external pressure from the Russian Federation. Of the major European powers, the British are the most sceptical (at least publicly) of Russian intentions in central and eastern Europe and the most preoccupied with the Russian ability to upset the European balance. The British strategy of inclusion in a Western-sponsored security architecture reflects this set of concerns; and the British strategy of inclusion reflects a preference for eventual NATO membership for those states.[7]

The continued ability of the British 'to punch above their weight' is largely derived in their own estimation from Britain's ability to project military power and its privileged position within the Western alliance system owing to German political disabilities, the French preoccupation with autonomy and the 'special relationship' with the United States. Any change in the character of the European security order would undermine that privileged position and further weaken the British position on affairs outside the compass of security, particularly in the realm of economic cooperation with the United States.[8]

The British security architecture makes room for all the major security institutions. NATO, the EU, the WEU, the OSCE and the UN are viewed as complementary institutions of security with functionally specific tasks. Each institution satisfies the need for multilateral solutions to common security problems, an imperative of the European security order reflecting the increased interdependence of political, economic and security interests. Like the French, however, the British reserve the right of sovereign control over their security and defence policy; they reserve the right to unilateral action to protect vital national interests. Nonetheless, the British also recognise that British security policy will be increasingly shaped within a multilateral context. From that perspective, there is much common ground between France, Germany and Britain. However, it is also the case that there is a starker institutional hierarchy in the British architecture that is at odds with France and Germany: NATO (and the American commitment to Europe it manifests) is and will remain the core security institution for Europe. The instrumental roles and aspirations of the subordinate security institutions are accented differently by the British in comparison with their European partners. The primary purpose of those alternative institutions is not to provide a mechanism for escaping American hegemony or providing a credible deterrent to the putative threat from the Russian Federation, but only to strengthen NATO and the American commitment to Europe.

The problem facing British policy-makers has been the integration of the alternative institutions of security within the NATO framework. The British are loath to entertain any architectural design that appears to diminish the primacy of NATO or threatens to attenuate the connection between the United States and European security. NATO is considered 'the only security organisation with the military means to back up its security guarantees. It secures the vital link between Europe and North America.'[9] The dependence upon NATO reflects both a political and a military calculation. The political dimension of the British dependence upon NATO reflects the disproportionate influence wielded by the British on security matters within NATO. This influence, derived from the British contribution to NATO, its status as the only other nuclear power within the integrated military command and its privileged relationship with the United States for most of the post-1945 period, enabled the United Kingdom to counter French pretensions to European leadership and offset the clear economic advantages possessed by the Federal Republic during the Cold War.[10] However, with the advent of the post-Cold War world British influence has waned. The American offer of 'partners in leadership' to Germany before German unification signalled a downgrading of the 'special relationship'. Nonetheless, the British calculation of privileging NATO over other security institutions reflects the historical success of NATO in maintaining balance on the European continent, a perceived community of interest with the United States within the NATO area, and a residual distrust of the foreign policy ambitions of a united Germany and perfidious France. Perhaps more important, however, the strategic preference for NATO reflects the British calculation that only American power can guarantee the unvarying British interest in thwarting hegemonic pretensions on the European continent. A confluence of enduring interests, past historical experience and calculation of potential threats to British vital interests leads inexorably in the British case to a preference for

NATO, but a NATO which remains an American-dominated institution unchallenged by either the WEU or the OSCE.

The European component of the British security architecture reflects the confluence of two forces: the recognition that British security and foreign policy interests are increasingly coincident with, if not identical to, those of its western European allies; and the series of NATO decisions that have recognised the importance of the European pillar of the alliance and provided institutional recognition of the EU and WEU. The Maastricht treaty recognised and codified the mutuality of security interests and committed the EU to creating a common foreign and security policy (CFSP) which 'might in time lead to a common defence'. The conditional 'might' in the Maastricht language reflected the British preference for leaving the question of a European defence identity open and providing the basis of a British opt-out. The British position that a CFSP should not necessarily produce or lead to a common defence policy reflects the British preference that the WEU, the designated agent of the EU in defence, should retain its intergovernmental character, remain independent of the EU, and remain subordinated to NATO on security and defence policies. British preferences appear to have been largely endorsed in successive NATO declarations, but it is also true that the British are conducting a rearguard action and lag behind the American desire for greater European cooperation in this area. Unlike the Americans, the British are not concerned only about fostering greater European cooperation to support NATO, but appreciate the consequences of institutional form.

The WEU is conceived of by the British as the bridge between the EU and NATO. The British view the CJTF concept as a mechanism that can maintain the dominant role of NATO within the European security area, yet provide the desirable flexibility that would enable the Europeans (and the British) to act in concert when the United States was unwilling to do so. In other words, the British desire some European autonomy from the United States, but want to ensure that the pan-Atlantic security order does not become a casualty of European autonomy. The acid test for the WEU from the British position, however, is that it must develop in such a way as to be compatible with NATO.[11] Yet the Major government also recognises that the development of an independent European capability *within* NATO is essential if an alternative security institution with a European character is to be avoided. The British concern, once again, is to prevent the loss of British influence *vis-à-vis* France or Germany within the European setting and, more important to forestall a premature abdication of American responsiblity for the stabilty and balance of the European continent.

The task of integrating the CEE states into the emerging security architecture is consigned to the NATO-sponsored NACC and PfP programmes and within the WEU-sponsored Forum of Consultation. The OSCE plays at best a residual role in the the British security architecture. The British assign the OSCE the Cold War tasks of confidence-building measures and arms control negotiations augmented by an extended role in peace-keeping and crisis management along the periphery of the Russian Federation.

Without intended understatement, NATO is the core institution of the British security architecture. It is at the core not only because it provides the best guarantee of British security, but because it provides an alternative to a Franco-German-dominated Europe. The British still function within a security universe dominated not only by the two world wars but by a traditional statecraft that has adhered to the imperative of ensuring a balance on the European continent. It is clear that Britain can no longer play that role; and it is equally clear that the United States can but is not keen to do so. Consequently, British efforts are directed at guaranteeing the American commitment to the European balance, of meeting American demands for the creation of a strengthened European pillar of the alliance, and of ensuring that the European pillar remains constrained by and subordinated to NATO. The British architecture, unlike that of France and Germany, is concerned less about ensuring the assimilation of the Russian Federation into a single European security order than with ensuring that once trouble arises along the eastern periphery of Europe the United States and a strong western Europe will be there to contain any threat to European stability. The self-proclaimed uninterest in 'institutional fantasies' demonstrates a public jadedness and smugness on security issues not evident in Paris, Bonn or Washington. The British architecture does possess the allure of addressing the familiar tasks of a security order; and the emphasis on NATO and the unwillingness to dilute substantially NATO competence for maintaining the European balance has the parochial advantage of maintaining British influence within the narrow compass of the Western alliance. What the British architecture lacks, however, is a clear appreciation of the the problem of integrating the CEE states into a European security order and the consequence of integrating those nations, presumably into NATO, for the relationship of the NATO countries with the Russian Federation.

The security architectures of the great powers: the United States

The post-Cold War environment has renewed American efforts to cajole its European allies into assuming greater responsibility for their own military and economic security and into paying a higher price for the changed and hedged American security guarantee. Yet the United States seeks to retain the benefits of hegemony. The post-Cold War environment has complicated the American security strategy. The Bush and Clinton administrations have been confronted with the challenges and opportunities of multipolarity. The American foreign policy establishment must manage the ambiguities of the new military-strategic imbalance, rather than the certainties of balance that characterised Soviet–American competition. The identification, calculation and weighing of both threats and advantages have become more complicated and at times counterindicative; containment no longer functions as the Rosetta stone of American foreign policy. The dissolution of the Soviet Union and its replacement by a politically enfeebled but dangerous Russian Federation has also exaggerated the divergences between the global responsibilities and interests of the United States and the parochial responsibilties and interests of the major European powers, particularly Germany.

Three objectives of the Nixon–Kissinger security strategy have resurfaced in the Bush and Clinton foreign policies.[12] First, there is the effort to establish a new division of labour within the Atlantic alliance that shifts burdens and responsibilities for regional stability on to America's NATO partners without forgoing American political predominance. Second, there is conditional support of European efforts to create an independent defence identity as a part of the Atlantic alliance. Yet both the Bush and the Clinton administrations, like that of President Nixon, are keenly aware of the potential role Europe could play as competitor of the United States and consistently hedge their support for greater progress towards a European security identity with the caveat that NATO must remain the preeminient security institution. And the third objective has been the linkage of the economic and military dimensions of the Atlantic alliance to lighten the burden of leadership without forgoing its prerogatives. The rhetoric of the Bush and Clinton administrations, while it differs at the margin, effectively rehearses the debate of the early 1970s. How does the United States retain its leadership role in Europe at a lower cost? The primary differences between the Nixon administration and the Bush and Clinton administrations are rhetorical and are located in the role ascribed to institutions and the changed international environment.

The New World Order served the long-standing American interest of preventing hegemony in Europe, sustaining the regional and global balances of power, and protecting an open international economic order. The United States retained the 'pivotal responsbility for ensuring the stability of the international balance' and NATO remained the core security institution in the Atlantic area.[13] In early 1990 the Bush administration described NATO as 'the natural framework for harmonizing Western policies on both security and diplomacy' and in 1995 NATO was described by Secretary of State Warren Christopher as the 'linchpin of Atlantic security'.[14] The primacy of NATO circumscribes the roles that can be played by the EU and WEU: although the creation of a more integrated Europe with a defence and security identity was expected and desired – the administration assumed that it would lead to a more balanced sharing of reponsiblities and burdens – American support is contingent upon the compatibility of that development with NATO.[15]

The Bush administration placed American foreign policy aspirations within the context of a new structure of power in the international system, particularly the emergence of Germany and Japan as new centres of power. Germany, within the European context, was elevated to the role of potential partner for the joint management of the Atlantic alliance, a role that the Chancellor

Kohl politely declined, but which for some remains a credible role for Germany.[16] The New World Order amounted to an effort to employ multilateral institutions in the service of American foreign policy objectives. The Bush administration's vision, while it carried with it a watered-down Wilsonianism informed by an appreciation of the national interest, reflected acute sensitivity to the changes that have taken place in the international system. And although Europe retained its supremacy as the core security preoccupation of the United States, the centrality of Europe was encroached upon by other areas of the world, particulary the Pacific rim. The strategy of the New World Order had a second component: dependence upon the cooperation of the great powers to manage regional conflicts as well as to monitor the overall stability of the international system. What the United States lacked in the post-Cold War world was a single state that could support (or challenge) it on a global basis. The rhetoric of the New World Order aside, the Soviet Union remained the most likely source of global and regional instability. Consequently, the European system still required the United States to function as 'a counterweight to Soviet military strength' and NATO remained essential in the face of a potential 'Weimar Russia' that could derail progress towards a cooperative European security order.[17]

The Bush and Clinton administrations also shared the assumption that American leadership in Europe and elsewhere was not only desirable but necessary. The Clinton administration's security strategy built upon the Bush administration's strategy of engagement and leadership. But the Clinton administration emphasised the enlargement of democracy at the expense of leadership. The chief American foreign policy objective became the expansion of democracy and the market economy to central and eastern Europe as well as to the republics of the former Soviet Union. The Clinton administration denied that this security strategy was a democratic crusade, but suggested that it was 'a pragmatic commitment to see freedom take hold where that will help us most'.[18] The Clinton administration grappled with the problem of enlargement that the Bush administration and NATO finessed with the NACC proposal. The continuing pressures of the CEE states to join NATO and the growing Russian resistance to such membership after September 1993 were met by former American Secretary of Defence Les Aspin's PfP proposal. The PfP programme possessed any number of virtues from the American perspective: first, it expanded the number of states that could become institutionally linked with NATO on a bilateral basis beyond NACC; second, it committed NATO to expansion without establishing a timetable; third, PfP provided a mechanism for judging the willingness and ability of individual states to seek NATO membership; and fourth, the PfP provides for consultation under Article 4 of the North Atlantic Treaty, but still falls short of an alliance or American security guarantee to PfP states. These advantages of the PfP, important as they are in lending greater legitimacy to a NATO-dominated security system, were overshadowed by another advantage from the American perspective: it transformed NATO into an institution that robbed the OSCE of its singular characteristic, non-exclusivity and the accompanying logic that NATO could eventually be abandoned in its favour.[19]

The Clinton strategy of engagement and enlargement has four key elements: first, a new division of labour must be established within the alliance; second, the United States must retain (and be granted) a leadership position within any Euro-Atlantic security order; third, the deepening and widening of the EU, particularly in the development of a CFSP, is to be encouraged so long as it produces a more equitable sharing of the burdens and risks within the alliance without encroaching on American policy prerogatives; and fourth, the future security of the Euro-Atlantic region depends upon the successful transitions to democracy and the market economy in the CEE states and the republics of the former Soviet Union, particularly the Russian Federation.[20]

The demand for a new division of labour within the alliance reflects the assessment that the community of interest in preserving a stable European security order competes with divergent interests out of area and along the southern periphery of Europe:

> Europe's post-Cold War security environment calls for an evolving division of labour between the United States and Europe, and between Atlantic and European institutions – a division which will insure full American involvement in the management of those aspects of European security which by reason of their scope and seriousness are clearly of vital interest to the United States, and are agreed to be beyond Europe's unaided efforts, while encouraging Europeans and European institutions to develop the capacity to handle challenges which fall below such a threshold.[21]

The Clinton administration, like the Bush administration before it, has made an effort to differentiate between American interests in the European theatre that touch primarily upon the vital interests of the Europeans and those which touch upon the vital interests of the United States. This differentiation of interests and areas of responsibilities appears to recast the burden-sharing arguments of the 1960s and 1970s, but in fact it resumes the failed effort of the Nixon administration to cope with the dilemma posed by the identity and diversity of interests within the NATO alliance.

The institutional solution to the dilemma of diversity and identity is located in the WEU. The administration's thinking on the WEU is complex and potentially contradictory: WEU is viewed as an institution providing a mechanism for the projection of European power outside the Euro-Atlantic area and in that respect supports the American objectives of lessening the burdens of regional security for the United States and engaging Europe out of area. Yet at the same time the United States wants to avoid the creation of a European military structure that would duplicate and compete with NATO.[22] It is not clear how the United States can have it both ways.

The final element of the American security architecture is the eastward expansion of NATO and continued security cooperation with the Russian Federation. The United States, and indeed the alliance, face the problem of assimilating the Russian Federation into the Euro-Atlantic security order if a new division of the European continent is to be avoided. The OSCE was initially seized upon as the institutional locus of cooperation between the Russian Federation, the United States and the other NATO countries at the onset of the post-Cold War period. However, the waning of both the New World Order and the common European house, along with the institutional innovations with NATO, have marginalised the OSCE. Yet the eastward expansion of NATO has become inextricably enmeshed with Russian security concerns. Both the Russian Federation and the NATO members, particularly the United States, are aware that the eastward expansion of NATO, to the eastern Europeans at least, represents a defensive foreign policy aimed against an expansionist Russian Federation; and the NATO countries, particularly the United States, also understand that the European security order requires an institutional basis for cooperation with the Russian Federation.

Expanding NATO without meeting the security needs of the Russian Federation would simply redivide the European continent and move NATO's defence perimeter farther east. The dangers of great-power competition in Europe and the creation of new spheres of military influence have moved the United States towards a policy of establishing a 'strategic relationship' with the Russian Federation within the context of the PfP.[23] The United States is pursuing a path of enlarging NATO while assuaging Russian security concerns. This strategy, however, falls far short of the Russian expectation that NATO will become a transformed institution; in effect that NATO will become what the OSCE had promised to be in the early 1990s.[24] Thus the strategy of 'engagement' initiated by the Bush administration and carried on by the Clinton administration falls short of the minimum demands of the Russian Federation. Yet it is also the case that the Clinton administration is committed to the expansion of NATO and has placed the Russians on notice that they will not be able to exercise a veto.[25]

The security architectures of the great powers: France

The French perception of French security interests in the post-Cold War world does not differ markedly from that of the post-war period. The parochial language of the national interest remains the idiom in which French security policy is expressed. But the content of French interests has been altered not only by the change in international context but by the change in France's weight and role in the European and global balances.

The French security architecture addresses the tensions produced by a tripolar world that is subject to the countervailing indications of the dual processes of integration and 'destructuration' in the international system. The

United States is viewed as the only military and economic superpower to emerge in the post-Cold War world; Asia is considered to be a fragmented and heterogeneous pole of power; and the EU is perceived as the 'vector of stability and integration for the whole of Europe'.[26] The stabilising process of integration between the economies of the EU and of other G-7 states is offset by the destabilising process of destructuration driven by the juxtaposition of tripolarity with the tripartite division of the world into 'rich states, buffer zones and poverty zones'.[27] The process of destructuration is not limited to the familiar North–South divide, but potentially includes economic and social unrest in the Russian Federation and Ukraine as well as the consequences of a failed transition to democracy and the market in central and eastern Europe.

The certainties of diplomacy and security evaporated with the collapse of the Cold War order. The dissolution of the Warsaw Pact, the redefinition of NATO's role in Europe, France's unsettled relationship with NATO, and the inability of the EU to fashion a CFSP have been complicated by the question of enlargement and the requisite assimilation and participation of all the (extra-) European states into a comprehensive security order. The French acknowledge the explicit security threats posed by the vulnerability of open societies to drug trafficking, Islamic extremism and terrorism. Yet the primary threat to European stability and French security remains the Russian Federation. The continued importance of the American presence in Europe – for at least two decades, in the French estimation – reflects this postulated Russian threat as well as the potential for regional conflict in Europe. The elements of change and continuity in the definition of French security interests have left untouched, however, the French penchant for autonomy.

The French security architecture addresses these concerns and trends in the international and European security system. France has set itself three aims with its security architecture. First, the European element of French security policy seeks the development of a credible European security identity that avoids the uncertainty of *ad hoc* coalitions among willing players and the loss of sovereign control over defence policy inherent in an integrated European military command. The second element of the French security architecture is to 'renew the transatlantic link' by adapting NATO to the new strategic context and to assure a long-term American commitment to Europe. And, third, the French security architecture provides for the assimilation of the Russian Federation into a comprehensive European security order. The French wish to prevent the reconstruction of antagonistic military blocs that will simply redivide the European continent and throw the western Europeans once again upon the mercy of the American security guarantee as well as subject the Europeans to American policy preferences.

The European element of the French security architecture anticipates the development of a European security identity housed in a WEU subordinated to the EU. It depends upon the intensification of the bilateral relationship between France and Germany which will give political substance to the CFSP, enhance the operational credibility of the Eurocorps, and consolidate the implicit bargain struck between Germany and France in 1988 that exchanges French leadership in defence and foreign policy issues for German leadership in economic and monetary affairs. The third element of the European dimension of the French security architecture is the intensification of the Anglo-French relationship and the creation of a European nuclear deterrent, without which European autonomy in the defence field is impossible.[28] Thus the European element of the French security architecture combines the old and the new: the foundation of the new security architecture consists of the effort to institutionalise military cooperation between France, Germany and Britain, with France playing a pivotal role;[29] and the mechanism for institutionalising that cooperation is located in the WEU, the anticipated defence component of the EU, which is to fashion and operationalise a European security and defence policy.

The French preference for a European security identity reflects, in part, abiding concern with German power in Europe but also concern with the divergence in the competences for economic and security policies within the EU: security and defence policy remains located in the national ministries of defence, while economic policy in all issue areas is increasingly made at the European level. The problem from the French perspective is that the conflict in the dynamic of economic and security policy counsels the elevation of EU competence in the realm of security and defence policy to ensure the coordination and compatibility of economic and security policies.[30]

The institutionalisation of European defence and security cooperation within the WEU provides for the linkage between the European and Atlantic elements of the security architecture. The joint sharing of facilities by NATO and the WEU and the double-hatting of allied forces provide a mechanism for minimising Euro-American conflicts over intervention in regional conflicts and out of area: when the United States declares itself uninterested in a regional conflict impinging upon vital European interests, the Europeans will be empowered to intervene without initiating an acrimonious debate with the United States. In the French calculation, it also provides a context for an autonomous European security policy that should eliminate corrosive debates over burden sharing and burden shirking in conflicts carrying different weights and importance for the American and European members of the alliance.

The perceived need for the development of an autonomous European defence capability is derived from what the French politely refer to as the 'more selective approach to Europe's security problems' taken by the United States.[31] In the French judgement, the dissolution of the Warsaw Pact and the enfeeblement of the Russian Federation have made Europe a less likely source of threats to vital American interests; and the United States has vital interests in the Pacific that will inevitably divert attention from Europe. The role of NATO, then, has become that of providing shelter and sustenance to the evolution of the budding European security and defence identity and to support the operational capabilities of the WEU. France has also made it a part of its policy to participate actively in the reshaping of the Atlantic alliance to meet the needs of the European security order and to service French interests in Europe. Towards that end, France has made an effort to retreat from the policy of distancing itself from the integrated military command of the alliance. The first important step towards a reconciliation with NATO was taken when the Franco-German Eurocorps was assigned to both NATO and the WEU; the next was when the French troops were placed under a NATO commander as a part of the IFOR.[32]

French support of NATO goes beyond the useful task of providing an institutional mechanism for committing the United States to the stability and security of Europe. NATO has emerged, ironically, as the most important security institution of post-Cold War Europe: it now plays the key role in the shaping of the emerging European security order; it is the guarantor of France's ambitions in Europe. The relative success of the NACC and the PfP programme has had the paradoxical effect of excluding France, one of the most important players in Europe, from deliberations over the future shape of the European security order. The viability of an effective European security identity depends upon the long-term health of NATO. Only NATO provides a forum where Europe and the United States can fashion a CFSP jointly and as equals. The French have not abandoned the position, however, that the long-term viability of NATO requires an independent and equal Europe acting in concert with the United States. NATO cannot survive if one of its (un)intended consequences is a Europe divided against itself and the perpetuation of American policy hegemony in security and defence.

The adaptation of NATO to the new international environment also suggests the need for the assimilation of the CEE states and the eastward extension of the NATO defence perimeter. The French security architecture envisages the expansion of both NATO membership and EU/WEU membership along the eastern periphery of the EU. The difficulty facing the western European countries, in the French view, is the process of embracing those nations and integrating them into the wealthier half of Europe without sparking the Russian fear of encirclement and thereby inadvertently recreating a division of the European continent into two antagonistic military blocs. The French recognise Russia as 'a European power indispensable to the stability and balance of Europe' which needs an institutionalised role in the new European security order. In exchange for meeting Russian security concerns, the French expect the Russians to acquiesce in the eastward expansion of the EU and subsequently of the WEU. The trick, then, becomes that of not violating the legitimate security concerns of the Russian Federation, particularly its well founded fear of isolation and encirclement, while securing Russian assurances that the EU and the WEU can expand eastwards in due course. The OSCE provides the institutional solution to the integration of the Russian Federation into the European security order and the avoidance of a Europe divided into two mutually antagonistic military blocs. It provides the forum for cooperation between the major European and extra-European powers on common security and defence issues.

The French security architecture places the EU/WEU at the centre of the European security order. The EU/WEU forges the primary connection between the western, central and eastern Europeans; the WEU forms the basis of a European defence identity that can strengthen the European pillar of the Atlantic alliance; and the extension of the WEU/EU provides a basis for expanding NATO membership eastwards without transforming it into a military alliance aimed explicitly at the Russian Federation.

The security architectures of the great powers: Germany

The content and direction of German security policy was narrowly circumscribed between 1949 and 1989 by the Federal Republic's membership of NATO and dependence upon the United States, and was defined by the need to contain Soviet power in Europe. The traditional preoccupation with guaranteeing Germany's territorial integrity has been pushed into the background by the changes that have taken place in the European state system. The Germans have refined and broadened their concept of security to conform with the pressures generated, and to exploit the opportunities offered, by the evolution of the European state system. Today German security is threatened not by an invasion of the Russian army but by the inability to control the flow of refugees in the event of mass migrations driven by political chaos or economic deprivation; by the proliferation of terrorist groups operating in Germany, both indigenous and foreign; and by threats to German economic security, defined not only in the traditional terms of access to foreign markets or of assured supply to raw materials, but in terms of protecting the post-war gains of the social market economy, the German preference for price stability and fiscal rectitude, and the European environment.

This broadened and evolving redefinition of German security interests also reflects a redefinition of the German state.[33] Germans have welcomed and embraced the notion that Germany must play the role of a 'civilian' power in Europe,[34] since the role of a great or middling power, defined militarily, has been proscribed by history, conscience, treaty, self-interest and until recently constitutional interpretation. The Germans remain hesitant contributors to the military requirements of regional and global stability; the United States, France and the United Kingdom retain a comparative advantage in the provision of military security. Germany has played the dominant role in financing the political and economic reconstruction of eastern Europe and has championed the eastward expansion of the EU and NATO. Germany remains satisfied to contribute primarily to the economic requirements of security and to accelerate the demilitarisation of inter-state relations, particularly in Europe – a development that plays to Germany's economic capacity and not coincidentally enhances German influence in the reconstruction and recasting of the European order.

Germany locates the greatest threat to European stability in the 'prosperity barrier' (*Wohlstandsgrenze*) between the nations of western and eastern Europe. The Germans argue that economic envy (*Wirtschaftsneid*) on the part of the immiserated nations of Europe, rather than the exercise or exploitation of Germany's economic power (*Wirtschaftsmacht*), is the important and very real threat to the stability of Europe, and consequently to the Germans.[35] The emphasis on the economic aspect of relations among the nations of Europe reflects the German redefinition of security. It also has the practical consequence of altering the calculus of power in the European area: it shifts attention away from the military potential of a state to its productive capability and rate of technological innovation, a development that would further strengthen German diplomacy at the expense of France and Britain. The German government views the transition to the market and democracy as the foundation of social stability in the CEE states and therefore for German and European security.

The redefinition of security and the changed (and changing) European state system have shaped and reshaped the role and promise of the existing institutions of European security. Germany, the key continental European partner of the United States in NATO, faced a choice in the procurement of its security: whereas NATO had the character of an automatic alliance over the course of the post-war period – the Germans had little choice but to support NATO in exchange for an extended American deterrent – the collapse of the Warsaw Pact and the absence of a countervailing order in the eastern portion of the European continent has had the unsettling affect of providing Germany with choice.[36] While it appeared in the early 1990s that NATO faced a longer-term challenge from the OSCE as the core security institution of the future, institutional innovation within NATO and political uncertainty in the Russian Federation have placed NATO firmly at the centre of the German security architecture.[37] The German security strategy envisions specific roles for NATO and the EC/WEU, but that strategy remains contingent upon the evolution of the European state system and the evolving redefinition of German interests, both of which will be influenced by the path taken by the Russian Federation and by the unfolding relations among the major European powers and between Europe and America in post-Cold War Europe.

NATO remains attractive to the Germans because it provides them with a number of positive externalities: first, NATO stabilises the periphery of western Europe;[38] second, NATO, NACC and the PfP programme provide an institutional mechanism for integrating all the nations of Europe into a single European security order; third, the changes in NATO strategy promise a more secure Germany with a greatly diminished exposure to nuclear war; fourth, NATO serves as a hedge against neo-isolationism in the United States;[39] and finally, as former defence Minister Stoltenberg noted, NATO is "the single functioning security structure in Europe" and serves as a yardstick against "fair-weather security structures" that are pretenders to NATO's role.[40] Within the German government there is general agreement that NATO, as the sole functioning security structure in Europe, is necessary for the foreseeable future. It is also clear that the Germans believe that without NATO (and to a lesser extent NACC and PfP), an independent European security identity and eventual European political union would be non-starters. This position answers in the affirmative the question 'Is NATO a key element of the German security strategy?' But it also raises two significant questions. Is NATO important because it remains part and parcel of a unified Germany's *Staatsraison* or because it is the only realistic alternative Germany has? Is NATO important because it is the only viable foundation upon which a collective security system from the Atlantic to the Urals can be safely constructed or has NATO merely become a 'traditional bridge of friendship across the Atlantic'?[41] The answer to these questions turns less upon the future (and indeterminate) relationship between NATO and the OSCE that seemed likely in the early 1990s than upon the expectations the Germans have of EC/WEU in the future European security order.[42]

German dependence upon NATO – as reinsurance against the unravelling of the reform process in eastern Europe and the Russian Federation and as the nexus for the coordination of policy on a broad array of issues from security to the environment to debt relief – has not precluded a European option for Germany, an option seen as complementary to rather than competitive with continued German membership of NATO or partnership with the United States.[43] The German government anticipates the absorption of the WEU by the EU as a major contribution to the stabilisation of Europe and the creation of an effective second pillar in the Atlantic alliance. The political unification of Europe requires progress towards the creation of a defence identity to complement the progress made towards a CFSP as well as European monetary union.[44]

The exact relationship between the EU and the WEU did not occupy an important place in the foreign policy agendas of the Atlantic states until October 1991, when France and Germany proposed the transformation of the WEU into the defence arm of the EU. The Germans have not strayed far from that position. The strengthening the WEU is treated as an essential component of the process of European integration, of a European security and defence identity, and as an essential complement to the CFSP. Whereas the British government prefers a WEU that continues to operate within an intergovernmental framework, to protect the privileged position of the United States within the alliance, to preserve the intergovernmental character of defence cooperation, and to facilitate cooperation out of area, the Germans (and French) clearly prefer a WEU that cooperates with NATO within Europe and out of area but is closely linked institutionally with the EU and forms the nucleus of a European defence identity. The Maastricht treaty provided that the WEU could be requested to 'elaborate and implement decisions and actions of the Union which have defence implications'.[45] Although language in the treaty provided that the evolution of this relationship between the WEU and the EU should be compatible with NATO, it is also clear that the Franco-German design for a separate security identity remains a blueprint for the future relationship between the EU and the WEU. The German government expects that progress will be made at the 1996 intergovernmental conference in strengthening the CFSP and moving towards the development of an autonomous EU defence policy. The German position at the intergovernmental conference now appears to favour a more ambiguous relationship between the WEU and the EU. Although it favours empowering the European Council to issue guidelines to the WEU, there appears to be greater acceptance of the Anglo-French position that defence policy should remain intergovernmental. Europe *à la carte* is the preferred option for defence policy.[46]

The OSCE held the promise of forming the primary institutional vehicle for creating a European security order based upon the principle of collective security. The German government's attitude towards the OSCE remains more ambivalent than at any time since 1989. The OSCE is clearly subordinated to NATO in the German security architecture: NATO provides insurance against any military threat to German territorial integrity, while the OSCE contribution to European security is located in the broad assimilation of the CEE states and the successor states to the former Soviet Union into the western economic and political orbit. Yet even this role has been compromised by the institutional innovations of NATO, the establishment of criteria for EU and NATO membership, and the expressed intention of NATO to establish a 'strategic partnership' with the Russian Federation. One important role the OSCE does play, however, is that of unburdening Russo-German cooperation. The OSCE diminishes the spectre of a second Rapallo, because the relations between the Russian Federation and Germany evolve within and are sanctioned by an established multilateral framework.[47]

The German architecture for Europe has three primary elements: the self-containment of German military power in order that Germany may use its economic power to influence its European neighbours in pursuit of German policy objectives; the creation of an independent Europe capable of negotiating on an equal basis with the United States on economic issues; and the continued demilitarisation of Europe, which depends upon the sustained growth of democracy and the free market in the former member states of the Warsaw Pact.

The economic dimension of German security depends first and foremost upon the consolidation of the EU's role as the economic and political magnet for central and eastern Europe, as the 'sheet anchor' of all Europe, as the core of a future European (con)federation, and as the vehicle for ensuring the pan-European adoption and codification of German economic *mores*, particularly the triple imperative of monetary independence from political interference, price stability and fiscal rectitude. The military-political strategy has five objectives: to create a pan-European security structure that integrates Germany into Europe as an equal if not a leading state; to accelerate the demilitarisation of the European area in order to create an environment favouring German economic interests, a development that would increase German leverage with the other European states and minimise Germany's historically dictated disadvantage in the military realm; to retain the American presence in Europe as reinsurance against the failure of a demilitarised pan-European security structure; to ensure the full participation of the Russian Federation in the institutions of the European security order; and to convince Germany's neighbours that it has renounced the objectives and instruments of *Realpolitik*.

The institutional solution to Germany's security dilemma – retaining the American extended deterrent, building a prosperous, politically stable and independent Europe, and creating an inclusive pan-European security system – cannot be found in a simple choice between NATO, OSCE, the EU or the WEU. The Germans in fact reject the notion that a choice must be made. All four security institutions are treated as if they are compatible and mutually reinforcing. Each serves specific and interrelated tasks for the Germans. NATO reinsures against the unravelling of the post-Cold War order as the Germans (and other Europeans) construct a (con)federal Europe and a European security identity. The primary advantage of the OSCE, its inclusiveness (both the United States and the Russian Federation are members), has evaporated. Yet the OSCE also serves other important tasks: it provides a framework for the continued demilitarisation of European foreign affairs with accelerated arms control and disarmament, it facilitates intensified Russo-German cooperation on security and economic affairs, and it furnishes Europe with embryonic regimes that lend support to the embrace of the market economy and democracy on a pan-European basis. The EU and the WEU provide the Germans with a mechanism for ensuring a German voice in the evolution of the European order; for providing the Germans with the consummation of the constitutionally dictated objective of European unification; for engendering a European economic space that conforms with German economic imperatives; for creating a European security identity capable of contesting American pretensions in Europe; and for constructing a political entity capable of withstanding pressure from a renascent Russia.

Yet NATO remains the key institution in the German strategy: NATO is considered essential to the creation of a European political and security identity; NATO is considered the only credible guarantor of European (and German) security; NATO serves as reinsurance against the misfiring of the political and economic liberalisation in eastern Europe or the political disintegration of Russian Federation; and NATO appears to be the only viable security institution capable of supporting order in the European security space. The Germans refuse to make an unambiguous choice between these institutions, partly because there is no compelling reason to make such a choice at this juncture and partly because these institutions are in fact complementary rather than competitive, at least for now. The German preoccupation with the institutional configuration of the post-Cold War security order reflects, no doubt, two lessons of history: first, peace and stability in Europe are possible only if Germany is closely tied to its neighbours in a manner that benefits each reciprocally; second, NATO has provided Germany and the other European democracies with the longest period of peace in contemporary history.

The German strategy offers Europe a bargain that Europe can hardly refuse: the most influential state in Europe, by virtue of geography, demography, economic capacity and putative military power, has offered to entrap itself in integrative and constraining political and military structures in exchange for the right to lead Europe on economic affairs and more critically to set the framework conditions of the post-Cold War European economy, particularly with respect to the targets and instruments of macroeconomic policy. This bargain yields tangible economic returns to the Germans, while the Europeans are left with the intangible military-political gain of resolving the German Problem – the full and irreversible integration of Germany into a European security order that banishes once and for all the prospect of a German diplomacy conducted in the pre-war idioms of war and territorial annexation. The potential cost of this strategy for Germany is a loss of national prerogative in the fashioning of its foreign policy on military and political issues, while the Europeans will bear the inevitable cost of a loss of national autonomy in economic affairs.

The architectures compared

The security architectures of the great powers demonstrate elements of convergence, divergence and parallelism. The relevant dimensions of comparison are the perception of threat to the European security order, the future role of NATO, the WEU and OSCE in the European security order, and future relations between those institutions, particularly the EU and WEU. The function of a security architecture ought to be the diminution of the anticipated threats to stability and order. The French and British consider an expansionist Russian Federation as the explicit and primary threat to the European security order. Although the United States does not ignore the potential threat posed by the Russian Federation to American and European security, it subordinates that concern – at least rhetorically – to the threat posed by the failure of the transitions to democracy and the market throughout the former Soviet imperium. The importance of the transition process drives the German security architecture; it explains the importance Bonn places on the economic requirements of security.[48] The German government, while aware of the military threat that the Russian Federation could pose to European (and German) security, seeks instead a new partnership that would bind Russia as closely to Europe as Germany was bound to western Europe after the Second World War. The new security agenda – migratory pressures, environmental threats, religious fundamentalism – remains subordinated to the old security agenda for the major European powers, once again with the exception of the Federal Republic. A second divergence between the major powers is located in the geographical orientation and reach of the security threat. The United States retains a global preoccupation with the requirements of security; the United Kingdom rests content with an unaltered Atlantic conception of security; the French are as concerned with the Mediterranean as they are with central and eastern Europe; and the Germans are particularly concerned with the evolution of the European system beyond their eastern border. These geographical orientations do not generate irreconcilable differences of interest, but they do lead to different reactions to the same security threat. It can help explain, for example, initial American indifference to the events in the Balkans and the German preoccupation with them; British indifference to the migratory pressures felt by France and the Federal Republic; and European indifference to the collapse of financial markets in Mexico. The absence of an immediate security threat, which the Soviet Union once posed, and an international context that allows parochialism to creep into foreign policy calculations, can corrode the willingness to cooperate even when common interests are at stake.

NATO has served as the key institutional feature of the Western security order since its founding in 1949. None of the major European powers is willing to abandon NATO at this juncture in history. The OSCE, the only viable competitor to NATO in post-Cold War Europe, has been outflanked by institutional innovations in NATO, particularly the effort to overcome NATO's initial disadvantage, its exclusivity. All four countries have consigned the OSCE to the residual role of assimilating states along the periphery of Europe, affording a permanent institutional forum for arms control and disarmament talks, providing a dispute settlement mechanism for its member states, and engaging in preventive diplomacy. NATO has been firmly endorsed as the core security institution of the European security order by the United States, France, the United Kingdom and Germany. The differences between the major powers revolve around the 'openness' of the institution to newcomers, the future role between NATO and the Russian Federation and, most important the relationship between the United States and the Europeans within NATO. The United States and the United Kingdom are reading off nearly identical scripts. Both countries want to perpetuate NATO predominance in the Atlantic order; both are comfortable with continued American dominance of the organisation if not leadership. The only schism between the two Anglo-Saxon powers derives from the enthusiasm for an autonomous European pillar that contributes to the alliance without competing with it or American policy preferences. The British are sceptical of the prospects for a European pillar within the alliance without that would inevitably lead to conflicts of interest between the United States and the Europeans. The British fear it could spark, in the end, American disengagement. The United States, on the other hand, welcomes a European defence identity that is capable of carrying a 'fairer' share of the burden of collective security without diminishing the American prerogative to set the security agenda. The French and the Germans are inclined to create an independent European security identity that enables Europe to act in concert with the United States as an equal; NATO then becomes the forum for the coordination of the security interests of the United States and Europe. France has become more willing to reconcile itself to NATO. This willingness is born largely of necessity, given the atrophied state of OSCE, the success of NACC and the PfP programme, and German resistance to a European solution that would jeopardise the American security guarantee. Germany, particularly during the stewardship of the Kohl–Kinkel government, has moved away from the earlier foreign policy logic that anticipated the eventual subordination of NATO to the OSCE. NATO has once again become the institutional address for German security cooperation.

The least settled dimension of the security architectures on offer by the four powers is the relationship between the EU and WEU and between the EU and NATO. The Federal Republic and France prefer the creation of a defence competence to complement the progress made towards the establishment of a CFSP. The French desire to subordinate the WEU to the EU represents the desire to provide an institutional basis for French foreign policy leadership in Europe; and for the Germans, the willingness to subordinate the WEU to the EU flows from the logic of creating a federal Europe and the need to complement progress towards economic and monetary unification. The French logic remains that of de Gaulle: only with an independent security and defence competence can Europe escape its subordination to the United States. Yet there is an element of change: a single European defence identity, and the attachment to autonomy and independence, would enable Europe to press its claims within NATO rather than in opposition to it. The United States supports the notion of a second European pillar; and it remains a standard element of the American foreign policy catechism that a united Europe will strengthen the United States and further American interests. The British are not so sure. It has been the British position that the WEU should remain independent of the EU and that the WEU should remain intergovernmental. As noted above, the British fear that any institutional subordination of the WEU to the EU would have a corrosive effect upon the alliance, encourage the dissociation of the United States and Europe, and degrade British security. There has been some movement towards a reconciliation of the British, French and German views: each country now reserves the right of ultimate control over the disposition and use of national armed forces. Residual autonomy in defence has not given way to the efficiencies and benefits of pooled sovereignty.

The 1996 intergovernmental conference of the EU, which is to review the Maastricht treaty, faces the difficult task of resolving the vexed issue of the relationship between the EU and the WEU as well as the more general question of reconciling the EC treaties with the foreign and security policy pillar of the EU. The foreign and security policy pillar of the EU is subject to intergovernmental procedures. The chief obstacle facing those who favour the deepening of a CFSP is the resistance to the introduction of qualified majority voting, particularly on the part of the major EU states. The European Commission favours closer integration of the WEU and the EU for several reasons: first, such a development would correct the anomaly that although NATO is represented at WEU meetings, the WEU is 'rarely' represented at Council meetings; second, the WEU has been recognised as an 'integral part of the development of the Union'; and, third, a closer institutional connection will provide a framework for structuring the debate over the future of the WEU when the treaty expires in March 1998.[49] The position of the European Commission, and the Franco-German position favouring the integration of the WEU and EU as well as the development of a European security identity, were endorsed at the NATO ministerial meeting at Noordwijk aan Zee in May 1995. At that time, the NATO ministers acknowledged that the WEU would strengthen the European pillar of the alliance and that the WEU 'is being developed as the defence component of the European Union'.[50] What has not been resolved, however, is the logic of national autonomy insisted upon by Britain, France and Germany with the logic of pooling sovereignty to parallel progress towards economic and monetary union.

The points of tangency and divergence between these architectures cannot obscure the extraordinary level of security cooperation that has occurred since 1989. Two developments suggest that progress has been made towards the multilateralisation and eastward expansion of the European security space. The Pact on European Stability arrested the initial tendency towards the 'spoke and hub' securitisation of the CEE states which was the inevitable outcome of the expansion questions, be it WEU, EU or NATO. Suggested initially by French Prime Minister Eduard Balladur, acted upon by the EU's CFSP, and deposited with the OSCE in March 1995, the Pact on European Stability established a network of bilateral treaties and multilateral programmes between the EU and the nine prospective members of the EU in central and eastern Europe. The pact sought to enhance regional economic cooperation, resolve outstanding minority issues, mitigate common environmental problems, and address other issues in order to facilitate a more cooperative set of relationships at Europe's geographical centre.[51] The Pact on European Security has contributed to the multilateralisation of the economic dimensions of security, to the creation of a common sense of destiny and to the identification of common interests.

NATO expansion is the second development giving shape to the future outline of the European security architecture. NATO has established three enlargement criteria. First, enlargement cannot weaken NATO from within. It must preserve the 'community of values' which have held the alliance together since its founding. The candidates for membership must enjoy democratic governance and the market economy, afford protection to civil liberties and the rights of minorities, and have firmly established civilian control over the military. Second, NATO expansion must enhance the security of the alliance and contribute to the security and stability of Europe. Outstanding territorial or ethnic disputes must be resolved before a candidate can qualify for membership. And third, it must be complemented by the parallel expansion of the EU.[52] The decision to enlarge NATO consolidates the centrality of NATO in the future European security order; it complements the integration of the CEE states into the (Western) economic institutions of security; and it provides a mechanism for reinforcing the transition process.

These developments, taken in conjunction with the preferred security architectures of the major European powers, suggest greater integration or gentle differentiation of the European security space. The American, British and German architectures are consistent with greater integration. This assessment reflects the long-lived interest of the Anglo-Saxon countries in, and the recent German advocacy of, an Atlantic free-trade area to complement security cooperation in NATO. The dividing line between the Anglo-Saxon and the German architectures is located, however, in the anticipated institutional form of the second pillar of the Atlantic alliance: the Germans favour a solution that parallels progress towards the pooling of sovereignty in the EU, which could have the unintended consequence of diplomatic drift and the eventual estrangement of the two pillars of the alliance, but meets France's minimum demand of some progress towards an independent European security identity. The French architecture clearly anticipates a security architecture that supports gentle differentiation of the North American and European pillars of the European security order. The French reconciliation with NATO does not carry with it abandonment of the 'principles of 1966' nor does it translate into support for an Atlantic free-trade area. Moreover, the acute sensitivity of the French foreign policy establishment to the economic and technological requirements of national autonomy and security suggests a continuing French preference for a Europe capable of acting independently of the United States. The German architecture appears to fit best the needs and present evolutionary path of the European security order; it meets the conflicting security requirements of the United States, the Russian Federation and the other European powers, particularly France.

And institutional choices

In the introduction, we identified the institutional requirements of a stable security order and outlined some of the problems associated with institutional choice. The overarching institutional question raised in the introduction revolved around regime congruence and regime interdependence. Regime congruence refers to the requirement that the norms governing the economic and security regimes should be mutually reinforcing and should not conflict in purpose. The interdependence of the military and economic security regimes refers to the requirement that the norms of military (economic) regimes should generate positive externalities that support the norms and institutions of the economic (military) regimes. It also implies that the regimes supporting the economic and military components of the overall security architecture are mutually dependent: the instability or incoherence of one element will undo the stability and coherence of the other. Both criteria have been met in the post-Cold War security order.

Three norms govern the issue clusters of the European security order:

democratic governance, collective security and conformity with the market. The post-Cold War security order has been effectively enveloped by the norms of the Bretton Wooods and NATO economic and security systems. As was the case with the American inspired security order, the macroeconomic, trade and exchange rate cluster facilitates the integration of national markets which not only enhances national economic welfare but creates a community of interest that translates into a source of support for the institution of collective defence, NATO. In the post-Cold War era, the universalism envisioned at Bretton Woods has been replaced with a more parochial construction that focuses upon the relationship between an enlarged EU and North America. The precise content of those norms with respect to macroeconomic and microeconomic policy is located in what we have called the Maastricht and Single European Act norms; the trading norms are an admixture of regionalism and multilateralism. The norms of the market economy and democratic governance suffuse and drive the financing regime. The nations in transition have been subject to the 'new conditionality' – project finance and balance of payments financing are contingent not only upon the standard criteria of feasibility or sound macroeconomic adjustment but upon progress towards the market and democracy. The norms of democratisation and marketisation govern the economic dimension of security and generate two externalities: they create a common frame of reference for identifying and resolving conflicts of interest; and they create a community of interest and values which supports the task of collective security.

The supply of collective security presupposes the presence of common or coincidental interests. These interests are generally presumed to be strategic and linked with matters of territorial integrity and the protection of national values. The demilitarisation of the European security space has reduced the urgency of these concerns, yet the problem of collective security has become more pressing owing to the change in the nature of the security threats posed to the nations of Europe. Drug trafficking, ethnic conflict, religious extremism and terrorism take the form of pan-regional threats to national security and consequently require cooperative solutions. Once again, the norms of democratic governance and the market supply a common frame of reference creating confidence in collective security. Moreover, collective security, particularly within the NATO framework, has paralleled the integration of economies with the integration of the military command structure. Cooperation in military security affairs reinforces and has been reinforced by the norms of comparative advantage, mutual dependence and mutual gain that are diffused throughout the economic institutions of cooperation.

The norms of marketisation, democratisation and collective security have contributed to the development of a common frame of reference for all the states occupying the European security space. These norms contribute to the development of an international context characterised by amity rather than enmity; blunt the divisive dynamics of multipolarity; and alter the calculation of benefit and gain in a way that supports cooperation. It is too early to assert with any certainty which norms have been successfully imposed upon the nations in transition and the extent to which those norms have been internalised. Yet the evidence of the first half the decade suggest that the norms have altered calculations of interest and action for the nations in transition.

Of more particular interest is the role institutions play in the process of norm adoption. It would appear that in the construction of the European security order the economic institutions of security have been the primary conveyors and enforcers of those norms. Those institutions have largely acted in conformity with the instrumental interests of the Western nations, particularly the belief in the elective affinity between the market, democracy and peace. Yet international institutions have mediated between the interests of the Western states and the states in transition. Moreover, these norms have functioned as criteria not only for membership of these institutions of security but for access to finance to underwrite the transition process itself.

The secondary institutional question that must be addressed is the problem of institutional choice. We decomposed the security order into three interlocking institutional clusters. A major consideration was the problem of coordination between and within clusters. The empirical evidence would suggest that there have been high levels of coordination within the institutional clusters on a periodic basis. In the economic clusters, coherence and coordination are supplied by three institutions: the market, the IMF and Maastricht. The market, given the openness of national economies and the reliance upon the market by national authorities to allocate resources within and between the economies of the Atlantic area, has reduced the control national authorities can exert over macroeconomic aggregates and has consequently created pressure for the coordination of economic activity. The IMF has contributed to the extension of western macroeconomic practices and policies in the nations in transition. The IMF leverages its key role in the debt regime to lessen the debt overhang retarding the process of transition, but extracts in exchange fidelity to restrictive macroeconomic norms. And the Maastricht norms have created a set of macroeconomic and exchange rate policy targets which discipline not only the EU nations but increasingly the nations along their eastern periphery.

The problem of coordination within the military cluster has been largely resolved with the emergence of NATO as the core security institution of the European security order, a development helped in large part by the institutional innovation that has broadened the participation in its deliberations by non-members, the prospect of eventual expansion, and the partial reconciliation of the Anglo-Saxon and French positions over the form and function of an independent European pillar. The NACC and PfP programme hold open the possibility of meaningful security cooperation between the two most important states in the European system, the United States and the Russian Federation; and the OSCE provides the basis for preventive diplomacy.

Coordination between the three clusters, or more generally between the economic and military dimensions of the security order, remains unsolved and may resist an institutional solution. The G-7 is ill equipped to serve the role of coordinating mechanism. The G-7 is an organisation with global reach but parochial concerns: just as the French are relatively indifferent to leadership changes on the Korean peninsula, the Japanese are nonplussed by the problem of North African migration to Europe. The exclusion of the Russian Federation from the G-7 and its inclusion in a political caucus is not tenable, particularly if the economic and military dimensions of security are as interdependent as we have argued. A new grouping, a G-4 consisting of the United States, Japan, the EU and the Russian Federation, might successfully perform the task of coordinating the two elements of the security order, but the problem of parochialism would remain, as would the awkwardness of an EU that cannot speak with one voice on economic and security problems.

The geographical scope of the primary institutions of economic security is global: the international financial and goods markets, the IMF, the World Bank, the IAEA, the G-7, the London and Paris Clubs and the WTO. Yet these institutions are overwhelmingly affected by the policies of the states comprising the European security area. Where geographical scope is most relevant, however, is in the area of military security. *The* problem of the European security order will be establishing the eastern boundary of NATO and the WEU. The NATO states must identify the outer limits of expansion which removes the strategic uncertainty facing the nations in transition without jeopardising the prospect of establishing a 'strategic relationship' with the Russian Federation.

Connected with the problem of geographical scope is the consideration of relations between institutions. Institutions may be ordered according to the principal of hierarchy or in accordance with the market metaphor. The financing regime is ordered according to the market metaphor; it has proved to be the least successful of the institutional clusters. The lack of progress towards resolving the nuclear safety problem reflects the inefficiency of an institutional market, as does the G-24 aid programme. Where institutional relations are ranked hierarchically the regime is more successful: this is particularly true in the case of macroeconomic policy, where the World Bank and regional institutions are subordinated to the IMF, and in the case of defence policy, where the WEU and OSCE are subordinated to NATO. While it is the case that these hierarchical relationships reflect the evolution of those institutions, and the institutions of transition are newly established and face an inherently less tractable set of policy problems, it appears that hierarchy rather than the market is the better ordering principle. The market metaphor is a flawed one for the organisation of security or the ordering of institutional relationships.

Conclusion

The problem of economic security is a temporal one within the European security space. The centrality of economic security to European stability is located in the urgency of completing and consolidating the transitions to democracy and to the market. The integration of the CEE states, particularly, into the heretofore Western institutions of security and prosperity is contingent upon their meeting those two criteria. Once these states make the transition to democracy and have economies irrevocably linked with the market norm, many of the economic security concerns identified in this book will be better approached from the perspective of welfare maximisation. But we are closer to the end of the beginning than to the beginning of the end; the problem of economic security will vex policy-makers into the next millennium.

The necessity of ensuring the parallel construction of the economic and military institutions of security is not only a theoretical proposition but has become a policy problem. There has been a formal linkage between the expansion of NATO and the expansion of the EU and WEU. The NATO countries have expressed the desirability of the contiguity of jurisdictional boundaries for the European members of NATO and the EU. There has been a remarkable degree of parallelism in the extension of the norms of the post-Cold War order. The economic institutions of security have enveloped the states in transition and the military institutions of security. NATO and the WEU have introduced institutional innovations that have reached out to the states in transition, and NATO has taken pains to establish a strategic relationship with the Russian Federation that privileges Russian security interests. The demand for the eastward expansion of NATO and the EU by the CEE states as well as by the United States and Germany presents the post-Cold War order with yet another dilemma: the expansion of NATO and the other security institutions presents fewer barriers to entry than does the most important institution of economic security, the EU.

NATO and the EU are both interlocking and interblocking. They are arguably interlocking by fiat: there is no compelling logic to dictate that all EU members must belong to NATO or that all the European NATO member states must belong to the EU. But this impulse towards institutional tidiness will be transformed into an institutional necessity if the EU develops a CFSP, transforms the WEU as the defence arm of the EU, and abandons intergovernmentalism in favour of pooled sovereignty. They are interblocking because NATO membership has been made contingent upon EU membership; and EU membership is unlikely in the medium term. The criteria for NATO membership reflect subjective political and strategic criteria, whereas the criteria of EU membership may be summarised as the ability of the petitioning state to enact the *acquis communautaire* and meet the Maastricht convergence criteria.

The logic embedded in this particular sequencing of expansion reflects the Western calculation that Russian resistance to the eastward expansion of NATO can be defused if the CEE states first become members of the EU and WEU. The Russians have not expressed any reservations about EU membership for the CEE states. Consequently, it would prepare the ground for the parallel expansion of NATO. It would have the double benefit of assuaging Russian security concerns while enhancing the security of Europe. This sequencing pattern possesses a compelling strategic logic, but it also postpones the expansion indefinately and leaves the European security architecture unsettled. It also suggests the consideration of security architectures that fall short of the parallel extension of NATO and the EU.

There are four credible architectural alternatives. The first, and potentially least stable, would be the encouragement of a new Russian zone of influence in central and eastern Europe. This option risks the redivision of the European continent and a new Cold War conducted in the idiom of geopolitics rather than ideological enmity. A second option would be to consign the CEE states to the purgatory of a *cordon sanitaire*. This option would privilege Russian security and economic interests and reflect the calculation that any security order that did not fully assimilate the Russian Federation would be fundamentally unstable and prone to conflict if not war. While the CEE states would have no alternative other than to accept membership in the global institutions of economic security and depend upon the great powers to protect their independence, the security order would be prone to periodic legitimacy crises. The third option would be the spoke-and-hub securitisation of central and eastern Europe. This option would be little more than a continuation of the *status quo* within the NACC and the PfP programme. It has the advantage of not precluding eventual membership of both NATO and the EU but at the same time does not infringe Russian security interests or entail a larger commitment by the United States to European security. The fourth and final alternative would be a two-speed Europe. In Chapters 4 and 5, it was argued that a two-speed Europe presented the best chance of including the CEE states in the EU without mortgaging their future prospects by locking them into a subordinate position economically and without holding progress towards economic and monetary union hostage to the lowest common denominator. And lowering the barrier to EU entry would pave the way for NATO membership. This solution would have a number of advantages: it would recognise the difficulty of full EU membership for the CEE states, it would remove the impediment to the parallel expansion of the EU and NATO, and it would lessen Russian security concerns attending NATO expansion.

The inter-war period provides a sobering comparison with and lessons for the post-Cold War world. The United Kingdom emerged from the Great War willing but unable to lead militarily or economically. The United States, which emerged as a hegemonic power, was unwilling to assume a leadership position on anything other than a set of narrow economic problems, particularly financial questions attending reparations. The peace agreement at Versailles lacked legitimacy, failed to assure the participation of the major states in the League of Nations, and lacked the support of collateral global economic institutions. At the end of the Cold War the United States may have emerged as the sole superpower but it is no longer a hegemon. It retains the ability to act independently on military matters. Only the United States can galvanise a collective Western response to a common military threat. The United States does not have that freedom of action or consistent leadership capability in economic affairs. The European security order is a double hegemony on the economic side of the equation. The Germans, like the Americans in the 1920s, are content to shoulder the economic burdens of security, but are hesitant to provide the military requirements of security and remain incapable of assuming a leadership position within Europe. One difference between the 1920s and the 1990s is the important role vested in and played by the international institutions of security. The post-Cold War order is populated by institutions that enjoy a high level of legitimacy and effectiveness. Two other institutional differences between the 1920s and 1990s are evident. First, the institutions of military security are grappling successfully with the problem of assimilation and inclusion. Second, the military institutions of security are buttressed by a collateral set of economic institutions.

Institutions have played an important role in recasting the European security order and will continue to facilitate cooperation on issues impinging upon both the economic and the military dimensions of security. But as the failure of Western institutions to halt the bloodshed and barbarism in Bosnia demonstrates, the effectiveness of institutions is contingent upon the willingness and ability of a state or group of states to exert leadership. With a little luck, the post-Cold War settlement will perpetuate the long peace built upon the rubble of Coventry, Dresden and Tokyo.

Notes

1 For an elaborate effort at scenario building see Adrian Hyde-Price, *European Security Beyond the Cold War: Four Scenarios for the Year 2010* (London: Royal Institute of International Affairs, 1991).
2 See Steve Weber and John Zysman, 'The Risk that Mercantilism will define the next Security System,' in Wayne Sandholtz et al. (eds), *The Highest Stakes: the Economic Foundations of the next Security System* (New York: Oxford University Press, 1992), pp. 172ff.
3 This argument is put by Barry Buzan, 'Economic Structure and International Security: the Limits of the Liberal Case,' *International Organization*, vol. 38, no. 4 (autumn 1984), pp. 587–624. Paolo Guerrieri and Pier Carlo Padoan argue that mercantilism carries with it the impulse both of securing welfare objectives and of promoting state power. Consequently, any form of regional mercantilism ultimately sharpens interstate competition and cannot be viewed as a strategy for promoting global stability, even in the absence of hegemony. Guerrieri and Padoan, 'Neomercantilism and International Economic Stability,' *International Organization*, vol. 40, no. 1 (winter 1986), pp. 29–42.
4 On the transition from Cold War to post-Cold War Europe see Stuart Croft, 'British Approaches to the European Security Debate,' *Arms Control*, vol. 12, no. 3 (December 1991), pp. 120–8.
5 N. H. R. A. Broomfield, Deputy Under Secretary, Foreign and Commonwealth Office, 'European Security: a British View,' speech to Federal Trust Conference on European Security, 4 November 1990. The perspective remains valid today; see Ministry of Defence, *Statement on the Defence Estimates*, Cmnd 2550 (London: HMSO, 1994), p. 9.

6   Broomfield, 'European Security'.
7   *Statement on Defence Estimates*, p. 11.
8   Progress towards a common security and foreign policy in the EU would necessarily reduce British visibility and influence in a procedural sense. It would also aggravate Britain's loss of influence in economic affairs, a situation driven by the loss of manufacturing and commercial clout in the international economy. See Will Hutton, 'Britain in a Cold Climate: the Economic Aims of Foreign Policy in the 1990s,' *International Affairs*, vol. 68, no. 4 (1992), pp. 619–32.
9   *Statement on Defence Estimates*, p. 9.
10 On the continued psychological importance of the 'special relationship' to both the United Kingdom and the United States see Christopher Coker, 'Britain and the New World Order: the Special Relationship in the 1990s,' *International Affairs*, vol. 68, no. 3 (July 1992), pp. 407–21.
11 On scepticism about the long-term compatibility of the EU/WEU security efforts with NATO see 'Europe – the Next Phase: New European Community Structures for Foreign Affairs and Defence,' *Research Note*, 92/44 (London: House of Commons Library, 1992).
12 On the Nixon administration's foreign policy and the consequences of this retrenchment see Robert Litwak, *Detente and the Nixon-Doctrine: American Foreign Policy and the Pursuit of Stability, 1969–1976* (Cambridge: Cambridge University Press, 1984); James Sperling, 'America, NATO, and West German Foreign Economic Policies, 1949–89,' in Emil J. Kirchner and James Sperling (eds), *The Federal Republic of Germany and NATO: Forty Years After* (London: Macmillan, 1992), pp. 157–93; and Terry Terriff, *The Nixon Administration and the Making of US Nuclear Strategy* (Ithaca: Cornell University Press, 1995).
13 *National Security Strategy of the United States* (Washington, DC: White House, March 1990), p. 2.
14 Warren Christopher, 'America's Leadership, America's Opportunity,' *Foreign Policy*, 95 (spring 1995), p. 19.
15 *National Security Strategy of the United States* (Washington, DC: White House, August 1991), p. 7; Department of Defense, *Report of the Secretary of Defence to the President and Congress. February 1992* (Washington, DC: Government Printing Office, 1992), p. 16.
16 See Wolfgang Schäuble, chair of the CDU/CSU Parliamentary Group, Deutsche Bundestag, 'The United States and the Future of Europe in an Era of Transition,' 13 November 1995, Georgetown University, reprinted in *Statements and Speeches*, vol. XVII, no. 18.
17 *National Security Strategy of the United States* (Washington, DC: White House, August 1991), p. 6; Department of Defense, *Report of the Secretary of Defense to the President and the Congress. February 1992* (Washington, DC: Government Printing Office, 1992), p. 5.
18 *National Security Strategy of Engagement and Enlargement* (Washington, DC: White House, February 1995), p. 23.
19 The PfP has supported 'NATO's central role in post-Cold War Europe while maintaining our role in shaping Europe's security architecture'. *National Security Strategy of Engagement and Enlargement*, p. 25; see also Richard Holbrooke, 'America: a European Power,' *Foreign Affairs*, vol. 74, no. 2 (March/April 1995), p. 42–4; and Warren Christopher, 'America's Leadership,' p. 19.
20 For a critique of the policy of 'enlargement' see Richard Haas, 'Paradigm Lost,' *Foreign Affairs*, vol. 74, no. 1 (January/February 1995), pp. 44–5. Haas argues that 'it remains unclear that "enlarging" democracy acutally qualifies as a paramount American interest'. The Clinton administration's assumption is that the successful transformation to democracy will provide the basis of membership in NATO as well as the EU, both of which provide mechanisms for resolving conflicts and protecting interests on a multilateral basis; and the more contested assumption that democracies are less likely to

resort to force of arms to settle conflicts of interest with one another. At least in the European context, the strategy of 'enlargment' remains plausible.

21   Ambassador James F. Dobbins, 'Europe and America in the post-Cold War Era: Agenda for a Euro-Atlantic Community,' Centre for European Policy Studies, 24 May 1993, Brussels, p. 8.
22   Holbrooke, 'America: a European Power,' p. 47.
23   Warren Christopher, 'America's Leadership,' p. 19.
24   Andrei Kozyrev, 'Partnership or Cold Peace?,' *Foreign Policy*, 99 (summer 1995), p. 12–14. For an extended discussion of Russian interests see James H. Brusstar, 'Russian Vital Interests and Western Security,' *Orbis*, vol. 38, no. 4 (fall 1994), pp. 607–19. The notion of creating a 'special relationship' between NATO and the Russian Federation is not limited to the Russian foreign minister. According to Zbigniew Brzezinski, the question of eventual Russian membership in NATO should be left open, the eastward expansion of NATO should be accompanied by a formal security treaty between NATO and Russia, security consultations should be institutionalised within the OSCE, and NATO should refrain from the stationing of NATO forces in the new NATO member states. Zbigniew Brzezinski, 'A Plan for Europe,' *Foreign Affairs*, vol. 74, no. 1 (January/February 1995), pp. 34–5.
25   For a critique of NATO expansion see Karl-Heinze Kamp, 'The Folly of rapid NATO Expansion,' *Foreign Policy*, 98 (spring 1995), pp. 116–31.
26   French Ministry of defence, *Livre Blanc sur la Défense 1994* (Paris: Ministry of Defence, 1994), pp. 8–9.
27   *Ibid.*, p. 10.
28   The French recently announced the shift in nuclear doctrine from a focus upon a national deterrent to *dissuasion concertée*.' The impact of this change on the prospects for the CFSP could, in Michael Stürmer's view be either positive or negative. Michael Stürmer, 'A Question of Balance,' *Financial Times*, 19 September 1995, p. 14.
29   France's uncertainty about its continued ability to balance a unified Germany may account for the desire to stake out common strategic interests with the United Kingdom. See Dominique Moïsi and Michael Mertes, 'Europe's Map, Compass, and Horizon,' *Foreign Affairs*, vol. 74, no. 1 (January 1995), pp. 132–3.
30   *Ibid.*, p. 132.
31   *Ibid.*, p. 32.
32   The importance of this step was argued by Pierre Lellouche in his 'France in Search of Security,' *Foreign Affairs*, vol. 72, no. 2 (spring 1993), p. 129.
33   For a discussion of the redefinition of state and nation in Germany see Ole Wæver, 'Three Competing Europes: German, French, and Russian,' *International Affairs*, vol. 66, no. 3 (July 1990), pp. 477–94.
34   See Hanns W. Maull, 'Germany and Japan: the New Civilian Powers,' *Foreign Affairs*, vol. 65, no. 9 (winter 1990/91), pp. 92–3; and Stephen Szabo, *The Changing Politics of Germany Security* (New York: St Martin's Press, 1990).
35   Chancellor Kohl, 'Die Rolle Deutschlands in Europa,' 13 March 1991, *Bulletin* 33 (22 March 1991), p. 245.
36   For an extended discussion of NATO as a 'fated community' (*Schicksalsgemeinschaft*) see Emil J. Kirchner and James Sperling, 'The Future Germany and the Future of NATO,' *German Politics*, vol. 1, no. 1 (April 1992), pp. 50–72.
37   Foreign Minister Klaus Kinkel, 'German Foreign Policy Five Years after Unification,' *Statements and Speeches*, vol. XVIII, no. 14 (3 October 1995).
38   Chancellor Kohl, 'Erstes Treffen des Rates der Aussenminister der Teilnehmerstaaten der KSZE,' 19 June 1991, *Bulletin*, 72 (22 June 1991), p. 579. This position reflected the outcome of the Copenhagen NATO summit on 6 June 1991, when the allies made an effort to reassure the nations of the former Warsaw Pact in terms that stopped short of

offering a unilateral security guarantee. *New York Times*, 7 June 1991, p. A1.
39 Bundesminister des Auswärtigen Hans-Dietrich Genscher, 'Eine Vision für das ganze Europa,' 3 February 1991, *Bulletin*, 14 (February 1991), p. 92.
40 Bundesminister der Verteidigung Gerhard Stoltenberg, 'Zukunftsaufgaben der Bundeswehr im vereinten Deutschland,' 13 March 1991, *Bulletin*, 29 (15 March 1991), p. 215. This theme is repeated in Foreign Minister Kinkel, 'Kernfragen deutscher Aussenpolitik,' 12 October 1995, *Bulletin*, 82 (16 October 1995), p. 801.
41 Kinkel, 'Kernfragen deutscher Aussenpolitik,' p. 801.
42 See Klaus Kinkel, 'Eine gerechte und dauerhafte Friedensordnung für ganz Europa,' 5 February 1995, *Bulletin*, 12 (16 February 1995), p. 96.
43 Chancellor Kohl, 'Verantwortung für das Zusammenwachsen Deutschlands und Europa,' 6 June 1991, *Bulletin*, 64 (7 June 1991), p. 513.
44 Volker Rühe, 'Rede von Bundesminister Rühe,' 17 November 1995, *Bulletin*, 97 (21 November 1995), p. 945.
45 *Economist*, 14 December 1991, No. 7737, p. 52. For a post-Maastricht statement on the WEU and the EC see Chancellor Kohl, 'Erklärung der Bundesregierung,' 13 December 1991, *Bulletin*, 142 (17 December 1991), p. 1156.
46 See Klaus Kinkel, 'Erklärung der Bundesregierung,' 22 June 1995, *Bulletin*, 51 (26 June 1995), p. 462; and 'Central Issues of German Foreign Policy,' pp. 3–4.
47 Less relaxed appraisals of the new German-Russian relationship can be found in W. R. Smyser, 'USSR–Germany: a Link Restored,' *Foreign Policy*, 84 (fall 1991), pp. 125–41; and Marian Leighton and Robert Rudney, 'Non-offensive Defense: toward a Soviet–German Security Partnership?' *Orbis*, vol. 35, no. 3 (summer 1991), pp. 377–94.
48 For a detailed discussion of the economic dimension of the German security architecture see James Sperling, 'The German Architecture for Europe: Military, Political and Economic Dimensions,' in Peter Merkel (ed.), *The Federal Republic of Germany at Forty-five* (New York: New York University Press, 1995), pp. 378–88.
49 European Commission, 'The 1996 Intergovernmental Conference (First Report),' B/9/95, pp. 4–8; and *Commission Report for the Reflection Group* (Luxembourg: European Communities, 1995), pp. 61–70.
50 'Communiqué,' Ministerial Meeting of the North Atlantic Council, Noordwijk aan Zee, the Netherlands, 30 May 1995, section 2.
51 See *The Pact on Stability in Europe*, Paris, 20–1 March 1995.
52 'Study on NATO Enlargement,' *NATO Review*, 6 (November 1995), p. 10; 'Wirre Angst,' *Der Spiegel*, 21 August 1995, pp. 32–3; and 'Communiqué,' Ministerial Meeting of the North Atlantic Council, section 4.

BIBLIOGRAPHY

Anderson, K. (1994), 'Implementation of the Agreement on Agriculture'. *The New World Trading System: Readings*, OECD, Paris, pp. 153–62.

Andrews, D. (1994), 'Capital Mobility and State Autonomy: Toward a Structural Theory of International Monetary Relations', *International Studies Quarterly*, XXXVIII, pp. 193–218.

Aron, R. (1973), *Peace and War: A Theory of International Relations*. Anchor Press, New York.

Asmus, R. D., Kugler, R. L. and Larrabee, F. S. (1993), 'Building a new NATO', *Foreign Affairs*, LXXII, pp. 28–40.

Atlantic Council of the United States (1990), Task Force on German Unification, *The United States and United Germany*. Atlantic Council of the United States, Washington, DC.

Axelrod, R. (1984), *The Evolution of Cooperation*, Basic Books, New York.

Axelrod, R. S. (1994), 'Subsidiarity and Environmental Policy in the European Community', *International Environmental Affairs*, VI, pp. 115–32.

Axilrod, S. H.. (1987), 'Treasury and Federal Reserve Foreign Exchange Operations', *Federal Reserve Bulletin*, LXXIII, pp. 48–53.

Beahr, P. R. and Gordenker, L. (1994), *The United Nations in the 1990s*, second edition, St Martin's Press, New York.

Baldwin, D. (1985), *Economic Statecraft*, Princeton University Press, Princeton.

Baldwin, R. E. (1989), 'US Trade Policy: Recent Changes and Future US Interests', *American Economic Review*, LXXIX, no. 2, pp. 128–33.

Baldwin, R. E. (1994), *Towards an Integrated Europe*, Centre for Economic Policy Research. London.

Banca d'Italia (1992), 'Recent trade agreements concluded by the EC with EFTA and certain Countries in Central and Eastern Europe', *Economic Bulletin*, vol. 14, pp. 59–9.

Bank of England (1990), 'The Advent of Trading Blocs', *Bank of England Quarterly Bulletin*, XXX, pp. 372–3.

Bank of England (1992), 'The Maastricht Agreement on Economic and Monetary Union', *Quarterly Bulletin*, XXXII, pp. 64–8.

Bank for International Settlements (1992), *Sixty-second Annual Report, 1st April 1991–31st March 1992*, BIS, Basle.

Bank for International Settlements (1993), *Sixty-third Annual Report, 1st April 1992–31st March 1993*, BIS, Basle.

Barbe, E. (1992), '*Spanish Responses to the Security Institutions of the new Europe: Mediterranean Objectives and European Instruments*', Working Paper, Centre d'Estudios sobre la Pau i el Desarmament, Autonomous University of Barcelona.

Bardehle, P. (1989), '"Blue Helmets" from Germany? Opportunities and Limits of UN Peacekeeping', *Aussenpolitik*, XL, pp. 372–84.

Bates, W. T. and Bianco, R. H. (1990), 'Cooperation by Design: Leadership, Structure, and Collective Dilemmas', *American Political Science Review*, LXXXIV, pp. 133–48.

Bauwens, W., Colson, B., De Haar, W., De Feyter, K., Paye, O. and Vertongen, N. (1994), 'The CSCE and the Changing Role of NATO and the European Union', *NATO Review*, XLII, no. 3, pp. 21–5.

Baylis, T. A. (1994), *The West and Eastern Europe: Economic Statecraft and Political Change*,

Westview Press, Boulder.
Bayoumi, T. (1992), 'The Effect of the ERM on Participating Economies', *IMF Staff Papers*, XXXIX, pp. 350–6.
Bhagwati, J. (1990), 'Multilaterialism at Risk. The GATT is dead. Long live the GATT', *The World Economy*, XIII, pp. 149–69.
Biersteker, T. J. (ed.) (1993), *Dealing with Debt: International Financial Negotiations and Adjustment Bargaining*, Westview Press, Boulder.
Blackwill, R. D. (1990), 'The Security Implications of a United Germany', II, 'America's Role in a Changing World', II, *Adelphi Papers* 257.
Bleaney, M. (1990), 'Some Trade Policy Issues in the Transition to a Market Economy in Eastern Europe', *The World Economy*, XIII, pp. 251–62.
Blejer, M. I., Calvo, G. A., Coricelli, F. and Gelb, A. H. (eds) (1993), *Eastern Europe in Transition: from Recession to Growth?*, World Bank Discussion Papers 196, World Bank, Washington, DC.
Borensztein, E. and Montiel, P. J. (1991), 'Savings, Investment, and Growth in Eastern Europe', *IMF Working Paper*, International Monetary Fund, Washington, DC.
Brandsma, A. S. and Pijers, J. R. (1985), 'Coordinated Strategies for Economic Cooperation between Europe and the United States', *Weltwirtschaftliches Archiv*, CXXI, pp. 661–81.
Brinkhorst, L. J. (1992), 'Nuclear Safety and the European Community: Broadening Perspectives', *IAEA Bulletin*, XXXIV, no. 2, pp. 41–3.
Broer, M. and Diehl, O. (1991), 'Die Sicherheit der neuen Demokratien in Europa und die NATO', *Europa Archiv*, XLVI, pp. 372–6.
Brown, N. (1989), 'Climate, Ecology, and International Security', *Survival*, XXXI, pp. 519–32.
Brusstar, J. (1994), 'Russian Vital Interests and Western Security', *Orbis*, XXXVIII, pp. 607–19.
Bryant, R. (1980), *Money and Monetary Policy in Interdependent Nations*, Brookings Institution, Washington, DC.
Bryant, R. (1987), 'Intergovernmental Coordination of Economic Policies: an Interim Stocktaking', in *International Monetary Cooperation: Essays in Honor of Henry C. Wallich*, Essays in International Finance 169, Princeton University, Princeton.
Brzezinski, Z. (1995), 'A Plan for Europe', *Foreign Affairs*, LXXIV, pp. 26–42.
Bull, H. (1977), *The Anarchical Society: a Study of Order in World Politics*, Macmillan, London.
Burghardt, G. (1994), 'The New Europe', paper given at sixteenth World Congress of the International Political Science Association, Berlin, 23 August 1994.
Butterfield, H. (1950), *History and Human Relations*, Collins, London.
Butts, K. H. (ed.) (1994) *Environmental Security: a DOD Partnership for Peace*, Strategic Studies Institute Special Report, US Army War College: Carlisle Barracks, PA.
Buzan, B. (1991), *People, States and Fear: an Agenda for International Security Studies in the post-Cold War Era*, second edition, Lynne Reinner, Boulder.
Buzan, B. (1993), ' From International System to International Society: Structural Realism and Regime Theory meet the English School', *International Organization*, XLVII, pp. 327–52.
Buzan, B. (1984), 'Economic Structure and International Security: the Limits of the Liberal Case', *International Organization*, XXXVIII, pp. 587–624.
Buzan, B., Jones, C. and Little, R. (1993), *The Logic of Anarchy: Neorealism to Structural Realism*, Columbia University Press, New York.
Cadiou, J-M. (1993), 'The Environmental Legacy of the Cold War', *NATO Review*, XLI, no. 5, pp. 33–5.
Cadiou, J-M. (1995), 'Meeting on Defence-related Cross-border Environment Problems', *NATO Review*, XLIII, no. 5, pp. 33–5.
Cahan, A. (1989), *The Western European Union and NATO: Building a European Defence*

Identity within the Context of Atlantic Solidarity, Brassey's, London.
Caldwell, L. K. (1990), *International Environmental Policy: Emergence and Dimensions*, second edition, Duke University Press, Durham, NC.
Calleo, D. P. (1982), *The Imperious Economy*, Harvard University Press, Cambridge, MA.
Calleo, D. P. (1987), *Beyond American Hegemony*, Basic Books, New York.
Calleo, D. P. (1987), 'NATO's Middle Course', *Foreign Policy*, no. 96, pp. 135–47.
Calleo, D. P. and Rowland, B. M. (1973), *America and the World Political Economy: Atlantic Dreams and National Realities*, Indiana University Press, Bloomington.
Canzoneri, M. and Gray, J. A. (1985), 'Monetary Policy Games and the Consequences of Non-cooperative Behavior', *International Economic Review*, XXVI, pp. 547–64.
Carment, D. (1994), 'The International Politics of Ethnic Conflict: A NATO Perspective on Theory and Policy', paper delivered at the APSA convention, New York, September.
Carré, H. and Johnson, K. H. (1990), 'Progress toward a European Monetary Union', *Federal Reserve Bulletin*, LXXVII, pp. 773–4.
Caves, R. E. and Jones, R. W. (1977), *World Trade and Payments: An Introduction*, second edition, Little Brown, Boston, MA.
Cecchini, P. (1988), *The European Challenge, 1992: the Benefits of a Single Market*, Gower, Aldershot.
Chan, S. (1985), 'The Impact of Defense Spending on Economic Performance: a Survey of Evidence and Problems', *Orbis*, XXIX, pp. 403–34.
Christopher, W. (1995), 'America's Leadership, America's Opportunity', *Foreign Policy*, no. 95, pp. 6–28.
Cizauskas, A. C. (1979), 'International Debt Renegotiation: Lessons from the Past', *World Development*, VII, pp. 199–210.
O'Cleireacain, S. (1990), 'Europe 1992 and Gaps in the EC's Common Commercial Policy', *Journal of Common Market Studies*, XXVIII, pp. 201–18.
Coker, C. (1992), 'Britain and the New World Order: the Special Relationship in the 1990s', *International Affairs*, LXVIII, pp. 407–21.
Commission of the European Communities (1990), 'One market, one Money: an Evaluation of the potential Benefits and Costs of forming an Economic and Monetary Union', Study of the Directorate-General for Economic and Financial Affairs, *European Economy*, European Community, Brussels.
Commission of the European Communities (1992), *The Maastricht Conclusions on EMU: Six Points*, European Community, Brussels.
Commission of the European Communities (1992), *Towards Sustainability: a European Community Programme of Policy and Action in Relation to the Environment and Sustainable Development*, COM (92) 23 final, II, European Community, Brussels.
Commission of the European Communities (1992), *Proposal for a Resolution of the Council of European Communities on a Community Programme of Policy and Action in Relation to the Environment and Sustainable Development*, I, European Community, Brussels.
Commission of the European Communities (1995), *Towards Greater Economic integration: the European Union's financial assistance and trade policy for central and eastern Europe and the countries of the Commonwealth of Independent States*, European Community, Brussels.
Commission of the European Communities (1995), White Paper. *Preparation of the Associated Countries of Central and Eastern Europe for Integration into the Internal Market of the Union*, COM (95) 163 final, 3 May.
Conybeare, J. A. C. (1987), *Trade Wars*, Columbia University Press, New York.
Cooper, R. N. (1968), *The Economics of Interdependence*, McGraw-Hill for the Council on Foreign Relations, New York.
Cooper, R. N. (1976), 'Worldwide versus Regional Integration: is there an Optimum Size of the Integration Area?' in F. Machlup (ed.), *Economic Integration, Worldwide, Regional,*

Sectoral, Macmillan, London.
Cooper, R. N., Eichengreen, B., Holtham, G., Putnam, R. D. and Henning, C. R. (1989), *Can Nations Agree? Issues in International Economic Cooperation*, Brookings Institution, Washington, DC.
Corden, W. M. (1986), 'Fiscal Policies, Current Accounts and Real Exchange Rates: in Search of a Logic of International Policy Coordination', *Weltwirtschaftliches Archiv*, CXXII, pp. 423–38.
Corrigan, E. G. (1989), 'Reflections on the 1980s', *Federal Reserve Bank of New York, Annual Report*, FRBNY, New York, pp. 5–22.
Croft, Stuart, 'British Approaches to the European Security Debate', *Arms Control*, XII, pp. 120–8.
Cowhey, P. F. (1993), 'Domestic Institutions and International Communication', *International Organization*, XLVII, pp. 299–326.
Curtis, M. (1993), 'Western European Security and the Third World', in M. Curtis, O. Diel, J. Paolini, A. Seydoux and R. Wolf (eds), *Challenges and Responses to Future European Security: British, French and German Perspectives*, European Strategy Group.
Dam, K. (1970), *The GATT: The Law and International Economic Organization*, University of Chicago Press, Chicago.
Dassu, M. (1990), 'The Future of Europe: the View from Rome', *International Affairs*, LXVI, pp. 302–3.
Deger, S. (1993), 'World Military Expenditure', *SIPRI Yearbook 1993*, Oxford University Press, Oxford, pp. 337–97.
Delors, J. (1991), 'European Integration and Security', *Survival*, XXXIII, pp. 99–110.
Deudney, D. (1990), 'The Case against Linking Environmental Degradation and National Security', *Millennium*, XIX, pp. 461–76.
Deudney, D. (1991), 'Environment and Security: Muddled Thinking', *Bulletin of Atomic Scientists*, April, pp. 22–8.
Deutsche Bundesbank (1984), *Annual Report of the Deutsche Bundesbank for the Year 1984*, Deutsche Bundesbank, Frankfurt.
Deutsche Bundesbank (1988), 'Forty Years of the Deutsche Mark', *Monthly Report*, XL, no. 5, pp. 13–24.
Deutsche Bundesbank (1989), *Annual Report of the Deutsche Bundesbank for the Year 1989*, Deutsche Bundesbank, Frankfurt.
Deutsche Bundesbank (1989), 'Exchange Rate Movements within the European Monetary System', *Monthly Report*, XLI, no. 11, pp. 28–37.
Deutsche Bundesbank (1990), 'Statement by the Deutsche Bundesbank on the Establishment of an Economic and Monetary Union in Europe', *Monthly Report*, XLII, pp. 40–4.
Deutsche Bundesbank (1990), 'Statistische Beihefte zu den Monatsberichten der Deutschen Bundesbank, Reihe 3', *Zahlungsbilanzstatistik*, Bundesbank, Frankfurt.
Deutsche Bundesbank (1993), *Annual Report of the Deutsche Bundesbank for the Year 1992*, Deutsche Bundesbank, Frankfurt.
Deutsche Bundesbank (1993), 'The recent Monetary Policy Decisions and Developments in the European Monetary System', *Monthly Report*, XLV, pp. 19–27.
Deutsche Bundesbank (1994), 'The Second Stage of European Economic and Monetary Union', *Monthly Report*, XLVI, pp. 23–9.
Deutsche Bundesbank (1995), 'Overall Determinants of the Trends in the real External Value of the Deutsche Mark', *Monthly Report*, XLVII, no. 8, pp. 17–38.
Diehl, P. F. (ed.), (1989), *The Politics of International Organizations*, University of Chicago Press, Chicago.
Dienstbier, J. (1991), 'Central Europe's Security', *Foreign Policy*, no. 83, pp. 125–7.
Diwan, I. and Saldanha, F. (1991), 'Long Term Prospects in Eastern Europe: the Role of External Finance in an Era of Change', *Working Papers*, World Bank, Washington, DC.

Dobson, W. (1991), *Economic Policy Coordination: Requiem or Prologue?*, Institute for International Economics, Washington, DC.
O'Donnell, R. and Murphy, A. (1994), 'The relevance of the European Union and European integration to the world trade regime', *International Journal*, XLIX, pp. 535–67.
Duke, S. (1994), *The New European Security Disorder*, Macmillan, London.
Dumas, L. J. (1986), *The Overburdened Economy*, University of California Press, Berkeley.
Economic Commission for Europe (1991), *Economic Survey of Europe in 1990–1991*, United Nations, New York.
Economic Commission for Europe (1992), *Economic Survey of Europe in 1991–1992*, United Nations, New York.
Economic Commission for Europe (1993), *Economic Survey of Europe in 1992–1993*, United Nations, New York.
Economic Commission for Europe (1994), *Economic Survey of Europe in 1993–1994*, United Nations, Geneva.
van Eekelen, W. (1993), 'WEU prepares the Way for new Missions', *NATO Review*, XLI, no. 5, pp. 19–23.
van Eekelen, W. (1994), 'WEU after two Brussels Summits: a new Approach to Common Tasks', paper presented at the Royal Institute for International Relations, London.
Eichengreen, B. (1990), 'One Money for Europe? Lessons from US Currency Union', *Economic Policy*, X, pp. 117–87.
European Bank for Reconstruction and Development (1992), *Environmental Procedures*, EBRD, London.
European Bank for Reconstruction and Development (1993), 'Harmonisation of Environmental Legislation and Standards', *Environments in Transition*, EBRD, London.
European Bank for Reconstruction and Development (1993), *EBRD Economic Review: Annual Economic Report*, EBRD, London.
European Bank for Reconstruction and Development (1993), 'Export Access to Western Markets; recent Issues and Developments', *EBRD Economic Review: Current Economic Issues*, EBRD, London, pp. 17–27.
European Bank for Reconstruction and Development (1994), *The Nuclear Safety Account: Central and Eastern Europe and former Soviet Union*, EBRD, London.
European Commission (1993), *PHARE and TACIS: Nuclear Safety in Central and Eastern Europe: Present and Future Activities*, European Commission, Brussels.
European Commission (1994), *Phare Funding, 1990–1994*, European Commission, Brussels.
European Investment Bank (1990), *Loans to Build the European Community*, EIB, Luxembourg.
European Investment Bank (1990), *Protection of the Environment*, EIB, Luxembourg.
European Investment Bank (1990), *Annual Report, 1990*. EIB, Luxembourg.
European Investment Bank (1991), *Annual Report, 1991*. EIB, Luxembourg.
European Investment Bank (1992), *European Investment Bank: The European Community's financial institution*, EIB, Luxembourg.
European Investment Bank (1992), *Annual Report, 1992*. EIB, Luxembourg.
European Investment Bank (1993), *Annual Report, 1993*. EIB, Luxembourg.
Evans, G. (1994), 'Cooperative Security and Intrastate Conflict', *Foreign Policy*, no. 106, pp. 3–20.
Falk, R. (1995), 'Appraising the UN at 50: the Looming Challenge', *Journal of International Affairs*, XXXXVIII, pp. 625–43.
Fazio, A. (1991), 'Role and Independence of Central Banks', *Banca d'Italia Economic Bulletin*, no. 12, pp. 73–85.
Federal Reserve Bank of New York (1994), 'Foreign Exchange Operations of the Treasury and the Federal Reserve, February–April 1994', *FRBNY Quarterly Review*, XIX, pp. 72–8.
Feinberg, R. E. (1988), 'The changing Relationship between the World Bank and the Inter-

national Monetary Fund', *International Organization*, XLII, pp. 545–60.
Finlayson, J. A. and Zacher, M. W. (1982), 'The GATT and the Regulation of Trade Barriers: Regime Dynamics and Functions', in S. Krasner (ed.), *International Regimes*, Cornell University Press, Ithaca, NY.
Frankel, J. A. (1990), 'International Nominal Targeting (INT): a Proposal for Monetary Policy Coordination in the 1990s', *The World Economy*, XIII, pp. 263–73.
Frankel, J. A. and Mussa, M.. (1980), 'Monetary and Fiscal Policies in an Open Economy', *American Economic Review*, LXX, pp. 374–81.
Frankel, J. A. and Rockett, K. (1988), 'International Macroeconomic Policy Coordination when Policymakers do not agree on the True Model', *American Economic Review*, LXXVIII, pp. 318–40.
Freedman, I. (1994), 'The Balkan Tragedy', *Foreign Policy*, no. 97, pp. 53–69.
French, H. (1991), *Green Revolutions: Environmental Reconstruction in Eastern Europe and the Soviet Union*, Worldwatch Paper 99, World Watch Institute, New York.
Garrett, G. (1992), 'The European Community's Internal Market', *International Organization*, XLVI, pp. 534–45.
Gerber, E. R. and Jackson, J. E. (1993), 'Endogenous Preferences and the Study of Institutions', *American Political Science Review*, LXXXVII, pp. 639–57.
Ghosh, A. R. and Masson, P. R. (1988), 'International Policy Coordination with Model Uncertainty', *IMF Staff Papers*, XXXV, pp. 230–58.
Gilpin, R. (1975), *US Power and the Multinational Corporation*, Basic Books, New York.
Gilpin, R. (1981), *War and Change in World Politics*, Princeton University Press, Princeton.
Glenny, M. (1992), *The Fall of Yugoslavia: The Third Balkan War*, Penguin Books, London.
Gleick, P. (1991), 'Environment and Security: the clear Connections', *Bulletin of Atomic Scientists,*, April, pp. 17–21.
Gleick, P. (1993), 'Water and Conflict: Fresh Water Resources and International Security', *International Security*, XVIII, pp. 79–112.
Gnesotto, N. (1994), 'Lessons of Yugoslavia', *Chaillot Papers* 14, WEU Institute for Security Studies, Paris.
Goldstein, M., Isard, P., Masson, P. R. and Taylor, M. P. (1992), *Policy Issues in the Evolving International Monetary System*, International Monetary Fund, Washington, DC.
González, A. J. (1992), 'Fundamental Principles of Protection and Safety for Nuclear Power', *IAEA Bulletin*, XXXIV, no. 2, pp. 10–14.
Gosovic, B. (1992), *The Quest for World Environmental Cooperation: the Case of the UN Global Environment Monitoring System*, Routledge, London.
Gow, J. (1992), 'The Use of Coercion in the Yugoslav Crisis', *The World Today*, XLVIII, pp. 198–202.
Gowa, J. (1989), 'Bipolarity, Multipolarity, and Free Trade', *American Political Science Review*, LXXXIII, pp. 1245–56.
Grasselli, G. (1992), 'Western Europe's Security after Maastricht', *European Access*, pp. 7–9.
Gretschmann, K. (1993), 'EMU: Thoughtful Wish or Wishful Thinking?' in Gretschmann, K. (ed.), *Economic and Monetary Union: Implications for National Policy-makers*, European Institute of Public Administration, Maastricht.
Grieco, J. (1990), *Cooperation among Nations: Europe, America, and Non-tariff Barriers to Trade*, Cornell University Press, Ithaca, NY.
Grimmett, J. J. (1994), 'World Trade Organization: Institutional Issues and Dispute Settlement', *CRS Report for Congress*, Congressional Research Service, Washington, DC.
Gros, D. (1989), 'Paradigms for the Monetary Union of Europe', *Journal of Common Market Studies*, XXVII, pp. 219–31.
Gros, D. and Thygesen, N. (1992), *European Monetary Integration: From the European Monetary System to European Monetary Union*, Longman.
Grosser, G. (1988), 'Empirical Evidence of Effects of Policy Co-ordination among Major

Industrial Countries since Rambouillet Summit of 1975', in Guth, W. (ed.), *Economic Policy Cooperation*, International Monetary Fund, Washington, DC.

Guerrieri, Paolo and Padoan, Pier Carlo (1986), 'Neomercantilism and International Economic Stability', *International Organization*, XL, pp. 29–42.

Guitián, M. (1992), *Rules and Discretion in International Economic Policy*, International Monetary Fund, Washington, DC.

Haas, P. (ed.) (1992), 'Knowledge, Power and International Policy Coordination', special issue of *International Organization*, XLVI.

Haggard, S. (1985), 'The Politics of Adjustment', *International Organization*, XXXIX, pp. 503–34.

Haggard, S. and Kaufman, R. (1989), 'The Politics of Stabilization and Structural Adjustment', in J. Sachs (ed.), *Developing Country Debt and The World Economy*, University of Chicago Press, Chicago.

Haigh, N. (1992), 'The European Community and International Environmental Policy', in A. Hurrell and B. Kingsbury (eds), *The International Politics of the Environment: Actors, Interests, and Institutions*, Clarendon Press, Oxford.

Halliday, G. D. (1993), 'GATT and Regional Free Trade Agreements', *CRS Report for Congress*, Congressional Research Service, Washington, DC.

Halverson, T. (1993), 'Ticking Time Bombs: Eastern Bloc Reactors', *Bulletin of Atomic Scientists*, no. 49, pp. 43–8.

van Ham, P. (1994), 'Can Institutions hold Europe together?' in H. Miall (ed.), *Redefining Europe: New Patterns of Conflict and Cooperation*, Royal Institute of International Affairs, London.

van Ham, P. (1994), 'Ukraine, Russia and European Security: Implications for Western Policy', *Chaillot Papers* 13, WEU Institute for Security Studies, Paris.

Hamada, K. (1976), 'A Strategic Analysis of Monetary Interdependence', *Journal of Political Economy*, LXXXIV, pp. 677–700.

Hamada, K. (1979), *The Political Economy of International Monetary Interdependence*, MIT Press, Cambridge, MA.

Hanink, D. M. (1990), 'Linder again', *Weltwirtschaftliches Archiv*, LXXVI, pp. 257–67.

Hanrieder, W. F. (1978), 'Dissolving International Politics: Reflections on the Nation-State', *American Political Science Review*, LXXII, pp. 1276–87.

Hartland-Thunberg, P. (1988), 'From Guns and Butter to Guns v. Butter: the Relation between Economics and Security in the United States', *Washington Quarterly*, XI, pp. 47–54.

Hathaway, D. E. (1994), 'New World Order in Agricultural Trade', *The New World Trading System: Readings*, OECD, Paris, pp. 167–9.

Heisbourg, F. (1991), 'Population Movements in post-Cold War Europe', *Survival*, XXXIII, pp. 31–44.

Heisbourg, F. (1993), 'The Future Direction of European Security Policy', in M. Wörner, H. Cetin, F. Heisbourg, S. Lunn and J. Onyszkiewicz (eds), *What is European Security after the Cold War?*, Philip Morris Institute for Public Policy Research, Brussels.

Herz, J. (1950), 'Idealist Internationalism and the Security Dilemma', *World Politics*, II, pp. 157–80.

High-level group of experts on the CFSP (1994), First Report on 'European Security Policy towards 2000: ways and means to establish genuine credibility', Brussels, 19 December, p. 16.

Hill, C. (1993), 'The Capability–Expectations Gap, or, Conceptualizing Europe's International Role', *Journal of Common Market Studies*, XXXI, pp. 305–28.

Hino, H. (1986), 'IMF–World Bank Collaboration', *Finance and Development*, XXIII, pp. 10–14.

Hirschman, A. O. (1969), *National Power and the Structure of Foreign Trade*, University of

California Press, Berkeley.
Hoda, A. (1994), 'Trade Liberalisation', *The New World Trading System: Readings*, OECD, Paris, pp. 47–54.
Hoekman, B. (1994), 'General Agreement on Trade in Services', *The New World Trading System*, OECD, Paris, pp. 177–83.
Hoeynck, W. (1994), 'CSCE works to develop its Conflict Prevention Potential', *NATO Review*, XLII, no. 2, pp. 16–22.
Hoffmann, S. (1966), 'Obstinate or Obsolete? The Fate of the Nation-state and the Case of Western Europe', *Daedalus*, LXXXXV, pp. 862–915.
Hoffmann, S. (1981), 'Security in an Age of Turbulence: Means of Response', in 'Third World Conflict and International Society' II, *Adelphi Papers* 167, International Institute of Strategic Studies, London.
Hoffmann, S. (1990), 'The Case for Leadership', *Foreign Policy*, no. 81, pp. 20–38.
Holbrooke, R. (1995), 'America, a European Power', *Foreign Affairs*, LXXIV, pp. 38–51.
Homer-Dixon, T. F. (1991), 'On the Threshold: Environmental Changes as Causes of Acute Conflict', *International Security*, XVI, pp. 76–116.
Homer-Dixon, T. F. (1994), 'Environmental Scarcities and Violent Conflict: Evidence from Cases', *International Security*, XIX, pp. 5–40.
Horne, J. and Masson, R. (1988), 'Scope and Limits of International Economic Cooperation and Policy Coordination', *IMF Staff Papers*, XXXV, pp. 259–96.
Howard, M. (1990), 'The Remaking of Europe', *Survival*, XXII, pp. 99–106.
Howorth, J. (1994), 'The Debate in France over Military Intervention in Europe', in L. Freedman (ed.), *Military Intervention in European Conflicts*, Blackwell, Oxford.
Huelshoff, M. G., Markovits, A. S. and Reich, S. (eds) (1993), *From Bundesrepublik to Deutschland: German Politics after Unification*, University of Michigan Press, Ann Arbor.
Huntington, S. (1965), 'Political Development and Political Decay', *World Politics*, XVII, pp. 386–430.
Hurrell, A. and Kingsbury, B. (1992), *The International Politics of the Environment: Actors, Interests, and Institutions*, Clarendon Press, Oxford.
Hutton, W. (1992), 'Britain in a cold Climate: the economic Aims of Foreign Policy in the 1990s', *International Affairs*, LXVIII, pp. 619–32.
Ikenberry, G. J. (1993), 'Salvaging the G-7', *Foreign Affairs*, LXXII, pp. 132–40.
Ilgen, T. (1985), *Autonomy and Interdependence*, Rowman and Littlefield, Totowa, NJ.
Inotai, A. (1994), 'Die regionale Zusammenarbeit der Visegrad-Staaten. Mehr Wettbewerb als Kooperation?' *Integration*, 1/94, pp. 21–9.
Inotai, A. (1994), 'Die Beziehungen zwischen der EU und den assoziierten Staaten Mittel- und Osteuropas', *Vierteljahreszeitschrift für Politik Wirtschaft und Zeitgeschichte*, XXII, p. 19–35.
International Atomic Energy Authority (1992), *The Safety of WWER-440 Model 230 Nuclear Power Plants*, IAEA, Vienna.
International Monetary Fund (1977), *Annual Report, 1977*, International Monetary Fund, Washington, DC.
International Monetary Fund (1989), *Annual Report, 1989*, International Monetary Fund, Washington, DC.
International Monetary Fund (1992), *Annual Report, 1992*, International Monetary Fund, Washington, DC.
International Monetary Fund (1993), *Annual Report, 1993*, International Monetary Fund, Washington, DC.
International Monetary Fund (1994), *Annual Report, 1994*, International Monetary Fund, Washington, DC.
International Monetary Fund (1994), *The Direction of Trade Statistics Yearbook*, International

Monetary Fund, Washington, DC.
Jackson, J. (1992), 'Regional Trade Blocs and the Gatt', *The World Economy*, XVI, pp. 121–31.
Jackson, J. (1994), 'Managing the Trading System: the World Trade Organization and the post-Uruguay Round GATT Agenda', in P. B. Kenen (ed.), *Managing the World Economy: Fifty Years after Bretton Woods*, Institute for International Economics, Washington, DC.
Jackson, J. (1994), 'Dispute Settlement Procedures', *The New World Trading System: Readings*, OECD, Paris, pp. 117–25.
Jacquemin, A. and Sapir, A. (1991), 'Europe post-1992: Internal and External Liberalization', *American Economic Review*, LXXXI, pp. 168–9.
Jannuzzi, G. (1993), 'NATO's Outlook: a Perspective from Italy', *NATO Review*, XLI, pp. 11–15.
Jervis, R. (1978), 'Cooperation under the Security Dilemma', *World Politics*, XXX, pp. 167–214.
Joffe, J. (1990), 'The Security Implications of a United Germany' I, 'America's Role in a Changing World' II, *Adelphi Papers* 257, pp. 84–91.
Johnson, W. and Young, T-D. (1994), *Partnership for Peace: Discerning Fact from Fiction*, Strategic Studies Institute, US Army War College, Carlisle Barracks, PA.
Junz, H. B. (1991), 'Integration of Eastern Europe into the World Trading System', *American Economic Review*, LXXXI, pp. 176–80.
Kahler, M. (1992), 'Multilateralism with small and large Numbers', *International Organization* XLVI, pp. 681–708.
Kahler, M. (1995), *International Institutions and the Political Economy of Integration*, Brookings Institution, Washington, DC.
Kahler, M. (ed.), (1986), *The Politics of International Debt*, Cornell University Press, Ithaca, NY.
Kamp, K-H., (1995), 'The Folly of Rapid NATO Expansion', *Foreign Policy*, no. 98, pp. 116–31.
Kapstein, E. B. (1992), *The Political Economy of National Security: A Global Perspective*, McGraw-Hill, New York.
Kaspar, M. (1993), *The Ecological Reconstruction of Central and Eastern Europe: International and Austrian Contributions*, Global 2000 Institute for Environmental Research, Vienna.
Kearney, C. (1993), 'The Creditor Clubs: Paris and London', in T. J. Biersteker (ed.), *Dealing with Debt: International Financial Negotiations and Adjustment Bargaining*, Westview, Boulder.
Keatinge, P. (1995), 'The Twelve, the United Nations and Somalia: the mirage of global intervention', paper delivered at the TEPSA workshop, Brussels, January.
Kehoe, P. J. (1989), 'Policy Cooperation among Benevolent Governments may be undesirable', *Review of Economic Studies*, LVI, pp. 289–96.
Kelleher, C. M. (1993), *A New Security Order: the United States and the European Community in the 1990s*, Occasional Paper of the European Community Studies Association, US–EC Relations Project.
Kenen, P. B. (1969), 'The Theory of optimum Currency Areas: an Eclectic View', in R. A. Mundell and A. Swoboda (eds), *Monetary Problems in the International Economy*, University of Chicago Press, Chicago.
Kenen, P. B. (1991), 'Transitional Arrangements for Trade and Payments among the CMEA Countries', *IMF Staff Papers*, XXVIII, pp. 235–67.
Kennedy, P. (1987), *The Rise and Fall of the Great Powers*, Random House, New York.
Keohane, R. O. (1984), *After Hegemony: Cooperation and Discord in the World Political Economy*, Princeton University Press, Princeton.
Keohane, R. O. (ed.) (1986), *Neorealism and its Critics*, Columbia University Press, New York.
Keohane, R. O. and Nye, J. S. (1977), *Power and Interdependence: World Politics in Transition*,

Little Brown, Boston, MA.
Kindleberger, C. P. (1973), *The World in Depression, 1929–1939*, University of California Press, Berkeley.
Kirchner, E. J. (1990), 'Genscher and what lies behind "Genscherism"', *West European Politics*, XIII, pp. 159–77.
Kirchner, E. J. (1994), 'The Impact of German Unification on the New European Order', in H. Miall (ed.), *Redefining Europe: New Patterns of Conflict and Cooperation*, Royal Institute of International Affairs, London, pp. 206–26.
Kirchner, E. J. (1995), 'A "Federal Republic of Europe"?', in Peter Merkl (ed.), *The Federal Republic of Germany at Forty-five: Union without Unity*, New York University Press, New York, pp. 389–406.
Kirchner, E. J. and Sperling, J. (1992), 'The Future Germany and the Future of NATO', *German Politics*, I, pp. 50–72.
Kirchner, E. J. and Sperling, J. (eds) (1992), *The Federal Republic of Germany and NATO: Forty Years After*, Macmillan, London.
Kirton, J. (1989), 'Contemporary Concert Diplomacy: the Seven-Power Summit and the Management of International Order', paper delivered at the London meeting of the International Studies Association.
Kirton, J. (1993), 'The Seven Power Summit as a New Security Institution', in D. Dewitt, D. Haglund and J. Kirton (eds), *Building a New Global Order*. Oxford University Press, Oxford.
Klein, T. (1992), 'Innovations in Debt Relief: Creditor Countries have increased Concessions in granting Debt Relief to reduce the Debt Burden of indebted Countries', *Finance and Development*, XXIX, pp. 42–3.
Knowles, C. (1992), 'The European Investment Bank', in *Conference on Energy and Environment in European Economies in Transition: Proceedings*, OECD, Paris.
Kozyrev, A. (1994), 'Leaders of World Diplomacy: a Strategy for Partnership', *International Affairs*, VIII, pp. 3–13.
Kozyrev, A. (1995), 'Partnership or Cold Peace?', *Foreign Policy*, no. 99, pp. 3–14.
Krasner, S. (ed.) (1983), *International Regimes*, Cornell University Press, Ithaca, NY.
Krugman, P. (1991), *Geography and Trade*, MIT Press, Cambridge, MA.
Kupchan, C. (1989), "Defence Spending and Economic Performance', *Survival*, XXXI, pp. 447–61.
Lamers, K. (1994), 'The future Shape of United Nations Military Operations: Lessons of past UN Peace Missions', *German Comments*, no. 35, July 1994, p. 59.
Layne, C. (1989), 'Superpower Disengagement', *Foreign Policy*, no. 77, pp. 17–40.
Lee Williams, A. and Lee Williams, G. (1995), *NATO's Future in the Balance: time for a rethink*, Atlantic Council of the United Kingdom, London.
Lee Williams, G. (1995), 'Does Europe need an American Ally?', *European Brief*, II, no. 6, pp. 27–8.
Leigh-Phippard, H. (1994), 'Remaking the Security Council: the Options', *The World Today*, C, pp. 167–72.
Leighton, M. and Rudney, R. (1991), 'Non-offensive Defense: Toward a Soviet–German Security Partnership?', *Orbis*, XXXV, pp. 377–94.
Leimbacher, U. (1992), *Die unversichtbare Allianz. Deutsch-französische sicherheitspolitische Zusammenarbeit, 1982–1989*, Nomos, Baden-Baden.
Lellouche, P. (1993), 'France in Search of Security', *Foreign Affairs*, LXXIV, pp. 122–31.
Lindbeck, A. (1978), 'Economic Dependence and Interdependence in the Industrialized World', *From Marshall Plan to Global Independence*, OECD, Paris.
Link, W. (1994), 'Serving World Peace as an Equal Partner in the United Europe: Germany's Stance in Europe', *German Comments*, XXXIII, January, pp. 13–19.
Lipschutz, R. and Holdren, J. P. (1990), 'Crossing Borders: Resource Flows, the Global Envi-

ronment, and International Security', *Bulletin of Peace Proposals*, XXI, pp. 121–33.
Lipson, C. (1981), 'The International Organization of Third World Debt', *International Organization*, XXXV, pp. 603–32.
Lipson, C. (1984), 'International Cooperation in Economic and Security Affairs', *World Politics*, XXXVII, pp. 1–23.
Lipson, C. (1985), 'Bankers' Dilemmas: Private Cooperation in Rescheduling Sovereign Debts', *World Politics*, XXXVIII, pp. 200–25.
Lipson, C. (1985), *Standing Guard: Protecting Foreign Capital in the Nineteenth and Twentieth Centuries*, University of California Press, Berkeley.
Litwak, R. (1984), *Detente and the Nixon Doctrine: American Foreign Policy and the Pursuit of Stability, 1969–1976*, Cambridge University Press, Cambridge.
Lodge, J. (ed.) (1993), *The European Community and the Challenge of the Future*, second edition, Pinter, London.
Lorenz, D. (1992), 'Economic Geography and the Political Economy of Regionalization: the Example of Western Europe', *American Economic Review*, LXXXII, pp. 84–8.
Lowi, M. R. (1993), 'Bridging the Divide: Transboundary Resource Disputes and the Case of West Bank Water', *International Security*, XVIII, pp. 113–38.
Lunn, S. (1993), 'A Reassessment of European Security', in M. Curtis, O. Diel, J. Paolini, A. Seydoux and R. Wolf (eds), *Challenges and Responses to Future European Security: British, French and German Perspectives*, European Strategy Group.
McGuire, M. C. (1990), 'The Revolution in International Security', *Challenge*, XXXIII, pp. 5–10.
McInnes, C. (ed.) (1992), *Security Strategy in the New Europe*, Routledge, London.
McKinnon, R. I. (1963), 'Optimum Currency Areas', *American Economic Review*, LIII, pp. 717–25.
McKinnon, R. I. (1988), 'Monetary and Exchange Rate Policies for International Financial Stability: a Proposal', *Journal of Economic Perspectives*, II, pp. 83–105.
Mahncke, D. (1993), 'Parameters of European Security', *Chaillot Papers* 10, WEU Institute for Security Studies, Paris.
March, J. G. and Olsen, J. P. (1984), 'The New Institutionalism: Organizational Factors in Political Life', *American Political Science Review*, LXXVIII, pp. 734–49.
Martin, L. L. (1992), 'Interests, Power, and Multilaterialism', *International Organization*, XLVI, pp. 765–93.
Martin, L. L. (1992), *Coercive Diplomacy: Explaining Multilateral Economic Sanctions*, Princeton University Press, Princeton.
Martin, L. and Roper, J. (1995), 'Introduction', *Towards a Common Defence Policy*, WEU Institute for Strategic Studies, Paris.
Martin, M. (1991), *The Crumbling Facade of African Debt Negotiations: No Winners*, St Martin's Press, New York.
Mastanduno, M. (1992), *Economic Containment: COCOM and the Politics of East–West Trade*, Cornell University Press, Ithaca, NY.
Mathews, J. T. (1989), 'Redefining Security', *Foreign Affairs*, LXVIII, pp. 162–77.
Maull, H. (1990), 'Germany and Japan: The New Civilian Powers', *Foreign Affairs*, LXIX, pp. 91–106.
Mearsheimer, J. (1990), 'Back to the Future: Instability in Europe after the Cold War', *International Security*, XV, pp. 1–56.
Mearsheimer, J. (1994), 'The False Promise of International Institutions', *International Security*, XIX, pp. 5–49.
Miall, H. (ed.) (1994), *Redefining Europe: New Patterns of Conflict and Cooperation*, Royal Institute of International Affairs, London.
Mikesell, R. F. and Williams, L. (1992), *International Banks and the Environment. From Growth to Sustainability: an Unfinished Agenda*, Sierra Club Books, San Francisco.

Milward, A. (1984), *The Reconstruction of Western Europe, 1945–51*, Macmillan, London.
Moïsi, D. and Mertes, M. (1995), 'Europe's Map, Compass, and Horizon', *Foreign Affairs*, LXXIV, pp. 122–34.
Moran, T. H. (1993), 'An Economics Agenda for Neorealists', *International Security*, XXXVIII, pp. 214–15.
Moran, T. H. (1993), *American Economic Policy and National Security*, Council of Foreign Relations Press, New York.
Mundell, R. (1961), 'A Theory of Optimum Currency Areas', *American Economic Review*, LI, pp. 657–64.
Mussa, M. (1979), 'Macroeconomic Interdependence and the Exchange Rate Regime', in R. Dornbusch and J. A. Frankel (eds), *International Economic Policy*, Johns Hopkins University Press, Baltimore.
Mussa, M. (1993), 'Making the Practical case for Freer Trade', *American Economic Review*, LXXXIII, pp. 372–76.
Mussa, M. (1995), 'Trade Liberalization is Linked to Global Prosperity', *IMF Survey*, XXIV, no. 10, pp. 157–8.
Myers, N. (1989), 'Environment and Security', *Foreign Policy*, no. 74, pp. 23–41.
NATO (1991), *The Alliance's New Strategic Concept*, Press Communiqué S-1(91)85, NATO Press Service, Brussels, 7 November.
NATO Press and information Service (1989), *Declaration of the Heads of State and Government participating in the Meeting of the North Atlantic Council*, NATO Press and information Service, Brussels.
NATO Press and Information Service (1990), *London Declaration on a Transformed North Atlantic Alliance*, NATO Press and Information Service, Brussels.
NATO Scientific Affairs Division (1992), *The Challenges of Modern Society*, NATO, Brussels.
Newhouse, J. (1993), 'No Exit, no Entrance', *New Yorker*, 28 June, pp. 44–51.
Niehaus, F. and Lederman, L. (1992), 'International Safety Review of WWER-440 Model 230 Nuclear Power Plants', *IAEA Bulletin*, XXXIV, no. 2, pp. 24–31.
Nordic Investment Bank (1991), *Annual Report, 1990*, Nordic Investment Bank, Helsinki.
Nordic Investment Bank (1994), *Annual Report, 1993*, Nordic Investment Bank, Helsinki.
Organisation for Economic Cooperation and Development (1994), *The OECD Jobs Study*, OECD, Paris.
Organisation for Economic Cooperation and Development (1994), *OECD Documents: The New World Trading System: Readings*, OECD, Paris.
Oudiz, G. and Sachs, J. (1984), 'Macroeconomic Policy Coordination among the Industrialized Economies', *Brookings Papers on Economic Activity*, I, pp. 1–64.
Oye, K. A. (1985), 'Explaining Cooperation under Anarchy: Hypotheses and Strategies', *World Politics*, XXXVIII, pp. 1–24.
Oye, K. A. (1992), *Economic Discrimination and Political Exchange*, Princeton University Press, Princeton.
Picco, G. (1994), 'The UN and the Use of Force: Leave the Secretary General out of it', *Foreign Affairs*, LXXIII, pp. 14–18.
Powell, R. (1991), 'Absolute and Relative Gains in International Relations Theory', *American Political Science Review*, LXXXV, pp. 1303–20.
Powell, R. (1993), 'Guns, Butter, and Anarchy', *American Political Science Review*, LXXXVII, pp. 115–32.
Predöhl, A. (1949), *Aussenwirtschaft. Weltwirtschaft, Handelspolitik und Währungspolitik*, Vandenhoeck & Ruprecht, Göttingen.
Putnam, R. D. (1984), 'The Western Economic Summits: A Political Interpretation', in C. Merlini (ed.), *Economic Summits and Western Decision-making*, Croom Helm, London.
Putnam, R. D. and Bayne, N. (1984), *Hanging Together: The Seven Power Summits*, Harvard University Press, Cambridge, MA.

Putnam, R. D. and Bayne, N. D. (1987), *Hanging Together: Cooperation and Conflict in the Seven Power Summits*, second edition, Harvard University Press, Cambridge, MA.

Quinlan, M. (1993), 'The Future of Nuclear Weapons: Policy for Western Possessors', *International Affairs*, LXIX, pp. 485–96.

Rambaut, P. (1992), 'Environmental Challenges: the Role of NATO', *NATO Review*, XL, no. 2, pp. 24–7.

Rappaport, E. (1994), 'Uruguay Round: Industry Issues', *CRS Issues Brief*, Congressional Research Service, Washington, DC.

Ravenal, E. C. (1990), 'The Case for Adjustment', *Foreign Policy*, no. 81, pp. 3–19.

Reed, D. (1990), 'The European Bank for Reconstruction and Development: an Environmental Opportunity', *International Environmental Affairs*, II, pp. 325–40.

Rees, G. W. (ed.) (1993), *International Politics in Europe: The New Agenda*, Routledge, London.

Reichel, H-C. (1990), 'Die Bonner Wirtschaftskonferenz und die Zukunft der KSZE', *Europa Archiv*, XLV, pp. 461–70.

Report submitted on behalf of the Committee for Parliamentary and Public Relations, by Mr Roman, Rapporteur, WEU Institute for Security, 31 October 1994.

Rieffel, A. (1985), 'The Role of the Paris Club in Managing Debt Problems', *Essays in International Finance* no. 161, Department of Economics, Princeton University, Princeton.

Rogoff, K. (1985), 'Can International Monetary Cooperation be Counterproductive?' *Journal of International Economics*, XVIII, pp. 199–217.

Rogoff, K. (1990), 'Bargaining and International Policy Cooperation', *American Economic Review*, LXXX, pp. 139–42.

Romm, J. J. (1993), *Defining National Security: The Nonmilitary Aspects*, Council on Foreign Relations, New York.

Rühe, V. (1993), 'Adapting the Alliance in the Face of great Challenges', *NATO Review*, XLIII, no. 6, pp. 3–6.

Rühe, V. (1994), *The Konrad Adenauer Memorial Lecture 1994: Germany's responsibility in and for Europe*, St Antony's College Oxford and Konrad Adenauer Foundation, 1994.

Ruggie, J. G. (1983), 'Continuity and Transformation in the World Polity: Toward a Neorealist Synthesis', *World Politics*, XXXV, pp. 261–85.

Ruggie, J. G. (ed.) (1993), *Multilateralism Matters: The Theory and Praxis of an Institutional Form*, Columbia University Press, New York.

Russett, B. (1955), 'Correspondence – the Democratic Peace', *International Security*, XIX, pp. 164–75.

Sachs, J. (ed.) (1989), *Developing Country Debt and the World Economy*, University of Chicago Press, Chicago.

Sandholtz, W. et al. (eds) (1992), *The Highest Stakes: the Economic Foundations of the Next Security System*, Oxford University Press, Oxford.

Schadler, S. M. (1994), 'Developing Countries and the Evolving Role of the IMF', *IMF Survey*, XXIII, pp. 223–6.

Schadler, S., Rozwadowski, F., Tiwari, S. and Robinson, D. O. (1993), *Economic Adjustment in Low-income Countries: Experience under the Structural Adjustment Facility*, IMF Occasional Paper 106, International Monetary Fund, Washington, DC.

Schmidt, P. (1993), *The Western European Union in the 1990s: Searching for a Role*, SSI Special Report, Strategic Institute, US Army College, Carlisle Barracks, PA.

Schmidt, P. (ed.) (1992), *In the Midst of Change: on the development of West European security and defence cooperation*, Nomos, Baden-Baden.

Scholl-Latour, P. (1995), 'Anti-Islamic Alliance of the former Superpowers? Europe must press for Dialogue and Containment: Eurocorps', *German Comments*, no. 38, April, pp. 11–20.

Scholz, R. (1990), 'Deutsche Frage und europäische Sicherheit. Sicherheitspolitik in einem

sich einigenden Deutschland und Europa', *Europa Archiv*, XLV, pp. 239–46.
Schott, J. J. (1991), 'Trading Blocs and the World Trading System', *The World Economy*, XIV, pp. 1–19.
Seidelmann, R. (ed.) (1989), *Auf dem Weg zu einer westeuropäischen Sicherheitspolitik*, Nomos, Baden-Baden.
Seydoux, A. and Paolini, J. (1993), 'From Western Security Interblocking to Institutional Evolutionism', in M. Curtis, O. Diel, J. Paolini, A. Seydoux and R. Wolf (eds), *Challenges and Responses to Future European Security: British, French and German Perspectives*, European Strategy Group.
Shea, J. (1993), 'Security: the Future', in J. Lodge (ed.), *The European Community and the Challenge of the Future*, second edition, Pinter, London.
Shiells, C. (1995), 'Regional Trading Blocs: Trade Creating or Diverting?', *Finance and Development*, XXXII, no. 1, pp. 30–2.
Shumaker, D. (1993), 'The Origins and Development of Central European Cooperation, 1989–92', *East European Quarterly*, XXVII, pp. 351–73.
Simpson, J. (1994), 'Nuclear Non-proliferation in the post-Cold War Era', *International Affairs*, LXX, pp. 17–39.
Sloan, S. (1990), 'NATO's Future in a new Europe: an American Perspective', *International Affairs*, LXVI, pp. 495–513.
Sloan, S. (1994), 'Transatlantic Relations in the Wake of the Brussels Summit', *NATO Review*, XLII, no. 2, pp. 27–31.
Sloan, S. (1994), 'Combined Joint Task Forces (CJTF) and new Missions for NATO', *CRS Report for Congress*, Congressional Research Service, Washington, DC.
Sloan, S. (1995), 'US Perspectives on NATO's Future', *International Affairs*, LXXI, pp. 217–32.
Smith, D. L. and Wanke, J. (1993), 'Competing in the Single European Market: an Analysis of the Impact on the Member States', *American Journal of Political Science*, XXXVII, pp. 529–54.
Smyser, W. R. (1991), 'USSR–Germany: a Link Restored', *Foreign Policy*, no. 84, pp. 125–41.
Snidal, D. (1985), 'The Limits of Hegemonic Stability Theory', *International Organization*, XXXIX, pp. 579–614.
Snidal, D. (1985), 'Coordination versus Prisoners' Dilemma: Implications for International Cooperation and Regimes', *American Political Science Review*, LXXIX, pp. 923–42.
Snidal, D. (1991), 'Relative Gains and the Pattern of International Cooperation', *American Political Science Review*, LXXXV, pp. 701–26.
Snidal, D. (1991), 'International Cooperation among Relative Gains Maximizers', *International Studies Quarterly*, XXXV, pp. 387–402.
Snidal, D. (1993), 'Relative Gains Problem for International Cooperation – Comment', *American Political Science Review*, LXXXVII, pp. 738–43.
Spear, J. (1993), 'The Environment Agenda', in G. W. Rees (ed.), *International politics in Europe: The New Agenda*, Routledge, London.
Sperling, J. (1992), 'The Atlantic Economy after German Unification', *German Politics*, I, pp. 201–7.
Sperling, J. (1992), 'America, NATO, and West German Foreign Economic Policies, 1949–89', in E. J. Kirchner and J. Sperling (eds), *The Federal Republic of Germany and NATO: Forty Years After*, Macmillan, London, pp. 157–93.
Sperling, J. (1993), 'A unified Germany, a single European Economic Space, and the Prospects for an Atlantic Economy', in C. Lankowski (ed.), *Germany and the European Community: Beyond Hegemony and Containment?*, St Martin's Press, New York.
Sperling, J. (1993), 'German Security Policy and the Future European Security Order', in M. G. Huelshoff, A. S. Markovits and S. Reich (eds), *From Bundesrepublik to Deutschland: German Politics after Unification*, University of Michigan Press, Ann Arbor.
Sperling, J. (1994), 'German Foreign Policy after Unification: the End of Cheque-Book

Diplomacy?', *West European Politics*, XVII, pp. 73–97.
Sperling, J. (1995), 'The German Architecture for Europe: Military, Political, and Economic Dimensions', in Peter Merkl (ed.), *The Federal Republic of Germany at Forty-five: Union without Unity*, New York University Press, New York.
Sperling, J., Louscher, D. and Salomone, M. (1995), 'A Reconceptualisation of the Arms Transfer Problem', *Defence Analysis*, XI, pp. 293–311.
Startup, J. (1994), 'An Agenda for International Investment', *The New World Trading System: Readings*, OECD, Paris, pp. 189–91.
Stein, A. (1982), 'Coordination and Collaboration: Regimes in an Anarchic World', in S. D. Krasner (ed.), *International Regimes*, Cornell University Press, Ithaca, NY.
Stein, A. (1990), *Why Nations Cooperate: Circumstance and Choice in International Relations*, Cornell University Press, Ithaca, NY.
Steinherr, A. (1984), 'Convergence and Coordination of Macroeconomic Policies: Some Basic Issues', *European Economy*, XX, pp. 69–110.
Szabo, S. (1990), *The Changing Politics of Germany Security*, St Martin's Press, New York.
Tangermann, S. (1994), 'An Assessment of the Agreement on Agriculture', *The New World Trading System: Readings*, OECD, Paris, pp. 143–51.
Tarschys, D. (1995), 'The Council of Europe: the Challenge of Enlargement', *The World Today*, LI, pp. 62–4.
Taylor, T. (1994), 'West European Security and Defence Cooperation: Maastricht and beyond', *International Affairs*, LXX, pp. 1–16.
Terriff, T. (1995), *The Nixon Administration and the Making of US Nuclear Strategy*, Cornell University Press, Ithaca, NY.
Teske, P., Schneider, M., Mintrom, M. and Best, S. (1993), 'Establishing the Micro Foundations of a Macro Theory: Information, Movers, and the Competitive Local Market for Public Goods', *American Political Science Review*, LXXXVII, pp. 702–16.
Thacher, S. (1992), 'The Role of the United Nations', in A. Hurrell and B. Kingsbury (eds), *The International Politics of the Environment: Actors, Interests, and Institutions*, Clarendon Press, Oxford.
Treverton, G. F. (1992), 'The New Europe', *Foreign Affairs*, LXXI, pp. 94–112.
Trolldalen, J. M. (1992), *International Environmental Conflict Resolution: The Role of the United Nations*, World Foundation for Environment and Development, Washington, DC.
Ullman, R. (1983), 'Redefining Security', *International Security*, VIII, pp. 129–53.
Ungerer, H., Evans, O. and Nyberg, P. (1983), *The European Monetary System: the Experience, 1979–82*, Occasional Paper 19, International Monetary Fund, Washington, DC.
Ungerer, H., Evans, O., Mayer, T. and Young, P. (1986), *The European Monetary System: Recent Developments*, Occasional Paper 48, International Monetary Fund, Washington, DC.
Ungerer, H., Hauvonen, J., Lopez-Claros, A. and Mayer, T. (1990), *The European Monetary System: Developments and Perspectives*. Occasional Paper 73, International Monetary Fund, Washington, DC.
United Kingdom, Ministry of Defence (1994), *Statement on the Defence Estimates*, Cmnd 2550, HMSO, London.
Vaubel, R. (1983), 'Coordination or Competition among National Macroeconomic Policies?', in F. Machlup, G. Fels and H. Mueller-Groeling (eds), *Reflections on a Troubled World Economy: Essays in Honour of Herbert Giersch*, Macmillan, London.
Vaubel, R. (1985), 'International Collusion or Competition for Macroeconomic Policy Coordination: A Restatement', *Recherches Economiques de Louvain*, CI, pp. 223–40.
Veen, H-J. (1991), 'Die Westbindung der Deutschen in einer Phase der Neuorientierung', *Europa Archiv*, XLVI, pp. 27–35.
Vierucci, L. (1993), 'WEU: a Regional Partner of the United Nations?', *Chaillot Papers* 12,

WEU Institute for Security Studies, Paris.
Viner, J. (1949), 'Power versus Plenty', *World Politics*, I, pp. 1–27.
Viner, J. (1950), *The Customs Union Issue*, Carnegie Endowment for International Peace, New York.
Wæver, O. (1990), 'Three Competing Europes: German, French, and Russian', *International Affairs*, LXVI, pp. 477–94.
Wæver, O., Buzan, B., Kelstrup, M. and Lemaitre, P. (1993), *Identity, Migration, and the New Security Agenda in Europe*, Pinter, London.
Wagner, R. H. (1983), 'The Theory of Games and the Problem of International Cooperation', *American Political Science Review*, LXX, pp. 330–46.
Walker, J. (1991), 'Keeping America in Europe', *Foreign Policy* no. 83, pp. 128–43.
Wallace, H. (1994), 'The EC and Western Europe after Maastricht', in H. Miall (ed.), *Redefining Europe: New Patterns of Conflict and Cooperation*, Royal Institute of International Affairs, London.
Waltz, K. (1979), *Theory of International Politics*, Random House, New York.
Waltz, K. (1993), 'The Emerging Structure of International Politics', *International Security*, XVIII, pp. 44–80.
Ward, M. D. and Davis, D. R. (1992), 'Sizing up the Peace Dividend: Economic Growth and Military Spending in the United States, 1948–96', *American Political Science Review*, LXXXVI, pp. 748–55.
Weatherford, M. S. (1988), 'The International Economy as a Constraint on US Macroeconomic Policy-making', *International Organization*, XLII, pp. 605–39.
Webb, M. (1991), 'International Economic Structures, Government Interests, and International Coordination of Macroeconomic Adjustment Policies', *International Organization*, XLV, pp. 309–42.
Webb, M. (1994), 'Understanding Patterns of Macroeconomic Policy Co-ordination in the Post-war Period', in R. Stubbs and G. R. D. Underhill (eds), *Political Economy and the Changing Global Order*, St Martin's Press, New York.
Weber, S. (1994), 'Origins of the European Bank for Reconstruction and Development', *International Organization*, XLVIII, pp. 19–21.
Weber, S. and Zysman, J. (1992), 'The Risk that Mercantilism will define the Next Security System', in Wayne Sandholtz *et al.* (eds), *The Highest Stakes: The Economic Foundations of the Next Security System*, Oxford University Press, New York.
van Well, G. (1990), 'Zur Europa-Politik eines vereinigten Deutschland', *Europa Archiv*, XLV, pp. 29–38.
Wettig, G. (1991), 'German Unification and European Security', *Aussenpolitik*, XLII, pp. 13–19.
Wettig, G. (1995), 'Controversial Foundations of Security in Europe', *Aussenpolitik*, XLVI, p. 46.
Williamson, J. and Henning, C. R. (1994), 'Managing the Monetary System', in David Dewitt *et al.* (eds), *Managing the World Economy*, Institute for International Economics, Washington, DC.
Winham, Gilbert R. (1986), *International Trade and the Tokyo Round Negotiation*, Princeton University Press, Princeton.
Winters, L. A. (1992), 'The Welfare and Policy Implications of the International Trade Consequences of "1992"', *American Economic Review*, LXXXII, pp. 104–8.
Wörner, M. (1991), 'NATO Transformed: the Significance of the Rome Summit', *NATO Review*, XXXIX, no. 6, p. 3.
Wörner, M. (1993), 'European security: political will plus military might', in M. Wörner, H. Cetin, F. Heisbourg, S. Lunn and J. Onyszkiewicz (eds), *What is European Security after the Cold War?* Philip Morris Institute for Public Policy Research, Brussels.
Wolfers, A. (1962), *Discord and Collaboration*, Johns Hopkins University Press, Baltimore.

World Bank (1993), *World Bank: Annual Report, 1993*, World Bank, Washington, DC.
World Bank (1994), *World Debt Tables, 1994–95*, World Bank, Washington, DC.
Wright, K. (1994), 'Open Skies', *Air Force Monthly*, VII, pp. 15–19.
Young, O. R. (1982), 'Regime dynamics: the rise and fall of regimes', in S. D. Krasner (ed.), *International Regimes*, Cornell University Press, Ithaca, NY.
Young, O. R. (1989), *International Cooperation: Building Regimes for Natural Resources and the Environment*, Cornell University Press, Ithaca, NY.
Young, T-D. and W. T. Johnson (1992), *Reforming NATO's Command and Operational Control Structures: Progress and Problems*, SSI Special Report, Strategic Studies Institute, US Army War College, Carlisle Barracks, PA.
Yuksel-Beten, D. (1991), 'CCMS: NATO's Environmental Programme is Expanded and Opened to the East', *NATO Review*, XXXIX, no. 4, pp. 27–32.

Index

Asia Pacific Economic Cooperation Forum (APEC) 133
Association of South East Asian Nations (ASEAN) 133

Baltic Council 66
Bank for International Settlements (BIS) 106, 112
Black Sea Cooperation Council 66
Black Sea Economic Cooperation (BSEC) 139–40
Bosnia 46, 52, 64, 66, 75
Brady Plan 169
Bretton Woods 1, 91
Bundesbank 95, 98–9, 101, 104, 108, 112–13, 115

Central European Free Trade Area (CEFTA) 139
Chernobyl nuclear plant 41, 219, 223, 226
  see also environmental security; European Union and nuclear power plants in eastern Europe
Combined Joint Task Forces (CJTFs) 36, 69–71, 77, 80, 240
comprehensive security system 16–19
Conference on Security and Cooperation in Europe (CSCE)
  environmental security 207–8
  see also Organisation for Security and Cooperation in Europe
Cooperation 13–16
Coordinating Committee for Multilateral Export Controls (COCOM) 130
Council of Europe 29, 31, 39, 75–6
Council of Mutual Economic Assistance (CMEA) 135–6, 139, 146–7, 175–6
crisis management 37

debt
  Bulgaria 176–8
  institutions of 164–72
  Poland 178–81
  Russian Federation 181–7
Deutschmark 95, 100, 102, 105, 107, 109, 113–14

Earth summit 211–12
East European Clearing Union (EECU) 139
environmental security 61, 201–233
  importance of 202–205
  and nuclear power plants 219–24
Eurocorps 33–4, 47, 71, 77, 80
European Bank for Reconstruction and Development (EBRD) 19, 191, 192, 210, 216–18, 235
European Defence Community (EDC) 29
European Economic Area (EEA) 135–6
European Free Trade Area (EFTA) 50, 135–6, 141
European Investment Bank (EIB) 19, 191, 214–16, 225
European Monetary System (EMS) 86, 94, 112, 115–16
European Recovery Programme (ERP) 163–4
European Security Identity (ESI) 75, 77
European state system
  changing attributes 3–6
  integration 11
European Union (EU)
  accession to 137–8
  common foreign and security policy (CFSP) 30, 32, 35, 46–7, 49, 240, 244–5, 247, 251
  Council of Economic and Finance Ministers (ECOFIN) 88, 93

economic and monetary union (EMU)
   93–4, 112–13, 115–18
environmental policy 208–10
Europe Agreements 136–7, 155
European Court of Justice 45, 208
European Monetary Institute (EMI)
   88, 93
European Political Cooperation (EPC)
   30, 45
exchange rate mechanism (ERM)
   112–13,
macroeconomic policy convergence
   111–19
and nuclear power plants in eastern
   Europe 221–2
Phare 226
Policy consistency 43–6
Single European Act 135
Tacis 223, 226
Treaty on European Union 32, 107,
   111–13, 116–19, 120
and WEU 46–50, 256–8
Europol 45

Federal Reserve Board 103, 107, 108, 110
France
   and NATO 69–71

G-7 87, 88–93, 95–111, 119, 166, 168,
   178, 182, 223, 247
   Nuclear Safety Fund 223–4, 226
G-24 191
General Agreement on Trade in Services
   (GATS) 145
General Agreement on Tariffs and Trades
   (GATT)/World Trade
   Organisation (WTO) 131, 132,
   133, 135, 140–3, 146, 261
   Uruguay Round 142, 144–6
Gulf conflict 35, 57, 64

hegemonic stability model 20

indebtedness 163–4
institutions
   and choices 258–61
   design 16–19

and security architectures 234–67
trade 135–43
International Atomic Energy Authority
   (IAEA) 207–8, 220, 222, 261
International Bank for Reconstruction
   and Development (IBRD) see
   World Bank
International Monetary Fund (IMF) 87,
   89–90, 99–101, 104, 107, 120,
   132, 142, 164–72, 177–8, 183,
   261

London Club 164–72, 177, 179, 187,
   261

macro-economic policy 11,
   convergence 88–94
   and European Union 111–19
   stability 85–129
   see also European Union
Marshall Plan 40, 85, 190

Neo-liberalism 3
Neo-realism 3
Nordic Council 66
Nordic Investment Bank (NIB) 212–14,
   225
North American Free Trade Agreement
   (NAFTA) 105, 133
North Atlantic Treaty Organisation
   (NATO) 59–61, 76–7, 121, 255–6,
   257, 260, 262–3
   Allied Rapid Reaction Corps (ARRC)
      68
   Committee on the Challenges of
      Modern Society (CCMS) 206
   Dayton Peace agreement 61
   and France 247–8
   and Germany 250–1, 252–3
   and Great Britain 239–40, 241
   North Atlantic Cooperation Council
      39, 59–60, 73, 75–6, 206, 243, 255
   Partnership for Peace (PfP) 59–60, 73,
      75–6, 235, 243
   Strategic Concept 59–60
   and United States 242–4
   and WEU 67–75

Organisation for Economic Cooperation and Development (OECD) 145, 146, 151, 176
Organisation for Security and Cooperation in Europe (OSCE) 64–7, 75–6, 235, 245, 253
  Conflict Prevention Centre 65, 66
  Forum for Security Cooperation 65,
  Office for Democratic Institutions and Human Rights 65, 66
  see also Conference on Security and Cooperation in Europe

Paris Club 164–72, 177, 179, 180, 184–7, 261
peace dividend 8

regional institutions *see* Council of Europe; European Union and WEU
Russian Federation
  debt profile 172, 181–7

security
  architectures 234–65
    compared 254–8
    France 245–9
    Germany 249–54
    Great Britain 237–41
    United States 241–5
  definitions of 4–5, 10–13
  dilemmas of 6–10
  economic dimensions 1–2, 130–61, 162–200
  environmental security 201–33
  military dimensions 22–3
Stability Pact 40, 48, 257

trade
  political power in 152–4
  see also institutions

United Nations (UN) 62–4
  United Nations High Commission on Refugees (UNHCR) 62
  United Nations Protection Force (UNPROFOR) 36, 62, 69
  UN Environmental Programme 211

Visegrad states 38, 136, 189

Western European Union (WEU) 29, 31, 32–5, 43, 80, 247, 255–6
  and EU 46–50
  and France 247–9
  and Germany 251–2
  and NATO 67–75
World Bank (IBRD) 19, 132, 142, 164, 261
World Trade Organisation (WTO) *see* General Agreement on Tariffs and Trades